INTERNATIONAL INTELLECTUAL PROPERTY

IN A NUTSHELL®

DANIEL C.K. CHOW
Frank E. and Virginia H. Bazler Chair in Law
The Ohio State University
Michael E. Moritz College of Law
Columbus, Ohio

WEST ACADEMIC

860 Blue Gentian Road, Suite 350
Eagan, MN 55121
1-877-888-1330

Published in the United States of America

ISBN: 978-0-314-15086-8

WEST ACADEMIC PUBLISHING'S LAW SCHOOL ADVISORY BOARD

PREFACE

This book examines the basic treaties and institutions that form the "system" of international intellectual property. Of these treaties, the most important is the Agreement on Trade-Related Intellectual Property Rights (TRIPS) of the World Trade Organization (WTO). Other treaties that are examined in detail include the Berne Convention on copyright, the Paris Convention on patents and trademarks, the Rome Convention on performance rights, the Patent Cooperation Treaty, and the Madrid Agreement and the Madrid Protocol on the international registration of trademarks. Of the international institutions examined in the book the most important are the WTO, although the book also examines the European Union, the United States Mexico Canada Trade Agreement, and the World Intellectual Property Organization, among others.

This book examines in detail all of the basic intellectual property rights in an international context: copyright, patent, trademark, geographical indications, and trade secrets. The book also discusses unfair competition and design protection. The last chapter of the book focuses on the private enforcement of intellectual property rights in a transnational context against trademark counterfeiting and gray market goods.

This book follows the structure and organization of the popular casebook Daniel C.K. Chow and Edward Lee, *International Intellectual Property:*

Problems, Cases, and Materials (West 4th edition 2022). A revised version of this book is now being prepared so that it can be used with the 5th edition of the Chow & Lee casebook that was published in 2025. This book can also be used with any international intellectual property casebook.

DANIEL C.K. CHOW
COLUMBUS, OHIO

March 18, 2025

OUTLINE

TABLE OF CASES

References are to Pages

INTERNATIONAL INTELLECTUAL PROPERTY

IN A NUTSHELL®

CHAPTER 1

THE FIELD OF INTERNATIONAL INTELLECTUAL PROPERTY

A. INTRODUCTION

This book is intended for an audience of students, lawyers, and academics interested in the field of international intellectual property law. The major substantive intellectual property rights that we will examine in a transnational context are copyright, patent, trademark, geographical indications, and trade secrets. We will also discuss unfair competition law, a branch of law related to trade secrets and business ethics, and design protection. This book examines these substantive intellectual property rights and related areas within the overall context and framework of the major international intellectual property institutions and treaties that form what we shall refer to in this book as the "system" of international intellectual property.

Of the international institutions, the most important that will be examined in detail is the World Trade Organization (WTO), a multilateral trade organization consisting of 166 countries as of 2024. Other organizations such as the European Economic Area, which is part of the European Union (EU) will also be discussed. The most important international treaty is the Agreement on Trade-Related Intellectual Property Rights (TRIPS) of the WTO, although several other intellectual property treaties, including the Berne Convention for the

Protection of Literary and Artistic Works (1886, revised 1971) and the International Convention for the Protection of Industrial Property (1883, revised 1967), known as the Paris Convention, are also very important and will be discussed in depth.

TRIPS sets forth minimum standards for all of the major intellectual property rights examined in this book. All WTO members have a duty to implement domestic intellectual property laws consistent with the standards set forth in TRIPS. This structure ensures harmonization of intellectual property laws on an international level to an extent never before achieved. While TRIPS sets out the minimum intellectual property standards that all WTO members must satisfy, many nations, including the United States, have exceeded the minimum standards in TRIPS in certain areas of intellectual property.

As part of our study, we also examine a topic of increasing importance to every modern intellectual property lawyer: the enforcement of intellectual property rights in the private sphere through domestic courts, administrative agencies, private investigation companies, and other means. Enforcement is a major topic because the theft and misappropriation of intellectual property is now a major global business problem. Contrast private law enforcement with enforcement in the public sphere, which in this book will refer to litigation in the WTO and, to some extent, the EU. Private parties, including corporations, have no standing to litigate in the WTO, which considers only disputes between governments. While this book will discuss many WTO cases (and some EU cases), we will not discuss strategies for litigating in the WTO. Our discussion of enforcement actions and enforcement strategies will be focused on private enforcement.

1. INTERNATIONAL INTELLECTUAL PROPERTY AS AN EMERGING FIELD OF STUDY

International intellectual property is a relatively new field of study in the law school curriculum. Just a few decades ago in the 1990s, most law schools did not offer a course on international intellectual property as it was not considered to be a separate course. Today, international intellectual property is not only recognized as a separate course in the curriculum in many law schools but the study of international intellectual property is now considered to be absolutely essential for every serious student of intellectual property. Why has international intellectual property emerged as a separate and serious field of study in the recent past? Why has intellectual property gone international?

To understand developments in intellectual property, we need to see that trends in international intellectual property are connected to and are part of the momentous developments in international economics, trade, and politics that mark the latter half of the twentieth century and that continue into the decades of the new millennium. We can trace the development of the modern global economy to the end of the Second World War when the United States led a small group of nations in a conference held in Bretton Woods, New Hampshire. The goal of the Bretton Woods Conference was to establish the modern international economic and legal institutions for the global economy that would also avoid the disastrous economic policies that contributed to the rise of the Second World War. In the 1930s, the period immediately preceding the Second World War, nations erected protectionist trade barriers for the purpose of restricting or preventing trade with each other. Many nations did not wish to trade with each other but instead viewed each other with mistrust and suspicion. One of the main lessons from this period is that where economic conflict exists, military conflict soon follows.

In order to prevent a reoccurrence of the disastrous pre-war policies that might lead to another world conflict, the United States and the other Bretton Woods countries planned to erect a tripartite structure of international institutions to bolster the post war global economy. The tripartite structure envisioned a role for the World Bank to lend money first for the reconstruction of Europe then to developing and least developing countries to alleviate poverty. A second organization, the International Monetary Fund, was to create stability in currency exchange rates and discourage currency manipulation in order to avoid the vicious cycle of currency devaluations marking the pre-war period. The third organization was to be the International Trade Organization, which would reduce trade barriers and promote free trade. To jump start international trade, the Bretton Woods countries also approved the General Agreement on Tariffs and Trade (GATT) in 1947 on a provisional basis. The GATT was designed to reduce tariffs (taxes) imposed at the border on imports. After the International Trade Organization failed to gain approval due to U.S. opposition, the GATT operated with a skeletal staff as a treaty without an organization in Geneva for nearly 50 years. When the WTO was established in 1995, it took on the role that was originally envisioned for the International Trade Organization. GATT 1947 was absorbed into and became part of GATT 1994, which continues to regulate trade in goods today.

By the time that the WTO came into existence on January 1, 1995, the GATT 1947 had been extremely successful in reducing tariffs on imports, contributing to a rapid rise in the trade in goods in the decades following the Second World War. Not only did merchandise trade increase but all areas of trade increased rapidly. In the modern world, all trade occurs in four channels: goods, services, technology (or intellectual property), and investment. Services trade (including legal services, accounting, insurance, and banking), technology trade, and investment trade have also risen to historical peaks in the post war years. By "technology" this book refers to information and knowledge protected by intellectual property laws. In the context of this book, the terms technology and intellectual property are synonymous and interchangeable.

Intellectual property has played a key role in facilitating the rapid rise of all channels trade in the modern global economy. Indeed, it is no exaggeration to say that information and knowledge (protected by intellectual property) is more important than ever in international business and trade. A strong intellectual property legal regime can encourage trade while a weak regime can harm trade.

Let us begin with the trade in goods. A major factor in a decision by a producer of goods to export to a target market is the level of intellectual property protection in that market. For example, suppose that Apex Company, located in the United States, wishes to export its products to a developing country. If the developing country does not have a rigorous intellectual property regime, Apex might be reluctant to export its products to that country. Apex's product might be a pharmaceutical product with a valuable patent and trademark. Pirates in the developing country can copy Apex's patent and trademark with impunity because the country does not have effective laws on its books or does not enforce its laws effectively. Lack of intellectual property protection becomes a trade barrier. On the other hand, if the developing country has a strong intellectual property legal regime, Apex might feel more confident in exporting its products there.

A similar analysis also applies to services, the second channel of trade set forth above. Assume that Elite Services corporation is an accounting, insurance, or financial services firm located in Texas that is seeking to provide professional services to a client in a foreign country. Elite might be reluctant to provide services that may contain trade secrets and confidential business information if the foreign country does not have a strong regime protecting intellectual property rights.

The third channel of trade is trade in technology or intellectual property. Technology trade occurs when the owner of proprietary technology gives a third party access to its technology. The access can be by way of assignment, i.e. the transfer of full ownership rights or by way of licensing, i.e. allowing the third party the right to use the technology while the licensor maintains ownership of the technology. Suppose that Mega-Soft Company wishes to license its technology to a manufacturer in a foreign country. The normal procedure to set up a licensing agreement is for Mega-Soft to register the patents and trademarks in its own name in the foreign country and then to license the use of the technology to a licensee in the foreign country that will manufacture the goods under contract with the licensor for sale in the foreign country. Any licensing arrangement creates risks because the licensee might misuse or misappropriate the licensed technology. The licensee might misuse the technology by using it to improve its own products that compete with those of the licensor or the licensee might retain the technology and continue to use it after the termination of the licensing agreement. Mega-Soft might not be willing to license its technology to a licensee in a foreign country if it does not have a legal regime that rigorously enforces licensing agreements.

For the fourth channel of trade, foreign investment, considerations related to the intellectual property legal regime in the host country are even more important than in the other channels of trade. A common definition of foreign investment is the acquisition of lasting ownership rights by a business entity located in one country in a business entity organized and established in another country. Ownership rights, usually acquired through an infusion of capital, also allow the owner to exercise management control over the foreign business entity.

An example of foreign investment is when Supreme Industries, a corporation organized and established in the United States, establishes a wholly or partially owned subsidiary in Germany, France, China, or another foreign country. In this case, the German subsidiary is a business entity that is formed and organized under German law but is owned by a U.S. company with its headquarters in the United States. In order for the subsidiary to operate effectively in Germany, Supreme Industries, the U.S. parent, will need to provide its subsidiary with access to its proprietary technology. If the product is laundry detergent, Supreme Industries will give its German subsidiary access to the formula and enzymes that allow the subsidiary's product to clean clothes effectively. If the product is a drug, then Supreme Industries will have to provide access to its patents and know how to the Germany subsidiary. Without access to the U.S. parent company's technology, the German subsidiary will not be able to manufacture the product for the foreign market.

In many cases, the level of technology involved in foreign direct investment is higher than that involved in a pure licensing agreement between Supreme Industries, the U.S. parent, and an unaffiliated or third party licensee. Suppose that Supreme Industries also licenses its detergent formula to an unaffiliated detergent company in Germany. Supreme Industries may be willing to license only its secondary technologies to a third party so as to avoid direct intra-band competition with Supreme Industries's most successful and technologically advanced products. On the other hand, in a foreign direct investment scenario in which Supreme Industries invests substantial equity and human capital in a subsidiary that it owns and controls, Supreme Industries might be willing to license its most advanced technologies in order to be as competitive as possible in the German market. As technology transfer plays a critical role in foreign direct investment, the strength of the intellectual property legal regime in Germany or other target markets becomes a major consideration in moving forward with the foreign investment.

In all of these transactions in the modern global economy, intellectual property or technology plays a critical role. Indeed, it is the often the case that a U.S. company's technology—not its capital or its physical assets—is the most business asset that it owns. In the modern global economy, the intellectual property assets of a U.S. or foreign company may be far more valuable than the capital, inventory, and brick and mortar assets of the company. Think of a multinational company that designs, manufactures, and sells consumer electronics, mobile phones, software, and servers or a pharmaceutical company with patents, trademarks, and trade secrets for its drugs. The technology or the intellectual property assets owned by the multinational company, not its capital, is what is critical to its success in any market. The multinational company might invest hundreds of millions or billions of dollars in manufacturing and office operations in a foreign country, but its technology can far surpass in commercial value the amount of its capital investments. The growing importance of intellectual property in business and trade of all kinds in the modern global economy is one important reason why intellectual property has gone international.

Foreign investment is now viewed as critical to economic development by all countries, including many developing countries. The reason is that foreign investment is the best method for developing nations to absorb advanced technology and move up in the manufacturing and industrial value chain. A multinational company with advanced technology that invests in a foreign nation will need to send scientists, engineers, business managers, lawyers, accountants, and financial experts to the foreign nation to set run up and operate the foreign subsidiary. These foreign experts will help train local employees on how to use and implement the technology. The local employees may be sent to the United States for extended training periods. In other words, the multinational company will expect their foreign experts to teach and help train local employees that will replace them when the foreign experts exit and return to the United States. By then, the local employees will have absorbed the foreign technology and it becomes a permanent part of the local economy. This process, if repeated in many different industries, will allow the foreign nation to close the technology gap in rapid order with advanced industrialized countries. This is exactly the process by which China has been able to leapfrog into the top ranks of the world's economies in a span of a few decades. For this scenario to unfold, however, the foreign nation should have intellectual property laws and a legal regime that will be attractive enough to the U.S. or other foreign multinational company that may be willing to invest its technology in that nation.

The importance of intellectual property was reflected during the Uruguay round of negotiations from 1986 to 1994 leading to the establishment of the WTO to create a general agreement on intellectual property, TRIPS. Developed countries, led by the United States, were able to have intellectual property issues integrated into other trade issues in the WTO. Developing nations wanted to keep intellectual property out of the WTO as a separate and isolated field. Under the WTO, trade in technology is connected to other channels of trade. For example, a nation that violates TRIPS might be subject to increased tariffs on its exports of goods to the complaining nation. By creating TRIPS, the WTO recognized that in the modern world intellectual property and technology are an integral part of international trade.

2. THE "SYSTEM" OF INTERNATIONAL INTELLECTUAL PROPERTY

a. The International "System": Institutions and Organizations

As already noted, we will be examining the "system" of international intellectual property. This term is a bit of a misnomer. On the international level, there is no system that is comparable to a system of intellectual property laws at the domestic level. A system at the domestic level implies that there is a legislative body, a judicial and administrative body, and law enforcement bodies. None of this exists at the international level in any comparable form. The closest entity to a legislative body is the WTO that has implemented TRIPS but TRIPS is a treaty that does not apply directly in most domestic legal systems but must be implemented into law through domestic legislation. (A few nations apply WTO agreements directly.) TRIPS also sets forth minimum standards that many nations may exceed in their domestic legislation. For example, TRIPS requires a copyright term of life of the author plus 50 years while the United States has a term of life of the author plus 70 years.

Outside of the WTO there are other international organizations that are associated with important intellectual property treaties. The World Intellectual Property Organization (WIPO), an inter-governmental organization located in Geneva and affiliated with the United Nations, administers a number of important intellectual property treaties, including the Paris Convention applicable to patents and trademarks, the Madrid system for the international registration of trademarks, and the Patent Cooperation Treaty, signed in 1970. WIPO also administers the Berne Convention on copyrights, the WIPO Copyright Treaty that deals with copyright in the digital environment such as the internet, and the Rome Convention dealing with rights of performers.

Outside of the WTO and WIPO, there are the many regional and bilateral trade agreements, discussed in a later section of this chapter, such as the United States Mexico Canada Trade Agreement, that provide for "WTO plus" benefits in intellectual property protection. These regional and bilateral trade agreements also create intellectual property rights on an international level.

On the international level, there is no judicial body that reviews international intellectual property laws. The WTO has a dispute settlement system that reviews laws of member states for consistency with TRIPS, but this system is currently disabled as further discussed in a subsequent section. Concerning other intellectual property treaties, including the ones discussed in the previous paragraph, there is no judicial body that has the power to review issues concerning those treaties. There is also no international body that enforces intellectual property laws similar to domestic judicial, administrative, or police entities. The WTO has enforcement powers but due to the disabling of the dispute settlement system, the WTO is currently unable to enforce its obligations and rules.

On the regional level, another important institution is the European Union, a free trade area and customs union consisting of 27 nations. The EU is not only a free trade area but is also a political and economic union, using a single currency and cooperating on matters of justice and security throughout the entire EU. An outstanding feature of the EU is the common market that allows goods to travel duty free throughout the entire EU. Freedom of movement of goods is one of the famous "four freedoms" of the EU, which also includes the freedom of movement of persons (including legal persons), capital, and services. Although the four freedoms do not explicitly include intellectual property, barriers to the free movement of goods can be justified as necessary to protect intellectual property. The EU is at the forefront of intellectual property and many of its innovations in the field will be discussed in this book. In addition to the EU, various other free trade areas, including the United States Mexico Canada Trade Agreement, create intellectual property rights on a regional level.

b. The "System": Treaties and International Agreements

The terms "international intellectual property" are also a bit of a misnomer as there are no substantive intellectual property laws that are international in character. (Except in those cases where some nations apply TRIPS and other international intellectual property treaties directly in their domestic legal systems.) All substantive intellectual property rights are created by the national or domestic legislation of each country. Each nation has substantive laws that govern patents, trademarks, copyright and other intellectual property rights. The role of international law, such as TRIPS, is to set forth the standards to which national legislation must conform.

The need for international standards arises because national legislation creating intellectual property rights (as well as all other legislation) is binding and effective only within the territory of the nation enacting the laws and not on an exterritorial basis, i.e. outside the territory of the nation enacting the laws, except on an exceptional basis. Each sovereign nation has the right to enact its own laws. National sovereignty means that in theory each nation can enact its own intellectual property laws that differ from those of other nations. Country A could enact a patent law, Country B could enact a totally different patent law, and so forth, creating the possibility of serious divergences in intellectual property laws. The possibility of differing national substantive laws creates the need for harmonization. National intellectual property regimes with different rules make it difficult to have transactions and trade across different legal regimes.

Early efforts to create harmonization were made through the Berne Convention that applied to copyright and the Paris Convention that applied to patents and trademarks, but these efforts fell short. In their early years, membership in these conventions were limited to mainly to western nations and their colonial territories so any treaty standards were not universal. In addition, in the case of patents, the Paris Convention did not actually require patent protection, leaving it up to each nation to decide for itself whether to have patent laws at all. This meant that prior to TRIPS, patent laws around the world could differ in the basic elements of patent, patent term, and field of patent protection. Some nations, such as India, excluded entire fields, such as pharmaceuticals, from patent protection. This situation meant that a drug protected by a patent in the United States could be copied with impunity in India as U.S. patent law did not extend extraterritorially to India. The lack of patent protection for pharmaceuticals led to a thriving generic drug industry in India.

The advent of TRIPS fundamentally changed the intellectual property landscape on the international level. First, each nation that joins the WTO must adhere to TRIPS. All WTO general agreements that apply to goods, services, and technology are mandatory for all members. Those nations that wanted the benefit of low tariffs for their goods under the GATT also had to adhere to TRIPS. At present, total WTO membership consists of 166 nations (out of a total of 195 nations in the world) all of which must follow TRIPS. Unlike all prior international intellectual property treaties, TRIPS sets uniform standards for the full range of intellectual property rights: copyrights and performance rights, patents, trademarks, geographical indications, industrial designs, lay-out designs of integrated circuits, and trade secrets. Returning to our earlier patent example, as a result of TRIPS, all 166 WTO member countries must have patent laws that require the same basic elements: novelty, inventive step (or non-obviousness), and capable of industrial application (or utility) and all patents must enjoy a minimum term of 20 years. This is a remarkable achievement of harmonization on a global basis. A similar achievement has been obtained in each of the other intellectual property rights.

TRIPS also deals with the problems of exclusion of fields from patent protection as in the case of nations refusing to provide patent protection to pharmaceuticals alluded to earlier. Under TRIPS, patents must be available in all fields of technology. Nations can no longer pick and choose which products to exclude from patent protection but must include all fields of technology, including pharmaceuticals, in their patent laws.

Aside from promoting harmonization, international intellectual property treaties serve a second function: they facilitate the acquisition of intellectual property rights in foreign countries. As noted earlier, national intellectual property laws have effect only within the nation's territory and have no effect in the territory of other nations. If a rights holder wishes to obtain intellectual property protection in a foreign nation, the rights holder must follow all of the laws and procedures of the foreign nation. A U.S. patent owner who wishes to obtain protection in Germany, France, or China must file a separate patent application in each of those countries. As some intellectual property owners seek patents and trademarks in many different countries, the process of filing separate applications can be very time consuming and expensive. To facilitate the acquisition of patent and trademark rights on an international level, the Patent Cooperation Treaty, a special treaty under the Paris Convention, and the Madrid system, consisting of two treaties, the Madrid Agreement and the Madrid Protocol, simplify the process. The Patent Cooperation Treaty allows for a single patent application to be effective in multiple states and the Madrid system creates an international registration system, administered by WIPO in Geneva, that creates trademark rights effective in designated states. We will examine the procedures under both of these treaties in detail as well as other similar treaties in later chapters of this book.

Based on this discussion, we can say that the system of international intellectual property consists of two main components. First, there are the international institutions consisting of a loose conglomeration of inter-governmental institutions that deal with intellectual property issues, the most important of which remains the WTO. These institutions developed separately over a long period of time in accordance with national interests and there was never an overarching design at work. Although efforts are underway to coordinate efforts among them concerning intellectual property, these are separate and independent institutions serving their members and sometimes they will work at cross purposes. Second, there are international intellectual property treaties administered by these international organizations. These treaties create international standards that are implemented in domestic legislation. Many of the disputes in this area deal with the extent to which national legal systems faithfully implement TRIPS and conflicts between domestic laws and TRIPS and other WTO agreements. International treaties also facilitate the acquisition of intellectual property right in foreign countries.

As this discussion implies this book will not examine the specific intellectual property laws of nation states in any systematic fashion. Issues of national intellectual property laws will arise as warranted by the discussion of specific cases or issues. There is no attempt to do a survey of national intellectual property legal systems. Such a survey would be too time consuming for a treatment such as that contained in this book and is not necessary to understand the system of international intellectual property as those terms are used in this book.

3. THE PRINCIPLE OF TERRITORIALITY

If we start with the fundamental premise that all substantive intellectual property laws are bound by the principle of territory, the next questions that arise concern the appropriate sphere of application of such national laws. A related issue concerns how to resolve conflicts among such laws in a world with many different nations with many different substantive laws. We can understand the scope of national law by starting with the principle of territoriality, which posits that each nation has the power or jurisdiction to enact valid and binding laws within its own territory but, in general, lacks the power to enact laws with binding effect outside of its territory. This principle gives rise the following corollary issues.

> Illustration 1-1: Country A enacts a national patent law. An inventor, Issac, obtains a patent under Country A's patent registration system. In the absence of an international treaty, Issac's patent is effective only within the territory of Country A. Issac's patent has no effect in Country B or any other country. If Issac wishes to obtain patent protection in Country B then Issac must obtain a patent under Country B's laws by meeting the requirements of Country B's laws and following its registration procedures. Fortunately, after TRIPS, the substantive requirements of Country B's patent laws are similar to those of Country A as they are both WTO countries. However, Issac must still follow Country's B's registration procedures. In the absence of an international treaty such as the Patent Cooperation Treaty, Issac must also follow the procedures for obtaining a patent in any other country of the world in which Issac wishes to obtain patent protection.

The principle of territoriality is part of the larger doctrine of jurisdiction to prescribe that deals with a nation's power to enact valid and binding laws. In international law, the principle of territoriality is well accepted as a basis of a nation's jurisdiction to prescribe. The principle applies not only to intellectual property laws but in general to all laws of a nation.

Aside from the territoriality principle, a second basis for jurisdiction to prescribe is based upon the principle of nationality, i.e. each nation has the power to enact valid and binding laws affecting its own nationals wherever in the world they may be located. For example, the United States has the power to enact laws affecting U.S. citizens no matter what nation its citizens happen to be in on a temporary or permanent basis. As U.S. law applies to its citizens in a foreign country, nationality provides the basis for exterritorial application of law but as the power of nations to bind their own nationals is viewed as sacrosanct, the exterritorial application of law based on the nationality principle is well accepted.

A third basis for jurisdiction to prescribe is a based on the effects principle, which holds that where activity or conduct outside of a nation has substantial effects within that nation, the nation has the power to prescribe valid laws concerning that activity or conduct. For example, suppose that a cartel of companies in a foreign nation agree on conduct such as price-fixing that has an anti-competitive effect within the United States. On the basis of the conduct's harmful effects in its territory, the United States can assert that its antitrust laws reach this conduct in a foreign nation and makes the conduct illegal and actionable in a U.S. court. The effects doctrine is controversial; the United States has asserted the effects doctrine as a justification for the exterritorial application of U.S. law in many situations causing tension with other nations. In the area of intellectual property, the principle of territoriality is the most often used basis for the enactment of valid and binding laws and it is a widely accepted norm of international law. Except in rare circumstances, such intellectual property laws do not have any extraterritorial effect.

Under the principle of territoriality, it becomes possible to have multiple intellectual property rights for the same subject matter owned by different entities in different countries. For example, it is possible to have a U.S. patent for an invention that is valid and enforceable in the United States, a German patent for the same invention that is valid and enforceable in Germany, a Brazilian patent, a Japanese patent, a Chinese patent and so on. Each of these patents is for the same invention but each is a separate and independent patent. Moreover, each patent may have a different owner. The inventor may be owner in the United States, but a different entity may own one or more of the foreign patents. This consequence of territoriality means that intellectual property holders need to file separately for intellectual property rights in each country in which they seek intellectual property protection (although this task is alleviated to some extent by international treaties that facilitate international applications and registrations, a topic we consider in detail later in this book). Many intellectual property holders have a portfolio consisting of hundreds or thousands of patents, trademarks, and copyrights registered in countries around the world.

An illuminating application of the principle of territoriality is provided by *Subafilms, Ltd. v. MGM-Pathé Communications Co.*, 24 F.3d 1088 (9th Cir. 1994) (en banc). In 1967, the Beatles through Subafilms, a joint venture with the Hearst Corporation, entered into a licensing agreement to distribute and finance the film, "Yellow Submarine." In the 1980s, the distributor, MGM/UA Communications, authorized the distribution of the film on videocassette for both the U.S. domestic and foreign markets.

Subafilms subsequently brought suit against MGM/UA for copyright infringement. Subafilms argued that the original distribution agreement did not authorize distribution of videocassettes of the film as videocassette technology did not even exist when the original distribution agreement was entered into in 1967. When MGM/UA authorized its subsidiary to distribute videocassettes of the film in the United States, MGM/UA infringed the Beatles' U.S. copyright in the film as the distribution rights to videocassettes were never licensed in the 1967 agreement. The district court held that both the domestic and foreign distribution violated the Beatles's U.S. copyright in the film. On appeal, a panel of the Ninth Circuit initially affirmed the district court decision as to both the domestic distribution and foreign distribution.

The Ninth Circuit opinion did not focus on the domestic distribution of the videocassette. All U.S.

copyright owners possess the right to distribute their works in the United States and MGM/UA's unauthorized distribution of the video cassette clearly violated this right. Rather the Ninth Circuit focused its opinion on the foreign distribution of the videocassettes. As U.S. copyright law is limited by the principle of territoriality, the Beatles had no right to control the distribution of Yellow Submarine videocassettes in foreign countries. However, the panel of the Ninth Circuit believed that it had to follow an earlier decision *Peter Starr Products Company v. Twin Continental Films, Inc.* 783 F.2d 1440 (9th Cir. 1986), which held that even though the activity itself—the foreign distribution—is not actionable because it takes place outside of the United States, the authorization of the activity that does take place in the United States constituted a contributory infringement. Relying on *Peter Starr*, the Ninth Circuit panel affirmed the district court decision.

In a rehearing en banc, the Ninth Circuit rejected the line of reasoning in *Peter Starr*. The Ninth Circuit held that there can be no liability for contributory infringement unless the authorized activity itself constituted an infringement. Since MGM/UA's distribution of the videocassettes in foreign countries is not an infringement of Subafilms's right of distribution, the authorization in the United States by MGM/UA cannot be contributory infringement.

The Ninth Circuit established a clear line of demarcation: U.S. copyright law governs distribution in the United States but does not govern distribution in foreign countries and no one can be held liable by the U.S. copyright holder for affecting distribution rights to its works overseas. The *Peter Starr* line of reasoning had blurred the clear lines drawn by the territoriality principle.

4. THE PRINCIPLE OF NATIONAL TREATMENT

The territoriality principle both empowers a nation to enact valid and binding laws within its own territory and limits its ability to enact laws outside of its territory. The limitations imposed by the territoriality principle can create problems for intellectual property owners as it can leave them open to infringing activity in foreign markets.

> Illustration 1-2: Anisa has intellectual property rights that are created by the law of Country A. Under the principle of territoriality, Anisa's intellectual property rights are valid and enforceable within Country A but have no effect in Country B. In the absence of a bilateral treaty between Country A and Country B requiring the latter to recognize Anisa's intellectual property rights in Country B, pirates in Country B can infringe Anisa's intellectual property rights by making unauthorized copies with impunity in Country B. Anisa has no legal recourse in Country B.

One approach was for Country A and Country B to enter into a bilateral treaty requiring each country to recognize the intellectual property rights of the other. Of course, this was a cumbersome method and would have to be repeated with many countries to afford effective protections on an international basis. Such an approach was not feasible on a long-term basis and a new approach was needed. The other problem with this approach was that the bilateral treaty used a principle of mutual reciprocity that was itself difficult to apply.

On the basis of a principle of mutual reciprocity set forth in a bilateral treaty, Country B would recognize Anisa's patent in its territory if Country A would recognize in its territory a patent acquired in Country B. The problem created by the principle of reciprocity was that it required Country B to apply the laws of Country A. This was not always an easy task. Country B had to interpret the laws of Country A, which might be in a foreign language, and apply the laws of a foreign legal system. Such an analysis could be difficult and time-consuming. Moreover, the principle of reciprocity required Country A to engage in the same analysis for each country where Anisa sought recognition of her patent, such as Country C, D, and so forth. This was a burdensome and complex task. The practical problems associated with the principle of mutual reciprocity prevented it from acquiring widespread acceptance as a norm of international law.

The current approach lies in the national treatment (NT) principle. The NT principle helps to overcome the limitations created by the principle of territoriality and is not plagued by the issues associated with the principle of mutual reciprocity.

In 1852, France issued a decree that a work of any origin would be entitled to the same copyright protection in France that French works received under French law. This decree, a bold move by France, established for the first time the use of the NT principle in intellectual property law. Under NT, foreign works are given the same intellectual property protections enjoyed by French works under French law. The effect of the NT principle is to assimilate foreign works to the laws of France; foreign works are treated as French works for the purposes of copyright protection.

Unlike the principle of reciprocity, NT is simple to apply. The host nation gives the foreign work the same treatment that it would receive under French law. This bold move by France sparked the beginning of a movement to accept NT as a basic principle of international intellectual property law. The national treatment principle was later incorporated into the Berne Convention applying to copyright in 1886 and the Paris Convention applying to patents and trademarks in 1883.

The national treatment principle as applied to the trade in goods was set forth in Article III of GATT 1947. With the establishment of the WTO in 1995, the national treatment principle was incorporated in TRIPS Article 3(1):

TRIPS

Article 3
National Treatment

(1) Each Member shall accord to the nationals of other Members treatment no less favorable than that it accords to its own nationals with regard to the protection of intellectual property, subject to the exceptions already provided in, respectively, the Paris Convention (1967), the Berne Convention (1971), the Rome Convention or the Treaty on Intellectual Property in Respect of Integrated Circuits. In respect of performers, producers of phonograms and broadcasting organizations, this obligation only applies in respect of the rights provided under this Agreement.

* * *

Illustration 1-3: Maria has a copyright for a work under the laws of Country A and seeks to sell the work to Country B but is concerned about unauthorized copying and piracy. Under the NT principle, if citizens of Country B have the right to prevent unauthorized copying of the work, Maria must be given the same protection in Country B. Assuming that nationals of Country B who own copyrights can prevent unauthorized copying of their works, Maria can prevent parties in Country B from violating her copyright and making unauthorized copies.

Note that the NT principle requires national treatment for the foreign work and for the foreign author or national. The foreign work is given the same rights as a domestic work and the foreign national is given the same right as a national of the country where protection is sought.

NT is not a principle of equality; it is a principle of non-discrimination. NT does not require equal treatment for foreign nationals and domestic nationals. Rather, a WTO member cannot treat foreign nationals *less* favorably than it treats its own nationals. So long as a nation does not treat foreign nationals less favorably, NT is satisfied even if the treatment of foreign and domestic intellectual property owners differs. A nation could also treat foreign nationals *more* favorably than it treats its own nationals without violating NT.

> Illustration 1-4: Country D grants a term of copyright protection to foreign authors of life of the author plus 70 years but grants a term of life of the author plus 50 years to its own authors. This differential treatment is *not* a violation of the NT principle. Countries are precluded under NT from treating foreign nationals less favorably with respect to intellectual property rights, but NT does not prevent countries from treating foreign nationals more favorably. Most countries, however, do not normally treat foreign intellectual property owners more favorably than their own nationals.

One example of a nation treating foreign works more favorably is the requirement under U.S. law that works of U.S. origin must be registered with the U.S. copyright office before the copyright holder can file a lawsuit in federal district court for copyright infringement. A work of foreign origin does not need to be registered for the rights holder to file an infringement lawsuit in federal district court in the United States.

A good example of how NT protects foreign works in the context of the European Union is provided by *Phil Collins v. Imtrat Handelsgesellschaft GmbH*, ECR 1–5145, C–92/92 (Oct. 30, 1993). Phil Collins, a musical performer and composer of UK nationality, gave a concert in the United States. During the concert, unknown parties recorded unauthorized or bootleg copies of Collins's performance on compact disks. Later, a German company sold and distributed the bootleg CDs in Germany. Phil Collins sought to enjoin the distribution of the bootleg copies in Germany.

Under applicable German law, German nationals had the right to prohibit the distribution within Germany of bootleg copies regardless of whether the performance took place in Germany or in another country. By contrast, under German law, foreign nationals could prohibit the distribution of bootleg copies within Germany only if the performance took place in Germany. As Collins, a UK national, gave the concert in the United States, Collins could not enjoin the distribution of the bootleg copies under applicable German law.

The case was first brought in a German court but as the issue was whether German law was consistent with the superseding national treatment principle of the EU, the German courts referred the case to the

European Court of Justice. The applicable EU rule in the case was the national treatment principle as set forth in the European Economic Community Treaty. The current version of the national treatment principle is contained in Article 18 of the Treaty on the Functioning of the European Union (2009), which reads as follows: "Within the scope of application of this Treaty, and without prejudice to any special provisions contained therein, any discrimination on the grounds of nationality shall be prohibited."

The ECJ found that the national treatment principle required that foreign nations be placed on "a completely equal footing with nationals of the Member State concerned. [I]t precludes a Member State from making the grant of an exclusive right subject to the requirement that the person concerned be a national of the State." *Phil Collins*, ECR 1–5145 at ¶ 32. In this case, Collins, a UK national, was denied the right to stop the distribution of the bootleg copies of the concert because the concert was given outside of Germany. German nationals would have been able to stop the distribution of the bootleg CDs as they have the right under German law to do so regardless of whether the performance was given in Germany or outside of Germany. The German law conditioned the right to stop bootleg copies of concerts given outside of Germany on having German nationality. This requirement constituted discrimination against foreign nationals in violation of the national treatment principle of the EU.

If Collins had been a U.S. national instead of a UK national, then Collins would have lost the case under

EU law. The United States is not a member of the EU so a U.S. national would not be entitled to the protection of the national treatment principle under EU law. The United States, however, is a member of the WTO and the EU is also a member in its own right and its states are also members individually of the WTO. While a U.S. national is not protected by the national treatment principle of EU law, a U.S. national is entitled to the benefits of the national treatment principle of TRIPS and the WTO. The German law discriminates against U.S. nationals and is inconsistent with TRIPS. The result in *Phil Collins* would have been the same for a U.S. national, but under TRIPS.

The holding of *Phil Collins* case concerned the national treatment principle of the EU and so it did not deal directly with the NT principle set forth in TRIPS. However, the reasoning of the *Phil Collins* case—discrimination against foreign nationals—is equally applicable within the context of the WTO and serves as a good example of how national treatment serves to protect intellectual property rights in the international context.

5. THE MOST FAVORED NATION PRINCIPLE

A second major principle applicable in the field of international intellectual property and international trade law as a whole is the most favored nation (MFN) principle. Together, the NT and MFN principles form the foundation of international intellectual property law and international trade law in general.

MNF was already well established in international trade before TRIPS, having been enshrined in Article I of the 1947 General Agreement on Tariffs and Trade, applicable to the international trade in goods. MFN is also a principle of non-discrimination: under MFN, a nation cannot give special benefits or preferences to one trading partner; any benefit or preference given by a nation to one of its trading partners must be given to all other countries of the WTO. Both NT and MFN are principles of non-discrimination. NT is a principle of internal non-discrimination prohibiting discrimination against foreign intellectual property owners in favor of domestic intellectual property owners in the internal market; MFN is a principle of external non-discrimination prohibiting discrimination among a nation's foreign trading partners.

Unlike the national treatment principle, MFN was not contained in the early major intellectual property agreements such as the Berne or Paris Conventions, although MFN did appear in some bilateral agreements. TRIPS is the first major international intellectual property agreement to contain MFN. Together NT and MFN are the foundational twin pillars within TRIPS.

TRIPS

Article 4
Most-Favored-Nation Treatment

With regard to the protection of intellectual property, any advantage favor, privilege of immunity granted by a Member to the nationals of any other country shall be accorded immediately and unconditionally to the nationals of all other Members. Exempted from this obligation are any advantage, favour, privilege or immunity accorded by a Member:

(a) deriving from international agreements on judicial assistance or law enforcement of a general nature and not particularly confined to the protection of intellectual property;

(b) granted in accordance with the provisions of the Berne Convention (1971) or the Rome Convention authorizing that the treatment accorded be a function not of national treatment but of the treatment accorded in another country;

(c) in respect of the rights of performers, producers of phonograms and broadcasting organizations not provided under this Agreement;

(d) deriving from international agreements related to the protection of intellectual property which entered into force prior to the entry into force of the WTO Agreement, provided that such agreements are notified to the Council for TRIPS and do not constitute an arbitrary or unjustifiable discrimination against nationals of other Members.

* * *

Illustration 1-5. Country A gives nationals of Country B an additional term of patent protection of five years beyond its normal term of 20 years. Country A must immediately and unconditionally extend the patent terms of nationals of all WTO members an additional five years.

MNF requires that *any* benefit given to nationals of another country with regard to intellectual property must be extended immediately and unconditionally to nationals of all WTO countries. The benefit may be purely procedural or administrative.

Illustration 1-6. Country A waives all fees and simplifies documents requirements for the registration of patents for nationals of Country B, a WTO country. Under Article 4 of TRIPS, Country A must immediately and unconditionally grant the same benefits to nationals from Country C, a WTO member, as well as to nationals from all other WTO members. Even though the waiver of fees and simplified documents requirements do not affect substantive patent rights these are benefits that must be accorded to all WTO members.

MFN requires any benefit given by a member of the WTO to the nationals of *any other* country—including countries that are members as well as non-members of the WTO—must be given immediately and unconditionally to the nationals of all other members of the WTO.

Illustration 1-7. Assume that Country B is not a member of the WTO. The results in Illustrations 1-5 and 1-6 remain the same. Country A must grant the same benefits given to the nationals of Country B to nationals from all WTO members. Article 4 requires that any benefit granted by a WTO member to "*any other country*," whether or not a WTO member, must be immediately and unconditionally granted to nationals of all WTO members.

Illustration 1-8. Now assume that Country C is not a member of the WTO. In the absence of a bilateral treaty requiring MFN treatment for Country C, Country A has no obligation to extend the same benefits given to nationals of Country B to Country C.

These illustrations indicate why so many countries wish to join the WTO. The prospect of receiving MFN treatment for intellectual property (as well as for the trade in goods and services) creates a powerful inducement for countries to join the WTO.

The term "most favored nation," although still commonly used, is a bit of a misnomer. The term seems to suggest that MFN treatment is preferential treatment reserved for a select few, but in practice MFN treatment is now the norm. The United States gives MFN treatment to most countries in the world. All WTO nations, 166 countries at this writing, receive MFN treatment from the United States not only in the area of intellectual property but in the areas of trade in goods and services. The MFN principle is also found in all recent bilateral or multilateral investment and trade agreements between the United States and its trading partners. Only certain pariah nations, such as North Korea, do not receive MFN treatment from the United States. For this reason, the United States now prefers to use the term "Permanent Normal Trade Relations" instead of MFN to describe its trade relations with its trading partners to avoid any confusion.

The WTO demonstrated how MFN applies to intellectual property rights in *United States—Section 211 Omnibus Appropriations Act of 1998,* WT/DS176/AB/R (January 2, 2002) decided by the WTO Appellate body. The case involved the 1960 confiscation by Fidel Castro and the Cuban government of the business assets and trademarks in Cuba for "Havana Club Rum" owned by the Arechabala family. Beginning in 1963, the United States imposed a trade embargo on Cuba. Although Cuba could not trade with the United States, Cuba-Export, the state trading company that owned the Havana Club Rum trademark in Cuba, was able to register the Havana Club Rum trademark in the United States and obtained a U.S. trademark registration in 1976.

In 1993, Cuba-Export entered into a joint venture with Pernod Ricard, a French company, and an international distributor of liquor. Although Cuba-Export and Pernod were still barred from selling products with the trademark Havana Club Rum in the United States, the joint venture renewed its U.S. trademark for Havana Club Rum in 1996. Meanwhile a competitor, Barcardi & Co. and its U.S. affiliate Barcardi-Martini, began selling rum under the Havana Club Rum trademark produced in Bermuda to the United States. The Cuban-French joint venture thereafter sued Barcardi for trademark infringement in the United States.

While the lawsuit was pending and in response to lobbying pressure, Congress passed § 211 of the U.S. Omnibus Appropriations Act of 1998. Section 211 contained a provision prohibiting a U.S. court from enforcing trademarks in the United States belonging to "designated nationals" (defined as "Cuba or any national thereof") that had been confiscated by the Cuban government unless the original owner gave its consent. The Second Circuit Court of Appeals held that § 211 barred the Cuban-French joint venture from enforcing its Havana Club Rum trademark rights in the U.S. because the Arechabalas had never given their consent to the Cuban-French joint venture to use the trademark in United States. To the contrary, the Arechabala family had sold all of its rights in the trademark to Barcardi instead.

The WTO Appellate Body held that § 211 violated the MFN principle contained in TRIPS. Section 211 applied only to "designated nationals" defined as "Cuba or its nationals." This singled out Cuban nationals for a special procedural burden not applicable to nationals from other WTO members. Only Cuban nationals had to demonstrate that they had obtained permission from the pre-confiscation owner of the confiscated trademark in Cuba. Under the terms of § 211, non-Cuban nationals were not burdened with this extra procedural hurdle. As the United States did not require nationals of France (or of any other WTO member) to obtain permission from the pre-confiscation owner, the United States was obligated under the MFN principle to extend the same benefit to nationals from all other WTO members. As Cuba was a member of the WTO, all Cuban nationals were entitled to the same benefits given by the United States to non-Cuban nationals of other WTO members, that is, the ability to enforce trademark rights in the United States freed from the burden of having to obtain permission from the pre-confiscation owner.

In *United States—Section 211*, the complainants did not argue that they were deprived of additional rights given to nationals of another WTO member. Rather, they complained that they were subject to an additional burden that did not apply to the nationals of any other WTO member and that they had the right to be free from that added burden. MFN not only requires that a WTO member extend additional rights given to any country to all WTO members but that a WTO member not impose a burden on one WTO country while exempting all others from the same burden. MFN prevents WTO countries from singling out a country for differential treatment whether it is beneficial or harmful. A WTO country wishing to mete out harsh treatment to one nation must do so for all WTO nations, a prospect that should deter singling out any one country for unfavorable treatment.

6. EXCEPTIONS TO MFN

The MFN principle is subject to a number of important exceptions in the WTO, including exceptions for essential security interests (GATT,

Article XXI(b)), general exceptions based on civil society concerns such as human, animal or plant life or health (GATT, Article XX(a)), and exceptions related to the conservation of exhaustible natural resources (GATT Article XX(g)). For example, the United States has placed export restrictions on certain advanced technologies to China. Restrictions aimed at China alone on their face violate MFN as they apply to China but to no other WTO member, but the restriction can be justified by the United States as necessary to protect its national security interests under GATT Article XXI(b).

For present purposes the most important exception to MFN is for free trade and preferential trade areas such as the EU and the United States Mexico Canada Trade Agreement (USMCA), which replaced the North American Free Trade Agreement on July 1, 2020. Free trade areas give trade preferences and benefits in the trade in goods, technology, services, and investment to members of the free trade area but not to non-members. For example, under the USMCA, the vast bulk of goods traded among its members are subject to zero tariffs. On their face, free trade areas are inconsistent with MFN as they extend preferential treatment to free trade area members only, leaving out the rest of the WTO. However, if free trade areas were required by MFN to provide the same preferences and benefits to non-members, then free trade areas would become impossible.

GATT Article XXIV provides an exception to MFN for free trade areas in goods. Article V of the General

Agreement on Trade in Services (GATS) also recognizes an exception to MFN for trade in services for free trade areas. TRIPS Article 4 (MFN principle) does not recognize the same exception for free trade areas but because the EU itself is a member of the WTO (as well as each EU nation), the nationals of the separate EU states are treated as a single group of nations for purposes of EU law. One could justify the preferences within the EU for intellectual property rights are those within a single WTO member and so no MFN issue arises. As the preferences are all within one member (the EU) and have not been extended to another member, they do not have to be extended to all other WTO members under MFN.

Other preferential trade areas, such as USMCA also enjoy an exception to MFN for intellectual property although the basis for such an exception is not clear as the USMCA is not itself a member of the WTO. At present, however, no one has challenged the exception to MFN for intellectual property rights in free trade and preferential trade areas.

TRIPS Article 4 also contains exceptions for obligations deriving from international agreements on judicial assistance or law enforcement of a general nature, for matters expressly excluded from national treatment under the Berne and Paris Conventions, for intellectual property agreements grandfathered in before the WTO was established, and for rights of performers, producers of phonograms and broadcasting organizations. TRIPS, Art. 4 (a)–(d). The latter category of performance rights is excluded due to the lower level of esteem accorded to performance rights as opposed to copyright. We return to the subject matter of copyright and performance rights in the next chapter.

7. THE PRINCIPLE OF TERRITORIALITY AND CHOICE OF LAW

The principle of territoriality is fundamental and has implications in many areas of intellectual property law. One of these areas is in choice of law issues for international intellectual property disputes. Choice of law issues arise in any case (not just intellectual property cases) that has contacts with more than one jurisdiction.

> Illustration 1-9. In a technology licensing contract that involves negotiations and other contacts that occur in both Country A and Country B, a dispute arises. An issue of choice of law, i.e. what law governs the contract is a preliminary issue in the dispute. As the contract has contacts with both Country A and Country B, under traditional choice of law analysis, the contract can be governed by the law of Country A or by the law of Country B or by a combination of both as to different issues in the case. A court will have to make a decision of the applicable law using the choice of law rules of the jurisdiction in which the court sits.

A strict application of the territoriality principle leads to a simple straightforward result in the choice of law in Illustration 1-9.

> Illustration 1-10. In the previous illustration, a strict application of the territoriality principle would require that the law to be applied is the law of the forum. If the lawsuit is brought in Country A, then a court of Country A should apply the law of Country A to the technology licensing contract. The laws of Country A are effective in the forum court. The laws of Country B have no extraterritorial effect in Country A.

If we now also apply the national treatment principle then the same result is reached.

> Illustration 1-11. Under the same facts as in the previous illustration, Country A now applies the national treatment principle. Under NT, the courts of Country A should treat the licensing contract as if it were a contract of Country A and extend the same intellectual property rights and treatment to the contract as it would extend to any technology licensing contract entered into in Country A. All rights and obligations should be treated as governed by Country A's laws even as to events that occurred in Country B that would otherwise be governed by the law of Country B.

The merits of this approach are its simplicity and ease of administration. Under the NT and territoriality principles, the forum court applies its own law to all aspects of the case, including to any events that occur in Country B. This allows the court to avoid applying the law of Country B, a foreign jurisdiction, which will always involve additional burdens for the court as the law may be in a foreign language and the court may not be familiar with foreign law and find it difficult to interpret. The merits of this approach also avoid having one set of issues subject to the law of the forum court and another set of issues subject to foreign law. This will prove difficult for any court to manage but could be particularly so if a jury consisting of laypersons is involved.

Although the application of the territoriality and the national treatment principles seem to dictate the result that the law of the forum should govern the contract, U.S. courts have not always followed this approach. Rather, some courts have undertaken a more complex approach. This is exemplified in the next case discussed below decided in the Second Circuit Court of Appeals, one of the most influential courts in the United States.

In *ITAR-TASS Russian News Agency v. Russian Kurier, Inc.*, 153 F.3d 82 (2d Cir. 1998), the defendant Kurier was a Russian language newspaper in the New York area. Kurier cut and pasted articles from the plaintiffs' Russian language newspapers in Russia and Israel. The plaintiffs in the case were all Russian newspapers and ITAR-TASS, a Russian government news agency. The district court found that the defendant had infringed the plaintiffs' Russian copyrights and enjoined the defendant from further copying the newspapers and awarded damages to the plaintiffs in the amount of $500,000.

On appeal the Second Circuit examined the choice of law issue and the effect of the national treatment principle on the choice of law analysis. The Second Circuit discussed the views of commentators such as

Nimmer and Stewart who claimed that under the national treatment principle, the case should be decided under the law of the state where the infringement occurred, the United States, and that all issues, including ownership, should be decided under U.S. law.

Note also that under the Berne Convention, the Russian plaintiffs were asserting a U.S. copyright claim under U.S. law. Under the Berne Convention, when the Russian plaintiffs acquired a Russian copyright, they also acquired a basket of national copyrights in each of the Berne countries at the same time. This follows from the Berne Convention's interpretation of the national treatment principle contained in Berne Convention Article 5(1). (We will return to an extended discussion of this concept in the next chapter on copyright.) As a result, the Russian plaintiffs also acquired a U.S. copyright under U.S. law for the contents of the Russian newspapers. In fact, the plaintiffs expressly asserted a U.S. copyright claim in the district court for the Russian newspapers. If the court had accepted the plaintiffs' position that they were asserting a U.S. copyright, then the court should have applied U.S. law to all issues, including the issues of ownership as well as infringement. As to ownership, under the U.S. work-for-hire doctrine, the court would have found that the newspapers were the owners of the copyrights in the articles as the newspapers were the employers of the reporters who wrote the articles. The court then would award damages for the illegal copying to the newspapers and ITAR-TASS, the news agency.

The Second Circuit, however, found that all the national treatment principle required was that the law of the forum state applied to issues of infringement and that the law should be applied even handedly to U.S. and foreign authors. Having disposed of the national treatment principle in this quick fashion, the Second Circuit then engaged in a choice of law analysis and found that Russian law governed the issue of ownership of the copyright for the articles and that under Russian law, there is an explicit exception to the work-for-hire doctrine in the case of newspapers. Under Russian law, the authors owned the copyright in the articles whereas the Russian newspapers could have a copyright in the selection and arrangement of the articles, assuming the selection and arrangement displayed a sufficient amount of creativity. As a result, the Second Circuit reversed the holding of the district court awarding damages to the newspapers (as the reporters, not the newspapers, owned the copyright and the reporters were not among the plaintiffs) and remanded the case for a determination of whether the newspapers might have a copyright in the selection and arrangement of the articles. ITAR-TASS was entitled to damages, however, as government news agencies, as opposed to newspapers, owned the copyright in the articles not the authors.

The Second Circuit's opinion seems to have given little weight to the national treatment principle. A basic feature of the Berne Convention is that its national treatment principle automatically gives any member with a copyright in any Berne Union country a basket of national copyrights in all other Berne

Union countries. This is a generally accepted interpretation of the Berne Convention. Under the Berne Convention, the Russian newspapers acquired a U.S. copyright at the same time they acquired the Russian copyright. The Second Circuit should have applied U.S. copyright law to determine the issues related to ownership of the copyright. Under the U.S. work-for-hire doctrine, the Russian newspapers owned the copyright in the Russian newspaper articles, thus supporting an award of damages to the newspapers. Under this approach, a U.S. court would simply have to decide the issue of ownership under U.S. law. However, the Second Circuit, without explanation, refused to accept the plaintiffs' claims under the Berne Convention.

Under the Second Circuit's approach, the court would have to decide the ownership issue under foreign law, in this case Russian law, with all of the attendant complexities involved such as the use of dueling experts engaged by the parties in *ITAR-TASS* on matters of interpretation of Russian law. Moreover, the Second Circuit further indicated that the issue of infringement, unlike the issue of ownership, would be decided by the principle of *lex loci delicti*, i.e. by the law of the place where the infringement occurred. Thus, under the Second Circuit approach, the ownership issue would be decided under Russian law whereas the infringement issue would be decided under U.S. law. Under an approach based upon the principle of territoriality and the national treatment principle, both the issues of ownership and infringement would be decided under U.S. law.

The approach by the Second Circuit is complex and time consuming as it bifurcates the applicable law into two national regimes, Russian law for ownership and U.S. law for infringement. Although the Second Circuit has been criticized for the *ITAR-TASS* decision, the case appears to be good law. The Second Circuit Court of Appeals is an important court; its decision is binding on federal district courts in the circuit and the decision may possibly carry weight in other circuits. So it is important to understand that its approach may be followed by other courts, even if it is at odds with how some experts would interpret the application of the national treatment and territoriality principles.

B. THE WTO AND REGIONAL FREE TRADE AGREEMENTS

Although this book referred to important international organizations earlier in this chapter in its discussion of the system of international intellectual property, several institutions merit a more in-depth discussion. These are the WTO, the EU, and other free trade agreements.

1. THE WORLD TRADE ORGANIZATION

The WTO came into existence on January 1, 1995 to serve the role that the International Trade Organization was originally intended to serve as a vehicle to facilitate trade between its member states. As noted earlier, the ITO never came into existence due to opposition from the United States. The GATT 1947 became a treaty without an administering organization that was managed by a skeletal staff in Geneva for nearly 50 years. The WTO now serves as the administrative organization for all of the WTO agreements, which includes GATT 1994, the updated version of GATT 1947, and TRIPS.

The WTO administers the three major agreements that cover trade in goods governed by the General Agreement on Tariffs and Trade, trade in services governed by the General Agreement on Trade in Services, and trade in technology governed by the Agreement on Trade-Related Intellectual Property Rights. For historical reasons, the WTO lacks a general agreement on investment trade. The WTO also administers a fourth major agreement, the Understanding on Rules and Procedures Governing the Settlement of Disputes also known as the Dispute Settlement Understanding (Dispute Understanding).

The WTO consists of 166 members as of this writing. The highest authority of the WTO is the Ministerial Conference, a meeting held every two years of all of the trade ministers of its members. When the Ministerial Conference is not in session, the highest body is the General Council, a permanent standing body that consists of the representatives of each member in Geneva. Most WTO members have a permanent delegation present in Geneva, Switzerland. For least-developed country members only about one third have a permanent delegation in Geneva. The chief U.S. representative in Geneva is the Deputy United States Trade Representative who also heads the U.S. mission to the WTO.

The WTO is designed to facilitate two fundamental goals: to provide a forum in which countries can negotiate new trade concessions and a forum in which countries can resolve trade disputes. All decisions in the WTO are made by consensus (i.e. a decision to which no member formally objects). The rationale behind the principle of consensus is that the majority will not ramrod decisions on an unwilling minority. Although the WTO agreements allow a majority vote to be taken when consensus is not possible, the WTO has never deviated from the tradition of decisions by consensus and is unlikely to do so in the near future. As consensus can be difficult to achieve, change in the WTO, such as amending one of the WTO agreements, occurs very slowly taking years or decades.

The WTO has separate councils set up to administer and monitor each of the major agreements. There is a GATT Council focusing the trade in goods and a GATS Council focusing on the trade in services. The TRIPS Council monitors the laws of each WTO member for compliance with TRIPS and is intended to identify issues early on in the drafting of a member's legislation so as to allow the TRIPS Council to work with members in resolving the problems before a trade conflict arises. Aside from the councils for the three major agreements, the WTO also has committees to study special topics. Directly under the General Council are committees on trade and the environment, trade and development (involving developing countries), among others. Under the GATT Council for the trade in goods are committees on market access, agriculture, sanitary and phytosanitary measures, technical barriers to trade, among others. Aside from committees are working parties and working groups that serve to negotiate issues directly with WTO members. At the moment, unlike the GATT and GATS Councils, TRIPS does not have any committees, working parties, or working groups.

The WTO also administers the WTO dispute settlement system, a major improvement over the prior system under the GATT. Under the GATT, the various aspects of the dispute settlement system were also subject to decision-making through the principle of consensus. Under the principle of consensus, all contracting parties, including the parties to a dispute, had to agree by consensus to establish a GATT dispute panel. A party to a dispute could effectively block the establishment of a panel by lodging a formal objection. The GATT panel, consisting of three arbitrators, decided the dispute but in order to become legally effective a panel decision had to be adopted by all of the contracting parties by consensus. A losing party also had the power to veto the adoption of a report.

Like the GATT, the WTO dispute system consists of panels, composed of three panelists, which operate like a trial court, but unlike the GATT, the WTO also includes an Appellate Body, which acts like a high court of international trade. The third entity in the dispute system is the Dispute Settlement Body, which must adopt panel or Appellate Body decisions before they become legally effective. The General Council of the WTO consisting of the entire WTO membership meets as the Dispute Settlement Body to consider adoption of panel or Appellate Body decisions. In a major departure from the GATT, WTO members can no longer block the establishment of panels. In addition, the Dispute Body operates under the principle of "reverse consensus", i.e. the Dispute Body must adopt a decision unless there is a consensus *not* to adopt the decision, meaning that a decision is adopted even if only one WTO member votes in favor of adoption. As a practical matter, all decisions are adopted by the Dispute Body. This is a major improvement over the GATT system.

In another major departure from its predecessor, the Dispute Body has enforcement powers to back its decisions. WTO decisions that find a violation of TRIPS (or other WTO obligations) make a "recommendation" to the offending member to bring its non-complying measures into compliance with WTO obligations. Most members comply with the "recommendations" of the Dispute Body due to peer pressure and a desire on the part of most members to maintain the effectiveness of the WTO system. While most countries comply, the WTO does have some options available to increase pressure on a non-complying member. The WTO can authorize the aggrieved member to receive compensation from the offending member. Compensation is not always possible as the offending member must agree to compensation. Where the parties cannot agree on compensation, the Dispute Body can authorize the aggrieved member to suspend trade concessions, i.e. to impose trade sanctions on a non-complying member.

Compensation in this context does not refer to a payment, but to the granting of additional trade concessions. For example, Country A, the offending country, would grant additional trade concessions such as lower tariffs on selected goods from Country B, the aggrieved member. The lower tariffs will allow the aggrieved member to increase its trade volume and earn more revenue serving to compensate the aggrieved member for the violation of its rights.

If compensation is not possible, then the suspension of trade concessions allows an aggrieved member to impose sanctions such as additional tariffs on imports from the offending member. While retaliation should first occur in the same sector of goods, services, or technology, the WTO also authorizes cross-retaliation in different sectors. For example, Country A, a developing country, has infringed Country B's intellectual property rights but Country A is not a producer of technology products. Country B may be authorized by the Dispute Body to impose tariffs on imports of textiles (clothing) from Country A, which is one of Country A's major exports. Both compensation and retaliation are viewed as intermediate steps only. The ultimate goal is always full compliance with WTO obligations. Only full compliance will remove the economic distortion to the system created by the non-compliance.

The enforceability of TRIPS within the WTO is a major distinction between the WTO and all other international intellectual property organizations, such as the World Intellectual Property Organization that administers the Paris and Berne Conventions and other important treaties. WIPO is a largely toothless organization as it lacks any enforcement power. The WTO is the only modern international trade and intellectual property organization that has enforcement power, although recent developments have put this power into doubt, as further explained at the conclusion of this chapter.

Decisions of the WTO panels and Appellate Body have no direct force or effect within the U.S. federal or state legal systems. U.S. federal and state courts are under no obligation to follow or recognize WTO decisions. By contrast, as a member of the WTO, the United States government has a duty to follow and implement WTO decisions adopted by the Dispute Settlement Body. If the United States fails to comply with WTO decisions the United States faces the prospect of having to provide compensation or be subject to trade sanctions. The obligation to follow WTO decisions, however, has been up-ended by the inability of the WTO dispute system to fully function as further explained below.

2. THE EUROPEAN UNION

The European Union is a political, economic, and monetary union of 27 European states. The EU has a total population of 446 million and has the world's third largest population after China and India. The EU has a $19.9 trillion dollar economy that constitutes 15.3 percent of world GDP. The size of the EU economy is nearly identical in size to the United States, which has a $20.5 trillion dollar economy and 15.8 percent share of world GDP. China has a $14.7

trillion dollar economy. Together these three economies represent about 50 percent of world GDP. Every other economy is far behind. The size of the EU economy and its population mean that anyone seriously interested in international business and intellectual property must learn about and deal with the EU. (The same can be said of China but China presents some special challenges further discussed in Chapter Six on enforcement of intellectual property rights.)

Like the GATT/WTO, the origins of the EU can also be traced to events after the Second World War. The first important initiative was taken by Robert Schuman, the foreign minister of France, who help create the European Coal and Steel Community of 1951, the first European Community. The Coal and Steel Community consisted of Belgium, France, Italy, Luxembourg, the Netherlands, and West Germany. Decisions concerning the use of coal and steel were to be made by the Community. As the use of coal and steel was necessary to produce the weapons of war, the Community provided a mechanism to prevent preparations for war. Two other communities followed, the European Economic Community (EEC) and European Atomic Energy Community were created by the Treaty of Rome in 1957. In 1993, the Maastricht Treaty on European Union created the EU in place of the EEC. In 2009, the Lisbon Treaty amended the Treaty of Rome and the Maastricht Treaty renaming them the Treaty on the Functioning of the European Union and the Treaty of European Union, respectively. The main governing bodies of the EU are the EU Commission, the executive arm, the Council of Ministers, which serves as the co-legislative arm along with the EU Parliament, the only branch with representatives directly elected by the people. The EU also has the European Court of Justice, also known as the Court of Justice of the European Union, which issues important decisions interpreting EU law.

For the purposes of this book, the most important feature of the EU is that it is a single common market subject to the "four freedoms", i.e. the free movement of goods, services, capital, and persons (including legal persons) throughout the EU. Once goods enter the EU, the goods can travel duty free throughout all the countries of the EU, which presents a single market. The same principle applies to the other three freedoms. Differences in national intellectual property laws can create barriers to the freedoms at the border. For example, suppose that the owner of a patent in Germany wishes to sell its patented products in France. In order to ensure that its patent is not copied in France, the German seller will wish to first register its patent in France. If the seller cannot register its patent because its patent does not qualify for patent protection in France due to differences in French law, the seller will not export its products to France. Or if administrative burdens in registering its patent in France create delays and additional expenses, these burdens can operate as a trade barrier. An important task of the EU is to harmonize intellectual property laws for all of its members to remove trade barriers. For this reason, harmonization of intellectual property laws in the EU is one of its major goals.

The EU is also an influential and leading innovator of intellectual property law. Some examples of the EU's recent innovative legislation, the EU Database Directive and the EU Copyright Directive are discussed further in Chapter Two. The EU is also the world's leading proponent of geographical indications that protect foods and wines known by their place of origin. Geographical indications are discussed in Chapter Four.

Although the United States and the EU are in the main politically friendly and share mutual security interests, they are also fierce economic competitors. The United States and the EU have sharp disagreements over intellectual property issues and other trade issues, many of which are litigated in the WTO.

3. OTHER FREE TRADE AREAS

Although the EU remains the world's most important free trade area, in recent years, there has been a proliferation of free trade agreements. Each of these agreements incorporates TRIPS and many go beyond TRIPS by adding additional benefits or by providing "TRIPS plus" benefits. Such agreements have now sprung up all over the world.

In North America, there is the United States Mexico Canada Trade Agreement; in the Asia and pacific region, there is the Regional Comprehensive Economic Agreement (2020), led by China and consisting of 10 ASEAN (Association of Southeast Asian Nations) members (Brunei Darussalam, Burma, Cambodia, Indonesia, Laos, Malaysia,

Philippines, Singapore, Thailand, and Vietnam) and China, Australia, New Zealand, Japan, and South America. There is also the Comprehensive and Progressive Trans-Pacific Partnership Agreement (2018) (CPTPP) between Australia, Brunei, Canada, Chile, Japan, Malaysia, Mexico, Peru, New Zealand, Singapore and Vietnam. The CPTPP is based on the Trans-Pacific Partnership (TPP) drafted and led by the United States. One of the earliest acts of the first Trump administration was to withdraw the United States from the TPP but the other nations remained and renamed the treaty as the CPTPP. In South America, there are two major free trade agreements: Mercosur (1991) consisting of Argentina, Brazil, Paraguay, and Uruguay and the Pacific Alliance (2011) consisting of Chile, Colombia, Peru, and Mexico. In Africa, there is the African Continental Free Trade Agreement (2021) consisting of 54 African states.

In addition to these regional trade agreements, the United States is a party to 20 bilateral free trade agreements with various individual countries. The United States enters in such agreements with countries that share common political and security interests. A full list of these treaties is available on the website of the United States Trade Representative. The EU has bilateral agreements with 78 states or territories and is in the process of ratifying or negotiating agreements with 13 other states or entities, including Mercosur, South Korea, and India. In total, there are now over 700 regional and bilateral free trade agreements and every WTO member is a party to at least one of them. No doubt over time, these entities will begin to play a more significant role in the regulation and enforcement of intellectual property rights on an international level.

C. INVESTOR STATE DISPUTE SETTLEMENT

A feature of some regional and bilateral free trade agreements is the availability of a mechanism that allows a private investor to bring a claim against a nation state. Dispute resolution in modern international business and trade generally falls into two major categories: (1) state to state disputes in the WTO, EU, or other international fora or (2) a private individual versus private business entities or individuals in domestic litigation. Investor state dispute settlement (ISDS) is the rare instance in which an individual or a private entity is allowed to sue a state directly. ISDS is available today in some of the regional trade agreements, including the Comprehensive and Progressive Trans-Pacific Partnership and the United States Mexico Canada Trade Agreement set forth in the preceding paragraph. ISDS is also available in some bilateral free trade agreements. The United States has numerous bilateral trade agreements (not listed in the previous section but available on the USTR website) that permits ISDS.

Investor state dispute settlement cases can be brought when an investor makes a foreign investment in a nation and then suffers a loss. The loss can be due to interference with intellectual property rights. For example, in *Eli Lilly & Co. v.*

Government of Canada, Case No. UNCT/14/2 (March 16, 2017), Eli Lilly unsuccessfully argued that Canada's invalidation of its patents violated NAFTA's articles on expropriation and fair and equitable treatment under international law. Although ISDS has risen in popularity in recent years, ISDS is controversial because it potentially allows a private individual or company to invalidate national laws, legal doctrines, and governmental actions.

Due to its controversial nature, the availability of investor state dispute settlement under NAFTA has been cut back under the USMCA, which replaced NAFTA on July 1, 2020. Under USMCA, ISDS is no longer available between the United States and Canada so the *Eli Lilly* case could not be brought today. These types of cases will have to be litigated under domestic law. While still available between the United States and Mexico, full ISDS is now restricted to certain economic sectors heavily regulated by Mexico (oil and gas, energy, telecommunications, transportation, and infrastructure). As to other areas, ISDS is available between the United States and Mexico but substantive rights have been cut down.

Full investor state dispute settlement is still available under other free trade agreements, but the USMCA's recent steps in scaling back ISDS may be a trend of the future. The main policy concern is that private disputes litigated through ISDS are able to invalidate public laws and regulations that are duly enacted by nation states.

D. THE CRISIS IN THE WTO PRECIPITATED BY THE UNITED STATES

When the United States led the Uruguay round of negotiations that resulted in the establishment of the WTO and its dispute settlement system, the United States worked under the assumption that its rights and obligations under existing U.S. and international law would not be disturbed by the WTO. Surely no one would believe that the United States would set up the WTO so that the latter could reject longstanding U.S. law and legal practices. The United States even insisted that the WTO include a provision in the WTO agreements that embodied this understanding. Article 3.4 of the Dispute Settlement Understanding states that "rulings made by the [Dispute Settlement Body] shall be . . . in accordance with the rights and obligations under this Understanding and under the covered agreements." The United States would find to its surprise that the WTO did not share the same policy or understanding.

Shortly after the establishment of the WTO, the United States became dissatisfied with the performance of the Appellate Body, which routinely struck down U.S. statutes, infuriating the United States. According to the United States Trade Representative in a Report to Congress issued in 2020:

> The proper functioning of the WTO Appellate Body has a disproportionate impact on the United States because more than one quarter of all disputes at the WTO have been challenges to

> U.S. laws or other measures. Specifically, 155 disputes have been filed against the United States, and no other Member has faced even a hundred disputes. According to some analyses, up to approximately 90 percent of the disputes pursued against the U.S. have led to a report finding that the U.S. law or other measure was inconsistent with WTO agreements. This means that, on average, over the past 25 years, the WTO has found a U.S. law or measure WTO-inconsistent between five and six times per year, every year.

The USTR report highlighted three shortcomings. The Appellate Body (1) routinely ignored its own procedural rules and repeatedly exceeded deadlines for rulings and appeals; (2) engaged in judicial activism by inventing new rights and obligations not based on the texts of the WTO; and (3) invaded the policy space of the United States by striking down U.S. statutes, some in existence long before the WTO. In its report, the USTR offered no solutions, noting that the purpose of the report was to expose the Appellate Body's failures.

Frustrations with the Appellate Body led the Obama administration in 2016 to block the reappointment of a member of the Appellate Body whose four-year term was expiring. The Trump administration continued this blockade by refusing to appoint new or reappoint existing members of the Appellate Body with the result on December 10, 2019, the number of members of the Appellate Body fell below that needed for a quorum. Without a quorum, the Appellate Body cannot convene and hear appeals. The Biden administration maintained this same approach blocking any efforts to install new Appellate Body members. For over five years, the Appellate Body has been paralyzed by the actions of three different U.S. administrations of both political parties.

The most significant consequence of the paralysis of the Appellate Body is that WTO obligations have become unenforceable. As noted earlier, no panel or Appellate Body decision becomes legally effective until it is adopted by the Dispute Settlement Body. Panel decisions that are not appealed are not affected by the Appellate Body's disability and can be adopted by the Dispute Body. Any panel decision that is appealed, however, falls into a legal abyss. The appeal cannot be completed because the Appellate Body cannot convene and the panel decision cannot be adopted until the appeal is concluded. DSU, Art. 16.4. The effect of an appeal then is to launch the panel decision into a legal limbo that nullifies its effect. Any party that loses a panel decision is able to nullify the decision by simply filing an appeal. In 2020, when China won a panel decision rejecting the Trump administration's punitive new tariffs on Chinese imports, the United States immediately appealed the decision, nullifying its effect. *United States—Tariff Measures on Certain Goods from China—Notification of an Appeal by the United States under Article 16 of the Understanding on Rules and Procedures Governing the Settlement of Disputes*, WT/DS543/10 (Oct. 27, 2020). The United States then continued the tariffs.

The paralysis of the Appellate Body has thrown the WTO into a crisis. An organization that is rules-based will have its very existence threatened if its rules are no longer enforceable. Adding to the crisis is that it is now in its sixth year, raising the possibility that through lack of political will and inertia the current impasse could become permanent and the status quo for the indefinite future. If that occurs, the WTO itself may fade away into irrelevance. Certainly, a crippled WTO will be significantly diminished in importance and will never again achieve the stature that it once possessed at the beginning of the new millennium.

Although the United States has publicly declared that it is committed to having a revived and fully functioning dispute system, many WTO nations view the U.S. statements with skepticism. What is clear is that no resolution of the crisis is possible without the agreement of the United States as all decisions in the WTO continue to be made by consensus. Prospects for a U.S. agreement do not seem promising based upon its actions so far. Invoking Article 25 of the DSU, the EU led efforts to create a substitute private Appellate Body under the Multiparty Interim Appeal Arbitration Arrangement. The substitute Appellate Body would carry on the functions of the defunct Appellate Body until the formal body can be resurrected. While some nations have joined the Interim Arrangement, the United States has not. As the United States is the most frequent litigator in the WTO both as a complainant and as a respondent, the Interim Agreement cannot be an effective response without the United States as a member.

So far the United States has steadfastly refused to seriously consider any proposal that would restore the Appellate Body to its former full powers and mandatory jurisdiction. Rather, the United States has recently floated proposals behind the scenes to require the consent of both parties in order to invoke the dispute settlement system and the use of the Appellate Body. Any party who has violated WTO rules can simply refuse to have the WTO review the dispute. Such a proposal would in essence preserve the status quo by making WTO rules unenforceable. These proposals have led some WTO members to question whether the United States' real intention is to destroy the WTO and not to save it. Unfortunately, at the moment, even after six years of an impasse, there does not appear to be a viable resolution of the Appellate Body blockade in sight and the WTO dispute system remains disabled. The future of the WTO remains under a cloud of uncertainty.

CHAPTER 2

COPYRIGHT AND NEIGHBORING RIGHTS

A. INTRODUCTION

Copyright law protects creative expression. Under U.S. law, copyright extends to any original work that exhibits a minimal level of creativity and is fixed in a tangible medium of expression. As distinguished from other intellectual property rights such as patent and trademarks, the hallmark of copyright is originality. In this sense, "originality" means that the work is independently created by the author and is not copied by the author from another work. If an author were to sit down and compose "Romeo and Juliet" from scratch that is word for word identical to Shakespeare's play, the work would be considered original within the meaning of copyright law because it is independently created and not copied from Shakespeare's masterwork. The work is not new but novelty is a requirement of patent and is not required for copyright.

U.S. law also requires that the work must be fixed in a tangible medium of expression, i.e. the work must be embodied in some permanent physical form, such as a book, a compact disk, or an optical drive and cannot be merely in an intangible form, which is not protectable by copyright. Fixation is required under U.S. law but is not required by the Berne Convention or TRIPS. Each nation can decide for itself whether to require fixation. Most nations require fixation but it is still necessary to check the laws of each nation.

1. THE UTILITARIAN AND NATURAL RIGHTS FOUNDATIONS OF COPYRIGHT

Modern copyright law can be traced to two traditions that are associated with England and continental Europe. In England, copyright grew out of a utilitarian tradition and was viewed as consisting mostly of economic rights. Under utilitarian theory, copyright is based upon a cost benefit analysis and economic incentives. Society will allow authors to enjoy a monopoly period in which they can obtain financial rewards for the work in exchange for encouraging authors to create works that will eventually enter the public domain after the expiration of the copyright term. The end goal is not to reward authors but to encourage the creation of works for society as a whole. This approach in England influenced the United States, which included the Copyright Clause in the U.S. Constitution providing that copyrights can be "granted for limited times" and for the purpose of "promot[ing] the Progress of Science and the Useful Arts." U.S. Const. art. I, § 8, cl. 8. The Anglo-American view of copyright is based on utilitarianism.

A second theory of copyright arose in continental Europe, which viewed copyright as derived from a theory of natural rights. This theory has a metaphysical dimension as it posits that copyright is part of a larger firmament of natural rights that exists in nature and is independent of human beings. By contrast, the utilitarian tradition is a creation of social science and economics and has no metaphysical dimension. The natural rights theory preferred to use the term "author's right" instead of copyright to emphasize that copyright emanated from the person of the author.

Countries such as France embraced the theory of the author's right that viewed copyright as a set of rights inherent in the author arising from the author's being. An author would infuse a work with his or her personality and it was viewed as a highly personal expression of the author's inner being. A consequence of the author's right approach is that these inherent rights included certain moral rights, i.e. non-economic rights that are inherent in all authors. One moral right is that of integrity, which is a right in authors to prevent others from altering their works in a way that would cause harm to their honor and reputation. A second moral right is that of attribution, i.e. the right to be known as the author of the work. As moral rights were a form of natural rights, some countries viewed moral rights as existing in perpetuity. Moral rights survived the death of the author and could be enforced by the author's heirs or successors in interest. Such rights were also inherent in the author and inalienable. In some continental countries, moral rights cannot be assigned but must always remain with the author.

Countries that follow a utilitarian theory of copyright, such as the United States, recognize few, if any moral rights. Even though the United States eventually joined the Berne Convention and came under its obligation to recognize moral rights, the United States continues to have weak protections for moral rights due to its view that copyright consists predominantly of economic rights.

The utilitarian theory and the natural rights theory of copyright also diverge on the treatment of performances and recordings. Authors create works but the work, such as a play or a musical composition, can be performed by actors or musicians. Whether the performer can acquire a copyright in the performance (fixed, for example, in a compact disk or recorded on a memory stick) or a lesser right know as a neighboring right depends upon a nation's approach to copyright law.

In the United States and the UK, both dominated by the utilitarian theory, performances and recordings are treated under the rubric of copyright, although performances and recordings might receive a shorter term of copyright protection. In continental Europe, however, performances and recordings are treated under a different category called neighboring rights or related rights, a lesser form of protection than copyright. In continental Europe with its strong tradition of the author's right, performers were viewed as less meritorious than authors and thus deserving of less protection. For example, a composer can write a musical work that is protected by copyright, but a performer of the music receives a lesser form of protection, called neighboring or related rights, reserved for performers. Of the two, only the composer is viewed as a true author deserving of full copyright protection. There are many persons who can perform Mozart's music but there are few, if any, persons throughout history who have attained Mozart's achievements as a composer. Many people can pick up a Shakespeare play and recite a part, but only a few persons in human history have the talent to compose works of such cultural and historical significance. Of course, not all authors need to attain the peak of achievement on a historical level to qualify for copyright. Even a more modest author, such as a composer of a pop song or a law professor, is deserving of copyright protection. For the natural rights theorist, the point is that there is a divide between even more modestly achieving authors who create the work and those who merely perform the author's work. Mere performers do not create and thereby do not arise to the level of authors deserving full copyright protection; nor do recording companies that fix the performances in records or compact disks. The recording companies do receive some protection in the recordings but only under the lesser regime of neighboring rights. Broadcasting companies that transmit a performance on television or radio also receive protection under the regime of neighboring rights. We will return to a discussion performance rights in a subsequent section of this chapter.

While there are two traditions underlying modern copyright law, you should not assume that they are a source of conflict in modern copyright law. It is more accurate to say that modern copyright law in most countries is a blend of both traditions with some countries emphasizing one tradition more than the other. For example, in the United States, a bastion of the utilitarian theory of copyright, the Berne Convention governing the acquisition of copyrights prevails due to its incorporation into TRIPS. Acquisition of copyrights under the Berne Convention is based on the natural rights theory. As a result of the Berne Convention's incorporation into TRIPS, the United States, a staunch proponent of the utilitarian theory, also applies the natural rights theory of how copyrights are acquired through the Berne Convention. TRIPS also incorporates elements of the utilitarian theory of copyright. Both traditions are consistent with TRIPS and are found embedded in TRIPS. The drafters of TRIPS did not believe that it was necessary to explicitly choose one tradition over the other and nothing in the text of TRIPS indicates that it was based on one tradition as opposed to the other. Elements of both traditions are found throughout TRIPS.

2. TRIPS AND THE BERNE CONVENTION

Article 9 of TRIPS incorporates Articles 1–21 of the Berne Convention, its basic substantive provisions. TRIPS also adds several important provisions of its own in Articles 10–14 dealing with copyright and neighboring rights. TRIPS follows the general overall approach of the Berne Convention in adopting the national treatment principle and minimum standards of rights and obligations.

TRIPS Article 9 excludes Article 6*bis* of the Berne Convention that explicitly recognizes moral rights. If Article 6*bis* were incorporated directly into TRIPS then one could argue that TRIPS had chosen sides and had imposed the natural rights theory on its members. Instead, TRIPS allows each country to decide for itself whether to recognize moral rights instead of requiring such recognition.

One reason why the United States insisted on the clause in Article 9 of TRIPS excluding moral rights from being incorporated into TRIPS is that moral rights can interfere with economic rights. An author of a novel that was made into a movie might have a claim that the right of integrity was damaged if the movie was not faithful to the novel. Such moral rights are inherent in the author and cannot be assigned to the movie studio. Such control left in the author could be damaging to the huge movie making industry in the United States. Note while the United States is not bound by TRIPS Article 9 to recognize moral rights due to its election not to be bound, the United States is still bound by the Berne Convention Article 6*bis* to recognize moral rights as the United States is a member of the Berne Convention. However, the United States realizes that as the World Intellectual Property Organization that administers the Berne Convention has no enforcement powers, failure to follow Article 6*bis* will not result in any serious consequences. The United States also believes that it is not necessary to explicitly recognize moral rights as U.S. tort doctrines protecting an author from misrepresentation offer similar protection.

TRIPS uses both the term "copyright" and "author's right" and explicitly states that the terms are synonymous. TRIPS recognizes both economic rights consistent with the utilitarian tradition and moral rights consistent with the natural rights theory of copyright. Today, being aware of the two traditions is helpful in understanding the originals of some aspects of copyright and why there remain some differences between copyright in the United States and parts of continental Europe.

As the foregoing discussion indicates, modern copyright law from the Berne Convention to TRIPS has been exclusively a western European and Anglo-American field of endeavor. Other traditions relevant to copyright existed at the time that the Berne Convention was created in 1886 but these were not reflected in the Convention. For example, Confucianism was a social and political theory that was already more than two thousand years old in China, its country of origin, by the late nineteenth century when the Berne Convention was being drafted and copyright law in Europe was in its infancy. Under Confucianism, copying was not viewed as wrong but as virtuous as copying the works of the masters of Chinese civilization helped to disseminate their contributions essential for all others in later generations to absorb. This theory of copying contrasts sharply with western theories. At least measured by the populations involved in China, India, Japan, and Korea, Confucianism was far more influential than either the utilitarian or natural rights theory. Yet, as the Berne Convention was dominated by western European nations, neither Confucianism nor any other non-western theory was reflected in the Convention.

Of course, larger events were also at work at the time. In the nineteenth century western European nations dominated the world economically, culturally, and militarily so little importance was given to other cultures or lines of thought. China, like most of Asia, was subjected to domination by European nations and was in no position to assert its traditions in the Berne Convention or anywhere else in Europe. No seat at the drafting table of the Berne Convention was offered to any non-western nation not under the domination of a western power. While historical events may explain why non-western theories found no place in the Berne Convention, perhaps what is more surprising is that even today after decades of membership in the GATT and the WTO, non-western countries have found little incorporation of their perspectives or traditions into the substantive copyright law set forth in TRIPS. We will return to a discussion of whether there is any space in modern copyright law for non-western traditions in a later part of this chapter.

B. POINTS OF ATTACHMENT UNDER THE BERNE CONVENTION

We now turn to how authors obtain protection for their works under the Berne Convention. All countries that are bound by the Berne Convention form the Berne Union. Prior to the WTO, the Berne Union consisted of all contracting states to the Berne Convention. As Articles 1–21 of the Berne Convention are incorporated into TRIPS by virtue of TRIPS Article 9, the Berne Union now consists of all WTO member states and all Berne Union countries that are not also members of the WTO. Every member of the WTO is subject to the analysis set forth below on points of attachment.

1. RATIONALE FOR POINTS OF ATTACHMENT

As the discussion below will make clear, the points of attachment analysis used in the Berne Convention is traceable to a natural rights theory of copyright. A country like United States does not subscribe to the natural rights theory but as the United States is a member of the WTO, the United States must accept the Berne Convention and incorporate elements of the natural rights theory into its copyright jurisprudence. The United States' unenthusiastic view of natural rights is one reason why the United States did not join the Berne Convention until 1989. The United States finally joined the Berne Convention when it became clear that the Convention would be incorporated into TRIPS and the WTO.

In order to obtain protection under the Berne Convention, the work must have a "point of attachment." The basic concept behind the point of attachment is that some event or condition must trigger the application of the Berne Convention. The concept of a point of attachment is unique to copyright and the Berne Convention and finds no corresponding or analogous concepts in patent or trademark law under the Paris Convention or other treaties. The reason why points of attachment are unique to copyright is because the acquisition of copyright is not subject to formalities. Berne Conv., Article 5(2). In the case of patents and trademarks, some formality, such as the filing of a patent or trademark application, is usually required to obtain the issuance of a patent or trademark registration conferring rights. The formalities of a patent or trademark application triggers the application of the Paris Convention. Paris Conv., Article 4(A)(1). Under Article 5(2) of the Berne Convention, countries are prohibited from requiring the filing of an application or any other formality for the acquisition of copyright.

For present purposes, the important distinction is that while formalities can trigger the application of the Paris Convention and other treaties for patents and trademarks, formalities cannot be used to trigger the application of the Berne Convention due to its prohibition of formalities. Formalities, such as the filing of a trademark or patent application, create highly visible and discrete events that make the application of the Paris Convention easily discernible. The lack of formalities means that the opposite is true of the Berne Convention so it became necessary for the Convention to set forth in Article 3 the events or conditions, i.e. the points of attachment, that would trigger the protections of the Berne Convention.

One might ask why the Berne Convention prohibits such formalities that would make determining the application of the Convention into a simple, straightforward matter instead of an abstract analysis relying on arcane concepts such as points of attachment. The answer is that the prohibition of formalities owes its origins to the natural rights theory of copyright that posited authors' rights as flowing from the creation of the work by the author. Such rights were part of the natural order and thus there can be no limitation placed on those rights by requiring formalities. This view of copyright, based on natural rights, continues to be a major component of the Berne Convention and, by incorporation, of TRIPS.

Article 3 of the Berne Convention sets forth three basic methods to establish a point of attachment.

Berne Convention

Article 3

(1) The protection of this Convention shall apply to:

(a) authors who are nationals of one of the countries of the Union, for their works whether published or not;

(b) authors who are not nationals of one of the countries of the Union, for their works first published in one of those countries or simultaneously in a country outside the Union and in a country of the Union.

(2) Authors who are not nationals of one of the countries of the Union but who have their habitual residence in one of them shall, for the purposes of this Convention be assimilated to nationals of the country.

As Article 3 indicates, there are three criteria for establishing a point of attachment: (1) nationality; (2) publication; and (3) habitual residence.

The first criterion of nationality suffices for all purposes, that is, a national of any Berne Union country automatically receives a copyright in any work upon creation. The publication of the work is unnecessary to create a point of attachment. Nationality and citizenship are synonymous in this context. Nationality/citizenship is determined by the laws of each country but it usually requires some type of formal recognition by the government of the nation involved. Once nationality is achieved, it becomes the critical element in a Berne Convention points of attachment analysis. Article 3(1)(a) only requires nationality and creation of the work for the Berne Convention to attach. The work does not need to be published or even ever shown to anyone. No record of the work's existence needs to be made. No one needs to know of the work. By virtue of the nationality of the author, copyright subsists in the work as soon as it is created.

The second criterion is publication, which applies when the first criterion is missing. In the case of an author who is not a national of a Berne Union country, the work can be protected and a point of attachment established if the work is first published in the Union or is simultaneously published in a non-Union country and a Union country. Simultaneous publication refers to publication in two or more countries within 30 days of first publication. Berne Conv., Article 3(4). The criterion of publication allows for nationals of non-Berne Union countries to receive the benefits of the Berne Convention. Publication was thus known as creating a "backdoor to Berne" and was controversial. For years, before the United States joined the Berne Convention in 1989, U.S. authors could receive Berne protection by first publication in Canada or simultaneous publication in the United States and Canada. Some advocates of the Convention believed that publication created incentives for some countries to take a free ride and to avoid joining the Berne Union. Nevertheless, the criterion of publication is well-established as creating a point of attachment.

Publication refers to works published with the consent of the author "whatever may be the means of manufacture of the copies, provided that the availability of such copies has been such as to satisfy the reasonable requirements of the public having regard to the nature of the work." Berne Conv., Article 3(3). The language of the Berne Convention needs to be updated to reflect the age of the internet but, as Article 3(3) is presently written, the terms "manufacture of the copies" seems to connote a hard copy of the work and raises the question whether posting a work on an internet website constitutes publication as there is no "manufacture" involved. Many authors today post their works on social sciences websites as a means of early dissemination. Posting may not constitute publication for an author from a non-Berne Union country. To meet the requirements of "manufacture" the author may be wise to have copies downloaded from the website in a Berne Union country. The download into a hard drive or in the form of a printed-out copy could satisfy the requirement of manufacture of copies in Article 3(3). Perhaps this ambiguity will be resolved when an opportunity arises for updating the Berne Convention text.

The third criterion of habitual residence applies when an author is not a national of a Berne Union country but establishes a habitual residence in a Union country; in that event, the author is "assimilated" to the nationals of the Berne Union country, i.e. is treated for purposes of the Berne Convention as if the author were a national of the country in which the author has his or her habitual residence. An author with a habitual residence in a Berne Union country will establish a point of attachment by virtue of his or her residence, which is treated as equivalent to being a national of a Berne Union country.

An author from a non-Berne Union country who establishes residence in a Berne Union country can acquire a point of attachment by merely creating a work just as in the case of a national of a Berne Union country. As in the case of nationality, habitual residence and creation are all that is necessary for copyright to subsist in a work. The criterion of habitual residence also extends the Berne Convention to nationals of a non-Berne Union country, raising the similar concerns of free riding as in the case of publication. One could say that these concerns are less serious in the case of habitual residence. Publication is a single act, but habitual residence requires a person to make a significant commitment of time and resources to assimilate to a Berne Union country in order to be able to enjoy the benefits of the Berne Convention. Habitual residence also benefits the Berne Union country where residence occurs as it allows creative persons who have assimilated to its nationals to enjoy rights under the Berne Convention.

Illustration 2-1. Alain is a national of a Berne Union country. Alain writes a novel in secret and shows it to no one. Alain is entitled to a copyright in the novel. The copyright arose when Alain wrote the novel.

Illustration 2-2. Beatrice is a national of a country that is not a member of the Berne Union. Beatrice writes the novel in her home country and then publishes the novel in Canada, a Berne Union country, or publishes the novel in Canada within 30 days of publishing the novel in her home country. When Beatrice publishes the novel in Canada, Beatrice receives a copyright in the novel. Beatrice is able to enjoy the benefits of the Berne Convention even though Beatrice's home nation has not joined the Berne Convention.

Illustration 2-3. Carlotta is a national of a country that is not a member of the Berne Union but lives in a Berne Union country, having established a habitual residence there. While on vacation in her home country, Carlotta writes a short story and publishes it there. Carlotta has a copyright in the short story due to her habitual residence in the Union country. Carlotta's copyright subsists in the work upon its creation. Writing the story in Carlotta's home country and publishing it there has no relevance for the Berne Convention. For the purposes of the Berne Convention, Carlotta's habitual residence in the Union country allows Carlotta to be treated as if Carlotta were a national of the Union country.

Article 4 of the Berne Convention provides special rules for two types of works: cinematographic works (motion pictures) and architectural works. In the case of motion pictures, the author (i.e. person or entity claiming a copyright) of the motion picture might be a national of a non-Berne Union country. In this case, if the production studio has its headquarters in a Berne Union country, the author can use the location of the production studio to establish a point of attachment based the location of the studio. In this case, the presence of the production studio in a Berne Union country establishes a point of attachment that the author can use to claim a copyright. In the case of architectural works created by an author who is a national of a non-Berne Union country, the erection of the work in a Berne Union country establishes a point of attachment that the author of the work can use to claim a copyright in the work. The presence of the production studio in a Berne Union country is similar to the criterion of habitual residence and the erection of the architectural work in a Berne Union country is similar to the criterion of publication.

2. BERNE CONVENTION NATIONAL TREATMENT

Once a point of attachment is established, the work in question is now entitled to the protections of the Berne Convention. The Berne Convention now governs the treatment that countries in the Berne Union *other than* the country of the origin of the work must provide to the work. Note carefully that the Berne Convention creates no direct substantive intellectual property rights and that these rights are all created by the domestic law of the countries of the Berne Union. What the Convention does require is national treatment (more on this soon) by Berne Union countries *other than* the country of origin of the work. The Berne Convention is concerned only with how Berne Union countries treat foreign works, i.e. works that have a country of origin other than the country in which protection is sought; the Berne Convention is not concerned with how Berne Union countries treat domestic works or works that have their origin in the country in which protection is claimed. How countries treat domestic works is an issue of domestic law and is of no concern to the Berne Convention.

Once Article 3 (points of attachment) is satisfied, the work in question is entitled to copyright protection in every country of the Berne Union under Article 5, the national treatment principle:

Berne Convention

Article 5

(1) Authors shall enjoy in respect of works for which they are protected under this Convention, in countries of the Union other than the country of origin, the rights which their respective laws do now or may hereafter grant to their nationals, as well as the rights specially granted by this Convention.

Article 5 requires all other Berne Union countries other than the country of origin of the work to extend to the work "the rights which their respective laws . . . grant to their nationals." This iteration of the national treatment principle makes explicit an obligation by a Berne Union country to extend the same substantive rights granted under domestic law for the work to its own nationals to any foreign work that has established a point of attachment. In other words, each country in the Berne Union must extend a copyright under domestic law to the foreign work.

The result of the combined effect of Article 3 (points of attachment) and Article 5 (national treatment) is that once an author achieves a point of attachment, the author acquires a "basket" of national copyrights from the entire Berne Union; the author's work is entitled to a German copyright under German law, a Japanese copyright under Japanese law, a French copyright under French law and so forth. Recall that the Berne Union today includes all WTO members who receive this benefit under Berne/TRIPS. As we shall see, such a benefit, the automatic acquisition of intellectual property protection, is not available for patents and trademarks.

Illustration 2-4. Wang, a national of Country C, a Berne Union country, composes an opera in Country C. Wang now has a copyright in each country of the Berne Union, including all 166 countries of the WTO.

Illustration 2-5. Liesel is a national of Country E, which is not a member of the Berne Convention and is not a member of the WTO. Leisel has a copyright for a novel under Country E's laws that Leisel published during the previous year. If Leisel wishes to obtain a copyright for the novel in Country G, a Berne Union country and WTO member, Leisel will have to satisfy the requirements of Country G's copyright law.

Illustration 2-6. Assume the same facts of Illustration 2-5 except that Leisel first publishes the novel in Country H, a Berne Union country, or simultaneously publishes the novel in Country E and Country H (i.e. within 30 days of publication in Country E). A point of attachment has now been established for Leisel's novel under the criterion of first (or simultaneous) publication in a Union country. Leisel has used the "backdoor to Berne." Leisel's novel is entitled to a copyright under the copyright laws of Country H as well as in every other country that is a member of the Berne Union or the WTO.

Illustration 2-7. Assume the same facts of Illustration 2-5 and 2-6 except that now Country E is a Berne Union country or is a WTO member. Since Leisel is now a national of a Berne Union country, Leisel's nationality establishes a point of attachment. At the instant of its creation, Leisel's novel became protected by a copyright under the copyright laws of Country E as well as under the laws of every other country that is a member of the Berne Union or the WTO.

3. THE INDEPENDENT TREATMENT OF COPYRIGHT

Article 5(2) of the Berne Convention states that the "enjoyment and exercise of" rights under the national treatment principle "shall be independent of the existence of protection in the country of origin of the work." Acquisition of a basket of national copyrights under the national treatment principle depends on establishing a point of attachment under Article 3; it does not depend on the acquisition of a copyright in the country of origin. (Country of origin is defined in Article 5(4) further discussed below.) Again, the Berne Convention is concern with how countries *other than* the country of origin treat the work. How the country of origin treats the work is of no concern to the Berne Convention. Even if the author does not acquire a copyright in the country of origin, the author will have a basket of national copyrights throughout the Berne Union so long as a point of attachment exists.

Illustration 2-8. Carmen publishes a work in Country M, a Berne Union country, but fails to comply with Country M's registration requirements for domestic works and, as a result, the work is not entitled to copyright protection but falls into the public domain in Country M. Under the Berne Convention, the publication of the work establishes a point of attachment and the work is entitled to the benefits of the national treatment principle regardless of the lack of copyright protection in the country of origin of the work. Carmen receives a basket of national copyrights under the Berne Convention even though Carmen does not have a copyright in the country of origin, i.e. the country where the work was first published.

The treatment of the work in countries other than the country of origin is independent of the treatment by the country of origin of the work under its domestic copyright law. This means that once a point of attachment is established, the existence or lack thereof of a copyright for the work in the country of origin is irrelevant to the requirement that all other Berne Union countries other than the country of origin of the work must extend copyright to the work.

4. BERNE CONVENTION PROHIBITION OF FORMALITIES

So far the concept of the country of origin has been used a number of times and has played a key role in the preceding discussion. This concept is examined in detail in this section in connection with the Berne

Convention prohibition on formalities. As noted earlier, the Berne Convention prohibition of formalities can be traced to the natural rights tradition of an author's right.

Article 5 of the Berne Convention provides:

Berne Convention

Article 5

(1) Authors shall enjoy, in respect of works for which they are protected under this Convention in countries of the Union other than the country of origin, the rights which their respective laws do now or may hereafter grant to their nationals as well as the rights specially granted by this Convention.

(2) The enjoyment and exercise of these rights shall not be subject to any formality . . . .

(3) Protection in the country of origin is governed by domestic law. However, when the author is not a national of the country of origin of the work for which he is protected under this Convention, he shall enjoy in that country the same rights as national authors.

(4) The country of origin shall be considered to be

(a) In the case of works first published in a country of the Union, that country; in the case of works published simultaneously in several countries of the Union which grant different terms of protection, the country whose legislation grants the shortest term of protection.

(b) In the case of works published simultaneously in a country outside the Union and in a country of the Union, the latter country;

(c) In the case of unpublished works or of works first published in a country outside of the Union, without simultaneous publication in a country of the Union, the country of the Union of which the author is a national. * * *

a. Berne Convention Article 5(2) Prohibition

Article 5(2) states that the enjoyment and exercise of *these* rights shall not be subject to any formality, referring us back to the rights set forth in Article 5(1). The reference is to the text in Article 5(1) is to rights of authors in respect of works for which they are protected in Berne Union countries *other* than in the country of origin.

The combination of Article 5(1) and 5(2) indicates that countries cannot subject foreign works, i.e. works that have as their country of origin in a country other than the country in which protection is being sought, to any formalities with respect to the acquisition or exercise of copyrights. Nothing in Article 5 prevents a country from subjecting works for which it is the country of origin to formalities, but not foreign works. This means that a country can require its own works to obtain a registration as a condition of obtaining copyright protection so long as it does not subject foreign works to the same requirement. Of course, most countries are not likely to subject their own works to greater burdens for obtaining copyright protection than foreign works. (An exception is the United States as further discussed below.) The point is that the Berne Convention is not concerned with how countries treat their own works under domestic law; the Convention is concerned with how countries treat foreign works.

The Berne Convention prohibition on formalities means that a country cannot require as a condition of granting copyright protection that the foreign work be subject to any type of formality such as registration of the work with a copyright office or the use of notice requirements, such as the placing of a copyright symbol © on the work. All of these requirements are formalities that violate Article 5(2). A Berne Union country can still provide for formalities such as registration but the registration cannot be a condition of granting copyright or enforcing a copyright. Most countries make registration of copyrights voluntary.

In addition, Article 5(2) prohibits subjecting the enforcement of copyrights to any formality. For example, a country cannot require that the copyright holder must first register a foreign work in order to enforce a copyright in the work. In the United States, an entity seeking to enforce a U.S. copyright in an infringement action in a federal court must first register the copyright with the U.S. copyright office. This formality is permitted as it applies to U.S. works; U.S. law does not require entities seeking to enforce rights in foreign works to register the copyright because such a requirement is prohibited by the Berne Convention. An entity can bring a lawsuit to enforce a copyright for a work that has its country of origin in a Berne Union country other than the United States without first registering the copyright. This anomaly exists in U.S. law because of the Berne prohibition against formalities for foreign works.

b. Berne Convention Article 4: Publication as the First Criterion for Country of Origin

Berne Convention Article 5(4) sets forth the tests for determining country of origin for works of authorship. The basic approach is to use the place of publication as a first criterion. Article 5(4)(a) provides that if the place of first publication is a Union country then that country is the country of origin. It further provides that if there is simultaneous publication in several countries of the Union then the country with the shortest copyright term is the country of origin.

> Illustration 2-9. Fredricka publishes a novel in Country G, which has a copyright term of life of the author plus 70 years. Country G is the country of origin of the work. But suppose that within 30 days Fredricka also publishes the novel in Country H, which has a copyright term of life of the author plus 100 years, and Country K, which has a copyright term of life of the author plus 50 years. Now Fredricka has simultaneously published the novel in Countries

G, H, and K. Which is the country of origin? The country of origin of the work is Country K, which has the shortest copyright term. Fredricka's nationality is irrelevant.

As the Berne Convention recognizes simultaneous publication, it had to create a rule to determine the country of origin when the work is published simultaneously in several Union countries. The rule of the country with the shortest term is an easy way to distinguish among several Berne Union countries and is easy to apply.

Article 5(4)(b) provides that in case of simultaneous publication in a country outside the Union and a country in the Union, the latter country is the country of origin. Finally, Article 5(4)(c) refers to unpublished works or works published outside the Union without simultaneous publication in the Union; in this situation the rule falls back on the nationality of the author if the author is a national of a Union country. The country of origin is the country of which the author is a national. In this case what happens if the author is not a national of a Union country? Then the work has no country of origin and the work is not protected by the Berne Union.

Note that in both Article 5(4)(a) and (b), a point of attachment exists through publication in a Union country. In Article 5(4)(c), because no point of attachment exists through publication the rule falls back on nationality to establish a point of attachment. If the author is not a national of a Berne Union country then no point of attachment exists and the Berne Convention does not apply. There is no country of origin and the work is not entitled to Berne protection.

c. Country of Origin Versus Nationality of the Author

In applying the Berne Convention rule on formalities, it is important to distinguish between the country of origin of the work and the nationality of the author. The Berne Convention's prohibition of formalities applies to foreign works regardless of the nationality of the author. For formalities, the key issue is the country of origin of the work not the nationality of the author. So in the United States, it would be possible for an author to be a U.S. national and the owner of a foreign work not subject any U.S. formalities; it would also be possible for an author who is a foreign national to be the owner of a U.S. work subject to U.S. formalities.

> Illustration 2-10. Joslin is a U.S. national who lives in the United States but who first publishes a work in France. Under Article 5(4)(a), the country of origin of the work is France because it is the country of first publication. The United States cannot impose any formalities on the work because it is a foreign work. Under U.S. copyright law, all U.S. works must be first registered with the U.S. copyright office before a lawsuit for infringement can be brought in a U.S. court. In this example, the United States cannot require the U.S. author to first register the copyright because the country of origin of the work is France and cannot be subject to a

formality in the form of the registration requirement. That the author is a U.S. national who lives in the United States is irrelevant to the country of origin of the work. Nationality and country of origin are two separate concepts.

Illustration 2-11. Yvette is a French national who first publishes a work in the United States, which under Article 5(4)(a) is the country of origin of the work. Under the Berne Convention, a country can impose formalities on its own domestic works. Yvette's work is subject to formalities under U.S. law and so the work would have to be first registered with the U.S. copyright office before the French author can bring an infringement action in U.S. courts. Again, the key issue is the country of origin of the work—in this example, the United States—not the nationality of the author.

The Berne Convention's prohibition on formalities can be traced to the natural rights theory of copyright. Under the natural rights theory, authors had a copyright through the operation of the laws of nature. There can be no prerequisite such as a formality for the acquisition of such a natural right. Such a requirement is self-contradictory. Copyright is created by natural law, not by positive human law. As the United States was never enthusiastic about the natural rights theory of copyright, the United States had a long history of requiring formalities as a condition of obtaining copyrights. This U.S. preference for formalities is one reason for the United States's reluctance to join the Berne Convention.

Once the United States joined the Berne Union in 1989, the prohibition of formalities became part of U.S. law and the United States had to revise its laws to remove formalities.

C. BERNE CONVENTION AND RETROACTIVITY

An issue that arises when a nation joins an international treaty such as the Berne Convention is whether the treaty applies prospectively only or also retroactively. If the treaty applies prospectively only then it will create intellectual property rights only after the effective date of the treaty and the application of the treaty tends to be straightforward. If the treaty also applies retroactively, then it will create intellectual property right on dates that precede the effective date of the treaty and raises some complexities. In the case of the Berne Convention, the retroactive application of the treaty for a new member of the Berne Convention can confer copyright on works that have fallen into the public domain of that new member. In this case, the retroactive application of the Berne Convention will remove these works from the public domain and restore them to copyright. This can occur many years after the works have fallen into the public domain. This can create problems in that country for those persons or entities who have relied on having those works in the public domain only to find that the works now are suddenly subject to private rights. This happened in the United States when it joined the Berne Convention in 1989. Scores of works, including movies that had fallen into public domain, were restored to copyright.

TRIPS Article 70 makes clear that TRIPS does not apply retroactively except with respect to copyright and neighboring rights, which are to be governed by Article 18 of the Berne Convention. As a result, TRIPS obligations with respect to patents, trademarks, trade secrets, and design protection do not apply retroactively. TRIPS obligations concerning copyright, however, are subject to the Berne rule of retroactivity as set forth in Berne Convention Article 18:

> **Berne Convention**
>
> **Article 18**
>
> 1. This Convention shall apply to all works which, at the moment of its coming into force, have not yet fallen into the public domain in the country of origin through the expiry of the term of protection.
>
> 2. If, however, through the expiry of the term of protection which was previously granted, a work has fallen into the public domain of the country where is protection is claimed that work shall not be protected anew.

For Article 18 to apply, several conditions must exist. Suppose that a work has fallen into the public domain in Country A, which now joins the Berne Convention. The work has fallen into the public domain of Country A for reasons other than the expiry of the copyright term. For example, the work failed to satisfy formalities in Country A, which were lawful before Country A joined the Berne Convention. The country of origin of the work is Country B in which the work is still protected by copyright. Under these conditions, Country A must restore the work to copyright protection and give the work the term of protection it would have received if it had not fallen into the public domain, even though it may have been in the public domain in Country A for many years.

In this situation, the work would have been entitled to copyright protection in Country A but for Country A's requirement of formalities. The work has been harmed by Country A's lack of participation in the Berne Convention. As the work is still in copyright in its country of origin then the work should be allowed to enjoy the term of copyright that it would have received in Country A but for the requirement of formalities. On the other hand, if the work had fallen into the public domain in Country A because of the expiry of its term then the work will not be protected anew. The work was not harmed by Country A's lack of membership in the Berne Union.

As the application of Article 18(1) will restore copyright to works in the public domain, its application can harm certain parties who relied on the public nature of the works. Article 18(3) allows Berne countries to mitigate the harshness of applying the rule of retroactivity: "[T]he respective countries shall determine, in so far as it is concerned, the conditions of the application of this principle." The *Dam Things* case further discussed below will examine how the United States chose to mitigate the negative impact of the rule of retroactivity.

The United States has implemented Article 18 of the Berne Convention in 17 U.S.C. § 104A, effective as of January 1, 1996, which provides that "an original work of authorship" is entitled to a term of copyright protection equal to what the work would have received if it never entered the public domain in the United States if the work

(B) is not in the public domain in its source country through expiration of term of protection;

(C) is in the public domain in the United States due to—

(i) noncompliance with formalities imposed at any time by United States copyright law, including failure of renewal, lack of proper notice, or failure to comply with any manufacturing requirements;

* * *

(D) has at least one author or right holder who was, at the time the work was created, a national or domiciliary of an eligible country, and if published, was first published in an eligible country and not published in the United States during the 30-day period following publication in such eligible country.

The application of Section 104A was involved in *Dam Things from Denmark, A/K/A Troll Company APS v. Russ Berrie & Company, Inc.*, 290 F.3d 548 (3rd Cir. 2002). In that case, the plaintiff Dam

Things, a Danish company, claimed that copyright was restored to its original troll doll design, a design for a type of plastic doll with a pudgy face and wild hair that proved very popular with consumers. The troll doll design fell into the public domain in the United States when Dam Things sought a U.S. copyright for the trolls in 1965 but published (i.e. sold) the dolls in the United States with improper notice. At the time, the United States was not yet a member of the Berne Convention and imposed formalities on the acquisition of copyright, including a formal notice requirement. As Dam Things published or sold the doll with improper notice, the doll design fell into the public domain in the United States and would remain there until it was restored to copyright some 34 years later after January 1, 1996 by Section 104A.

As the troll doll design fell into the public domain due to lack of proper notice, the troll satisfied the requirement of Section 104A(C) above that the doll fell into the public domain due to lack of compliance with formalities. A second requirement is that the troll doll must be still protected in Denmark, its country of origin. This element was satisfied because Dam Things still had a valid copyright for the basic troll doll design (as well for other troll doll designs). The last requirement under Section 104A(D) above is that at least one author was a national of Denmark (an eligible country as it was a member of the Berne Union) and that the work was first published in Denmark and not simultaneously in the United States. The first publication in Denmark would make Denmark the country of origin of the work; the requirement that the author be a foreign national of a Berne Union country would mean that the foreign author must be the right holder of the foreign work. In enacting Section 104A, the United States did not want to restore copyrights to U.S. works but only to foreign works; hence the requirement that the work be first published in a Berne Union country other than the United States. In addition, the United States did not want to restore copyright in a foreign work owned by a U.S. author, which is the reason for the requirement that the author be a national of a Berne Union country other than the United States. The United States wanted to restore copyright only in foreign works owned by a foreign author.

The case revolved around the last issue: place of first publication. The plaintiff Dam Things argued that the doll was first published in Denmark while the defendant Russ Berrie, who had built his own business by copying the troll doll design in the United States, argued that the troll doll was first published in the United States, making the United States the country of origin of the work; if the United States were the country of origin, then the troll doll design would be ineligible for restoration to copyright under Section 104A and Article 18 of the Berne Convention as both only applied to foreign works. The Third Circuit Court of Appeals resolved the issue in favor of Dam Things finding that Denmark was the place of first publication for the original troll doll design.

The holding by the court meant that the defendant Russ Berrie was in breach of the copyright owned by Dam Things in the troll doll as the copyright was retroactively restored to 1965. Section 104A states that the "copyright shall subsist for the remainder of the term of copyright that the work would have enjoyed if the work never entered the public domain in the United States." This holding could seem harsh since Berrie copied the troll doll design when it was in the public domain.

Section 104A alleviates the harshness of the retroactivity rule by providing some protection for reliance parties. Section 104A provides a 12-month grace period for reliance parties starting from the date of filing of a notice of intent to enforce the restored copyright in the work. In addition, if the reliance party has made derivative works based on the restored work, the party retains the right to exploit the derivative work for the remainder of the copyright term if the party pays the copyright owner reasonable compensation. The purpose of Section 104A in restoring copyright to works that have fallen into the public domain in the United States is the long-term goal of having other nations do the same—restore to copyright in their territory U.S. works that have fallen into the public domain. The goal is to have as much copyright protection for U.S. works around the world as possible even if the short-term effects of the goal is to create a disadvantage for some U.S. parties, such as Berrie, who copied some foreign works that have now been restored to copyright.

Berne Convention Article 18, the rule of retroactivity, has been incorporated into TRIPS through TRIPS Article 9 (incorporating Berne Articles 1–21). As the WTO now has 166 members, or most of the nations of the world, new members of the WTO and/or the Berne Convention may become fewer in number and the rule of retroactivity may see less application in the future.

D. NEIGHBORING AND RELATED RIGHTS

Let us now turn to an examination of rights of performers in sound or digital recordings of performances. This would include the performance by an orchestra of a canon written by Bach or Mozart, a concert given by a rock band of songs written by a composer, or a group of actors performing a Shakespearean play. The performing artist performs a work composed by another, the person who would be viewed as a true author. Assume that a musical band gives a concert that is recorded and then is made into compact disks by the band's production company. What are the rights of the band in the recording? The answer to this question turns on whether the country extending protection treats the recording under the rubric of copyright or under a lesser regime of rights known as neighboring or related rights. The Berne Convention is silent on how to treat neighboring rights and leaves it up to each country to decide how to treat recordings of performances. As noted earlier, some countries, such as the United States, treat sound recordings under the rubric of copyright while other countries, such as France and Germany, treat sound recordings under the doctrine of neighboring rights.

In the United States, rights in sound recordings are treated under copyright although the protection is somewhat narrower than copyright for musical works that are original compositions by a composer. What remains unclear is whether a country that treats sound recordings under the rubric of copyright must apply the national treatment principle of the Berne Convention to those recordings. The Berne Convention applies to "literary and artistic works." Berne Conv., Article 2(1). If a sound recording is not a literary or artistic work then it does not qualify for national treatment under Article 5, which states that authors shall enjoy national treatment "in respect of works for which they are protected under this Convention." Berne Conv., Article 5(1). If a sound recording is not a literary or artistic work, then a point of attachment cannot be created for the sound recording. Points of attachment are created only when a "work" is created by a national of a Berne Union country or when a "work" is published in a Berne Union country. Without a point of attachment, other Berne Union countries are not obliged to provide national treatment for the sound recording. By contrast, if a country considers a sound recording to be a literary and artistic work within the meaning of Berne Convention Article 2(1), then sound recordings enjoy national treatment under the Berne Convention.

The United States considers sound recordings to be artistic works under the Copyright Act. For the United States, the treatment of a performer's sound or digital recordings will proceed under the Berne Convention.

> Illustration 2-12. A rock band from the UK gives a concert in Belgium of songs written by a third party composer. The concert is recorded and compact disks are later manufactured from the recording in France. Belgium and France are Berne Union countries. The manufacture of the compact disks is a publication within the meaning of the Berne Convention. The publication of the concert in France creates a point of attachment under the Berne Convention and the United States must extend national treatment to the recording, i.e. the United States must extend a U.S. copyright to the compact disks. Any other Berne Union country treating performance rights under the rubric of copyright and sound recordings as artistic works must do the same. The nation in which the band gives the performance is irrelevant under the Berne Convention. The key event is the publication of the disk, which occurred in a Berne Union country. The band's rights to the compact disk are determined by copyright.

What if the country involved, such as Germany, does not treat sound recordings under copyright but under the regime of neighboring rights? Then foreign sound recordings cannot be given protection under the Berne Convention. In this case, protection can be extended under another treaty, the International Convention for the Protection of Performers, Producers of Phonograms and Broadcasting Organizations (1961) (the Rome Convention).

Illustration 2-13. Under the same facts of the previous illustration, Germany will determine the rights of the band under the Rome Convention, not the Berne Convention. Belgium and France are also Rome Union countries. Under the Rome Convention, unlike the Berne Convention, the decisive event is the place in which the performance was given, not the publication of the disk. When the band gave its performance in Belgium, a point of attachment to the Rome Convention was established and the band become entitled to the Rome Convention's requirement that national treatment must be given to performers in Germany and all other Rome Union countries. The band's rights to the compact disk are determined by the doctrine of neighboring rights.

The Rome Convention has 92 members as of this writing, including most of the states of Europe but not including the United States. Like the Berne Convention, the Rome Convention deals with the recognition of rights of foreign works—in the case of the Rome Convention, foreign recordings and foreign broadcasts—and does not deal with how countries protect domestic recordings and domestic broadcasts.

The formal title of the Rome Convention recognizes that in the case of performances there are often three entities involved that need protection: the performer, the producer of the phonogram or compact disk (the recording studio), and the broadcasting company that is transmitting a broadcast of the performance. All three entities receive protection under the Rome

Convention although the scope of that protection varies for each entity.

The Rome Convention, like the Berne Convention, is rooted in a natural rights tradition. The Berne and Rome Conventions both use the concept of points of attachment because formalities are prohibited under both conventions. No formalities can be required if the rights are embedded in the natural order so a different theory—points of attachment—must be used to determine when rights are acquired. The approach of the Berne and Rome Conventions are similar in this regard. Where they differ is that the natural rights accorded to authors are of a higher level than the natural rights accorded to performers who are less meritorious than authors and who receive lesser rights under natural law.

Unlike the Berne Convention, the Rome Convention has not been incorporated into TRIPS so WTO members are not bound by the Rome Convention. For the Rome Convention to apply in a country, the country must be a member of the Rome Union. TRIPS does provide for some recognition of performance rights under TRIPS Article 14. The rights recognized under the Rome Convention are more extensive than the rights under TRIPS so joining the Rome Convention can still provide additional benefits for those countries willing to join.

1. POINTS OF ATTACHMENT UNDER THE ROME CONVENTION

Protection under the Rome Convention, like the Berne Convention, is acquired by a point of attachment that triggers an obligation of members to provide national treatment. However, points of attachment under the Rome Convention are even more complicated than under the Berne Convention because there are three entities involved: the performer, the recording studio, and the broadcasting company, each of which receives different types of protection.

Article 4 of the Rome Convention provides:

Rome Convention

Article 4

Each Contracting State shall grant national treatment to performers if any of the following conditions is met:

(a) the performance takes place in another Contracting State;

(b) the performance is incorporated in a phonogram which is protected under Article 5 of this Convention;

(c) the performance, not being fixed on a phonogram, is carried by a broadcast which is protected by Article 6 of this Convention.

Article 4(a) indicates that a performer can acquire a point of attachment and thus trigger Rome protection by giving a performance in a Rome Union country. Note that the nationality of the performer does not create a point of attachment; this is one distinction between the Berne and Rome Conventions. Under the Berne Convention, the nationality of the author establishes a point of attachment so long as the author creates the work regardless of whether the author published the work in a Berne Union country, in a non-Berne Union country, or did not publish the work at all. Under the Rome Convention, the decisive criterion is the place of performance. The performance must occur in a Rome Union country for a point of attachment to exist. Even if the performer is a national of a Rome Union country, the performer must still give the performance in the Rome Union (or acquire protection through a point of attachment established by a producer of a phonogram or a broadcasting companying under Article 4(b)–(c)). One possible explanation for why the nationality of the performer does not confer the same benefits as under the Berne Convention may be linked to the lower esteem with which performers were held as opposed to true authors.

> Illustration 2-14. M2, a rock band from Cleveland, Ohio, gives a concert in Argentina, a Rome Union country. As the performance is in a Rome Union country, M2 is entitled to national treatment for its performance in all Rome Union countries. Although the United States is not a member of the Rome Convention and M2 is not a national of a Rome Union country, M2 receives Rome protection because its performance was given in a Rome Union country.

If the performer did not give the performance in a Rome Union country, it is still possible for the performer to receive national treatment for its performance in other Rome Union countries if the producer of the phonogram or the broadcasting company can establish a point of attachment under Articles 5 and 6 respectively. Article 4(b) states that a point of attachment also occurs if the performance is recorded in a phonogram under the conditions set forth in Article 5 (further discussed below). Article 5 allows the producer of a phonogram to establish a point of attachment for itself. If the producer establishes a point of attachment under Article 5, the performer can also assert the producer's point of attachment and receive national treatment from Rome Union countries. In other words, the performer can piggyback onto the point of attachment established by the producer. Article 4(c) provides that the same holds true for the broadcasting company. If the broadcasting company establishes a point of attachment under Article 6, then the broadcasting company receives national treatment for its broadcast under the Rome Convention. The performer is also allowed to piggyback on the point of attachment established by the broadcasting company.

Establishing a point of attachment on its own by the performer and piggybacking on the point of attachment of the producer or broadcasting company do not provide equivalent rights. If the performer establishes its own point of attachment, then the performer enjoys national treatment by Rome Union countries of rights given to performers. If the performer piggybacks on the producer or broadcasting company, then the performer receives a dependent protection only, i.e. the performer can only assert whatever rights the producer or broadcasting company can assert. Most countries provide different rights for performers, producers, and broadcasting companies. Illustrations 2-15, 2-16, 2-17, and 2-18 below provide some examples of how rights of performers, producers, and broadcasting companies differ.

The reason why performers are allowed to piggyback is because the drafters of the Rome Convention did not want to a producer or a broadcasting company to receive protections for the performance that the performer does not also receive. If a record producer could sue an infringer for unauthorized copies of its compact disk, it seemed unfair if the performer could not do the same as, after all, the compact disk was a recording of its performance. Hence a mechanism was established to allow the performer to piggyback.

Note that how the point of attachment for the producer or the broadcasting company is established is done under a different set of rules set forth in Articles 5 and 6. These rules are not the same as that for the performer's point of attachment. Let us turn now to a detailed examination of points of attachment for producers (Article 5) and broadcasting companies (Article 6).

Article 5 provides:

Rome Convention

Article 5

1. Each Contracting State shall grant national treatment to producers of phonograms if any of the following conditions is met:

(a) the producer of the phonogram is a national of another Contracting State (criterion of nationality);

(b) the first fixation of the sound was made in another Contracting state (criterion of fixation);

(c) the phonogram was first published in another Contracting State (criterion of publication).

2. If a phonogram was first published in a non-contracting state but if it was also published, within thirty of its first publication, in a Contracting State (simultaneous publication), it shall be considered as first published in the Contracting State.

3. By means of a notification deposited with the Secretary-General of the United Nations, any Contracting State may declare that it will not apply the criterion of publication or, alternatively, the criterion of fixation.

A producer of phonograms, defined as the person or legal entity that first fixes the sounds of a performance (Article 3(c)), can establish a point of attachment using any one of three criteria set forth in Article 5(1)(a)–(c).

Under Article 5(1)(a), the criterion of nationality, if the producer is national of a Rome Union country, then the nationality of the producer establishes a point of attachment and it does not matter where the fixation or publication of the performance occurred. For the producer, nationality suffices for all purposes, similar to how nationality functions under the Berne Convention. Recall that the criterion of nationality was not available for performers. This difference may be due to the greater lobbying and economic power of the record producer. The same will hold true for broadcasting companies that will also enjoy the criterion nationality (or its equivalent).

If nationality is unavailable, then Article 5 establishes a point of attachment if the fixation occurred in a Rome Union country (Article 5(b)) or if the publication (i.e. the manufacture of the compact disks) occurred in a Rome Union country (Article 5(c)).

> Illustration 2-15. M2, the rock band from Cleveland, gives a performance in Dallas, Texas, USA. M2's record company, Vista Records, a Delaware company, fixes and produces a compact disk in Germany. M2's performance occurs in a non-Rome Union country so M2 cannot establish a point of attachment (Article 4(a)). However, Vista Records fixed and published the compact disk in a Rome Union country and is entitled to national treatment under the Rome Convention for its compact disk

(Articles 4(b), 5(b)–(c)). M2 can piggyback on Vista's point of attachment.

Illustration 2-16. In piggybacking on Vista's point of attachment, M2 can only assert whatever rights that Vista can assert. In Rome countries, performers generally have the right to prevent "bootleg" copies of their performances, i.e. an authorized copy of a live performance by someone with a video camera in the audience that is later made into a compact disk and sold. This is not a right that most countries give to production companies. Production companies will receive rights to prevent the unauthorized copying of their compact disks. So if M2 can establish its own point of attachment, it can interdict bootleg copies and sales of bootleg copies of its live performance; if M2 is piggybacking on Vista's point of attachment, M2 will only be able to assert a right against sales of unauthorized copies of the compact disk, same as Vista.

A broadcasting country can establish a point of attachment under Article 6:

Rome Convention

Article 6

1. Each Contracting State shall grant national treatment to broadcasting organizations if either of the following conditions is met:

> (a) the headquarters of the broadcasting organization is situated in another Contracting State;
>
> (b) the broadcast was transmitted from a transmitter situated in another Contracting State.
>
> 2. By means of a notification deposited with the Secretary-General of the United Nations, any Contracting State may declare it will protect broadcasts only if the headquarters of the broadcasting organization is situated in another Contracting State and the broadcast was transmitted from a transmitter situated in the same Contracting State.

Under Article 6(1)(a), the location of the headquarters of the broadcasting organization in another Contracting State establishes a point of attachment. Location in a member of the Rome Union is similar to having a permanent residence in a member of the Rome Union and assimilates the broadcasting organization to the nationals of the member. As in the case of producers, the nationality (or its equivalent) of the broadcasting organization is sufficient to establish a point of attachment. Both producers and broadcasters are treated better than performers under the Rome Convention for reasons already discussed. Article 6(1)(b) also creates a point of attachment if the broadcasting company uses a transmitter in a Rome Union country. Many broadcasting companies have transmitters located in numerous countries.

Illustration 2-17. M2 gives a concert in India. Vista Records fixes and produces a compact disk in Atlanta, Georgia, USA. A broadcasting company with its headquarters in Japan broadcasts the concert live in parts of Asia. As India is not a member of the Rome Convention, M2 cannot establish a point of attachment through the performance of its concert. The United States is also not a member of the Rome Convention so Vista cannot establish a point of attachment based on fixation and manufacture in the United States. Japan is a member of the Rome Convention and the broadcasting company's headquarters in Japan does establish a point of attachment under Article 6(1)(a). M2 is allowed to piggyback on this point of attachment and is entitled to national treatment for its performance. M2 can now assert the same rights as the broadcasting company in the broadcast.

Illustration 2-18. In the previous illustration note that Vista is not allowed to piggyback on the broadcasting company's point of attachment. Piggybacking is allowed for the performer only. M2 can now assert whatever rights the broadcasting company can assert. Under the Rome Convention, broadcasting companies have the right to prohibit rebroadcasting and fixation of their broadcasts without their consent. Rome Conv., Article 13. M2 will have the same rights to the broadcasts. M2 will not have the right to prohibit the sales of any bootleg copies of its concert (a performer's right) or the right to prohibit any sales of unauthorized copies of Vista's compact disks (a production company's right).

Note carefully that it is not necessary for piggybacking by the performer that the performer cannot establish his own point of attachment. Article 4 allows for the possibility that the performer, the producer, and the broadcasting company can all establish points of attachment under Articles 4, 5, and 6. Or that the performer and only either the record company or broadcasting company can assert a point of attachment. If all three can assert points of attachment, then the performer will be able to assert performer's rights, producer's rights, and broadcaster's rights in the performance but the producer can only assert producer's rights and the broadcasting companying can only assert broadcaster's rights. Piggybacking is allowed for performers only.

2. DEPENDENT NATURE OF RIGHTS

The dependent nature of the rights of the performer who piggybacks on the rights of a broadcasting company is illustrated in *Bruce Springsteen and His Band*, Case No. 1 ZR 205/95, (April 23, 1998), decided by the Germany Federal Court of Justice. Shane Fontayne, a UK national and a member of Bruce Springsteen's band, sought to prohibit the distribution of bootleg compact disks in Germany. The compact disks were unauthorized copies of a concert given by Springsteen and his band in Los Angeles in 1992.

As the United States is not a member of the Rome Convention, Fontayne could not establish a point of attachment based on giving a performance in a Rome Union country. Rather Fontayne argued that a point of attachment was created because a number of radio broadcasting companies had broadcast the performance live on radio. The broadcasting companies were located in Argentina, Brazil, Austria, Paraguay, and Uruguay, all of which are Rome Union countries. As a performer, Fontayne would then piggyback on the broadcasters' points of attachment and assert a claim against the bootleggers.

A point of attachment was indeed established under Article 6 because radio broadcasts were made by broadcasting companies with their headquarters in Rome Union countries. But as Fontayne was piggybacking on the points of attachment of the broadcasting companies, he could only assert the same claims that the companies themselves could assert. For Fontayne to piggyback he had to show that rights of the broadcasting companies in the broadcasts had been violated. For the broadcasting companies to be able to assert that the sale of the compacts disks violated their rights, the disks had to be copies of the broadcast transmissions. However, Fontayne failed to offer any evidence that the disks were copies of the transmissions. It was also possible (and probably more likely) that the copies were made of the live performance itself by someone with a recording device sitting in the audience or hidden backstage. But as Fontayne was piggybacking the rights of the broadcasting company, Fontayne did not have the right to prohibit the recording of the band's live performance and the distribution of the compact disks made from copies of the videotape. Fontayne would have those rights only if he asserted a point of attachment as a performer, which was impossible as the performance took place in the United States, a non-contracting state to the Rome Convention. As Fontayne failed to prove that the compact disks were copies of the radio transmissions, the German Supreme Court rejected Fontayne's claim under the Rome Convention.

Although the claim based on the Rome Convention failed, the German Federal Court of Justice found that the national treatment principle contained in Article 6(1) of the EC Treaty protected Fontayne and Springsteen's band. In other words, the EC Treaty's national treatment principle created rights in performers. Citing the *Phil Collins* case (discussed earlier in this chapter) as precedent, the court found that Fontayne, a UK national, must be treated as least as favorably as German nationals under German law. No doubt the plaintiffs were aware of this argument under EU law, which is why Fontayne brought the action, not Springsteen, a citizen of the United States. German performers had the right to prohibit the distribution of bootleg copies whether the performance was given in Germany or outside of Germany. The German law at issue in *Phil Collins* provided that foreign nationals could prohibit bootleg copies only if the performance had been given in Germany. The *Phil Collins* case held that this discriminatory treatment violated the national treatment principle of the EC Treaty. The court found that under *Phil Collins*, Germany had to give the same treatment to Fontayne that German nationals enjoyed, allowing Fontayne to ban the distribution of the bootleg copies.

What if Bruce Springsteen, not Shane Fontayne, had brought the lawsuit? Springsteen is a U.S. national and so would not be entitled to assert the national treatment principle of the EC Treaty. Springsteen could, however, assert the national treatment principle under TRIPS Article 3 and achieve the same result. The national treatment analysis under TRIPS would follow from the *Phil Collins* case involving similar facts and previously discussed on pages 30–32 in Chapter One of this book.

Note that while we have discussed the national treatment principle because it is so important to understanding the international protection of intellectual property, there is no need for Springsteen in this context to rely on the national treatment principle in the EC Treaty or TRIPS. Springsteen can rely directly on performance rights required by TRIPS. Article 14 of TRIPs provides that "[i]n respect of a fixation of their performance on a phonogram, performers shall have the possibility of preventing the following acts when undertaken without their authorization: the fixation of their unfixed performance and the reproduction of such fixation." TRIPS Article 14 requires Germany to directly extend rights to Springsteen to interdict bootleg copies.

E. SUBSTANTIVE RIGHTS CONFERRED BY COPYRIGHT

So far the discussion in this chapter has focused on the acquisition of copyrights and neighboring rights. By necessity the discussion of acquisition of rights has been extensive due to the Berne and Rome Conventions' roots in natural rights theory. By prohibiting formalities, natural rights theory required the use of elaborate theories of points of attachment to explain how copyrights and related rights can be acquired without the simple use of a formality such as filing an application or registration.

At this point, we now assume that a copyright has been acquired. For the remainder of this chapter we will turn to the substantive issues of the subject matter of copyright and the rights conferred by copyright. As a preliminary matter, however, we will make a brief detour to discuss the issue of ownership of copyrights.

1. OWNERSHIP

Ownership concerns who or what entity has the initial ownership of the copyright. Under the Berne Convention, the "author" owns the copyright (Article 5(1)) with a presumption that the author is the name that appears on the work "in the usual manner." Berne Conv., Article 15.

Although most ownership issues are relatively straightforward, there is one area where the United States and some European states differ: corporate ownership and the work made for hire doctrine. In following the utilitarian theory of copyright, the United States had little difficulty in finding that a corporate entity can be the initial owner of a copyright. Under the work made for hire doctrine, generally applicable in the United States, ownership of the copyright would vest in the corporation, as employer, of a work created by an employee. Under the work made for hire doctrine, corporate ownership of copyrights in the United States and the UK is common; indeed, in the United States, the employee is not even considered to be the author of the work; the employer (i.e. the corporation) is the author. The U.S. position can avoid problems that arise in corporations over who owns rights in software, music, motion pictures or inventions (subject to patents discussed in the next chapter) created as part of the main enterprise of the corporation. If an employee creates a work during the course of employment, the ownership of the copyright vests in the employer, the corporation. The reward to the employee may consist of a pay increase, a promotion, or just a few words of praise and a slap on the back, but the work belongs to the corporation.

Countries in Europe have difficulty accepting this position because of their allegiance to the natural rights theory, which views authors as flesh and blood human beings, not an impersonal corporation. For this reason, the work made for hire doctrine has not achieved widespread acceptance in Europe. Certain countries, such as Germany, protect flesh and blood authors by prohibiting the complete assignment of their copyright to corporations. As European countries vary on how much allegiance they give to the natural rights theory and how the theory affects corporate ownership of copyrights, it is necessary to check local domestic laws carefully when a dispute arises.

2. SUBJECT MATTER OF COPYRIGHT

The subject matter of copyright concerns what types of works are entitled to copyright protection. TRIPS Article 9 states: "[c]opyright protection shall extend to expressions and not to ideas, procedures, methods of operation or mathematical concepts as such." This statement sets forth the basic idea/expression dichotomy in copyright law. Copyright protection extends to expressions not to ideas themselves. No one can copyright an idea as withdrawing ideas from the public domain would impoverish it severely. No one can copyright a mathematical theorem. Copyright would create private rights in the theorem or mathematical concept and no one would be able to copy or use it without authorization from the owner of the copyright. Such privatization of mathematical concepts could severely damage the ability of the public to freely use ideas, to commercialize the results of the use of such concepts, and to engage in further research. In theory at least, none of these activities could occur without permission from the copyright owner.

While ideas or concepts cannot be the subject matter of copyright, expressions of ideas can be protected by copyright. An author can write a novel about a heroic liberator who leads a beaten down people to freedom; the details of the plot of the story and the dialogue can be subject to copyright protection, but the idea of a heroic liberator cannot. Any other author can write a novel, short story, or play about a heroic liberator of beaten down peoples so long as the author does not copy the specific plot line or dialogue in the novel.

A similar distinction is drawn between "facts" and "compilations of facts." Some compilations of facts may be subject to copyright protection but facts themselves are not. This distinction is set forth in TRIPS Article 10:

> **TRIPS**
>
> **Article 10**
>
> Compilations of data or other material, whether in machine readable or other form, which by reason of their selection or arrangement of their contents constitute intellectual creations shall be protected as such. Such protection, which shall not extend to the data or material itself, shall be without prejudice to any copyright subsisting in the data or material itself.

While facts are not eligible for copyright protection, compilations of facts are eligible if their selection or arrangement constitute "intellectual creations," i.e. show a certain level of creativity. Although the term "creativity" does not appear in TRIPS or the Berne Convention, the term "intellectual creation" implies some mental element of creativity. The copyright protection extended to compilations of facts protects only the creative selection and arrangement of the facts or data; the underlying facts or data themselves are not protected by copyright but are free for all to use and copy at their pleasure. In this context, the terms "fact" and "data" are synonymous.

The minimum level of creativity necessary to protect the selection and arrangement of a compilation of facts was the main issue in *Feist Publications, Inc. v. Rural Telephone Service Company, Inc.*, 499 U.S. 340 (1991). Feist Publications published an area wide telephone book whereas Rural, a public utility, published a telephone book for its local service area. Feist's telephone book encompassed 11 different telephone service areas offering users the convenience of having one comprehensive telephone book and making it unnecessary to use multiple books to find numbers.

As Feist was not a telephone company, Feist had no access to telephone numbers other than by obtaining the numbers from the telephone companies for a licensing fee. Of the 11 telephone companies, only Rural refused to license its telephone entries to Feist. Rural viewed Feist as a rival as Rural was a keen competitor with Feist for yellow pages advertising. Feist knew that its area wide telephone book would not be very useful if it lacked one of the telephone service areas so Feist decided to copy Rural's entries without permission. Believing that Feist might do this, Rural planted four fictitious entries in its directory to detect copying.

Feist's justification for copying Rural's entire telephone book without permission was that the individual telephone number entries and the alphabetical ordering of the entries were not protected by copyright. The Supreme Court accepted this argument on appeal.

In deciding whether Rural had a copyright in its telephone directory, the U.S. Supreme Court started with the premise that originality is the touchstone of copyright. Originality means independent creation by the author plus a modest level of creativity. *Feist* elaborates on the creativity component of originality. Turning to the facts of *Feist*, the Court distinguished between the individual entries and the arrangement of the entries in alphabetical order. The individual entries were "facts" not eligible for copyright protection. The originality element of copyright requires that the author independently create the work. Facts are not created by the author but already exist in the world and are "discovered." As facts the telephone entries were free to anyone to copy.

While facts are not eligible for copyright protection, the selection and arrangement of facts can be eligible if original, i.e. arranged by *Feist* with a modicum of creativity. While the constitutionally required level of creativity is modest, arranging telephone entries in alphabetical order does not meet even this minimal level. An arrangement in alphabetical order not only lacks creativity but is almost inevitable. As a result, Feist had no copyright in its telephone book and Rural was entitled copy the individual entries as facts as well as the alphabetical ordering of all of the entries as a selection and arrangement done without any creativity.

Why weren't the fictitious entries inserted by Rural to detect copying considered creative? The trick was clever but a total of four entries scattered in a telephone book with thousands or tens of thousands of entries did not affect the overall selection and arrangement and is too minute of a contribution to satisfy even the modicum of creativity requirement.

Assuming that Rural had made a selection and arrangement of the entries that did satisfy the requirement of creativity, copyright protection extends only to the selection and arrangement not to the entries themselves. Anyone could copy the discrete telephone entries because as "facts" they are not entitled to copyright protection.

Feist's approach to creativity can be compared with the approached used by the Canadian Supreme Court in *CCH Canadian Ltd v. Law Society of Upper Canada*, 2004 SCC 13 (March 4, 2004). The Law Society of Upper Canada, an organization involved in the regulation of the legal profession in Ontario, offered a copying service for its members of legal materials available at the Great Library at Osgood Hall in Toronto. The Law Society copied legal materials published by CCH Canada Ltd, which publishes law reports and other materials. CCH claimed a copyright in the materials copied and the legal issue turned on whether the materials were original works within the meaning of the Copyright Act of Canada.

The Canadian Supreme Court used the case as an opportunity to review various approaches to originality. At one end of the spectrum was the "sweat of the brow" or "industriousness" standard of originality. Under the sweat of the brow doctrine, the only requirement for copyright was industriousness or effort in making the work. No creativity was required. This doctrine led to the criticism that the sweat of the brow standard could lead to copyright protection in the facts or data as such. If all that the author needed for copyright is to exert industrious effort then a hardworking author could obtain a copyright for a work totally devoid of creativity. An author who worked industriously to make a compilation of facts would have a copyright in the facts as such beyond their selection and arrangement. The court believed that this approach set the bar of creativity too low. At the opposite extreme, according to the court, was the *Feist* standard, which requires creativity. According to the court, this was too high a standard as the *Feist* standard indicates that work must be creative in the sense of being novel or unique. The court's characterization of *Feist* seems to overstate its requirement of creativity. The *Feist* standard is a modicum of creativity; nowhere does *Feist* require novelty or uniqueness.

The Canadian Supreme Court decided to chart a middle course between what it argued were the extremes of the sweat of the brow and the *Feist* creativity approaches. The court stated that in Canada originality required the "exercise of skill and judgment." In this context, skill refers to knowledge and ability; judgment refers to discernment and the ability to form opinions. This would be a mid-point in a scale with sweat of the brow at one extreme and

Feist's creativity in the sense of being novel or unique at the other extreme.

Using this standard, the court then examined the various works that CCH claimed were protected by copyright. The court concluded that the headnotes, case summary, topical indexes, and reported judicial opinions all required the exercise of skill and judgment and were entitled to copyright protection. All of these works were more than mere copies of facts but required the exercise of skill and judgment to create. With respect to the judicial opinions, the headnotes, case summary, catch lines, case title, and case information required the exercise of skill and judgment and the selection and arrangement of all of the items with the judicial opinion also required skill and judgment. The judicial opinion itself, devoid of these accompanying works, was not an original work.

Although the *CCH* case attempted to create a scale of creativity with the sweat of the brow doctrine at one extreme and *Feist* at the other, it seems doubtful that the *Feist* standard and the standard in *CCH* differ greatly in actual application. Using the *Feist* standard, the result in the *CCH* case would likely have been the same. Each of the works described in *CCH* required enough intellectual input from the author to meet the modest creativity requirement required by *Feist*.

Other jurisdictions have originality requirements that may have different labels but are likely in practice to be quite similar to the standards in both the United States and Canada. Although it is often assumed that civil law countries in Europe require a higher level of creativity, in practice the approach in these countries may not differ greatly from *Feist*. For example, France, which accepts the natural rights tradition, requires that the work be an expression of the "author's personality" made through "creative choices." This might seem at first to establish a high standard of creativity, but French legal commentators indicate that the test is not difficult to meet and that originality is present so long as authors show some creativity and the work is not a slavish copy. Overall, while the labels may differ, most countries seem to require some creativity for copyright, but only a modest amount.

3. THE EU DATABASE DIRECTIVE

In the modern age, databases containing various types of information are more important than ever in scientific and industrial research. In the area of pharmaceuticals, databases are essential for gathering information from clinical trials and other phases needed for national regulatory approval of drugs in many countries. Biomedical industries rely on databases to further genetic research. Databases can also be used by consumer products companies to discern trends in consumer tastes. With the increasing importance of databases, the question also arises whether databases must be given more protection than traditionally given under copyright law.

TRIPS Article 10 provides that databases are subject to protection under copyright law but the originality requirement limits the scope of protection available. Article 10 states: "[c]ompilations of data or other material . . . which by reason of the selection or arrangement of their contents constitute intellectual creations shall be protected as such. Such protection . . . shall not extend to the data or material itself." TRIPS Article 10 articulates a standard of protection for databases that is entirely consistent with copyright. The selection and arrangement of a database is protected by copyright if there is a sufficient level of creativity but the underlying data are not protected and free for all to copy. Article 10 maintains the expression/idea dichotomy by providing that the selection and arrangement—the expression of the data—is subject to copyright but the data (the ideas or the facts) are not subject to copyright protection.

TRIPS sets forth minimum standards for all of the major intellectual property rights, including copyright, but there is nothing in TRIPS that prevents WTO members from going beyond its minimum standards. A WTO member can provide for a heightened level of protection for any of the intellectual property rights recognized by TRIPS as well as provide protection for a new intellectual property right not recognized in TRIPS.

In the case of databases, the European Union believed that it was necessary to create a *sui generis* right that went beyond what was available under copyright. In 1996, the EU passed the Directive on the Legal Protection of Databases, Directive 96/9/EC of the European Parliament and of the Council of 11 March 1996 on the Legal Protection of Databases.

The EU directive is a significant innovation in intellectual property law and it pits the EU directly against the United States in the area of competition for intellectual property protections and investment in industrial development.

The EU directive consists of two different parts. Article 3 deals with copyright protection for databases:

EU Database Directive

Article 3
Object of protection

1. In accordance with this Directive, databases which, by reason of the selection or arrangement of their contents, constitute the author's own intellectual creation shall be protected as such by copyright. No other criteria shall be applied to determine their eligibility for that protection.

2. The copyright protection of databases provided for by this Directive shall not extend to their contents and shall be without prejudice to any rights subsisting in those contents themselves.

Article 3 is consistent with TRIPS Article 10 on compilations of data. Copyright protection extends to the creative selection and arrangement of data but no copyright exists in the underlying data. This part of the EU directive is not controversial.

Article 7 of the EU directive sets forth a *sui generis* right in databases as follows:

EU Database Directive

Chapter III: *Sui Generis* Right

Article 7
Object of Protection

1. Member States shall provide for a right for the maker of a database which shows that there has been qualitatively or quantitatively a substantial investment in either the obtaining, verification or presentation of the contents to prevent extraction and/or re-utilization of the whole or of a substantial part, evaluated qualitatively and/or quantitatively, of the contents of that database.

2. For the purposes of this Chapter:

(a) "extraction" shall mean the permanent or temporary transfer of all or a substantial part of the contents of the database to another medium by any means or in any form;

(b) "re-utilization" shall mean any form of making available to the public all or a substantial part of the contents of a database by the distribution of copies, by renting, by on-line or other forms of transmission. The first sale of a copy of a database within the Community by the right holder or with his consent shall exhaust the right to control resale of that copy within the Community. Public lending is not an act of extraction or re-utilization.

> 3. The right referred in paragraph 1 may be transferred, assigned or granted under contractual license.
>
> 4. The right provided for in paragraph 1 shall apply irrespective of the eligibility of that database for protection by copyright or by other rights. Moreover, it shall apply irrespective of eligibility of the contents of that database for protection by copyright or by other rights. Protection of databases under the right provided for in paragraph 1 shall be without prejudice to rights existing in respective of their content.

Article 7 of the EU Database Directive creates a *sui generis* right in the data, beyond anything available under copyright law. Article 7(3) makes it clear that the *sui generis* right "shall apply irrespective of the eligibility of the contents of that database for protection by copyright or any other right." The condition for obtaining such a right is that the maker of the database has made "qualitatively or quantitatively a substantial investment in the obtaining, verification, or presentation" of the contents of the database. The touchstone of the *sui generis* right is a substantial investment; there is no requirement of any creativity or intellectual effort. The EU Database Directive is reminiscent of the sweat of the brow doctrine, but it has been modernized by requiring a "substantial investment" instead of industriousness or effort. The terms "qualitative or quantitative" are given further elaboration in the *British Horseracing Board* case discussed below.

Article 10 creates the prospect of an indefinite term of protection under the EU directive, which further intensifies concerns about granting proprietary rights to raw data or facts.

EU Database Directive

Article 10
Term of Protection

1. The right provided for in Article 7 shall run from the date of completion of the making of the database. It shall expire fifteen years from the first of January of the year following the date of completion.

2. In the case of a database which is made available to the public in whatever manner before expiry in the period provided for in paragraph 1, the term of protection by that right shall expire fifteen years from the first of January of the year following the date when the database was first made available to the public.

3. Any substantial change, evaluated qualitatively or quantitatively, to the contents of a database, including any substantial change resulting from the accumulation of successive additions, deletions or alterations, which would result in the database being considered to be a substantial new investment, evaluated qualitatively or quantitatively, shall qualify the database resulting from that investment for its own term of protection.

Article 10(3) provides that any substantial change to an existing database that can be considered to be a substantial new investment will qualify the database for a new term of protection. This creates the potential for a perpetually protected database. Suppose that a database has been completed and receives a 15-year term of protection. A multinational company can periodically update the database, ensuring that it invests substantial resources in doing so. Under this scenario, the company can have a database that is protected indefinitely. The contents of the database have been withdrawn from the public indefinitely perhaps even permanently.

Once the *sui generis* right is created through a substantial investment, the maker of the database acquires the right to prohibit the extraction or reutilization of the whole or a substantial part of the database. Article 7(2)(a) of the EU directive defines extraction to mean "the permanent or temporary transfer of all or a substantial part of the contents of a database to any other medium by any means or in any form." Article 7(2)(b) defines reutilization to mean "any form of making available to the public all or a substantial part of the contents of a database by the distribution of copies, by renting, by on-line or other forms of transmission." The extraction right prohibits unauthorized users from copying the contents of the database. The reutilization right would apply where the maker of a database gives authorization to a third party to access its database. Suppose, for example, that the maker of the database has a website containing a database that subscribers can access for a fee; the subscriber is prohibited from making the contents of the database available to third parties.

Critics of the EU Database Directive worry that it eliminates the distinction between creation and discovery. Facts are not subject to copyright protection because they are not created by the author. Facts exist in nature and are discovered. If it is possible to have private rights in facts then parts of nature become private property and are withdrawn from the public domain. Such privatization would withdraw the essential tools necessary for scientific progress. As the data are protected as such, others cannot use the data without permission or the payment of a royalty. Scientific progress occurs when researchers are able to use existing data as the building blocks for further progress, which occurs incrementally. Without a substratum of facts and data that is in the public domain free for all to use, scientific progress might be impeded as the building blocks of progress have been removed and privatized. Scientific researchers cannot stop and inquire every time a fact is used in research to determine whether it is private property. That would seriously impede the process of scientific discovery. Critics also worry that some database owners may not be willing to license their data in order to impede their competitors. If that occurs then society as a whole suffers because scientific progress will be harmed by private entities acting in their own self-interests.

Another concern about the EU directive are the incentives created in the competition between the

United States and the EU for investment dollars. If a multinational company is faced with the option of locating a research and development center in the United States or the EU, the EU directive might tilt the choice in favor the EU. Critics worry that the EU will become more attractive as an investment destination than the United States due to the high level of protection for databases. Under Article 11(2) of the EU directive, a business can obtain EU protection only if its "registered office, central administration or principal place of business [is] within the community; however, where such a company or firm has only its registered office in the territory of the Community, its operations must be genuinely linked on an ongoing basis with the economy of a Member State." The EU wanted to ensure that foreign companies could not receive the benefits of the EU directive by setting up a small office in the EU to receive data transmitted from the company's headquarters in the United States or other country. To receive the benefits of the EU directive, a U.S. company must establish a genuine business operation such as a foreign subsidiary within the EU.

The EU directive appears to create an advantage in the ongoing competition between the United States and the EU for which territory has the more attractive investment climate created by intellectual property protections. Concerned about this development, the U.S. Congress has made efforts to introduce similar legislation for *sui generis* database protections in the United States. Others in Congress worry that the costs of private rights and monopolies in databases will outweigh the benefits. So far all efforts at passing legislation similar to the EU Database Directive in the U.S. Congress have been unsuccessful and the fervor for such legislation appears to have subsided. Database protection in the United States, at least for now, is governed by copyright.

The European Court of Justice might have addressed at least some of the concerns about the EU directive when it adopted a narrow reading of the EU Database Directive in the *British Horseracing Board Ltd. v. William Hill Organization Ltd.* (2004) ECR I–10415, Case C–203/02 (Nov. 9, 2004). The case concerned the database generated by the British Horseracing Board (BHB) for the horse racing industry. Among its other duties, the BHB organized horse races. Through its call center manned by about 30 operators, the BHB collected information from persons entering a horse in a race, checked on whether the characteristics of the horse met conditions for entry, decided whether the horse could race depending on the number of slots assigned to other horses, assigned a saddle cloth number to each horse, and assigned a stall from which it will start to each horse. The BHB also registered information concerning owners, trainers, jockeys, and horses and also provided weight added and handicapping for the horses entered in various races. The BHB made this information available through the internet as well as in hard copy form. The information was useful not only to persons who bet on races but also to various media that broadcast the races or commented on them. The cost of running BHB's database was approximately $6 million per year.

William Hill Organization Ltd. was a subscriber to BHB's internet feed and to the hard copy publication. Hill was also a leading provider of off-course betting services through Hill's own website. Hill displayed information on its website obtained from the BHB's internet feed and hard copy publication and Hill's customers were then able to make bets on Hill's website. If BHB's database were protected by the EU directive's *sui generis* right then BHB could prevent Hill from displaying the information (which constitutes a reutilization of the data) without BHB's authorization.

The European Court of Justice (ECJ) held that BHB's database did not qualify for *sui generis* protection. The key to the decision was the ECJ's interpretation of the substantial investment requirement. Article 7 of the EU Database Directive requires "a substantial investment in the obtaining, verification, and presentation of the contents" of a database. The ECJ interpreted this language to mean a substantial investment in the obtaining, verification, and presentation of *existing* data, not in the *creation* of new data. In this case, BHB created the data through its horse racing operations. As the database was not the result of a substantial investment in existing data, the database did not qualify for the *sui generis* right.

The ECJ decision did significantly narrow the types of databases eligible for protection. Databases based on data that is created or generated by the database maker is outside the scope of the EU directive. Horse racing and other sports gambling databases fall into category. Databases created by pharmaceutical companies to obtain regulatory approval also fall into this category and are also ineligible for the *sui generis* right. However, scientific databases that gather existing data fall within the protections of the EU directive so the basic criticism of the EU Database Directive that it creates private rights in facts or data remains. Creating intellectual property rights in facts or data remains controversial and is one reason why proposals to enact a similar law for databases in the United States have so far stalled.

F. COPYRIGHT PROTECTION FOR TRADITIONAL CULTURAL EXPRESSION

The previous section dealt with databases and data, areas that were not historically given copyright protection. This section examines whether another area not historically given copyright protection, folklore or traditional cultural expression, is or should be protected by copyright. Both databases and traditional culture do not meet all of the requirements for copyright. In the case of databases, the main issue was that data or facts are not eligible for copyright protection. In the case of traditional culture, additional obstacles to copyright protection exist as will be further discussed below.

Protection for traditional culture has become an important issue because some business entities have appropriated and commercialized traditional culture without offering compensation or credit to the indigenous groups from which the culture has been taken. For example, some elements of traditional folk songs and music have been commercialized in the form of pop music. A related concern is that multinational companies have also been known to patent ingredients found in traditional medicines for commercialization without compensating any indigenous groups. This practice has come to be known as "biopiracy" to distinguish it from commercial piracy, the unauthorized copying of products protected by trademarks. Traditional culture and traditional use of bioresources also raise the issue of whether there is any space in modern copyright and patent law for non-western traditions and values.

The World Intellectual Property Organization's Intergovernmental Committee has drafted articles (WIPO/GRTKF/IC/19/4) that define folklore or traditional cultural expression. In this context, traditional cultural expression refers to tangible and intangible forms of culture that can be passed from one generation of indigenous peoples to another. Traditional cultural expression can take intangible forms: verbal expressions, such as stories, poetry, and other narratives, musical or sound expressions such as songs or music, and expressions by action such as dance, ceremonies, games, and rituals. Tangible expressions include artwork, handicrafts, architecture, and sacred places.

From this definition, we can see that there are several hurdles that can prevent traditional cultural expression from obtaining copyright protection. First, modern copyright laws require an author of a work. In the case of traditional culture, identifying a single author or a group of persons as authors can be difficult or impossible. Traditional culture might have been passed from generation to generation for hundreds years without any records of who might have been the author of the works. Second, copyright requires originality, i.e. independent creation, not copying. Traditional culture may have passed through generations with no records so it becomes impossible to show that it was independently created by an author. Third, most copyright laws require fixation in a tangible medium. Some traditional culture is non-tangible, such as songs, dance, and rituals.

These obstacles to protection for traditional culture do not mean that it can never be protected by copyright. A notable success is an Australian case, *Milpurrurru and Others v. Indofurn Pty Ltd and Others*, [1994] 54 FCR 240 (Gen. Div.: Northern Terr. Dist. Registry). In this case, the court found the owners of an import trading company in Australia were liable for the breach of the copyrights in traditional paintings owned by Australian aboriginal artists. The importers had made arrangements with factories in Vietnam to copy paintings created by the artists as designs to be used on carpets without first getting permission from the copyright owners. The use of the designs on carpets was highly offensive to the indigenous groups because it meant that others would walk on their artwork, some of which had great cultural significance. The Australian court found that the owners violated the copyright of the artists, awarded damages, and enforced the rights of the artists in prohibiting the imports.

Although *Milpurrurru* resulted in a judgment based in copyright for the indigenous artists, the facts of the case were usually favorable to the plaintiffs and should not be taken as an indication that courts are receptive to protecting traditional culture in copyright. The copied works at issue were paintings, which are fixed in a tangible form. The artists were well-known so proving authorship and originality did not present obstacles. The artists were also represented by a statutorily created public body, the Aboriginal Arts Management Association. The same confluence of favorable facts may not exist in future cases.

For traditional culture to acquire effective protection against unwanted commercialization and piracy, it might be necessary—as in the case of databases—to create a *sui generis* right. In addition, to be effective on more than just a local basis, the right would have to be embodied in a multilateral treaty signed by numerous countries. However, such a possibility seems remote as there will be many interests opposed to such a treaty and many political obstacles. Some developed countries might oppose a *sui generis* right as it would empower groups within their territories to assert new property rights for which they might seek compensation for historical grievances. These new rights could open old wounds so the whole issue could become a political hot potato that no one will want to touch. The indigenous groups themselves might be unable to agree on issues of ownership and compensation. For example, will the group as a whole, a subset of the group, a few or a single individual own the *sui generis* right and the accompanying right to compensation? The realities of national and tribal politics might intrude to prevent the completion of a multilateral treaty even if there is an impetus to create one.

Another obstacle is that most of the interest groups supporting intellectual property rights in traditional culture and indigenous resources lack any real political power. Contrast their position with the interests in the EU behind protection for databases. The EU Database Directive was the result of efforts by powerful lobbying groups supported by multinational business interests in the EU, an entity that itself possessed legislative powers. Indigenous groups and individuals interested in traditional culture have none of these advantages.

The weak political position of indigenous peoples and their interest groups is highlighted by the decision by nations to delegate intellectual property issues dealing with traditional culture to the World Intellectual Property Organization. A similar area of concern, intellectual property rights in traditional medicines has also been delegated to WIPO. It is no accident that these issues concerning indigenous groups have been relegated to WIPO and not assigned to the WTO and TRIPS. The WTO is a much more prestigious organization and, until the recent disabling of the dispute settlement system discussed in Chapter One of this book, the WTO had effective enforcement powers. WIPO has never had enforcement power and is a largely toothless organization. Nations follow WIPO edicts only when they want to. The political reality is that nations delegated these issues to WIPO because any decisions or recommendations by WIPO calling for the recognition of intellectual property rights in indigenous resources can be ignored with impunity.

G. ECONOMIC RIGHTS REQUIRED BY THE BERNE CONVENTION

While the Berne Convention is rooted in the natural rights tradition, the Convention also sets forth a set of economic rights that all Berne Union countries must to provide to authors. (TRIPS sets forth additional rights.) The economic rights are scattered in piecemeal fashion throughout a number of Berne Convention articles. The piecemeal nature of these articles is due to the addition of new economic rights over time. The economic rights are set forth in Article 2*bis* (protection for political and public speeches); Article 8 (translations); Article 9 (reproductions); Article 11 (public performance of musical works); Article 11*bis* (public communications); Article 11*ter* (public recitation); Article 12 (adaptions, arrangements, and alterations); Article 14 (cinematographic adaptations); and Article 14*ter* (resale right or droite de suite). As all of these Berne Convention articles have been incorporated into TRIPS, all WTO members must implement these economic rights.

The United States sets forth economic rights under § 106 of the U.S. Copyright Act. Some of the rights in U.S. law correspond to those in the Berne Convention, while others exceed them. Set forth below is § 106 of the U.S. Copyright Act with the corresponding Berne Convention provision in brackets.

Under § 106, the owner of the copyright has the "exclusive rights to do and authorize any of the following":

(1) to reproduce the copyrighted work in copies or in phonorecords; [Berne Conv., Article 9]

(2) to prepare derivative works based upon the copyrighted work; [Berne Conv., Article 8 (translation rights); Article 12 (adaptations, arrangements, and other alterations)]

(3) to distribute copies or phonorecords of the copyrighted work to the public by sale or other transfer of ownership, or by rental, lease, or lending; [No general distribution right in the Berne Convention exists, but a specific right for the distribution of cinematographic adaptations is set forth in Berne Convention Article 14(1)]

(4) in the case of literary, musical, dramatic and choreographic works, pantomimes, and motion pictures and other audiovisual works, to perform the copyrighted work publicly; [Berne Conv., Articles 11, 11*bis*, 11*ter*, and 14]

(5) in the case of literary, musical, dramatic, and choreographic works, pantomimes, and pictorial, graphic, or sculptural works, including the individual images of a motion picture or other audiovisual work, to display the copyrighted work publicly; [no corresponding provision in the Berne Convention]

(6) in the case of sound recordings, to perform the copyrighted work by means of a digital audio transmission. [No corresponding provision in the Berne Convention]

Like all other Berne Union countries, the United States is required to implement, at a minimum, all economic rights required by the Berne Convention (TRIPS also requires this as all of these Berne Convention provisions have been incorporated into TRIPS). The United States has met the minimum requirements, except for the resale right under Berne Convention Article 14*ter*, but that provision is optional. (The resale right is compensation to the author when an original painting or manuscript is resold for a much higher price after the author achieves fame – sometimes after the death of the author.) As with the laws of many other countries, the U.S. statute also exceeds Berne Convention requirements in several respects, such as providing for a public display right and a right to perform a sound recording by digital audio transmission.

The U.S. Copyright statute also creates a general distribution right that is absent in the Berne Convention. Although most domestic copyright laws contain a general distribution right (which includes the right to sell the work), the Berne Convention does not because countries were unable to reach agreement on when a sale would exhaust the copyright in the work. Most countries agree that a first sale in the country of origin of the work exhausts the copyright. For example, if a U.S. author sells a book in the United States, then the copyright in that particular copy of the book is exhausted. The purchaser can lend or resell the book without the permission of the author. However, countries could not reach agreement on what happens when the first sale occurs abroad. Some countries took the position that the first sale of the book anywhere in the world exhausts the copyright (i.e., international exhaustion) while other countries took the position that only first sales in the country of origin of the work exhausts the copyright and the first sale abroad does not (i.e., national exhaustion). Whether a country follows national or international exhaustion is significant because of the common problem of gray market goods or parallel imports that arises in the following situation.

Let us assume that a U.S. copyright owner seeks to establish a foreign market and sells its products abroad. A foreign distributor purchases the products abroad and taking advantage of price and currency fluctuations imports the products back into the United States to sell at a discount. The U.S. copyright owner wishes to block the importation of the products because the products were intended for a foreign market and because the owner does not wish to have the products sold at discount prices in the United

States creating intra-band competition with products sold at full price. The imported products are known as gray market goods or parallel imports. The goods are genuine products originally intended for sale in a foreign market that have found their way back into the United States without the permission of the copyright owner. (A similar situation exists for trademarked products but the rules in the United States are different.) In the United States, and most countries, gray market goods can be lawfully sold if they have been lawfully imported.

A copyright usually includes the right of importation as part of the right of distribution. Whether the copyright owner can exercise the right of importation to block the imports depends on whether the country of origin follows a doctrine of national or international exhaustion. If the country follows a doctrine of national exhaustion only first sales in the country of origin exhausts the copyright. The first sale of the copy abroad does not exhaust the copyright in the products and the owner can exercise the right of importation to block the imports. If the country follows a doctrine of international exhaustion then the sale of the copies abroad exhausts the copyright in the products and the owner cannot block their importation. Countries could not agree on whether a doctrine of national or international exhaustion should be the prevailing rule and so the Berne Convention decided not to include a general right of distribution. Even today, countries cannot agree on a general position with respect to exhaustion. Article 6 of TRIPS states that

TRIPS takes no position on exhaustion, leaving exhaustion up to individual WTO members.

In addition to the economic rights required by the Berne Convention, TRIPS creates rental rights for the author in computer programs and cinematographic works. Article 11 of TRIPS gives authors the right to authorize or prohibit the commercial rental of the originals of these works. Rental rights for cinematographic works are optional unless rental has led to widespread copying harming the authors' reproduction rights. In that case, countries cannot offer rental rights. In the case of computer programs, the rental right does not exist if the computer program itself is not the essential object of the rental.

1. COPYRIGHT PROTECTION AND CONTENT REVIEW

An issue arose in a dispute between the United States and China on whether a country can condition the granting of the minimum economic rights required by the Berne Convention on a review of the content of the works. In *China—Measures Affecting the Protection and Enforcement of Intellectual Property Rights*, WT/DS362/R (January 26, 2009), the United States challenged China's intellectual property laws in three areas: thresholds for criminal penalties, disposal of goods seized by customs authorities for infringing intellectual property rights, and denial of all copyright protection to censored works. Our present discussion of this case focuses on the third issue—denial of copyright based on content.

(We will return to a discussion of the two other issues in a later section of this book.)

Article 4(1) of China's Copyright Law provided as follows:

> Works the publication and/or dissemination of which are prohibited by law shall not be protected by this Law.

The Chinese government regularly reviews the content of all audiovisual products including books, films, music, and software for content and will prohibit the publication and dissemination of works that the government deems objectionable. The government censors works for any number of reasons, including for legal, political, or cultural reasons. Works that are censored under Article 4(1) cannot be lawfully distributed in China. The United States challenged Article 4(1) on the grounds that it denied copyright protection to censored works in violation of the Berne Convention.

China argued that Article 4(1) of its Copyright Law denied authorization to publish but did not deny copyright protection. The WTO panel disagreed with China's characterization. The panel found that banned works under China's Article 4(1) were denied all of the rights enumerated in Article 10 of the Berne Convention, which sets forth four moral rights and 13 economic rights.

China also argued that Article 17 of the Berne Convention authorized Berne Union countries to deny copyright in certain works. Article 17 provides:

> The provisions of this Convention cannot in anyway affect the right of the Government of each country of the Union to permit, to control, or to prohibit, by legislation or regulation, the circulation, presentation, or exhibition of any work or production in regard to which the competent authority may find it necessary to exercise that right.

The panel found that the right of a government "to control or prohibit" the "circulation, presentation, or exhibition" of any work authorized censorship but did not authorize the denial of rights. The terms "circulation, presentation, or exhibition" were not the same terms used by the Berne Convention to define rights so these terms must refer instead to censorship not the denial of rights. Berne Union countries have the authority to interfere with an author's copyright for censorship reasons but do not have the authority to deny copyright in the work altogether. The panel concluded that China was in breach of Berne Convention Article 5(1), which states: "Authors shall enjoy [national treatment for their] works . . . as well as the rights specifically granted by this Convention." The rights specifically granted by the Berne Convention are economic rights. Article 4(1) of China's Copyright Law denied those rights in violation of Berne Article 5(1).

2. U.S. RATIONALE FOR PRESERVING COPYRIGHT IN CENSORED WORKS

One might ask why the United States insisted on preserving copyright in censored works since the banned works could not in any event be legally sold in the Chinese market. Was it for the purpose of making a political point to China that it cannot deny copyright just because it does not like the content of materials or was there a more practical objective? Was the United States primarily interested in teaching China a U.S. civics lesson? No, the objective was a practical one.

On the practical side, consider that while China can prevent objectionable U.S. works from lawfully entering its market under its censorship power, many banned works are still easily accessible in China. Maintaining copyrights in censored works is important for U.S. copyright owners as a protection against authorized copying and piracy. A good example concerns Hollywood movies. China maintains a screen quota for films from the United States; only those films authorized by the Chinese government for distribution in China are permitted to be shown in Chinese theaters or streamed through the internet. All other U.S. films cannot be lawfully screened. But banning the films does not prevent the films from being accessed in China as anyone who has spent any time in China knows.

Many banned Hollywood films are lawful for public consumption in nearby Hong Kong other parts of Asia. These films have added Chinese language subtitles and are easily accessible in China. Banning films also does not prevent pirates from copying them and then making the pirated copies available for sale in China. If banned films were denied copyright, then it is not illegal to copy them and sell the copies. When the U.S. film studio or copyright owner brings enforcement actions against the infringers, they can raise the defense that the banned films are not protected by copyright. Maintaining a copyright in banned works allows the United States to enforce its copyrights against pirates and other unauthorized users. Other than movies, China also bans some books, music, entertainment software, and websites such Youtube, Facebook, and Instagram. If all banned content were denied copyright protection then the content of all of these audio-visual products would also be free to all to copy in China. The WTO decision was very important to the United States for enforcement of intellectual property rights.

H. EXCEPTIONS TO EXCLUSIVE RIGHTS

Article 13 of TRIPS allows countries to make exceptions to copyright:

TRIPS

Article 13
Exceptions and limitations

> Members shall confine limitations or exceptions to exclusive rights to certain special cases which do not conflict with a normal exploitation of the work and do not unreasonably prejudice the legitimate interests of the right holder.

Article 13 recognizes the need to allow countries to make exceptions and to limit copyright protection in order to further other needs of society such as access to the copyrighted works for educational or scientific reasons. The United States has recognized a relatively broad exception to copyright under the doctrine of fair use, which is based upon First Amendment traditions. In addition to fair use, which is an open-ended exception, the United States has also issued specific exceptions. In *United States—Section 110(5) of the US Copyright Act*, WT/DS160/R (June 15, 2000), a WTO panel considered the validity of two specific exemptions set forth in § 110(5) of the U.S. Copyright Act in light of the requirements of TRIPS Article 13. The *United States—Section 110(5)* case helped to established that Article 13 creates a three-part test for exceptions and how to interpret elements of the test.

United States—Section 110(5) concerned two different exemptions to copyright contained in § 110(5)(A) and § 110(5)(B). Under the home style or *Aiken* exemption set forth in § 110(5)(A), owners of eating, drinking, and retail establishments smaller than 1,055 square feet (the size of the restaurant involved in *Twentieth Century Music Corp v. Aiken*) that used a single receiving apparatus commonly used in private homes (e.g., a radio) were exempt from having to pay royalties to owners of the music copyrights. Under the business exemption set forth in § 110(5)(B), owners of eating and drinking establishments under 3,750 square feet and retail establishments under 2,000 feet using up to six loudspeakers or four audiovisual devices were exempted from having to pay royalties. As many of the copyright owners were EU copyright agencies representing EU performing artists, the EU challenged the U.S. law in the WTO.

The WTO panel held that the exemptions were permitted if they satisfied the requirements of TRIPS Article 13, which the panel held constituted a three part test: limitations and exceptions (1) that were confined to certain special cases; (2) that do not conflict with a normal exploitation of the work; and (3) that do not unreasonably prejudice the legitimate interests of the right holder. The three conditions applied on a cumulative basis, meaning that all three had to be satisfied and the failure to satisfy any single condition meant that the exception was not justified.

The panel found that the business exemption applying to restaurants and bars under 3,750 square feet did not satisfy Article 13 because it was not a special case. A "special case" is one that has a limited application or purpose. A survey conducted by Congress in 1995 indicated that a substantial number of U.S. retail, eating, and drinking establishments would have fallen below the area size required by the business exemption. An exception is not limited if a substantial number of establishments fall within its scope. As the business exemption failed to meet the first prong of the three-part test, it cannot be justified under Article 13. There was no need to examine the second and third conditions.

By contrast, the home style exemption was a "special" case since relatively few U.S. eating (16 percent), drinking (13.4 percent), and retail (18 percent) establishments were the same size or smaller than the Aiken restaurant of 1,055 square feet. In addition, the scope of the exemption is narrow because it only applies to certain types of music. The first sentence of § 110(5)(A) stated that it was subject to an exception contained in § 110(5)(B), which referred to "nondramatic musical works" that could be played under the business exemption. The United States argued that the exception language contained in § 110(5)(A) meant that only those works that did not fall into the category of "nondramatic musical works," that is, "dramatic musical works" were permitted to be played under the home style exemption of § 110(5)(A). Dramatic musical works include operas, operettas, and musicals. As the home style exemption only exempted operas, operettas, and musicals from copyright royalties, it was a "special case."

Although the United States argued that the home style exemption applied only to operas, operettas, and musicals, this appears to be a deliberate misreading of the statute; it is unlikely that the drafters of § 110(5)(A) intended for the exemption to limited to only such works. It is difficult to imagine that Congress believed that mom and pop restaurants like the one in *Aiken* regularly played operas for their customers and that they should be able to play operas without having to pay royalties. More likely, § 110(5) was poorly drafted so that it could be read to mean that § 110(5)(A) applied only to works not covered by § 110(5)(B). As § 110(5)(B) covered nondramatic musical works, § 110(5)(A) must cover dramatic musical works—i.e. operas, operettas, and musicals. The United States took advantage of the poor drafting of § 110(5) to make this disingenuous argument before the WTO. The argument was effective because it really narrowed the application of the home style exemption, but the United States must have known that Congress never intended the statute to be read this way.

The EU also did not attempt to refute this argument despite its rather forced interpretation. The reason may be that the EU was not really concerned about the homestyle exception because the relevant establishments were very small in size with less than 1,055 square feet and they were probably not able to license the copyrights from the EU owners in any event. This meant that the loss of royalties from the home style exception was minor, even trivial. The EU was more concerned about the business exemption that applied to much larger restaurants and bars and on this issue, the EU was victorious. As the EU did not challenge the U.S. argument on the home style exemption, the panel accepted it.

The home style exemption also satisfied the last two prongs of Article 13. The exemption did not interfere with a normal exploitation of the work. The panel found that an exemption causes a conflict if it allowed a third party to enter into economic competition with the way that the copyright owners normally extract economic value from the work. In the context of dramatic musical works, however, the copyright owners do not normally license those works; the home style exemption would conflict with the normal exploitation of the work if the home style exemption decreased the opportunities that the copyright owners had for licensing their dramatic musical works. The panel found, however, that there was no evidence of any market for the licensing by eating establishments of operas or other dramatic musical works. As a result, the home style exemption did not conflict with the normal exploitation by the right holders of dramatic musical works.

The third prong requires that the exception cannot unreasonably prejudice the legitimate interests of the right holder. The panel interpreted the legitimate interests of the right holder to refer to its right in the economic value of the copyrights. The home style exemption did not interfere with these rights because the mom and pop restaurants that were entitled to make use of the exemption would not have otherwise entered into a commercial licensing agreement for the operas with the right holders. These establishments did not have the financial resources to license these operas and so these establishments would not have been a source of licensing fees for the EU copyright management organizations.

1. COUNTRIES' APPROACHES TO COPYRIGHT EXCEPTIONS

Countries take different approaches to exceptions under TRIPS Article 13 that can be best summarized as follows. All countries enumerate specific exceptions to copyright. For example, Argentina has a law that specifically exempts extracts of up to 1,000 words for scientific or literary works or eight bars for musical works. Other countries, such as the United States and the UK, have open ended exceptions that require a case-by-case analysis of the exception. In the United States, the fair use doctrine requires the weighing and balancing of a number of factors in determining whether the use is justified. In a limited number of cases, the United States does have specific exceptions enumerated in statutes (e.g., the *United States—Section 110(5)* case) but these cases are very small in number. In general, countries fall into one of two categories: some countries have only specific exceptions while other countries have general, open-ended exceptions and a few specific exceptions.

2. PAYMENT TO RIGHT HOLDER

Countries also differ on whether a payment to the right holder is required when an exception applies. Even where an exception is recognized, a country may require the right holder to receive some form of compensation. In the United States, if an exception is recognized the right holder receives no compensation. The EU takes the opposite position. The European Union Directive on Copyright and Related Rights in the Information Society, 2001/29/EC allows EU countries to recognize a copyright exception for private copying but also requires that the right holders receive fair compensation.

In *Padawan SL v. Sociedad General de Autores Y Editores de España (SGAE)*, C–467/08 (Oct. 21, 2010), the European Court of Justice considered a Spanish tax on equipment used for private copying that was used to provide compensation for copyright holders. The court required a link between the equipment and the use of the equipment for private copying (authorized as an exception to copyright). If all equipment was used solely for private copying then the tax might be justified as fair compensation. However, the tax did not distinguish between whether the purchaser of the equipment was a private individual, a commercial entity, or a business. As commercial entities and private businesses normally do not engage in private copying, those entities would be taxed even though they did not engage in any activity that was an exception to copyright. The court concluded that the application of the levy to them violated the fair compensation requirement.

I. COPYRIGHT TERM AND THE RULE OF THE SHORTER TERM

Article 7(1) of the Berne Convention sets forth the general minimum standard term of copyright protection: life of the author plus 50 years or 50 years p.m.a. (*post mortem auctoris* (after the author's death)). It is now also the standard of TRIPS. This is a minimum standard and countries are free to exceed it. Both the EU and the United States currently have minimum terms of protection of life of the author plus 70 years. The term starts on January 1 of the year following the author's death. For example, if the author dies on February 3, 2024, the term of protection starts on January 1, 2025. In the United States and the EU, the term will end on January 1, 2095. In countries with the Berne Convention term of life of the author plus 50 years, the term will end on January 1, 2075.

An author who establishes a point of attachment under the Berne Convention will have a basket of national copyrights. Berne Conv., Article 5(2). As nations offer different copyright terms, it is possible to have different terms for the same work. For example, an author may seek protection in a country with a different copyright term than the country of origin of the work or an author may seek copyright protection at the same time in several different countries with different copyright terms. The Berne Convention provides a rule to resolve these discrepancies called the rule of the shorter term contained in Article 7(8), which provides:

Berne Convention

Article 7

* * *

(7) In any case, the term shall be governed by the legislation of the country where the protection is claimed; however, unless the legislation of that country otherwise provides, the term shall not exceed the term fixed in the country of origin of the work.

The rule of the shorter term provides that the term of protection is determined by the country where protection is sought but if the term of protection in the country of origin of the work is shorter then in that case the country of protection is allowed to cut back its term to the length of the term in the country of origin.

The starting point for applying the rule of the shorter term is to determine the country of origin of the work. That determination must be done in accordance with Article 5(4), which provides as follows:

Berne Convention

Article 5

* * *

(5) The country of origin shall be considered to be:

(a) in the case of works first published in a country of the Union, that country; in the case of works published simultaneously in in several countries of the Union which grant different terms of protection, the country whose legislation grants the shortest term of protection;

(b) in the case of works published simultaneously in a country outside the Union and a country of the Union, the latter country;

(c) In the case of unpublished works or of works first published in a country outside the Union, without simultaneous publication in a country of the Union, the country of the Union of which the author is a national . . . [special rules for films and architectural works follow here]

Note do not confuse the rule of the shorter term set forth in Article 7(7) with Article 5(4)(a) providing that in the case of simultaneous publication in several countries the country of origin is the country with the shortest term. Article 5(4)(a) is a rule to determine which country is the *country of origin* of the work. Article 5(4)(a) articulates a convenient way to determine the country of origin for the work in the event of simultaneous publication in several countries. This rule in Article 5(4)(a) is not the same as the rule of the shorter term, which determines the *term of protection* that must be given to a foreign work by a country in which the work is seeking protection.

Oncc the country of origin of the work is determined, then it is necessary to compare it to the term of the country where protection is sought. The country where protection is sought must normally extend treatment at least as favorable to the foreign work as the country extends to domestic works under the national treatment principle; however, the rule of the shorter term, as an exception to national treatment, allows the country where protection is sought to cut back the term of protection to that in the country of origin if it is shorter. Note carefully that not all countries recognize an exception to national treatment for copyright term. A major exception is the EU as illustration 2-20 below demonstrates.

> Illustration 2-19. Yang is author of a novel. The country of origin of the novel is China, which has a term of life of the author plus 50 years. Yang also has a U.S. copyright for the novel and seeks to enforce the copyright in the United States,

which has a term of life of the author plus 70 years. Although the United States would normally be bound under the national treatment principle to give Yang treatment at least as favorable as it gives to U.S. nationals, the rule of the shorter term is an exception to the national treatment principle. The United States is allowed to cut back its term of protection for the novel to life of the author plus 50 years, the term in its country of origin.

Illustration 2-20. In 1965, Adeline, a French national, writes a novel in France and receives a term of the life of the author plus 50 years. On July 1, 1966, Germany enacts new legislation extending its copyright term to life of the author plus 70 years (France did the same on July 1, 1995). Adeline established a point of attachment when she wrote the novel in France and, as a result, received a German copyright in the novel. In September 1966, Adeline seeks to enforce a German copyright in her novel. Adeline is entitled to full national treatment under EU law and a term of life of the author plus 70 years in Germany. The EU does not recognize an exception to the national treatment principle for copyright term and does not apply the rule of the shorter term.

Not only is the rule of the shorter term an exception to the national treatment principle, it is also an exception to the rule of independent treatment of copyrights under Article 5(2) of the Berne Convention. In Illustration 2-19, Article 5(2) would normally require the United States to ignore the copyright treatment of the novel in China in determining the protection to be given to the work in United States, but the rule of the shorter term, as an exception, allows the United States to apply the shorter term in China, the country of origin, to the work in the United States.

The most common justification given for the rule of the shorter term is that it was created to give countries incentive to raise their terms to 50 years p.m.a. The 1908 Berlin version of the Berne Convention specifically allowed parties to have a term shorter than 50 years p.m.a. Under the rule of the shorter term, countries would be disadvantaged unless they raised their own terms of protection to 50 years p.m.a. However, the current version of the Berne Convention (Paris 1971) no longer permits countries to have a term less than 50 years p.m.a., so there appears to be no justification for maintaining the rule of the shorter term. Perhaps the rule continues to exist simply due to inertia, that is, the failure of the Berne Union parties to delete the rule from Article 7. Or perhaps the rule continues exists to create pressure on countries to enact a term equal to the highest term enacted by any Berne Union country. Although its policy justification is no longer clear, the rule continues to exist.

The key to applying the rule of the shorter term is to correctly apply Article 5(4) to first determine the country of origin.

Illustration 2-21. Triana, a national of Country E, first publishes a work in Country F. Country

E is a Berne Union country but Country F is not. Country E has a term of life of the author plus 50 years while Country F has a term of life of the author plus 100 years. Triana now seeks protection for the work in Country G, a Berne Union country, which has a term of protection of life of the author plus 80 years. Under Article 5(4), the country of origin of the work is Country E. Country F cannot be the country of origin because it is a non-Union country; under Article 5(4)(c), where a work is first published in a non-Union country, the country of origin is the country of the nationality of the author—in this case, Country E, which has a term of life of the author plus 50 years. Country F, the country in which protection is sought, has a term of life of the author plus 80 years so Country F is entitled to apply the rule of the shorter term and cut back the term of protection given to Triana's work to life of the author plus 50 years.

J. SPECIAL RULES IN THE EU APPLICABLE TO COPYRIGHT TERM

1. COPYRIGHT TERM AND THE EU COPYRIGHT DIRECTIVE

A discussion of copyright term is not complete with a consideration of some special rules that apply to copyright term and related rights term in the EU. Effective on July 1, 1995, the EU Copyright Directive extended the term of copyright protection to life of the author plus 70 years from the Berne Convention standard of life of the author plus 50 years. (The

United States followed with the same extension on October 27, 1998 with the Sonny Bono Copyright Term Extension Act.) For works created by corporate authors the term of protection in the EU is a term of 70 years in gross from the time that the work is made available to public. In the case of cinematographic works (e.g., films), the director is considered to be the author and the term begins at the death of the last of the following whether or not these persons are designated as co-authors: the principal director, the author of the screenplay, the author of the dialogue, and the composer of music for the film. EU Copyright Directive Art. 2(1). After a term extension granted in 2011, performers are given a term of protection for neighboring and related rights of 70 years for their performances as measured from either the date of the performance or the date of fixation of the performance.

In all cases, the starting point is on January 1 of the year following the event that gives rise to the term of protection. For example, for a film that is distributed to theaters on March 1, 2024 the term of protection of 70 years p.m.a. begins on January 1, 2025 if all relevant persons died in 2024. In the case of flesh and blood authors, the 70 p.m.a. term begins on January 1 of the year following the death of the author.

2. EU RULE OF RETROACTIVITY

Under the EU Copyright Directive, the longer 70 p.m.a. term applies to all works in the EU created after July 1, 1995. For older works created prior to

July 1, 1995 the EU Copyright Directive applies a rule of retroactivity that is similar to the rule of retroactivity under the Berne Convention that we examined in an earlier section of this chapter. Article 10(2) of the EU Copyright Directive states: "The term of protection provided for in this directive shall apply to all works and subject matter which are protected in at least one Member State on [July 1, 1995]."

3. APPLICATION OF THE EU RULE OF RETROACTIVITY

Under this rule, a work that has fallen out of copyright protection in any EU country, including its country of origin, will be restored to copyright protection throughout the entire EU, including its country of origin, if the work is still in copyright in any other EU country.

Illustration 2-18. Charles writes a novel and publishes it in France in 1937, establishing a point of attachment resulting in a basket of national copyrights for the novel in all Berne Union countries. Subsequently, Charles dies in 1940. Under France's copyright law, the term of protection was 50 years p.m.a. at the time (until it was changed by legislation on July 1, 1995 to 70 years p.m.a.) The term in France begins on January 1, 1941 and ends on January 1, 1991. On January 2, 1991 the novel fell into the public domain in France.

On July 1, 1966, Germany enacted a copyright term of life of the author plus 70 years. Germany's new copyright term applied to existing copyrights and upgraded their terms from 50 years p.m.a. to 70 years p.m.a. As of July 1, 1966, under Germany's new Copyright Law, the copyright term in Charles's novel was upgraded from 50 years p.m.a. to 70 years p.m.a. Although France's term is still 50 p.m.a., Germany must give the novel a term of 70 years p.m.a. because the EU recognizes no exception to the national treatment principle and will not allow Germany to apply the shorter term of 50 years p.m.a. in the novel's country of origin. Charles died in 1940 so the term of copyright in Germany began on January 1, 1941 and ends on January 1, 2011. As of January 2, 1991, Charles's novel fell into the public domain in France but it was still protected by copyright in Germany until January 1, 2011.

On July 1, 1995, Article 10(2) of the EU Copyright Directive became effective and required France to restore Charles's novel to copyright protection in France because the novel was still subject to copyright protection in Germany. The novel was out of copyright in France from January 2, 1991 to July 1, 1995 but restored to copyright after that by Article 10(2) of the EU Copyright Directive and expired in France and the rest of the EU on January 1, 2011.

The enactment by Germany of its 70 years p.m.a. copyright term on July 1, 1966 at a time when other nations in Europe had a 50 years p.m.a. gave rise to the possibility of retroactive restoration of copyrights. Due to Germany's longer term, copyrights that expired in countries such as France would still be valid in Germany. With the enactment of the EU Copyright Directive, expired copyrights in those other EU countries would be restored to copyright because the work was still in copyright in Germany.

This is an example of the retroactive effect of Article 10(2). This example illustrates the basic lesson that in determining whether a work is entitled to copyright protection in the EU, it is not enough to examine whether it is entitled to copyright protection in its country of origin. It is necessary to determine whether the work is still in copyright in any EU country; if it is, then it must be restored to copyright protection in all countries of the EU.

K. MORAL RIGHTS UNDER THE BERNE CONVENTION

An earlier section in this chapter examined the economic rights associated with copyright. In this section, we examine moral rights. We start with Article 6*bis* of the Berne Convention, which sets forth the two basic moral rights, the right of paternity and the right of integrity:

Berne Convention

Article 6*bis*

(1) Independently of the author's economic rights, and even after the transfer of the said rights, the author shall have the right to claim authorship of the work and to object to any distortion, mutilation or other modification of, or

> other derogatory action in relation to, the said work, which would be prejudicial to his honor or reputation.
>
> (2) The rights granted to the author in accordance with the preceding paragraph shall, after his death, be maintained, at least until the expiry of the economic rights, and shall be exercisable by the persons or the institutions authorized by the legislation of the country where the protection is claimed.

Although Article 9 of TRIPS incorporates Articles 1 through 21 of the Berne Convention, the last clause of Article 9 states that "[m]embers shall not have rights or obligations under this Agreement in respect of the rights conferred under Article 6*bis* of that Convention or of the rights derived therefrom." This provision was added into Article 9 of TRIPS at the behest of the United States. The result of this provision is that WTO members have no obligation to recognize moral rights in the WTO. Of course, WTO members can choose voluntarily to do so, but the United States wanted to ensure that recognition was not mandatory.

The United States is also a contracting party to the Berne Convention so as a member of the Berne Union, the United States has a separate obligation to recognize moral rights as required by Article 6*bis*. So the United States has a Berne Convention obligation to recognize moral rights but not a WTO obligation to do so. The result is that no WTO Member can challenge the United States over its stance on moral rights in the WTO; any challenge must occur within

WIPO, the administering authority of the Berne Convention. Of course, the United States is aware that WIPO has no enforcement power so there are no real consequences for failing to recognize moral rights for the United States. As further discussed in the next section, the United States has made a half-hearted effort to comply with Article 6*bis* in order to satisfy its Berne Convention obligations.

The United States is unenthusiastic about moral rights because they interfere with the exercise of economic rights. An illustration of how this occurs is *Huston v. Société Turner Entertainment*, Cours de Cassation (France), 1991 Bull. Civ. I, No. 172 (May 28, 1991). Turner Entertainment had acquired the rights to "Asphalt Jungle," a 1950 black and white crime film directed by John Huston. Apparently, Huston purported to assigned all of his rights, including moral rights, to the original movie production studio. After Turner acquired the rights, Turner made a colorized version of the movie and attempted to show it in France. Huston's heirs sued in France and attempted to enjoin a French television channel from airing the film but lost in the lower court. The lower court held that U.S. law governed the contract and that Huston had relinquished all of his rights under the contract. France's highest court, the Cours de Cassation, reversed holding that Huston retained his moral rights, including the right of integrity. The Cour de Cassation remanded the case to the lower courts in France.

Under most choice of law rules, a contract made in the United States between two U.S. parties (Huston and the movie studio) concerning a film made in the United States would be governed by U.S. law. Most countries around the world would probably follow this approach when all of the contacts are within a single jurisdiction. The Cours de Cassation, however, found that natural law is superior to man-made law and displaces it; in this case, natural law displaces U.S. law. The natural law of authors' rights applied regardless of where the contract was negotiated and where the work was first published.

Natural rights can disrupt commercial transactions based on economic rights. Huston had made a contract in which he assigned all of his economic and moral rights to the movie production studio. He was compensated for this transfer by the movie studio which believed it was receiving these rights in return. This was a free market transaction between sophisticated parties but the transaction is undermined by the natural rights theory, which holds that moral rights cannot be assigned away by contract. Berne Convention Article 6*bis*(1) makes this clear: "Independently of the author's economic rights, and even after the transfer of the said rights, the author shall have the right to claim authorship of the work." The rights of paternity and integrity are inalienable in the author and cannot be assigned. If Houston retained his moral rights of paternity and integrity then his heirs might be able to enjoin the screening of the colorized movie in France.

Following a theory of moral rights would place many movie studio contracts with authors of books made into movies in jeopardy as authors would retain their moral rights of paternity and integrity even if they expressly assigned away those rights in the contract itself. In addition, under the works made for hire doctrine popular in the United States, the employer becomes the owner of the copyright in works created by an employee; however, applying natural rights theory to a U.S. employer/employee relationship, the employee would still retain moral rights that can be exercised to interfere with the economic rights to the work. The problems created by moral rights is one reason why the United States was reluctant to join the Berne Convention and did not join until 1989. By 1989, the United States knew that the Berne Convention would be incorporated into TRIPS and so finally joined the Berne Union.

1. MORAL RIGHTS IN EUROPE

In Europe, most countries adopt either a dualist or monist approach to moral and economic rights. Under a dualist approach, moral rights and economic rights are separate rights existing independently of each other with moral rights being superior. An author (or successors in interest) can continue to exercise moral rights even after economic rights have been terminated by assignment or through the lapse of the copyright term. In countries that adopt a dualist approach such as France, moral rights can last in perpetuity or at least as long as the work exists.

By contrast, countries that adopt the monist approach, such as Germany, moral rights and economic rights are two aspects of a single set of rights subject to one set of legal rules; the termination of copyright by the lapse of the term terminates both moral and economic rights together. Although these two different approaches appear to dictate a certain position on the duration of moral rights, in practice countries that have adopted either the dualist or monist approaches are not uniform in how they treat the duration of moral rights. It is necessary to review the individual laws of each country.

The right of paternity and the right of integrity, the two moral rights set forth in the Berne Convention are the most widely recognized in Europe, but countries differ on specific aspects of those rights. There is no agreement, for example, on whether rights of paternity can be effectively waived by contract as in ghost writer agreements. There are different approaches on whether a successor in interest to the author must exercise the right of paternity in furtherance of the interests of the author only or whether the successor in interest can exercise the right as it sees fit or even in furtherance of its own interests. Concerning the issue of integrity, countries differ on whether it is an unconditional right or a conditional one. An unconditional right of integrity allows the author to object to any distortion, mutilation, or modification of the work regardless of whether such change is prejudicial to the author's honor or reputation. By contrast, a conditional right only prohibits changes to the work that adversely affects the author's honor or reputation. A special problem concerning the right of integrity is raised by the unauthorized destruction of the work as one could argue that destruction is the most extreme form of distortion, mutilation, or modification. Specific legislation in some countries, such as Switzerland, provide that in some circumstances involving a unique original work the owner cannot destroy it without first offering to return it to the author.

There is also no unanimous agreement on the scope of two other moral rights: the right of divulgation or the right to make the work available to the public and its corollary the right to repent or withdraw the work. The level of disagreement among civil law countries in Europe that recognize moral rights means that one needs to look at the laws and approaches of each individual country when dealing with an issue of moral rights. Perhaps the many different approaches and disagreements among countries provide an additional reason why the United States remains unenthusiastic about moral rights.

2. U.S. APPROACH TO MORAL RIGHTS

The United States takes the position that it meets the requirements of the Berne Convention to protect the rights of paternity and integrity through various provisions in the U.S. Copyright Act, the Lanham Act, various state statutes, and common law doctrines such as libel, defamation, misrepresentation, and unfair competition. Although U.S. laws contain what would be viewed as economic rights, the United States believes that these various economic rights create a patchwork that together serves to protect the moral rights required by Article 6*bis* of the Berne Convention.

An example of how U.S. law protects moral rights is *Gilliam v. American Broadcasting Companies, Inc.*, 538 F.2d 14 (2d Cir. 1976). In 1975, Monty Python, a group of British writers and performers, sought to enjoin the American Broadcasting Company (ABC) from airing a truncated version of three separate programs originally aired by the British Broadcasting Company (BBC). Time Life Films had acquired licensing rights from BBC to broadcast the programs in the United States. ABC agreed to air three separate 30 minute programs in a 90 minute time slot. In order to include commercials, Time Life deleted 24 minutes of the programs' content and ABC aired the first of the specials on October 3, 1975. Monty Python was apparently appalled by the "mutilation" of the program that resulted from the editing and sought to enjoin the second special that was scheduled to air on ABC on December 15, 1975. The district court denied Monty Python's application for a preliminary injunction because a number of legal issues were unresolved.

On appeal, the Second Circuit directed the district court to issue the preliminary injunction. The Second Circuit held that Monty Python owned the original copyright in the scripts that were used by BBC to create the original programs. BBC owned the copyright in the dramatizations of the scripts but that did not change Monty Python's ownership of the copyright in the underlying script. Time-Life might have acquired permission from BBC to edit BBC's programs but the editing also violated Monty Python's copyright in the underlying script. As no use could be made of Monty Python's script without its permission, the unauthorized editing of the script violated Monty Python's copyright. The Second Circuit also held that the airing of the edited program violated § 43(a) of the Lanham Act, which proscribes misrepresentation of goods or services. By airing a truncated version of the programs, ABC misrepresented the distorted or mutilated work as that of Monty Python.

Gilliam is an example of how the United States can use its existing laws to protect moral rights. When the United States joined the Berne Convention in 1988 a few years after *Gilliam* was decided, the United States declared that existing U.S. law was sufficient "to satisfy U.S. obligations under Article 6*bis* and that no further rights or interests shall be recognized or created for that purpose." Berne Convention Implementation Act of 1988, Senate Report No. 100–352.

The United States does specifically recognize moral rights for a limited class of visual arts under The Visual Artists Act, 17 U.S.C. § 106A, but this statutory right applies only to a small number of works of art and photography. Since the United States is not bound by TRIPS to recognize moral rights and is bound only by the Berne Convention, which is administered by WIPO with no enforcement powers, no country is likely to challenge the U.S. assertion that it meets all Berne Convention requirements on moral rights.

L. ANTI-CIRCUMVENTION RIGHTS AND THE INTERNET

The last sections of this chapter examine new rights created in copyright owners to protect them from unauthorized copying in the age of the internet and new digital technologies. Copyright owners have always been concerned about piracy but the emergence of the internet in the past several decades creates significant new challenges. Pirates who make unauthorized tangible copies of a work are subject to some physical limitations. For example, anyone who makes pirated compact disks of a movie must procure blank CDs, make copies, package the CDs, and sell and distribute the CDs through a physical network so they can reach the end use consumer. By contrast, copies of a digital file can be shared on the internet with no such physical limitations and these copies can circulate instantaneously around the world.

To deal with these new threats to copyright owners, WIPO included within the WIPO Copyright Treaty (Dec. 20, 1996) provisions to deal with unauthorized copying on the internet. Article 11 of the WIPO Copyright Treaty provides:

WIPO Copyright Treaty

Article 11
Obligations concerning Technological Measures

Contracting parties shall provide adequate legal protection and effective legal remedies against the circumventing of effective technological measures that are used by authors in connection with the exercise of their rights under the Treaty or the Berne Convention and that restrict acts in respect of their works, which are not authorized by the authors concerned or permitted by law.

As a contracting party to the WIPO Copyright Treaty, the United States has an obligation to implement Article 11 into U.S. law. The United States has implemented Article 11 through the Digital Millennium Copyright Act of 1998 (DMCA), 17 U.S.C. § 12 *et seq*. The DMCA implements Article 11 of the WIPO treaty by including an anti-circumvention provision and then goes beyond the requirements of the WIPO treaty by including anti-trafficking measures.

Section 1201(a)(1)(A), the anti-circumvention provision of the DMCA, prohibits a person from "circumvent[ing] a technological measure that effectively controls access to a work protected under" the U.S. Copyright Act. For example, if someone is able to use a software program to circumvent a password control for a protected website and gain access to that website, then that person has violated this provision.

The DMCA also contains two anti-trafficking provisions. One provision prohibits the trafficking in programs that circumvent passwords and access controls and the other provision prohibits trafficking in programs that can circumvent controls that prevent copying of protected content.

Digital Millennium Copyright Act of 1998

Section 1201

* * *

> (a)(2) No person shall manufacture, import, offer to the public, provide, or otherwise traffic in any technology, product, service, device, component, or part thereof, that . . . is primarily designed or produced for the purpose of circumventing a technological measure that effectively controls access to a work protected under this title . . . .

This provision would prevent a person from distributing a software program that can circumvent password controls either in hardcopy form or by posting the software program on the internet.

A second anti-trafficking provision is contained in § 1201(b)(1), which prohibits trafficking in technology that can circumvent "protection afforded by a technological measure that effectively protects a right of a copyright owner under" the U.S. Copyright Act. This provision would prohibit a person from trafficking in technology that circumvents a measure that prevents the copying of the contents of a website. For example, suppose that a website is not protected by a password so there is no need to circumvent a measure that prevents access. Suppose further, however, that any attempt to copy the contents of the website will result in copies with scrambled contents that are useless. If a person were to traffic in a technology that can prevent the anti-copying technology from scrambling the contents of copies so that perfect copies can be made, then that person would be in violation of § 1201(b)(1)—although not in violation of § 1201(a)(1). In practice, there may not be much of a difference between cases that arise under § 1201(a)(1) and § 1201(b)(1) since the same encryption technology often controls both access and copying.

The United States added the anti-trafficking provisions in addition to the anti-circumvention provision because in most cases trafficking is a more serious offense than the anti-circumvention itself. A person who circumvents encryption technology has gained access to a protected website or is able to make an unauthorized copy, but a person who makes available an anti-encryption technology through the internet could enable many thousands of users to circumvent an encryption technology.

The ability of the anti-trafficking provisions of the DMCA to withstand a constitutional challenge was the subject of *Universal City Studios, Inc. v. Corley*, 273 F.3d 429 (2d Cir. 2001). Movie production studios prevent unauthorized viewing or copying of movies by using an encryption technology called CSS (Content Scramble System). An attempt to copy a compact disk of a movie encrypted with CSS either in a digital format to be stored on a hard drive of a computer or on to a blank compact disk will result in a useless copy with scrambled content. Shortly after CSS was invented, a teenage hacker in Norway created a program that could circumvent CSS that was appropriately named "deCSS." Defendants Corley and his company posted a copy of "deCSS" on their website and a link to other websites containing "deCSS." Universal City Studios, Inc. obtained an injunction from the federal district court prohibiting Corley from engaging in these activities.

On appeal of the injunction before the Second Circuit, Corley argued that the anti-trafficking provisions of the DMCA violated the U.S. Constitution by eliminating the fair use of copyrighted materials. The Second Circuit rejected this argument by noting that Corley was not engaged in fair use of copyrighted materials. He was trafficking in anti-circumvention technology. In addition, there was no evidence to indicate that the anti-trafficking provisions of the DMCA would prevent others from making fair use of copyrighted materials. The Second Circuit also rejected an argument by Corley that fair use of DVD format movies requires that copying be made of the movies in their original digital format. The court noted that the DMCA did not prevent others from making a variety of fair uses of DVD movies such as commenting on content, quoting excerpts from the screenplay or even in making various copies by using a camera pointed at a monitor as it displays the DVD movies. That the copies made would not be in the same perfect digital form was no basis for a claim of unconstitutional limits on fair use.

M. SAFE HARBORS FOR INTERNET SERVICE PROVIDERS

A related issue that causes concern for copyright owners in the age of the internet concerns the liability of internet service providers (ISPs) for the infringing activity of users of the ISP. This issue arises because ISPs such as Facebook, Google, Twitter, and Youtube allow users to share and post content without a prior content review by the ISP of the posts. Some of the posts may contain content that violates the rights of copyright owners. For example, Youtube allows users to post unauthorized videos of movies that may infringe the copyright of movie production studios. The copyright owner can proceed against the individual user of the ISP who has made the post but there may be thousands or more of such users and some of these users may be judgment proof, i.e. have no financial assets against which the copyright owner might proceed. The copyright owner might find proceeding directly against the ISP itself to be a more attractive option as the ISP is likely to have substantial financial assets, more importantly, and controls all postings by infringing users.

To hold the ISP liable, however, the copyright owner will need to proceed on a theory of contributory negligence, which is a form of vicarious or secondary liability. The user of the ISP is the party that is primarily liable as it has engaged in the infringing activity, i.e. the post. The ISP may be liable because it has aided and abetted the infringing user but what constitutes aiding and abetting is a matter of debate. Not surprisingly, copyright owners and ISPs are divided on the where the lines are to be drawn on the issue of the vicarious liability of the ISP. Some copyright owners argue that ISPs should have an active duty to monitor their sites for infringing activities. By contrast, ISPs argue that saddling them with duties to actively supervise their websites would impose prohibitive costs and could lead to the shutdown of the sites.

As neither TRIPS nor the Berne Convention deals with the issue of vicarious liability for ISPs, this issue is one that is up to each country to decide. The United States has dealt with this issue in the DMCA that we considered in the previous section. The DMCA has established a system of "safe harbors," which is essentially a compromise reached between the ISPs and copyright owners. So long ISPs engage in certain prescribed conduct, ISPs can claim the immunity of safe harbors and be shielded from liability for the illegal actions by users of their websites. Under the DMCA, ISPs enjoy safe harbors for four different activities: (1) providing access to the internet (i.e. acting as a conduit); (2) caching or offer temporary storage for digital files on the internet; (3) providing storage for content posted by third parties called hosting; and (4) providing information tools such as search engines. 17 U.S.C. § 512. The DMCA does not create a general duty on the part of the ISP to monitor their services or to seek out infringing activity. 17 U.S.C. § 512(m)(1).

Under the DMCA, a "notice and takedown" procedure set forth in 17 U.S.C. § 512 provides the main safe harbor for ISPs from liability for infringing content. The notice and takedown procedure is available in the main only for the ISP activities of hosting and providing information tools and not available for providing access to the internet or for caching except under some limited circumstances.

Under the notice and takedown procedure, a copyright owner files a DMCA notice with the ISP that alleges copyright infringement due to third party conduct such as posting. The ISP must then remove the allegedly infringing content in order to fall with the safe harbor of the DMCA. After the takedown, the ISP must give notice to the user who posted the alleged infringing content subject to the takedown. The user can then file a counter-notification that the alleged infringing content was erroneously removed. The ISP then must repost the content between 10 and 14 business days following receipt of the counter-notification from the user unless the copyright owner informs the ISP that the copyright owner has filed an action with a court seeking an order restraining the reposting. At that point, the ISP does not need to repost the content as the copyright infringement issue is now before a court that will resolve the issue.

Section 512 also provides protection for users against abusive conduct by copyright owners. If a copyright owner misrepresents that the user has infringed a copyright the user has a cause of action for misrepresentation against the copyright owner.

The EU has enacted its own version of a "safe harbor" under the EU Directive on Electronic Commerce, 2000/31/EC (June 8, 2000). The EU directive differs from the DMCA in that it does not have a formal notice and takedown procedure. The EU directive leaves it to the parties and member states to voluntarily agree on a procedure that creates a safe harbor. The fundamental approach of the EU, however, is similar to that of the DMCA. So long as the ISP adheres to certain conduct, it is immunized from liability for the infringing activities of ISP users. Like the DMCA, the EU directive does not impose a duty on ISPs to monitor their services for infringing activities.

China has adopted a safe harbor notice and take down procedure based on that of the DMCA. *See PRC Regulation on Protection of the Right to Network Dissemination of Information* (2006). Under China's notice and takedown procedure, once the copyright owner files a takedown notice, the user is allowed to file a counter notification with supporting materials indicating that there is no infringement. At this point, the ISP must repost the material and there is no additional step under the notice and takedown procedure that will allow the copyright owner to require an additional takedown of the post. Rather, the copyright owner is then relegated to an action in a court for the removal of the material. Under China's legal system, courts do not have the same authority or stature as courts in the United States. It is unclear that an ISP will obey a court order to remove offending materials.

While the notice and takedown procedures (NTDs) based on the DMCA provide a procedure for intellectual property owners to challenge infringing content, in practice many right holders claim that the use of NTDs is cumbersome and frustrating. Right holders who have dealt with Amazon, for example, have claimed that using Amazon's NTDs is like being trapped in "Amazon purgatory." An intellectual property owner is confronted with a vast, faceless, and non-human bureaucracy with labyrinthine and convoluted NTD procedures.

In practice the gathering of information and documents to file a NTD claim can take months and one false step could require restarting the process from the beginning. Many companies also use a "three strikes" policy. A user who posts infringing content cannot be permanently banned from the ISP unless the right holder can demonstrate three instances of infringing conduct. Such a process can take months or years of intensive and frustrating work involving many stops and starts if a small detail is missing.

Even when an intellectual property owner manages to have an infringing user banned, the user can assume a new cyber identity and be back in business in short order. Right holders find dealing with infringing users who can hide in cyberspace is already frustrating but that the amount of time and resources spent in using NTDs set up by Amazon, Alibaba and other ISPs adds an additional layer of misery. Some intellectual property owners wonder if some ISPs are even sincere in cracking down on infringing content or are really just protecting infringing users. Many exasperated right holders have organized into industry groups and are concentrating their efforts in working with ISPs to simplify NTDs.

CHAPTER 3

PATENTS

A. INTRODUCTION

Patent law provides rights to inventors (or their assignees) for their inventions. Section 101 of the U.S. Patent Code sets forth five requirements for patents: (1) novelty; (2) non-obviousness; and (3) utility. Fourth, the patent must fall within the subject matter of patentable inventions and fifth, the inventor must provide an adequate written description of the patent to enable one skilled in the art to make the invention. All of these elements are required by TRIPS. The first four elements above are found in TRIPS Article 27(1) and enablement is found in Article 29(1).

While originality was the criterion of copyright, novelty is the touchstone of patent. Novelty is a much higher standard and more difficult to satisfy but the rights granted under a patent are far more extensive than those under copyright.

A U.S. patent grants the patentee the following rights: to exclude others from making, using, selling, offering for sale, and importing the patented invention without the permission of the patent owner. 36 U.S.C. § 271. Unlike copyright, U.S. patent law contains few limitations on patent rights and does not contain a major exception for fair use. For this reason, patent rights are considered to be the strongest of all of intellectual property rights. A patent term in the United States is 20 years from the date of the filing of the patent in accordance with the minimum requirements of Article 33 of TRIPS.

For many years, the United States used a first to invent criterion in order to resolve priority claims among competing patent applications as opposed to the first to file approach followed by most countries in the rest of the world. In 2011, the United States finally changed its approach to a first to file system under the America Invents Act (AIA) to bring U.S. practice into line with the practice of most countries. We will examine filing under the AIA in a later section of this chapter.

The U.S. Patent Code also recognizes a special kind of patent called a "design" patent for "new, original and ornamental" designs on an article of manufacture. The term for a design patent is 14 years from the date of the grant. 17 U.S. §§ 171, 173. The key distinction between a design patent and a utility patent is that a design patent protects the article's ornamental aspect, that is, its appearance; if a design is primarily useful or functional, the design cannot be protected by a design patent.

On the international level, the most important patent treaty other than TRIPS is the International Convention for the Protection of Industrial Property, popularly known as the Paris Convention, first signed in 1883 and subsequently amended six times. The current version of the Paris Convention is the 1967 Stockholm revision and that is the version that we will refer to in this chapter. The Paris Convention covers "industrial property," a term commonly used in Europe to refer to patents, trademarks, trade secrets, and unfair completion. Just as TRIPS incorporated the bulk of the Berne Convention, TRIPS also incorporates the main substantive provisions of the Paris Convention (Articles 1–12 and Article 19).

A major difference between the Berne and Paris Conventions is that the latter has relatively few minimum substantive standards for patent rights. The members of the Paris Convention were unable to reach agreement on minimum standards for patents. Countries did not want to relinquish control over patent standards as patents were deemed too important. For example, some countries did not wish to grant patent protection to pharmaceuticals and some agricultural chemicals. These countries believed that these products relate to issues of public health and should not be the subject of a private monopoly. Prior to TRIPS, countries such as India refused to extend patent protection to pharmaceuticals. A multinational pharmaceutical company might have a patent for its drug in the United States but due to the principle of territoriality this patent had no effect in India. The company had to obtain a patent in India in order to protect the drug against copying in India. As India did not recognize patents for pharmaceuticals, nothing prevented companies in India from copying the drug. Allowing copying in India led to the development of a generic pharmaceutical industry making cheap copies of drugs for export.

Today, under TRIPS, countries can no longer exclude entire fields of technology from patent protection. TRIPS Article 27 provides that "patents shall be available and patent rights enjoyable without discrimination as to . . . the field of technology."

The basic rights granted by the Paris Convention are the right of priority and national treatment. The right of priority allows a patent application to assert the earliest filing date in a Paris Union country as the date of the filing of subsequent applications in all other Paris Union countries if the subsequent applications are filed within 12 months of the original filing. The date of the filing is important because all countries now use a first to file approach in awarding the patent to competing patent applications. The ability to claim an early filing date will allow the patent application to prevail over all other applications that were filed at a later date. The early filing date will also protect the application from other events, such as a publication of the invention, that would otherwise defeat it. We will return to a detailed consideration of Paris priority in a later section of this book.

The second basic right under the Paris Convention is national treatment set forth in Article 2:

Paris Convention

Article 2
National Treatment for Nationals of Countries of the Union

(1) Nationals of any country of the Union shall, as regards the protection of industrial property, enjoy in all the other countries of the

> Union the advantages that their respective laws now grant, or may hereafter grant, to nationals; all without prejudice to the rights specially provided for by this Convention. Consequently, they shall have the same protection as the latter, and the same legal remedy against any infringement of their rights, provided that the conditions and formalities imposed upon nationals are complied with. * * *

The national treatment principle of the Paris Convention differs significantly from its counterpart in the Berne Convention. You will recall that under the Berne Convention, once a point of attachment is established the Berne Convention's national treatment principle will automatically create a basket of national copyrights consisting of individual copyrights of each country of the Berne Union. Under the Paris Convention, the national treatment principle does not have this effect. Instead, under the Paris Convention, an applicant must file an application in each Paris Union country in which patent protection is sought and each country has the right to decide on its own whether to issue the patent. In other words, the Berne Convention's national treatment principle has the effect of overcoming the principle of territoriality in creating a basket of national copyrights. Under the Paris Convention, the national treatment principle does not overcome territoriality. The patent owner must separately file and apply for a patent in each Paris Union country. Another treaty, the Patent Cooperation Treaty (PCT), a special treaty entered into under the auspices of the Paris Convention, provides a mechanism that simplifies the filing and acquisition of patent rights in Paris Union countries. Even under the PCT, though, each country ultimately decides whether to grant the patent.

The reason why the Paris Convention's national treatment principle cannot overcome the territoriality principle is due to the requirement of formalities. A basic rule of the Berne Convention, traceable to the natural rights tradition, is that the acquisition of copyright cannot be subject to formalities. Patents have never been associated with a natural rights theory. As patents deal with inventions that have an industrial and commercial character, it seemed to defy common sense to posit that patents were a natural right that embodied the personality of the inventor. As a result, patents are not acquired through natural rights but have been subject to formalities from the very beginning. The Paris Convention assumes that formalities exist with respect to patents as it refers to patents "that are applied for" in Article 4*bis*(1). No patent rights can be obtained in any Paris Union country without first filing an application. Then it is up to each country to decide whether to grant the patent. The requirement of formalities in every Paris Union country stands as a barrier to using the national treatment principle to create a basket of national patents in a manner similar to the operation of the national treatment principle under the Berne Convention.

The effect of the national treatment principle under the Paris Convention is to protect the patent and the patent owner from discriminatory treatment.

Suppose that a national of Country A, a Paris Union country, applies for a patent in Country B, also a member of the Paris Convention. Country B cannot impose substantive or administrative requirements on the nationals of Country A, including the payment of fees, that are more onerous than those that apply to Country B's own nationals.

Article 2 of TRIPS incorporates "Articles 1 through 12, and Article 19, of the Paris Convention (1967)." These are the major substantive provisions of the Paris Convention, including the right of priority and national treatment. In addition, TRIPS also imposes substantive minimum requirements with respect to patents. TRIPS, Articles 27–33. We will examine these requirements in detail in a later section of this chapter. The result of the Uruguay Round of negotiations is that WTO countries reached an agreement that the countries that negotiated the Paris Convention could not: a set of minimum substantive standards for patents that apply in all countries of the WTO.

B. PATENTS AND ECONOMIC DEVELOPMENT

1. RELATIONSHIP BETWEEN INTELLECTUAL PROPERTY LAW AND FOREIGN INVESTMENT

From the time of the earliest patent statute enacted in Venice in 1474, patents have been used to attract foreign investment and to increase foreign trade. The Venetian patent statute had as its purpose the attraction of foreign investment to Venice. The statute gave a patent to "every person who shall build any new and ingenious device in this City, not previously made in this Commonwealth." The statute did not require that the invention be absolutely novel only that it must be new in "this Commonwealth." An inventor could previously have made an invention in England and have acquired a patent for the invention in England. So long as the invention was novel in Venice, the inventor could also obtain a patent for the same invention in Venice. Today the general standard is absolute novelty with no geographical limitations, but when Venice enacted its patent statute all that was required was local novelty in Venice. Granting patent rights became a way to attract foreign capital and investment to Venice. The inventor would be able to exploit monopoly rights in the invention and Venice would reap the benefits of an infusion of capital to build a factory to produce the invention in Venice and also gain access to the technology.

Several hundred years later, the relationship between intellectual property rights, foreign trade, and economic development continues to be debated. During the Uruguay Round of negotiations (September 1984 to April 1994) that led to the formation of the WTO, nations debated the wisdom of including stronger intellectual property rights in the WTO. Advanced industrialized countries led by the United States argued that stronger intellectual property rights would help all nations in developing their economies, especially poor countries. Stronger intellectual property rights would allow the innovators of technology to protect their rights against thieves, infringers, and pirates. Technology innovators could then earn a profit and reap a return on the substantial resources used in research and development to create the technology and other innovators will be encouraged to create more new technology. Stronger intellectual property rights will lift the tide for all nations and eventually everyone will benefit.

By contrast, developing countries argued for weaker intellectual property rights. They also wanted to designate the World Intellectual Property Organization, an entity without enforcement power, to be the main organ for administering intellectual property rights. Developing countries were suspicious of the motives of industrialized countries. They feared that industrialized countries would use stronger intellectual property laws to deny them access altogether to advanced technologies or to make such access dependent on the payment of onerous licensing fees. Developing countries believed that strong intellectual property laws would be used to prevent them from modernizing and industrializing their economies and keep them from catching up to advanced developed countries. Strong intellectual property laws would be used to maintain the gap between developed and developing countries.

In the end, the United States and developed countries prevailed for the most part. TRIPS was approved in the WTO and created strong standards of protection for all of the major fields of intellectual property. While TRIPS was at first viewed as a significant victory for developed countries, recent developments in TRIPS indicate that developing countries may be making important strides to promote their interests.

The debate over intellectual property rights between the North (i.e. industrialized countries) and the South (developing and least developed countries) still continues today. An important discussion of the international economics of intellectual property rights is contained in an article written by Professor Keith Maskus, *Lessons from Studying the International Economics of Intellectual Property Rights*, 53 Vand. L. Rev. 2219 (2000).

Based on a study of data from the 1980s, Maskus makes the argument that stronger intellectual property rights help developing countries to increase all aspects of foreign trade, resulting in higher levels of economic development. The argument is based on both a short term and a long term perspective. In the short term, an increase in the level of intellectual property protection will result in an immediate increase in the revenue that the United States (and other developed countries) will earn from increased licensing fees. This immediate jump occurs because U.S. persons and entities hold patents in many foreign countries. If these countries increase their level of intellectual property protection up to the minimum standard of TRIPS then the United States will be able to more effectively prevent unauthorized uses of its patents. Those persons and entities who previously used U.S. patents without authorization must now seek permission from U.S. patent owners in the form of licenses to continue such use. The new licenses will result in a jump in royalties paid to U.S. patent owners. Maskus estimates that the increase in rents to the United States will bring in about $5.85 billion in additional revenue inflows to the United States in the short term. Developing countries will not see an immediate increase in reciprocal revenue inflows because most developing counties do not own many patents in the United States or other countries. Those who do own patents will not see a major increase in licensing revenue because U.S. intellectual property laws were already in substantial compliance with TRIPS so bringing U.S. laws into full TRIPS compliance would not make much of a difference in increasing licensing fees.

While the biggest winner from increased intellectual property rights in the short term is the United States, stronger intellectual property rights will help developing countries in the long term. Once stronger intellectual property rights have been implemented in developing countries, after a number of years developing countries should gradually see an increase in technology intensive imports. Countries like the United States will be more willing to ship technology intensive goods to developing countries because the United States will have greater confidence that it can prevent others from making unauthorized copies of the goods. Access to larger amounts of technology intensive goods, such as software and computers, will allow developing countries to absorb the technology. In addition, the United States will be more willing to license its technologies to developing countries because it can enforce those licensing agreements and protect its intellectual property from unauthorized use. In the area of foreign direct investment, stronger intellectual property laws will encourage the United States and other developed countries to invest in developing countries. U.S. companies will invest capital in setting up new factories and business headquarters. U.S. companies will also transfer technology to developing countries as the new factories can manufacture goods only if they have access to the know how (protected by patents and trade secrets) necessary to make such products. Foreign companies will also hire local employees and teach them how to use the technology. Implementing stronger intellectual property rights will eventually allow developing countries to have increased opportunities in foreign trade and greater access to technology that will lead them to higher levels of economic development.

One can understand why some developing countries remain skeptical about arguments that they benefit from stronger intellectual property laws. The short term benefits to the United States and other developed countries occur immediately and one can even put a dollar figure on the amount of increased licensing fees ($5.85 billion) that the United States will reap right away. By contrast, developing countries are told that they will benefit in the long term but no one knows for sure how many years will have to go by before they see any tangible benefits or whether they will see benefits at all. The United States will receive an additional $5.85 billion but no one can come up with a quantifiable figure, not even in ballpark terms, of how much increased revenue developing countries can expect to receive. All developing countries are told is that they will benefit sometime in the future and will earn high revenues in some amount. Developing countries might be asking themselves why does the United States get such a good deal while they get stuck with such a lousy bargain? Why shouldn't they be able to get the same deal as the United States and other developed countries?

Developing countries must also realize that many variables are considered by multinational companies making a foreign investment. While strong intellectual property laws are an important consideration, other variables also exist that are hard to predict. For example, multinational companies are not likely to invest in a country with an unstable economy plagued with problems of inflation and a currency that is not freely convertible into U.S. dollars. Multinational companies are also wary of governments that have serious corruption issues, true of many countries in the developing world. In the modern age, due to laws against corruption such as the U.S. Foreign Corrupt Practices Act, 15 U.S.C. §§ 78dd–1 et seq., no one wants to deal with a government that demands continuing pay offs in order to do business. Multinational companies are even more apprehensive about nations that are politically unstable. Such countries could face an outbreak of violent protests, political reprisals, the overthrow of a sitting government, and the chaos that will ensue. All of these are factors that could dissuade a multinational company from investing in a county no matter how strong its intellectual property laws may be. Many of these factors and how any multinational company might react to them are also unpredictable. Predictions that stronger intellectual property laws will result in higher inflows of foreign capital are far from certain.

These considerations may lead some developing countries to conclude that while stronger intellectual property laws are a good deal for the United States, vague promises and uncertain variables mean that stronger intellectual property laws are not a good deal for them. Developing countries might feel that developed countries are trying to exploit them by making false promises as has occurred so repeatedly in the past. Developing countries may conclude that weaker intellectual property laws allow them access to foreign technology and tangible benefits in the present. This is a better bargain than a promise of uncertain benefits in some unknowable future. As this discussion indicates, the North-South debate over the effects of intellectual property rights on economic development is far from over. This is a theme that we will revisit throughout this book.

2. TRANSITIONAL PROVISIONS IN TRIPS

Recognizing that developing and least developed countries may have difficulties in complying with TRIPS requirements, TRIPS contains so-called transitional provisions that delay the time in which developing and least developed countries are required to implement their TRIPS obligations.

All developed countries were given one year from the date that the WTO came into existence on January 1, 1995 to comply with TRIPS or by January 1, 1996. Developing countries were given until January 1, 2000 to comply with TRIPS, except for its national treatment and most favored nation provisions (TRIPS Articles 3, 4, and 5) that applied immediately. Least developed countries were given until January 1, 2006 to comply with TRIPS. The transition period for least developed countries has been extended three times with the most recent extension running until July 1, 2034 or until the date that the country is no longer "least developed," if that is earlier. (Least developed countries receive this designation from the United Nations.) Pursuant to the Doha Declaration on Public Health, a separate transition period for least developed countries applies for pharmaceuticals, which currently runs until January 1, 2033.

TRIPS Article 65(4) allowed qualifying developing countries to delay patent protection for pharmaceuticals and agricultural chemicals until January 1, 2005. Article 65(4) provided that a developing country that did not provide patent protection for a particular area of technology when the TRIPS Agreement came into force on January 1, 1995 had up to ten years to introduce the protection.

Developing countries using Article 65(4) to delay patent protection for pharmaceuticals were required by Article 70(8) to create a "mailbox" to preserve the priority of applications for pharmaceutical patents made during the transition period. The mailbox would protect the applications from otherwise invalidating subsequent events.

Illustration 3-1. Using Article 65(4), India delayed extending patent protection to pharmaceuticals until January 1, 2005. Assume that India has effectively implemented a "mailbox" required by Article 70(8). Mega-Pharma files a patent application in the mailbox of the India patent office on January 1, 2000. Six months later, an article published in a scientific magazine in India fully discloses the patented pharmaceutical that would defeat the novelty of the invention. India's mailbox preserves the novelty of Mega-Pharma's patent application that would otherwise be defeated by the publication. At the time that Mega-Pharma filed the application on January 1, 2000 the invention was novel and the mailbox immunizes the application from an event such as the later publication that would otherwise defeat it.

Illustration 3-2. After Mega-Pharma files its application on January 1, 2000, Euro-Pharma files an application for the same drug on January 1, 2002 with the India patent office. India must have a mailbox mechanism that preserves these filings dates. When India's new patent law comes into effect and India is ready to process the applications, the mechanism must recognize that Mega-Pharma's patent application was filed prior in time to Euro-Pharma's application.

The issue of whether India complied with the mailbox rule was the subject of the decision of the Appellate Body in *India-Patent Protection for Pharmaceutical and Agricultural Chemical Products*, WT/DS50/AB/R (Dec. 19, 1997). India was bound to implement TRIPS as a member of the WTO, but it faced an internal political problem. Opposition groups in Parliament adamantly refused to extend patent protection for pharmaceuticals. India had a thriving generic drug industry and enacting patents for pharmaceuticals was a serious threat to the industry. India's president first attempted to out-maneuver the opposition by amending India's Patent Act to create a TRIPS mailbox while Parliament was out of session. The president used his emergency constitutional powers to promulgate an ordinance amending the Patents Act to create a TRIPS mailbox.

Under India's laws, the emergency ordinance expired six weeks after the reassembly of Parliament. The president then attempted to implement the expired ordinance permanently through a bill introduced in Parliament. Efforts to steer the bill through Parliament were blocked by the opposition and Parliament disbanded before the bill could pass.

This setback left India's president in a serious quandary. Setting up the TRIPS mailbox was important because the availability of the TRIPS extension to January 1, 2005 to provide patent protection for pharmaceuticals required the mailbox. If India did not have an effective mailbox, India might be required to provide patents for pharmaceuticals immediately or be in breach of TRIPS. But as Parliament refused to set up the mailbox, the president had to find some other means.

Following this setback, India claimed that it implemented the mailbox through administrative measures. A skeptical United States challenged India's measures in the WTO. U.S. suspicions were confirmed when without explanation India refused to show copies of the administrative measures to the United States, the WTO panel, or the Appellate Body.

The WTO panel ruled and the Appellate Body agreed that India's attempt to satisfy the mailbox rule through the administrative measures did not meet India's obligations under TRIPS. The panel and Appellate Body made this decision without ever seeing the measures. The mailbox rule in TRIPS Article 70(8)(a) requires that India establish a "means" by which the priority of patent applications can be preserved. The Appellate Body noted that the Patents Act is a mandatory law and that various provisions of the Patents Act made it clear that pharmaceuticals were not eligible for patents and patent applications for pharmaceuticals had to be rejected. The Appellate Body was skeptical that administrative instructions could prevail over the mandatory law of the Patents Act. Of course, an amendment to the Patents Act could satisfy the mailbox requirement but efforts to amend the Patents Act failed in Parliament. The Appellate Body found that Article 70(8)(a) requiring a mailbox was not satisfied by India's elusive administrative measures, assuming they ever existed.

India-Patent Protection illustrates the political realities of different interest groups vying for control over intellectual property resources in rapidly industrializing countries such as India. Even if the national government is committed to strong intellectual property laws, not all constituencies may agree. Without having lined up sufficient political support for TRIPS, the national government of India found itself caught in an embarrassing quandary on an international stage.

C. OBTAINING PATENTS

1. FIRST TO FILE RULE

Unlike copyrights which cannot be subject to formalities except in the country of origin of the work, patents are subject to formalities in all countries of the world. These formalities, which vary from country to country, must be complied with before a country will issue a patent. All modern patent systems require a written patent application that is subject to review, although the level of review varies significantly from country to country. Some nations still require that the applicant hire a local patent agent to handle the application.

All modern patent systems follow a first to file rule in deciding disputes among competing patent applications. This rule is simple, easy to administer, and now universally followed: in a dispute among competing patent applications, the first in time, i.e.

the application that is first filed, assuming all other requirements are met, will be awarded the patent over a later filed patent application. For over 200 years, the United States followed a different rule, the first to invent rule, but with the enactment of the America Invents Act, Pub. L. No. 112–29, 125 Stat. 284 (2011), the United States has joined the rest of the world in following a first to file rule, although there are still some complications with the U.S. approach that we will further examine in a later section below.

The first to file rule can create some problems for an inventor. Suppose that an inventor who has acquired a patent in one country wishes to acquire patents in foreign countries. Since all countries follow a first to file rule and a principle of territoriality, a patent owner is under pressure to file foreign patent applications as quickly as possible to prevent a second inventor form acquiring the patent in a foreign country.

> Illustration 3-3. Anya obtains a patent in Country X. Subsequently, Friedrich independently invents the same invention in Country Y. Under the principle of territoriality, Anya's patent has no effect in Country Y. If Friedrich files for a patent application in Country Y before Anya, then Friedrich will obtain the patent for the same invention in Country Y. Anya will own the patent in Country X and Friedrich will own the patent in Country Y.

To avoid this problem, an inventor or an assignee can immediately file for patents in many different countries, but this can create many difficulties for the inventor. Any reasonable inventor will want to first evaluate the commercial viability of the invention in foreign markets before filing. The invention may not be suitable for some countries. To effectively evaluate the market for the invention, the inventor will need sufficient time to do research and make an informed evaluation.

2. PARIS PRIORITY

To deal ameliorate these difficulties, the Paris Convention creates a right known as "Paris priority" set forth in Article 4. The priority right preserves the priority of the patent filing for one year while the inventor decides whether to file in other countries.

Article 4 of the Paris Convention provides:

Paris Convention

Article 4

A.

(1) Any person who has duly filed an application for a patent . . . in any one of the countries of the Union . . . shall enjoy, for the purpose of filing in the other countries, a right of priority during the periods hereinafter fixed.

(2) Any filing that is equivalent to a regular filing under the domestic legislation of any country of the Union . . . shall be recognized as giving rise to the right of priority.

(3) By a regular national filing is meant any filing that is adequate to establish the date on which the application was filed in the country concerned whatever may be the subsequent fate of the application.

B.

Consequently, any subsequent filing in any of the other countries of the Union before the expiration of the periods referred to above shall not be invalidated by reason of any acts accomplished in the interval, in particular, another filing, the publication or exploitation of the invention . . . .

C.

(1) The periods referred to above shall be twelve months for patents and utility models, and six months for industrial designs and trademarks.

(2) These periods shall start from the date of filing of the first application; the day of filing shall not be included in the period.

(3) If the last day of the period is an official holiday, or a day when the Office is not open for the filing of applications in the country where protection is claimed, the period shall be extended until the first following working day.

Paris priority gives the patent owner an additional period of 12 months from the date of the filing of the first application to assess whether the patent is commercially viable in foreign markets. If the patent owner decides that the patented invention is commercially viable the patent owner can assert the date of its first filing as its filing date in all other Paris Union countries so long as the owner files additional patent applications within one year.

> Illustration 3-4. On January 10, 2024, Leni files a patent application in the United States. On March 1, 2024, Elke files a patent for the same invention in Germany. Leni then files a patent application in Germany on January 10, 2025. So long as Leni has filed within 12 months of her U.S. application, Leni is allowed to assert the U.S. filing date—called the Paris priority date—as her date of filing in Germany. Leni has a filing date of January 10, 2024 in Germany which is prior to Elke's filing date of March 1, 2024 so Leni wins the priority dispute and wins the patent.

The 12-month period starts on the date of filing, but the day of filing is not included in the period. Paris Conv., Article 4(C)(2). So in our example above, Leni files in the United States on January 10, 2024. We do not include January 10 in the 12-month period. We start with January 11 and then count one year, which ends on January 10, 2025. Leni has until January 10, 2025 to file in order to assert a priority filing date of January 10, 2024.

To be entitled to Paris priority, the filing must be a "regular" national filing, i.e. the filing must be adequate under the domestic laws of the country to be considered a national filing in order to establish Paris priority. The country's domestic laws or regulations will contain the details of what is required for a regular application. Some countries allow for a provisional application under a simplified procedure. For example, the United States allows for provisional patent applications to establish an early filing date in the United States if the provisional patent application is later converted into a non-provisional patent application.

> Illustration 3-5. On January 5, 2025, Summit Corporation files a provisional application for a patent under a simplified procedure in Country Z, a Paris Union country. Under applicable law, a provisional application must be later converted into a non-provisional application in order to obtain a patent. Summit converts the provisional filing into a regular filing on March 1, 2025. Summit has a Paris priority date of March 1, 2025, the conversion date. If Summit never converts the provisional filing into a regular filing then Summit never receives a right of Paris priority.

A patent application can establish a Paris priority date even if the application is later rejected. Article 4(A)(3) provides that a regular national filing establishes a Paris priority date "whatever may be the subsequent fate of the application."

> Illustration 3-6. On April 10, 2025, Ramesh files a regular national patent application in India. On August 5, 2025, the India patent office rejects the application for lack of novelty and failure to satisfy documentation requirements. Ramesh has a Paris priority date of April 10, 2025 in all

countries of the Paris Union. The filing of the national application established the priority date; that the application was eventually rejected and the reasons for its rejection are irrelevant. The result would be the same if India eventually granted the patent. Whether India grants or denies the patent is irrelevant to establishing Paris priority. The fate of the patent application in India is also irrelevant to whether other Paris Union countries will eventually grant the patent.

Article 4(A)(3) can be understood as another iteration of the independence principle that we have already seen in the Berne Convention. The existence of rights under the Paris Convention is independent of rights in the country of origin. The right of the inventor to Paris priority is established by the filing of the application not by the granting of the national patent. Like the Berne Convention, the Paris Convention is not concerned with how countries treat patents as a matter of domestic law. The Paris Convention is concerned with how countries treat foreign patents, and in this case, foreign patent applications.

In every instance in which Paris priority is asserted there must be two patent applications: (1) the first application in a Paris Union country establishes the Paris priority date; and (2) the second application in a second Paris Union country filed within 12 months of the first application is entitled to assert the benefit of the date of filing of the first application, i.e. the Paris priority date, in all Paris

Union countries. The filing date of the second application must be within 12 months of the first. If so, then the second application is allowed to assert the Paris priority date as its effective filing date in the second Paris Union country and all other Paris Union countries. If, for any reason, the second application is not entitled to assert the Paris priority date, then the filing date of the second application is its actual filing date.

> Illustration 3-7. Kiet files a patent application in Thailand on February 5, 2024. Kiet later files a patent application in India on January 1, 2025 and asserts a Paris priority date of February 5, 2024, the Thai filing date, in India. Later it is discovered that Kiet never submitted the filing fees for the Thai application so the application was never accepted by the Thai patent office. Kiet must now fall back on the January 1, 2025 actual filing date as his filing date in India.

The Paris priority date immunizes the patent application from events that would otherwise defeat the application occurring within 12 months after the application is filed. Article 4(B) provides:

Paris Convention

Article 4

* * *

B. [A]ny subsequent filing in any of the other countries of the Union before the expiration of the periods referred to above [i.e., Paris priority] shall not be invalidated by reason of any acts

> accomplished in the interval, in particular, another filing, the publication or exploitation of the invention . . . .

The Paris priority date immunizes the application from otherwise invalidating events occurring in other Paris Union countries. One situation we have already examined is that a subsequent filing in another Paris Union country will normally defeat the application. This occurs when Andrea files a patent application in the United States on January 1, 2024 and Bianca files an application for the same invention in Germany on February 1, 2024. Bianca's application would normally defeat any subsequent filing by Andrea in Germany but the first filing in the United States immunizes Andrea's subsequent filing in Germany from Bianca's filing so long as Andrea's subsequent filing in Germany occurs with 12 months of January 1, 2024.

The inventor's application is also immunized from other events committed by the inventor himself or by third parties in other Paris Union countries that would otherwise defeat the inventor's application.

> Illustration 3-8. Anatoly files his application in the United States on January 10, 2024. Anatoly publishes an article in a German scientific magazine with a full disclosure of Anatoly's invention in Germany on June 15, 2024 and Anatoly sells the invention at a trade show in Germany on July 1, 2024. Anatoly then files an application for the invention in Germany on January 10, 2025. The disclosure in the German publication and the sale of the invention would

normally invalidate Anatoly's subsequent patent application because it is not novel—the invention was disclosed to the public on June 15, 2024—and commercially exploited by sale on July 1, 2024. Because Anatoly is allowed to assert a Paris priority date of January 10, 2024, however, the publication and sale do not invalidate the German application as the application is deemed to have a filing date in Germany of January 10, 2024 or at least four months before the disclosure and sale. As the effective date of the Germany patent application is January 10, 2024, all events after that date, such as the disclosure and sale, are disregarded.

3. THE U.S. APPROACH TO RESOLVING PRIORITY DISPUTES

For over 200 years the United States adopted a first to invent approach instead of the first to file approach adopted by almost every other country in the world for granting patents. A first to invent approach grants the patent to the first inventor who conceives the invention and who reduces it to actual or constructive practice. As its name suggests, the first to file approach awards the patent to the first to file a patent application regardless of who was the first to invent. A first to file approach favors corporations with many lawyers and a staff ready to churn out patent applications. The United States approach was based on the notion that a first to invent approach would help small time inventors who might lack the resources to win a race to file.

As already noted in an earlier part of this chapter, the United States has now adopted a first to file approach to resolving competing patent disputes consistent with the rest of the world. However, it is still important to understand and to be able to apply the first to invent approach because this approach still applies in the United States to all patent applications filed before the effective date of the America Invents Act, i.e. March 16, 2013. All patent applications filed on or after March 16, 2013 are subject to the first to file approach. All patent applications filed before March 16, 2013 are still subject to the first to invent approach. As many existing patents in the United States are based on applications filed before March 16, 2013 any challenges to the validity of these patents based on competing patents must use the first to invent approach. For these reasons, we examine the first to invent approach in detail below.

To understand the difference between the first to invent and the first to file approach, we begin by noting that there are three important dates in patenting an invention: (1) the date of conception, (2) the date of actual reduction to practice, and (3) the date of constructive reduction to practice. The date of conception is the date that the inventor first conceived of the invention in its complete form. The date of actual reduction to practice is the date that the inventor built a working model or prototype. The date of constructive reduction to practice is the date that the inventor filed a patent application.

In a first to file approach only step (3) is important. This approach does not consider steps (1) and (2). In the first to invent approach all three steps are important. Step (1) represents the earliest date related to the invention. If the inventor satisfies all of the elements of the approach (i.e. step (1) plus either step (2) or (3)) the inventor is allowed to assert (1) the conception date as its priority date in a dispute between competing claims to the patent called an interference proceeding. To be entitled to assert the conception date, the inventor either (2) builds a working prototype known as an actual reduction to practice *or* (3) files a patent application known as a constructive reduction to practice. In addition, the inventor must not abandon, suppress, or conceal the invention. The inventor must also produce adequate evidence of the conception of the invention in the interference proceeding. If the inventor does not keep adequate records the inventor may have to fall back on constructive reduction to practice, i.e. the filing date.

Illustration 3-9. Fang conceives an invention on January 1 and files a patent application on April 1. Independently, Peng conceives the same invention on February 1 and files a patent application on March 1. If Fang has kept contemporaneous records of her conception then Fang will have a priority date of January 1 and win the patent. If Fang does not have good records, then Fang will have to fall back on her filing date of April 1 and Peng will win the patent.

Illustration 3-10. Cortez conceives an invention on May 1 and builds a working model on August 1 but does not file a patent application. Delores independently conceives the same invention on July 1 and files a patent application on September 1. If Cortez has adequate evidence of his conception and actual reduction to practice, then Cortez will be entitled to a priority date of May 1 and will prevail over Delores in an interference proceeding even though Cortez never filed a patent application. Cortez can now file a patent application and obtain the patent.

Many patent disputes involve competing applications. Under the first to invent approach, the first step is to compare the dates of the applications. Then the second step is to see whether either applicant is entitled to an earlier priority date based upon conception. To assert the conception date, the applicant must have adequate evidence (more on this point below). If both have adequate evidence then the next step is to compare the conception dates with the patent going to the applicant with the earliest conception date. If only one has adequate evidence then the comparison is between the conception date and the date of filing for the other application. If neither has adequate evidence then the comparison is between the filing dates alone. In many cases in practice, the first to invent approach does not differ from the first to file approach. Suppose that in Illustration 3-9 neither Fang nor Peng kept contemporaneous records. In that case, both parties must fall back on their constructive reduction to practice, i.e. the filing date and the inquiry resembles a simple who was first to file approach.

The advantage of the first to invent approach is that it rewards the first to invent, not the first to win a race to the patent office. The disadvantage of the first to invent approach is the potential costs in time and money of the interference proceeding to determine which of two inventors first conceived the invention. An inventor will have to produce evidence in the form of contemporaneous records corroborating the conception of the invention. The inventor's own testimony may not be enough. Contemporaneous documentary evidence and testimony by third persons may be necessary. Producing such evidence can be expensive and time consuming. It is quite possible that the costs of the interference proceeding will lead some small inventors to abandon the patent. Ironically, the first to invent approach intended to help small time inventors might harm them instead.

While the first to file approach can reward someone other than the real inventor, its advantage is that of utter simplicity. The inquiry is limited to examining the dates of the applications. (Note, however, that the inquiry may also have to take into account Paris priority dates.) In the end, the simplicity of this approach and its adoption by almost every other country in the world led the United States to change course and adopt a modified first to file approach.

On September 16, 2011, the United States enacted the America Invents Act, which switched the United

States to a modified first to file approach for all applications filed on or after March 16, 2013. The practical effect of the America Invents Act is that patent applications in the United States are subject to two different approaches in resolving priority disputes: (1) for all existing patents on March 16, 2013 and all patent applications that were filed before March 16, 2013, the first to invent approach still resolves priority disputes; (2) for all patent applications filed on or after March 16, 2013, the first to file approach is used to resolve priority disputes.

Under the America Invents Act, it is possible that a patent that existed as of March 16, 2013 or one that was filed before March 16, 2013 will be the subject of a challenge as of this writing in 2025 and for nearly the next decade.

> Illustration 3-11. Ajax corporation filed for a patent on January 1, 2013 that was eventually granted. The term of the patent ends on January 1, 2033 or twenty years from the filing date. In 2025, Ajax sues Borax corporation for infringement of the patent. Borax defends on the grounds that it owns the patent and that Ajax's patent is invalid. Borax filed a patent for the same invention on March 1, 2013 but Borax claims that its scientists fully conceived the invention by December 1, 2012, which it asserts as its priority date. To resolve this lawsuit in 2025, the court must apply the first to invent approach.

The first to invent approach applies not only to U.S. inventors but also to foreign inventors applying for U.S. patents. The key is whether the applications were filed on or before March 16, 2013 in the U.S. patent office.

Illustration 3-12. In 2012, Dieter and Maria both conceive the same invention independently in Germany. Dieter files a patent application with the U.S. patent office on February 1, 2013 and Maria files a U.S. patent application on March 10, 2013. Maria has kept contemporaneous records of her conception of the invention on December 1, 2012 while Dieter has lost all of his records. Maria will win the patent in the United States because she will be able to claim a priority date of December 1, 2012. As Dieter has no records, he must fall back on his filing date of February 1, 2013. Maria wins the patent even though she is a foreign inventor who conceived the invention in a foreign country.

As 2013 recedes into time, the first to invent approach will become less applicable in resolving priority disputes but for at least about the next decade or so, lawyers must still understand how the first to invent approach applies in U.S. priority disputes.

For patent applications filed on or after March 16, 2013, the United States uses a modified first to file approach. Unlike a "pure" first to file approach used by other countries with no exceptions, the United States gives the inventor a one year grace period before the filing of the patent for certain disclosures made by the inventor that would otherwise invalidate the patent. A disclosure that is made within one year before the filing date does not constitute disqualifying prior art if "(A) the disclosure was made by the inventor or joint inventor or by another who obtained the subject matter disclosed directly or indirectly from the inventor or a joint inventor; or (B) the subject matter disclosed had before such disclosure been publicly disclosed by the inventor or a joint inventor or another who obtained the subject matter disclosed directly or indirectly from the inventor or a joint inventor." American Invents Act, § 3(b).

> Illustration 3-13. After Norman creates an invention, Norman fully discloses the invention on March 1, 2024 at an academic conference. On January 1, 2025, Norman files a patent application in the U.S. patent office. Although the full disclosure of the invention at the academic conference will normally defeat the patent for lack of novelty, the one year grace period in the America Invents Act immunizes Norman's invention from the defeating effects of the disclosure. Norman's filing date is January 1, 2025 and the disclosure is given no effect by the U.S. patent office.

The rationale for the one year grace period for certain disclosures can be traced to considerations underlying the first to invent approach. Under that approach, an inventor does not need to be in a hurry to file a patent application after conception of the invention. If the inventor has kept good contemporaneous records of his conception in written notes then the inventor is protected against the claims of a subsequent independent inventor. The inventor can discuss his ideas with others, publish a paper, and present the ideas at a conference. This process should help the inventor refine his conception and improve the invention. Once the inventor has refined his ideas, the inventor can file a patent application. By contrast, in a first to file jurisdiction, the inventor would be hesitant to discuss his ideas with anyone for fear that someone will realize that the ideas can be patented and will win the race to the courthouse. The inventor will face strong pressure to file as soon as possible even before the conception can be refined. The first to file approach can lead to a lot of applications for half-baked and untested ideas. The purpose of the one year grace period is to allow inventors an incubation period to discuss and improve their inventions without fear of losing the patent. Not all jurisdictions have a one year grace period so that is why the U.S. approach is a called a modified first to file jurisdiction.

4. THE PATENT COOPERATION TREATY

Paris priority creates an important benefit for inventors, but the inventor must still face the burden of filing a separate patent application in each country in which protection is sought. This can create both financial and administrative burdens for the inventor. Each nation will also establish its own filing procedures so differences in national filing systems could add to the costs and complexity of international filings. To ease the burden of filing multiple patent applications in foreign countries, members of the Paris Union signed the Paris

Cooperation Treaty (PCT) in 1970 as a special agreement under the auspices of the Paris Convention.

The PCT provides a streamlined process for the filing of a single international application that is designed to ease the administrative burden of multiple filings. Whether the PCT creates cost savings is another matter as the available statistics indicate that using the PCT can be as expensive as filing separate applications. The PCT is a special agreement among Paris Union countries under Article 19 of the Paris Convention. Article 19 permits Paris Union countries to make separate agreements among themselves for the protection of patent and trademark rights so long as the agreements do not contravene the Paris Convention. In 1970, 28 countries were members of the PCT. As of 2025, 158 countries are members of the PCT. The growth in membership and use of the PCT reflects its popularity and success.

All WTO countries are bound to apply Articles 1-12 and 19 of the Paris Convention but as the PCT is a special agreement under Article 19, WTO members are not automatically members of the PCT. WTO members must separately join the PCT to be able to use its streamlined process.

A filing under the PCT has two significant advantages over separate foreign filings. The first advantage is that the PCT extends the period of priority in which an inventor can decide on the commercial viability of the invention in foreign markets. Most users of the PCT believe that the extension of the period of priority is its most important benefit. Under Paris priority, the inventor receives a 12-month period in which the inventor can decide whether to proceed to file a foreign patent application; Paris priority preserves the ability of the inventor to use the first filing date for all additional applications filed within 12 months. The PCT extends the period for an additional 18 months during which Paris priority will be preserved. The PCT allows the inventor up to a total of 30 months to decide whether to file additional foreign applications. In other words, the inventor is allowed the use the first filing date—the Paris priority date—for up to 30 months for all additional patent applications in other PCT countries. This is a major benefit of the PCT.

The second advantage is that the PCT uses a single application form that must be accepted by all PCT countries. This reduces the administrative burden for the inventor who would otherwise have to comply with multiple different application form requirements. PCT applications can be filed in any language accepted by the receiving office (i.e. a national patent office designated to receive PCT applications) but for publication, the application must be translated into one of the ten official languages recognized by the PCT: Arabic, Chinese, English, French, German, Japanese, Korean, Portuguese, Russian, and Spanish.

a. PCT Application

To understand how a PCT international patent application works, we begin by noting that there are two different routes for a PCT application: (1) a PCT international application based on a prior national patent application called the "traditional route" and (2) a PCT international application not based on a prior national application called the "PCT route." The traditional route is more commonly used.

Under the traditional route, like any other set of applications involving Paris priority, there are two applications: (1) a national application establishing the Paris priority date and then (2) a PCT application asserting the benefit of the Paris priority date.

An inventor first files a patent application with a national patent authority. Within 12 months of the original filing, the inventor then files a PCT international application with either the international bureau of WIPO or in a national patent office that has been designated as an International Search Authority. The patent offices of the United States, Australia, Canada, Japan, Korea, China and others have been designated as search authorities. The European Patent Office is another important search authority.

The PCT international application automatically identifies all PCT countries as designated countries in which the applicant will seek a national patent. If the applicant is seeking a patent in only some countries of the PCT, the applicant must specifically designate those countries or, by default, the PCT will designate all countries.

The PCT international application, like any other patent application, is entitled to claim the benefit of

Paris priority based on a prior filing in a Paris Union country. So long as the PCT application is filed within 12 months of the first national filing, the PCT international application can assert the benefit of the Paris priority date, i.e. the filing date of the national application.

As the second filing is a PCT international application, the inventor has an additional 18 months in addition to the 12 months from the Paris priority date to decide whether to seek national patents in other Paris Union countries. Or the inventor has a total of 30 months from the first filing date to seek national patents based on the Paris priority date of the first filing in the national patent authority. Most patent owners find the additional 18 months to the most important benefit conferred by the PCT.

> Illustration 3-14. On March 1, 2024 Ultra-Soft corporation files a patent application in the UK patent office. Ultra-Soft also wants patents in Australia, Belgium, Korea, and China. If Ultra-Soft files separate national applications in each country, Ultra-Soft will have until March 1, 2025 to file the applications and be able to assert a Paris priority date of March 1, 2024 for each of the national applications.

> Illustration 3-15. After filing for a UK patent on March 1, 2024, Ultra-Soft corporation files a PCT international application with the Canadian International Search Authority designating Australia, Belgium, Korea, and China as countries for the PCT application. If

Ultra-Soft files the PCT application with 12 months of the UK application, Ultra-Soft will have a total of 30 months from the UK filing date or until August 1, 2026 to file national applications in the designated countries. When the international application enters national stage in the designated countries, the national applications will have a Paris priority date of March 1, 2024. Ultra-Soft can use the extra 18 months to decide whether it makes business sense to pursue patents in the additional countries.

The second type of application is a PCT international application that is not based on a prior national application, known as the "PCT route." This type of application is rare; most inventors will first file a patent application in a national patent system before filing for international patents under the PCT. Under the PCT route, the filing date of the PCT international application establishes the priority date. The inventor has a total of 30 months from the priority date to seek national patents in other PCT countries based on the first filing date of the PCT international application.

Illustration 3-16. On March 1, 2024, Ultra-Soft corporation files a PCT international application with the Canadian International Search Authority designating Australia, Belgium, Korea, and China. Ultra-Soft has 30 months or until August 1, 2026 to file national applications in each of these countries. In this illustration the first filing is a PCT international application. In

Illustration 3-8, the first filing is a national application in the UK. In both cases, the initial filing date establishes the PCT priority date. The initial filing date triggers the 30-month clock that starts on March 1, 2024 and ends on August 1, 2026.

Under either route, the first filing date, known as the "PCT priority date" begins the 30-month period, whether it is a national application or a PCT international application. For the traditional route there are two applications, the national application and the PCT international application. For the PCT route there is only one application, the PCT international application. In either case, it is the first filing date that starts the 30-month clock. Everything that occurs from this point forward is measured from the first filing date, i.e. the PCT priority date.

With this starting point in mind, we can now review the important stages in the PCT application. Keep in mind that for the purposes of the discussion below, it does not matter whether the application uses the traditional route or the PCT route. All references are to the starting point, the PCT priority date, which is the same regardless of the route chosen.

b. Stages in the PCT Application

Stage One: International Stage:

- **0 months** from PCT priority date: The date of the first filing starts the 30-month period under the PCT. Under the traditional route, the first filing is an application in a Paris Union country; under the PCT route, the first filing is a PCT international application. Under either route, once the PCT international application is filed, the International Search Authority will conduct a non-binding prior art search and will issue an opinion on patentability.

- **16 months** from PCT priority date: The International Search Authority forwards the prior art search and patentability opinion to the World Intellectual Property Organization in Geneva.

- **18 months** from PCT priority date: WIPO publishes a search report, opinion, and the PCT application.

- **22 months** from PCT priority date or 3 months from receipt of search report and patentability opinion, whichever is later: Applicant can decide whether to request an international preliminary examination from an International Preliminary Examination Authority. The preliminary examination is non-binding on national patent authorities but will be given consideration by national authorities. A preliminary examination also allows the applicant another opportunity to make amendments to the application.

- **28 months** from PCT priority date: The Preliminary Examination Authority issues preliminary examination report, if one was requested.

- **30 months** from PCT priority date: Applicant must decide whether to enter national stage.

Stage Two: National stage

- **30 months** from PCT priority date: If the PCT application enters national stage within 30 months of the PCT priority date, the PCT application will be given the PCT priority date that started the 30-month period as the filing date of the national application.

- If the applicant decides to enter national stage, the International Search Authority will forward the PCT application to the national patent offices of each designated country. The PCT application will be treated as a national application. The filing date of the national application is the PCT priority date that begun the 30-month period.

- National patent authorities will review the PCT application and decide whether to issue the patent.

Note carefully that the filing of the national application is considered to be part of one single PCT application that has both an international stage and a national stage. The filing of the national application is the entry of the PCT international application into the national stage, not the filing of a separate national application.

> Illustration 3-17. On June 1, 2024, Green Power corporation files a patent application with the China patent office. On June 1, 2025, within the period of Paris priority, Green Power files a PCT application with the Canadian patent office, an International Search Authority. On January 1, 2026 or 30 months from June 1, 2024, Green Power enters national stage in the United States. The PCT priority date of June 1, 2024 is considered the actual filing date of the U.S. patent application.
>
> In particular do not make the mistake of thinking that the U.S. application is a separate application that is claiming Paris priority based on a prior filing. The U.S. application is part of a single application that has a PCT priority date of June 1, 2024 and that has an international stage and a national stage. Everything that occurs up to 30 months from June 1, 2024 is the international stage of the PCT application. Everything that occurs from January 1, 2026 is the national stage of the PCT application. There is only one single PCT application and the U.S. application is part of that single PCT application. There is not a PCT application and a separate U.S. application.

The result in Illustration 3-17 is made clear under Article 11 of the PCT, which states that a properly filed PCT international application that is accorded "an international filing date shall have the effect of a regular national application in each designated State as of the international filing date, which shall be considered to be the actual filing date in each designated State." In our example, the PCT international application was able to assert the June 1, 2024 filing date based on Paris priority. As June 1, 2024 is the filing date of the PCT international application, under Article 11 of the PCT the date of June 1, 2024 also becomes the "actual filing date" in the U.S. patent office when the PCT application enters national stage.

By all accounts the PCT has been a resounding success. In the 1990s, there were 20,000 PCT applications per year. By 2010, this number had grown to about 163,000 annual PCT applications. In 2011, the two millionth PCT application was filed. The top five countries by PCT filings are in order: the United States, Japan, Germany, China, and South Korea.

5. THE EUROPEAN PATENT CONVENTION AND THE EU UNITARY PATENT

The European Patent Convention (1973) (EPC), modeled after the PCT, allows the use of one application to obtain a single European patent that has the effect of a national patent in all members of the EPC designated in the application. The applicant files a single application with the European Patent Office in Munich, Germany. A branch of the European Patent Office in The Hague in the Netherlands conducts a single prior art search.

As an example, if an applicant for a European patent designates Spain, Portugal, Germany, Belgium, and Italy and obtains the European patent, the single patent has the effect of a national patent in each of those countries. If the patent designates all 38 members of the EPC then the European patent has the effect of 38 national patents.

Members of the EPC do not have to be European states. At present there are 38 member states, including all 27 states of the EU. The European patent does not displace national patent systems. An applicant can also apply for national patents using the procedures in each state's domestic patent system. Rather, the EPC creates a parallel system to facilitate the acquisition of national patent rights.

Under the Patent Cooperation Treaty, the international application can designate the European patent as one of the application's designated states. This would allow a single filing under the PCT to obtain a European patent along with other patents in other designated PCT states.

Unlike the European patent, the EU unitary patent is not a collection of national patents but a supranational patent that has the same effect throughout its member states. The EU unitary patent is based on a harmonized patent law effective in all member states that is set forth in the Agreement for a Unified Patent Court, 2013/C 175/01, that entered in force June 1, 2023. At present there are 18 members of the agreement with other members that are expected to ratify the agreement in the future. EU unitary patents issued and registered by the European Patent Office on or after September 1, 2024 will take effect in the 18 EU member states.

6. PRIORITY DISPUTES FOR U.S. PATENT APPLICATIONS

Cases that involve Paris priority disputes are regularly litigated in the United States. The basic issue in many of these cases is whether the applicant can rely on the Paris priority date in an interference proceeding or must fall back on the actual filing date in the United States. A good example is *Frazer v. Schlegel*, 498 F.3d 1283 (Fed. Cir. 2007).

The dispute concerned an interference action between two competing applications for a cancer virus vaccine. Frazer filed a patent application for the vaccine in Australia on July 19, 1991 and then a PCT international application on July 20, 1992 claiming the Paris priority date of the Australian application. (Under the Paris Convention, the date of filing is not included for the purposes of determining the 12-month period (Article 4(C)(2)) so the period expired at the end of business on July 20, 1992.)

Frazer filed a U.S. patent application on January 19, 1994 or within 18 months of the PCT international filing date of July 20, 1992 and within 30 months of the July 19, 1991 PCT priority date. Asserting Paris priority and the PCT, Frazer claimed July 19, 1991 as his priority date for his U.S. patent application in the interference proceeding in the United States.

The other applicant, Schlegel had a U.S. filing date of June 25, 1992. If Frazer could assert a Paris priority date of July 19, 1991, he would win the patent. The U.S. patent board refused to allow Frazer to assert the July 19, 1991 date so Frazer had to fall back on his actual filing date in the United States of January 19, 1994. As Schlegel had an earlier U.S. filing date of June 25, 1992, the patent board awarded the patent to Schlegel.

The patent board found that Frazer could assert the PCT priority date only if the invention was fully disclosed in the Australian patent filing on July 19, 1991 in a manner that would allow a person of ordinary skill in the art to make the vaccine. This disclosure requirement is set forth in § 112 of the U.S. Patent Code and in Article 29(1) of TRIPS. In his Australian application, Frazer mistakenly assumed that the expression of both the L1 and L2 genes in the same plasmid was required for the vaccine, but in his PCT application, Frazer later indicated that only the expression of the L1 gene was necessary. The patent board found that the Australian application was not a full disclosure of the invention and so refused to allow Frazer to assert the filing date of the Australian application as the filing date of this application in the U.S. patent office.

On appeal, the Federal Circuit reversed. The Federal Circuit disagreed with the patent board, holding that given that the invention occurred in an unpredictable field of technology in the early stages of development, the disclosure of the invention in the Australian application would enable a person of ordinary skill in the art to make the invention as required by § 112 of the U.S. Patent Code. The Federal Circuit found that the disclosure in the Australian application, although not precisely accurate, was still sufficient as a full disclosure because it would allow a person skilled in the art to make the vaccine. The Federal Circuit seemed to find that some leeway was available when the invention involved a new field of technology in the early stages of development. Such an approach would benefit inventors in areas of emerging technologies, such as the biomedical technology field. As the Australian disclosure met U.S. patent law requirements, Frazer was allowed to assert the Australian filing date of July 19, 1991 so Frazer won the patent.

Note that this dispute arose while the United States followed the first to invent approach, but it proceeded based on an analysis of who was first to file. Neither of the inventors kept adequate contemporaneous records of the conception or actual reduction to practice. Without contemporaneous records, the parties fell back on constructive reduction to practice, i.e. the filing dates. As many inventors, especially foreign inventors, may not have kept contemporaneous records of the conception of the invention, many disputes during the first to invent era may not as a practical matter differ from first to file disputes.

D. LOCAL WORKING REQUIREMENTS

Local working requirements refer to policies in some countries that require the owner of a patent to work or use the patent in the country granting the patent or else be subject to a compulsory license or forfeiture. Many of these countries are developing countries and impose these policies because they are wary of being exploited by multinational companies holding patents.

Illustration 3-18. Mega-Pharma corporation files for a patent for a drug that treats a widespread health problem in a developing country. Once the patent is secured, Mega-Pharma manufactures the drug in the United States and exports the drug to the developing country, charging monopoly prices. The developing country receives the social benefits of the drug but the bulk of the economic benefits of the patent accrue to Mega-Pharma, which earns huge profits due to its high prices.

Illustration 3-19. Lawmakers in the developing country pass a new law imposing local working requirements on foreign owned patents. The patent must be worked locally or be subject to forfeiture or compulsory licensing. After the passage of the law, Mega-Pharma injects millions of dollars in capital into the local economy to build manufacturing and office facilities. Mega-Pharma also creates dozens of new jobs. Among the employees hired by Mega-Pharma are scientists and engineers from the local university who learn how to use the patent and the new technology. Later some in this group will set up their own drug companies in the local economy. Mega-Pharma's local operations earn profits and pay taxes to the local government. People in the developing country still benefit from the drug, but by working the patent locally, Mega-Pharma shares the economic benefits of the patent with the developing country.

Although the Paris Convention imposed some limits, both compulsory licenses and forfeitures are allowed in the event that the patent is not worked locally. Paris Conv., Article 5(A)(3)–(4). The Paris Convention is also administered by the World Intellectual Property Organization, which has no enforcement powers. Many nations believed that additional international rules outside of the Paris Convention were needed to deal with the issue of working requirements. When nations drafted the TRIPS agreement as part of the Uruguay round of negotiations to establish the WTO, the issue of working requirements was one of the issues addressed. Countries tend to divide on local working requirements along the North-South line with developing countries in favor of local working requirements and developed countries opposed to them.

To deal with the lack of enforceable standards on working requirements, the drafters of TRIPS included a clause in Article 27(1), which states that "patents shall be available and patent rights enjoyable without discrimination as to the place of invention, the field of technology and *whether the products are imported or locally produced.*"

The last part of Article 27(1) can be read to prohibit local working requirements. This clause states that the enjoyment of patent rights cannot depend on whether the products are imported (i.e. the patent is not worked locally) or locally produced (i.e. worked locally). Article 27(1) appears to allow patents of the type involved in Illustration 3-11 where the patent owner uses the patent overseas to produce exports for the local economy. Imposing a forfeiture requirement on such a patent would be a form of discrimination that is prohibited by Article 27(1).

While TRIPS appears to have sided with developed countries on working requirements, the legality of local working requirements has not been settled. Some developing countries still have patent laws containing local working requirements on the books despite the language contained in TRIPS Article 27(1). Whether the WTO will interpret Article 27(1) to prohibit local working requirements is also unclear. As will be discussed in a later section, the WTO has adopted a flexible interpretation of compulsory licenses in the context of pharmaceutical patents that may permit some local working requirements. As of this writing, no case has been brought in the WTO challenging any national laws containing local working requirements.

E. OWNERSHIP OF PATENTS

The issue of who owns the patent is not one that is subject to specific requirements by TRIPS or the Paris Convention. The inventor can be the owner of the patent, but that is not always or even usually the case. The inventor may also not even be the applicant in a patent filing. The applicant can be the employer of the inventor because the employee has assigned its rights to the patent as part of the employment contract. Any person or entity can be the owner of a patent.

The ownership of patents can become an important issue in employment situations. In the preceding chapter on copyright, we examined a similar issue. In the United States, the work for hire doctrine in copyright holds that the employer is the owner of a work created by an employee. In the patent context, a similar issue can arise over whether an employer owns a patent to an invention created by an employee. In these situations, the United States adopts the position that the employer owns the patent if there is an express or implied contract that the employee will assign the rights to the invention to the employer. *See Teets v. Chromalloy Gas Turbine Corporation*, 83 F.3d 403, 407 (Fed. Cir. 1996). An express contract is an agreement that is oral or in writing that is contained in an employment contract. Since many jobs are at will in the United States, a written employment contract may not exist. At this point, the doctrine of implied contract becomes important.

An implied contract exists when an "employer specifically hires an employee [to make the invention] or directs the employee to exercise inventive faculties." *Id.* at 407. Such contracts usually apply to inventions made during the course of employment, i.e. when the employee makes the invention in the normal course of work. If the employee makes the invention outside the scope of employment then the invention belongs to the employee in the absence of an express contract. For example, a person working in the mailroom of a pharmaceutical company who invents a new drug will be the owner of the invention. Or, if a scientist in the pharmaceutical company invents a new product in the consumer electronics field in his spare time the employee will own the invention. If the employee inventor uses the facilities of the employer, such as laboratories, to make the invention, the employer might acquire a shop right, i.e. a right to use the employee's invention without liability for infringement and without having the duty to compensate the employee for the use.

The U.S. position on the ownership of the patent in an employer-employee situation as based on express or implied contract is similar to that of countries in Europe and Japan. In Europe, ownership of patents by employers of inventions created by employees does not involve the issues that prevented the work for hire doctrine in copyright from gaining wide acceptance. The natural rights theory of copyright followed by many European countries rejected the idea that an impersonal corporation could be the owner of a copyright to a work of authorship. Only flesh and blood authors were copyright owners. No such hurdles exist in the case of patents as patents were never the subject of a natural rights tradition in Europe.

Where the United States seems to differ from all other countries is on the issue of renumeration to the employee for the assignment of the invention. The U.S. position is that the employee is not entitled to any additional compensation for the assignment of the patent to the employer, whether by express or implied contract. The employee is compensated by receiving a salary as part of his or her employment. To the extent that the employee has excelled in creating a valuable new invention, the employer might reward the employee with a bonus, a pay raise, or a promotion with higher pay but that is up to the employer. In the United States, the employer is not required to do anything to reward the employee. While the U.S. position may seem harsh at first sight, it is also the case that many U.S. companies pay higher compensation than companies in Europe or Japan for similar positions. For example, software engineers in Silicon Valley are paid significantly higher than counterparts in Japan or Europe.

In Europe and Japan, an employee receives additional remuneration in the form of a statutory right to compensation in exchange for assigning the patent to the employer. Although countries in the EU vary on whether and under what circumstances the employee must assign the invention to the employer, all EU countries are in agreement that the employee has a statutory right to compensation. Even the UK, which usually shares positions with the United States on many employment issues, recognizes a statutory right to compensation in the employee.

A right to compensation can become problematic when it results in a huge windfall to the employee. In *Nakamura v. Nichia Kagaku Kôgyô K.K.*, a case decided in 2004 by the Tokyo District Court, translated and published in 35 IIC 941, 941–43 (2004), the inventor, Nakamura, invented a blue light-emitting diode for his employer. The court found that Nakamura had by contract agreed to assign the right to the invention to his employer but that Nakamura had a right to reasonable remuneration under statutory law. The court found that the employer was likely earn over USD $1 billion in profits from the invention and determined that Nakamura was responsible for a 50 percent contribution to the invention and so was entitled to 50 percent of the profits. The court ruled that Nakamura was entitled to USD $534 million from his employer. Since Nakamura's complaint only sought USD $180 million in damages, the court awarded $180 million to Nakamura. After the case, Nakamura settled for $8 million and moved to the United States to become a professor. Perhaps he settled the case for only $8 million because he was concerned that the judgment might have been seen as excessive on appeal and overturned or reduced. Japan subsequently amended the law to allow the employer to set the amount of remuneration. The employee is bound unless the amount of remuneration is unreasonable in which case the employee can seek statutory remuneration.

The situation in *Nakamura*, while extreme, is one reason the United States does not recognized a mandatory right to remuneration. A requirement to pay hundreds of millions of dollars to an employee would be a burden for most companies. The U.S. position is a bright line rule that is easy to administer. Agreeing on an appropriate amount of remuneration in Japan and Europe could be a contested issue and lead to litigation, which will also be disruptive to business. The U.S. position can be seen as more employer and business friendly (and more profitable so in the long run so employees will receive higher salaries according to the theory) while the positions in Japan and Europe place greater emphasis on the rights of the individual employee.

F. PATENT REQUIREMENTS

TRIPS establishes the following requirements for patents: (1) novelty; (2) inventive step or non-obviousness; (3) capable of industrial application or utility; and (4) enablement. The first three requirements are the minimum requirements for patents under TRIPS Article 27. The enablement requirement is found in TRIPS Article 29(1), which states "[m]embers shall require that an applicant for a patent shall disclose the invention in a manner sufficiently clear and complete for the invention to be carried out by a person skilled in the art."

TRIPS also deals with the subject matter of patents in Article 27. As this is a preliminary issue, we first turn to this topic and then will examine each of the required elements of patent in turn.

1. SUBJECT MATTER OF PATENTS

In examining the subject matter of patents, we begin with Article 27 of TRIPS, which states that "patents shall be available for any inventions, whether products or processes, in all fields of technology." This broad definition of patents to include "all fields of technology" means that countries can no longer exclude patents for entire fields, such as pharmaceuticals, chemicals, and various processes from patents. Historically many countries in Europe excluded drugs and medical methods from patent protection and, until this century, India did not recognize patents for pharmaceuticals. These types of exclusions were possible under the Paris Convention but are not permitted under TRIPS.

Article 27(2) allows countries to exclude inventions from patents for purposes of "*ordre public*" (public order) and morality provided that "such exclusion is not made merely because the exploitation is prohibited by their law." Under Article 27(2), countries must have a genuine ground based on considerations of public order or morality to exclude an invention from patent and cannot just say that the invention is against the law. Under Article 29(3), countries are allowed to exclude medical, therapeutic, and surgical methods for the treatment of humans and animals. Countries may consider these inventions as too important to society to protect by the grant of a private monopoly created by a patent.

a. Patents and Lower Life Forms

An ongoing controversy concerns the availability of patents for life forms and genetic materials. *Diamond v. Chakrabarty*, 447 U.S. 303 (1980) was the first case anywhere in the world to recognize a patent for a life form, a genetically altered micro bacterial organism that was used to clean up oil spills. *Chakrabarty* suggested that the patent laws were broad and expansive and could "include anything under the sun that is made by man." 447 U.S. at 309.

Chakrabarty's broad pronouncement of patent eligibility sparked the development of the biotechnology industry in the United States. Soon a flood of biotechnology patent applications inundated the U.S. patent office. Biotechnology firms from around the world were attracted by the prospect of being able to obtain a U.S. patent for their inventions and eagerly flocked to the United States to do business. By contrast, in the 1980s the EU fell well behind the United States in developing a biotechnology industry. The EU took an uncertain position on the patentability of life forms, influenced perhaps by the history of medical experimentation by Nazi doctors during the Second World War. The uncertainty surrounding the patentability of biotechnology inventions in the EU led to the EU falling behind the United States in attracting foreign investment. By 1996, an EU study found that the United States had issued 65 percent of the world's patents for biotechnology inventions and had 1,300 biotechnology firms while the EU had only a 15 percent share of biotechnology patents and only 485 firms. The EU was falling seriously behind the United States in biotechnology investment due to the more attractive U.S. patent laws. The huge lead by the United States in the global race for biotechnology investment dollars due to its patent legal regime once again confirmed the relationship between intellectual property and foreign investment.

In response, on July 6, 1998, the EU passed a new law, the EU Directive on the Legal Protection of Biotechnological Inventions, 98/44/EC. The EU Biotechnology Directive is meant to clarify EU standards on biotechnology patents and to dispel any confusion that might create a deterrent to applying for biotechnology patents in the EU. However, Article 6(1) of the EU directive provides that inventions "shall be considered unpatentable where their commercial exploitation would be contrary to *ordre public* or morality." Article 6(2) of the EU directive provides that processes for cloning human beings and processes that modify the genetic identity of animals that cause them harm without any substantial benefit are unpatentable.

The EU Biotechnology Directive injects ethical and moral factors into the decision on whether to grant a patent. The directive appears to require patent authorities in EU member states to engage in a moral and ethical calculus as part of the patent granting process. The requirement that inventions are unpatentable when "contrary to public order or morality" uses a standard that appears to be unmoored to any objective criteria.

The EU approach differs radically from the U.S. approach. Nothing in U.S. patent law refers to these considerations in decisions by the U.S. patent office that is to base decisions on technical factors alone. To the extent that moral and ethical considerations become part of the decision to grant biotechnology patents in the EU, obtaining patents in the EU will be more unpredictable than in the United States and could continue to be a disadvantage to the EU in the biotechnology race with the United States.

b. Patents and Higher Life Forms

Diamond v. Chakrabarty broke new ground when it upheld a patent for a life form, a micro bacteria organism. Subsequently, the United States and other countries issued patents for higher life forms such as animals. These patents were more controversial, raising ethical and moral concerns. One such controversy involved the so-called "onco-mouse," a genetically altered mouse that was more susceptible to cancer and useful for cancer research.

In *Havard College v. Canada Commissioner of Patents*, 4 S.C.R. 45 (2002), the Canadian Supreme Court refused to approve a patent for the onco-mouse. The majority recognized a patent for the process of creating the genetically altered mouse but refused to recognize a patent for the mouse itself. Based on the court's textual exegesis, the court concluded that a higher life form was outside the scope of the existing Canadian patent law. The majority found that if patents were to be issued for higher life forms, the decision was one for the legislature not the courts.

In a dissent, Justice Binnie warned that Canada was dangerously out of step with other countries of a comparable level of industrial development. He noted that the onco-mouse received patents in Austria, Belgium, Denmark, Finland, France, Germany, Greece, Ireland, Italy, Luxembourg, the Netherlands, Portugal, Spain, Sweden, the United Kingdom, and the United States. Similar patents had been issued for genetically altered mice in Japan and New Zealand. Given the mobility of capital and technology, biotechnology industries might move their operations from Canada to other countries that are more hospitable to protecting their inventions. The dissent once again identified the relationship between patent law and foreign investment. Note that while the EU had previously been a laggard in biotechnology patents, the largest economies in the EU have issued patents for the onco-mouse. Now it is Canada's turn to worry about falling behind in the global race for investment and technology.

Perhaps the Canadian Supreme Court recognized the sentiments expressed in the dissent by the time it revisited the issue in *Monsanto Canada Inc. v. Schmeiser*, 2004 S.C.C. 34 (2004). *Monsanto* was a 5–4 decision involving a patent for the process for creating a genetically engineered canola plant that was resistant to the herbicide "Roundup" also a Monsanto product. The Canadian Supreme Court recognized a patent for the cell created by that process but not for the genetically modified plant itself. As in the *Harvard College* case, the Canadian Supreme Court also upheld the patent for the process. The Canadian Supreme Court then found that under the precedent of the *Harvard College* case, the organism, the plant itself, was a higher life form that was not eligible for patent but that the gene or cell could be patented.

In holding that a cell was patentable, the *Monsanto* decision seems to be at least in tension if not in outright conflict with the Canadian Supreme Court's prior decision in *Harvard College*. Recognizing a patent for a cell in a genetically engineered plant seems to open the door to a patent for a cell in a genetically engineered animal as there does not seem to a principled way of distinguishing the two cases. In addition, if Harvard owned a patent for a cell in the mouse, then Harvard could exercise its rights under the patent to prevent others from manufacturing, using, and selling the mouse containing the cell. A patent in the cell of the mouse would achieve the same objectives for Harvard as a patent in the mouse itself. The *Monsanto* decision may be a signal that Canada has been swayed by the realities and pressures of the modern global economy for broad patent law protection in biotechnology.

c. Patents for DNA Sequences

Although the United States has been at the forefront of recognizing patents for life forms, some observers began expressing concern that U.S. patent law had become too expansive for life forms. In the United States, concerns with patenting life forms arose with special force in the area of patents for the human genome. In 1982 the United States granted the first patent on an invention involving a human gene. The U.S. patent office allowed patents for DNA sequences of genes that had been isolated from their occurrence in the human body. DNA sequences were useful to researchers for predicting disease and for finding cures for diseases. Eventually both Japan and the EU also recognized patents for gene sequences. By 2005, gene patents had been issued by various countries for 20 percent of the human genome. This development led courts to question the continuing patentability of gene sequences.

The policy issue for the courts had to do with the ability of the patent owner to block off whole areas of research. If a company had a patent for a DNA sequence then no third party can use the sequence in research without authorization from the patent owner. As 20 percent of the human genome had been patented, a large area of research was subject to private control. Other researchers either had to avoid using the DNA sequences, which seemed unlikely, or pay royalties to the owners of the patents. One serious concern was that owners of DNA patents might refuse to license the DNA sequences so as to block the research efforts of their competitors. This possibility was disturbing to policy makers because the purpose of recognizing patents in life forms was to promote research not to impede it.

In 2013, the U.S. Supreme Court weighed in on patents for DNA sequences in *Association for Molecular Pathology v. U.S. Patent and Trademark Office*, 569 U.S. 576 (2013). Myriad Genetics, Inc. had obtained patents for the DNA sequences for two genes associated with a higher risk for developing breast cancer. The Court of Appeals for the Federal Circuit upheld the validity of the patents on the grounds that the patents were for isolated human genes or DNA sequences that were not found in nature.

This last finding was essential because it is an axiom of patent law that patents are not available for products of nature. *Diamond v. Chakrabarty*, 447 U.S. 303 (1980) read § 101 of the U.S. Patent Code to implicitly prohibit the patentability of "laws of nature, physical phenomena, and abstract ideas." 447 U.S. at 309. Products of nature are not inventive or new. A researcher does not invent or create a product of nature but discovers it. The product of nature is also not novel because it previously existed in nature. To be eligible for patent, DNA sequences cannot be products of nature.

Lower courts in the United States had found that DNA sequences were not products of nature because the DNA sequences were cut or "cleaved" from the DNA in the human body. The DNA sequences had to be detached and isolated from the DNA in the human body by severing their chemical bonds at specific locations. The process of cleaving also altered the chemical composition of the severed DNA into a form not found in nature. These findings led lower courts to hold that isolated DNA sequences are not found in nature but are inventions and novel.

On appeal, the Supreme Court rejected this analysis and held that the isolated DNA sequences were products of nature and not subject to patent. The Court found that the patent claims are related to the genetic information contained in the genes and are not related in any way to the chemical changes that occur when the gene is severed and isolated. The genetic information contained in the genes is not altered by the cleaving and as this aspect is the critical element in the DNA sequence for research, not its altered chemical composition, the sequence must be considered to be a product of nature. On a second issue, the Supreme Court found that synthetically created complimentary DNA also known as cDNA is eligible for patent. The synthetically created cDNA removes parts of the DNA molecule found in the human body so cDNA is not naturally occurring.

The Supreme Court's decision seems to create a legal bar to the future patenting of gene sequences. The decision may also act as a signal to the lower courts to put a stop to the expansive reading of the U.S. Patent Code that allowed patents for isolated gene sequences for many years.

d. Patentability of Business Methods

The previous section considered patents for life forms, a non-traditional area of patent protection. This section turns to another non-traditional area: business methods. As in the case of life forms, business method patents also face doctrinal obstacles to patent protection.

Like laws of nature and physical phenomenon, abstract ideas are also excluded from patent protection under § 101 of the U.S. Patent Code. *Diamond v. Chakrabarty*, 447 U.S. at 309. Abstract ideas are part of the building blocks of human ingenuity and withdrawing them from the public domain would impoverish the essential tools needed for scientific progress. This means that business methods that are purely abstract ideas cannot be patented. The test is whether the business method consists of purely abstract ideas or consists of abstract ideas that are connected with or integrated with something that has physical effects in the real world, such as a machine or a computer. In the latter case, business methods are eligible for patent in the United States. The most difficult part of the test is to identify the nature of the required link of the abstract ideas to physical effects. As the cases discussed below indicate, the courts have tried to articulate the nature of this linkage but the tests are still unclear.

In 1998, the United States Court of Appeals for the Federal Circuit decided *State Street Bank & Trust Co. v. Signature Financial Group, Inc.*, 149 F.3d 1368 (Fed. Cir. 1998), which held that business methods are eligible for patent protection. The Federal Circuit sits in Washington, D.C., and has appellate jurisdiction over patent law issues from all federal district courts.

State Street Bank distinguished a business method from an unpatentable abstract idea. *State Street Bank* held that so long as the application of an abstract idea or mathematical formula produced "a useful, concrete, tangible thing," then the abstract idea that was part of a business method was patentable. The court was attempting to make a distinction between pure abstract ideas that were unpatentable and abstract ideas that had a practical application that could be patented as part of a business method. The expansive scope of *State Street Bank* was controversial; if every abstract idea with a practical application was a patentable business method then the floodgates for business method patents in the United States would be flung wide open. Two years after *State Street Bank*, the number of patents issued for business methods by the U.S. patent office doubled to 1,006.

In 2008, the Federal Circuit seemed to reign in the expansive scope of *State Street Bank* in its decision in *In re Bilski*, 545 F.3d 943 (Fed. Cir. 2008). The *Bilski* court rejected the "useful, concrete, and tangible result" test of *State Street Bank*. Instead, the court adopted the machine or transformation test, which holds that a business method is patentable if "(1) it is tied to a particular machine or apparatus, or (2) it transforms a particular article into a different state or thing." 545 F.3d at 954–55. This approach seems to be considerably more narrow but also easier to apply than the broader but also more ambiguous "useful, concrete, and tangible result" test of *State Street Bank*. The machine or transformation test also seems to make it more difficult to obtain a business method patent.

In *Bilski v. Kappos*, 561 U.S. 593 (2010), the U.S. Supreme Court upheld the decision of the Federal Circuit in rejecting the business method at issue in the case as an unpatentable abstract idea. However, the Supreme Court stated that "[t]he machine-or-transformation test is not the sole test for deciding whether an invention is a patent-eligible 'process.'" *Id.* at 604. That is, some business methods that do not satisfy the machine or transformation test might nevertheless be patentable. The Supreme Court also specifically stated that it did not endorse the "useful, concrete, and tangible result" test of *State Street Bank*. The Supreme Court did make clear that U.S. patent law contemplates the existence of at least some business method patents and that this is acknowledged by sections of the U.S. Patent Code.

The claimed invention in *Bilski* concerned a hedging method for buyers and sellers of commodities in the energy market to protect against price fluctuations. Claim 1 involved a series of steps on how to hedge risk. Buyers who are concerned that the cost of energy will rise can hedge risk by buying futures contracts for energy at a fixed rate based on historical averages. Sellers then identify market participants who have a counter-risk position, i.e. buyers who are concerned that the price of energy or a closely related commodity will go down. The seller then enters into commodity contracts with buyers of the second group that balances out the risk positions of both groups of buyers. Claim 4 then articulated the concepts in Claim 1 into a mathematical formula.

The Supreme Court found that both Claim 1 and Claim 4 were not eligible for patent. The basic concept of hedging or protecting against risk is a fundamental concept taught in any introductory economics course. All the applicant had done in this case was to apply the concept of hedging to the energy commodities market. Hedging is an abstract idea described in Claim 1 and reduced to a mathematical formula in Claim 2. Abstract ideas are unpatentable.

The Supreme Court's decision in *Bilski* leaves many questions unsettled. The Court did not give clear direction on what test should be applied to determine the patentability of business methods. The Court rejected the machine or transformation test as the exclusive test but also did not endorse the *State Street Bank* "useful, concrete, and tangible result" test.

What we can say is that *Bilski* indicates methods that meet the machine or transformation test will qualify for patent but what is unclear is what happens to business methods that do not meet this test. Such methods may still qualify for patent under the "useful, concrete, and tangible result" test of *State Street Bank*. The Supreme Court did not endorse this test, but it also did not reject it. The Supreme Court stated that "we by no means foreclose the Federal Circuit's development of other limiting criteria that further the purposes of the Patent Act and are not inconsistent with its text." *Id.* at 613. At present, the tests for determining how to distinguish an unpatentable pure abstract idea and a patentable business method are unclear and it is left to the Federal Circuit and the U.S. Supreme Court to give further guidance in future cases.

A useful comparison to the U.S. approach is the approach in the EU. Article 52 of the European Patent Convention states that "methods for . . . doing business" are not eligible for patents. The EU Patent Office has qualified Article 52 by stating it refers to business methods "as such," i.e. business methods that are pure abstract ideas, but that methods of doing business can be patentable if they display a "technical character." *Hitachi, Ltd.*, T 0258/03–3.5.1, Technical Board of Appeal, European Patent Office (April 21, 2004).

By a "technical character," "technical feature," or "technical solution," countries in Europe refer to some physical implementation of the business method in the real world. That is, the business method must have some physical effect or manifestation in the real world that serves to distinguish it from a pure abstract idea. "Technical" also means concerned with applied and industrial sciences; the term connotes an artificiality that is human added as opposed to what is found in nature. The "non-technical feature" of the business method refers to its nature as a pure abstract concept. If a business method consists only of "non-technical features," it is unpatentable.

The business method patent in *Hitachi* concerned using computers to collect bids under a so-called Dutch auction in which the price is set and then successively lowered until it matches a bid. The EU patent office stated that the business method was more than an abstract idea because the computers gave it a technical character, i.e. a physical implementation. However, while the business method satisfied the requirement that it was more than an abstract idea, the business method of using a computer to perform a Dutch auction failed to qualify for a patent because it did not involve an inventive step, i.e. it was obvious.

The EU approach has been criticized by commentators as allowing a business method to pass the Article 52 test as long as it is attached to "any hardware." If all that is required to be eligible for patent is that the business method can be expressed as a computer program and then run on a computer then most business methods will qualify. If attachment to any hardware is all that is required, then the laws of nature and theorems of mathematics can also be patented. There must be some limits to the "any hardware" approach, but so far the EU has not addressed this issue. The EU patent office did rule, however, that even if the business method can overcome the abstract idea barrier, it must still satisfy the other requirements of a patent.

e. Patentability of Computer Programs

The discussion of business method patents raises issues that are similar to those first raised in connection with patents for computer programs. The issue was whether a computer program that was based on a mathematical algorithm, an abstract idea, is patentable. In *Diamond v. Diehr*, 450 U.S. 175 (1981), the Supreme Court ruled that a patent for a computer program can be granted "when a claim containing a mathematical formula implements or applies that formula in a function which the patents laws were designed to protect (e.g. transforming or reducing an article to a different state or thing)." *Id.* at 192. Following *Diehr*, in *In re Alappat*, 33 F.3d

1526 (Fed. Cir. 1994), the First Circuit ruled that the physical effects of a computer program on a computer can distinguish it from an abstract idea. A computer program is eligible for patent if running the computer program creates a "new machine, because a general purpose computer becomes a special purpose computer once it is programed to perform particular functions pursuant to instructions from program software." *Id.* at 1545. A patentable computer program is one that is distinguished from a computer program that contains an abstract idea because the former physically transforms a computer from a general purpose to a special purpose computer. The physical transformation that occurs is the practical application that distinguishes a patentable computer program from an unpatentable program that states an abstract idea.

The Federal Circuit seemed to adopt a very lenient standard. Nearly all computer programs provide instructions to a computer to perform particular functions. If that is all that is required to qualify for patent then many software patents will be issued, some for dubious software applications. In fact, for many years, U.S. courts were quite permissive in issuing patents for software programs leading to the criticism that this approach would stifle innovation.

The Supreme Court weighed in on patents for computer programs in *Alice Corp. Pty. Ltd. v. CLS Bank International*, 573 U.S. 208 (2014). The patents in the case were issued for a computer program implementing a scheme for mitigating settlement risks, i.e. the risk that only one party to a financial transaction will pay what it owes. The computer program at issue mitigated the risk by using an intermediary that acts as a "clearinghouse" between the two parties by keeping up to date financial records and permitting only those transactions for which the parties had sufficient funds. At the end of each day, the intermediary issues instructions to carry out only the permitted transactions. The issue for the Court was whether the computer program involved an abstract idea and was unpatentable.

In deciding this issue, the Supreme Court followed a two-step test first enunciated in *Mayo Collaborative Services v. Prometheus Laboratories, Inc.* 566 U.S. 66 (2012). First, the Court determined whether the claim involved the laws of nature, natural phenomena, and abstract ideas, which are patent ineligible areas. Second, if so, then the Court will ask "[w]hat else is there in the claims before us?" There must be additional elements or the claim is ineligible for patent. The Court is searching for an "inventive concept," that is, an inventive element or elements that go beyond the pure abstract idea so that the patent is not just a patent on the ineligible abstract idea.

The Supreme Court found that under the first prong of the test, the concept of intermediated settlement, like hedging in *Bilski*, is a basic economic practice and an abstract idea. As to the second prong, no inventive concept was added by the computer program, which required only generic computer implementation. The computer program expressed the concept of intermediated settlement and then instructed the computer to apply it. No additional inventive elements were added. As a result, the computer program was ineligible for patent protection.

The approach adopted by the Supreme Court in *Alice Corp. v. CLS Bank International* appears to narrow the permissive approach of the Federal Circuit's approach set forth in *In re Alappat*. The Federal Circuit indicated that any computer software program that involves instructions to perform specific functions could qualify for patent protection. The Supreme Court's approach requires that the program do more than provide instructions for specific functions but must also possesses an inventive concept, which sets a higher bar. No doubt many observers are hoping that the lower courts and the Supreme Court will provide further guidance on what constitutes an inventive concept that will qualify computer programs for patent.

2. NOVELTY

The most basic requirement of patent is novelty. An invention must be new or add to the sum of human knowledge to be eligible for patent. Existing knowledge and information that is publicly available is known as prior art. To be novel, an invention cannot be disclosed in or be part of the prior art.

a. Geographical Limitations on Prior Art

A question that arose in the first formal patent statute enacted in Venice in 1474 is whether there should be any geographical limitation on prior art.

The Venetian patent statute granted patents "not previously made in this Commonwealth." This statute restricted relevant prior art to that within Venice. It did not matter that the invention was disclosed in the prior art outside of Venice. So long as the invention was not part of the prior art within the territory of Venice, the invention was novel and entitled to patent protection. The purpose of this geographical limitation on prior art was to attract foreign investment to Venice. Owners of inventions made in other countries were rewarded with a patent if they brought their inventions to Venice.

In modern times, two different approaches developed concerning geographical limitations on prior art. One approach is that of the EU, which placed no geographical limits on prior art. This approach is set forth as follows below:

European Patent Convention

Article 54

* * *

(2) The state of the art shall be held to comprise everything made available to the public by means of a written or oral description, by use or in any other way before the filing date of the European patent application.

Under the EU approach, prior art consists of all publicly available information anywhere in the world, whether written or oral or by made available by use. Contrast the EU position with the position followed by the United States before the America Invents Act went into effect on March 16, 2013:

U.S. Patent Code § 102. Conditions for patentability; novelty and the loss of the right to patent

A person shall be entitled to a patent unless—

(a) the invention was known or used by others in this country or patented or described in a printed publication in this or a foreign country, before the invention thereof by the applicant for patent . . . .

This approach divides prior art into two categories: (1) in the United States prior art consists of information contained in written form in a patent or a printed publication as well as information not in written form if known by or used by others; and (2) in a foreign country prior art consists only of information contained in a patent or a printed publication. In a foreign country information that is not in a patent or printed publication cannot constitute prior art. One rationale for the distinguishing between U.S. and foreign non-written prior art is that U.S. authorities are in a better position to assess evidence of non-written prior art in the United States than non-written prior art in a foreign country. Claims based on written prior art in a foreign country in the form of patents and printed publications are viewed as reliable, but not those based on non-written events.

Under the EU position and the U.S. approach prior to the America Invents Act, inventors will be able to obtain some patents in the United States but not in the EU. A good example is *European Patent Office, Position Division Decision Revoking the European Patent No. EP–B–0436257* (Feb. 13, 2001). In that case, W.R. Grace had obtained a patent in the United States for a pesticide derived from the Neem tree, a tree found in India. W.R. Grace then filed for a patent in the EU on December 20, 1990 that was eventually granted. Two non-governmental organizations then sought to revoke the W.R. Grace EU patent on the ground that the patent was part of the prior art at the time of W.R. Grace's application and therefore the application lacked novelty. The organizations were able to demonstrate that local farmers made field tests of W.R. Grace's Neem tree insecticide in India in 1985 and 1986. One of the farmers submitted an affidavit and a list of corroborating witnesses. The EU found the evidence to be credible and revoked the patent.

In the EU, the field tests made using the Neem pesticide constituted prior art that defeated the W.R. Grace patent. In the United States, at the time of the W.R. Grace application, the field tests were not prior art. To constitute prior in a foreign nation, the prior art must be in written form, i.e. a patent or a printed publication. The field tests did not satisfy these conditions.

The position of the United States as exemplified in the *Neem* case results in more patents being granted by the U.S. patent office than by its EU counterparts. By limiting prior art in foreign countries to patents and printed publications, the United States has disqualified a wide range of activities that would qualify as prior art under the EU approach that would defeat patents. W.R. Grace was able to obtain a patent for the Neem tree pesticide in the United States but not in the EU. The United States was able to grant more patents and to attract more foreign inventors to file and invest in the United States.

Effective March 16, 2013, the America Invents Act brought the U.S. position into line with the EU. The current version of § 102(a) describes prior art as circumstances in which "the claimed invention was patented, described in a printed publication, or in public use, on sale, or otherwise available to the public before the effective filing date of the claimed invention." The current statute contains no geographical limit on "public use, sale, or information otherwise available to the public." Oral representations and non-printed writings can qualify as prior art as information "otherwise available to the public." The same standard applies to prior art in the United States and the EU. Under the current version of § 102(a), the field tests of the Neem tree pesticide in India would constitute a "public use" and disqualifying prior art.

It is important to emphasize that currently the United States follows two approaches to foreign prior art. For all patents based on applications on or after March 16, 2013, i.e. the effective date of the America Invents Act, prior art includes both U.S. and foreign activities that are "in public use, on sale, or otherwise available to the public." For all patents based on applications filed before March 16, 2013, foreign prior art consists only of patents or printed publications. If a U.S. patent is being challenged for lack of novelty it is important to determine its filing date in order to apply the proper test of prior art. For the next decade or so at least, it is necessary to understand the two different U.S. approaches to foreign prior art.

b. Patent Filings as Prior Art

The discussion in the previous section indicates that a patent can constitute prior art. Of course, this makes sense as an invention cannot be novel if a patent for the invention has already been issued. The question then becomes what is the effective date that a patent becomes a prior art reference? Since the term of the patent begins on the filing date, the filing date should be the date that the patent becomes prior art. The filing date, however, can be divided in three separate topics: (1) domestic patent filings, (2) foreign filings that occur alone, and (3) foreign filings that occur as part of a pair of filings that assert the Paris priority date of the first filing as the date the filing becomes a prior art reference.

i. Domestic Filings

In most countries, a patent application filed in that country's patent office becomes prior art on the date of filing so long as the application is later published or the patent is granted. (Some countries that are not members of the Patent Cooperation Treaty may not publish applications. Even under the PCT there can be exceptions to publication.) Even though the information in the patent application is not publicly available until it is published or the patent is granted, the publication or granting of the patent relates back to the filing date, which is deemed to be the date the application becomes prior art. When a patent is granted the patent term is measured starting with the date of filing so it makes sense to use the filing date as the date the patent becomes prior art. Sometimes this is referred to as "secret prior art" because the patent filing operates as prior art during the period between its filing and publication even though it is unknown to the public.

ii. Foreign Filings

The approach to foreign filings is more complicated. Let us start with a foreign filing that occurs alone, i.e. that does not serve as the first filing to establish a Paris priority date for a second filing. We discuss the latter situation in the next section. Most countries treat foreign filings as prior art on the date that the application is published or on the date that the patent is granted, whichever occurs first.

There is no ready explanation why countries treat foreign and domestic filings differently except to say that most countries have more confidence in their own patent systems than in foreign systems.

iii. *Foreign Filings That Are Used to Establish Paris Priority for Prior Art Purposes: Offensive and Defensive Uses of Paris Priority*

Now let us examine a foreign filing that is a part of a pair of filings and that is used to establish Paris priority. Recall that in any situation involving Paris priority there are two patent applications (1) the first filing in a Paris Union country establishes a Paris priority date and (2) the second filing in a different Paris Union country, if filed within 12 months, claims the benefit of the Paris priority date. In a situation involving two patent applications when can the second application claim the Paris priority date of the first filing as the date on which the patent application becomes prior art?

> Illustration 3-20. Gisela files a patent application in Japan on January 1, 2012 that is subsequently published. On January 1, 2013, within the 12-month period of Paris priority, Gisela files patent applications in Germany and in the United States. In Germany and the United States, when does Gisela's patent application become a prior art reference, January 1, 2012 or January 1, 2013?

In Germany, Gisela's patent application becomes prior art on January 1, 2012, the Paris priority date. In the United States prior to the America Invents Act, Gisela's patent application becomes prior art on January 1, 2013, its actual filing date in the United States, not on its Paris priority date. After the America Invents Act, the result in the United States is the same as in Germany: the application becomes a prior art reference on the Paris priority date.

Note that we are now using Paris priority dates in a different sense than we used the dates in our discussion of Paris priority in an earlier part of this chapter. Previously, we had used Paris priority to establish the earliest filing date of an application that is competing with another application to win the patent. In this context, Paris priority is being asserted by an application that is in competition with another application for the patent based upon the first to file approach used to resolve priority disputes. This is known as *defensive use* of Paris priority, which is how Paris priority is most often used.

> Illustration 3-21. Albrecht files a patent application in Germany on January 1, 2024. Cato files an application for the same invention in the United States on August 1, 2024. On January 1, 2025 Albrecht files a patent application in the United States. Albrecht claims a U.S. filing date of January 1, 2024, the Paris priority date. Albrecht argues that Paris priority immunizes or protects his January 1, 2024 filing from events in other Paris Union countries that would otherwise defeat his patent application for a period of 12 months, such as Cato's filing in the United States on August 1, 2024. Abrecht is engaging in a defensive use of Paris priority. Albrecht is using Paris priority to establish the priority of his own patent

application and will win the patent in the United States.

In the defensive uses of Paris priority, the claimant is arguing that its *own* patent application has the benefit of the Paris priority date in a priority dispute with another patent application. All countries in the Paris Union have agreed from the beginnings of the Paris Convention that in a defensive context, the applicant is allowed to assert the Paris priority date.

In the present context of viewing patent applications as prior art, we are examining the *offensive use* of Paris priority. Asserting that a patent application is prior art is always done for the purpose of invalidating another's patent or patent application and not for the purpose of claiming priority for one's own application, which is defensive use of Paris priority. In the context of offensive use of Paris priority, a third party is using the Paris priority date of *someone else*'s patent application to "knock out" a patent that the third party is challenging.

Illustration 3-22. Ajax corporation sues Bello company for patent infringement in U.S. federal district court. In response, Bello argues that Ajax's patent is invalid because it was disclosed in a previously filed patent application by Nemo. Nemo filed a patent application in Italy on July 1, 2010 which was later published and granted and then Nemo filed a U.S. patent application on June 8, 2011. Ajax filed its patent in the United States on May 5, 2011. Bello argues that Nemo's Italian patent application became prior art in the United Sates on July 1, 2010, its Paris priority date, and that it defeats the Ajax patent for lack of novelty as Ajax's application was filed later on May 5, 2011.

Bello is attempting an *offensive use* of Paris priority. Bello is arguing that someone else's patent application, i.e. Nemo's application, became prior art in the United States on July 1, 2010, its Paris priority date, in order to "knock out" the Ajax patent. As this case arose prior to the effective date of the America Invents Act of March 16, 2013, the federal district court rejects Bello's claim and holds that the Nemo application's actual U.S. filing date of June 8, 2011 is the date on which the Nemo application becomes prior art in the United States. As Ajax's U.S. patent application was earlier filed on May 5, 2011, the Nemo filing is not a prior art reference.

Unlike in the case of defensive use, countries could not agree on the offensive use of the Paris priority date. The EU and most countries allowed the offensive use of Paris priority, i.e. a third party is allowed to assert the Paris priority date of someone else's patent application as the date that it became a prior art reference. Prior to the America Invents Act, the United States took a different approach. In cases of offensive use, the actual filing date in the United States, not the Paris priority date, is the date that the filing becomes prior art. In Illustration 3-15 above, Nemo's actual patent filing date in the United States of June 8, 2011 is the date the application becomes a prior art reference so Ajax's patent application, previously on filed on May 5, 2011, is valid.

Studiengesellschaft Kohle MBH (SGK) v. Eastman Kodak Co., 616 F.2d 1315 (5th Cir. 1980) involved both offensive and defensive uses of Paris priority in the same case. SGK sued Eastman Kodak for patent infringement. In response, Kodak claimed that SGK's patent was invalid because it had been disclosed in a patent application filed by Professor Natta in Italy on July 27, 1954. Within the 12-month period of Paris priority, Natta then filed for a U.S. patent on June 8, 1955. Kodak claimed that Natta's Italian patent application became a prior art reference in the United States on July 27, 1954, its Paris priority date. Note that Kodak did not own the Natta patent but was attempting to use it as a prior art reference to "knock out" the SKG patent. This is an offensive use of Paris priority.

The inventor of SGK's patent filed a German patent application on August 3, 1954 and then a U.S. application on June 8, 1955 within the period of Paris priority. SGK claimed a U.S. filing date for its patent of August 3, 1954, the German filing date, which is also the Paris priority date. SGK is asserting the Paris priority date for the benefit of its own patent application in the United States. This is a defensive use of Paris priority.

The court found that SGK was entitled to a U.S. filing date of August 3, 1954, its Paris priority date. SGK's defensive use of Paris priority was successful. Following the approach set forth in *Application of Hilmer*, 359 F.2d 859 (Fed. Cir 1966) (*Hilmer I*), the court rejected Kodak's attempted offensive use of the Paris priority date of the Natta Italian patent application for prior art purposes. The court found that the Natta patent was not entitled to a U.S. filing date of July 27, 1954, the Italian filing date, which is also the Paris priority date, but had to fall back on its actual filing date in the United States of June 8, 1955. As the SGK patent had a U.S. filing date of August 3, 1954, its novelty was not defeated by prior art because the Natta patent did not become a prior art reference until its actual U.S. filing date of June 8, 1955.

SGK was entitled to assert its Paris priority date because SGK was engaged in a defensive use of Paris priority. Kodak was not allowed to assert the Paris priority date of the Natta patent application because Kodak was engaged in an offensive use of Paris priority. (If Kodak had owned the Natta patent then Kodak could have asserted the July 27, 1954 Paris priority date because Kodak would have been asserting a defensive use of Paris priority.)

Under the U.S. approach as set forth in *Hilmer I*, fewer U.S. patents will be "knocked out" as *Hilmer I* requires the use of the U.S. filing date as the effective date of the prior art reference instead of the earlier Paris priority date. Recall that the United States had also imposed a geographical limit on prior art. There appears to be a consistent theme in U.S. patent law before the America Invents Act: U.S. patent law permitted more U.S. patents to be granted and fewer U.S. patents to be "knocked out" by prior art references, favoring the United States over the EU (and other jurisdictions) as a place to file patents and to invest.

iv. The U.S. Approach After the America Invents Act

The America Invents Act now harmonizes the U.S. approach to prior art with the approach in the EU. Once again it is important to understand that for about the next decade, the United States has two approaches to the offensive use of Paris priority dates for prior art purposes.

For all patent applications filed in the United States before the effective date of the America Invents Act on March 16, 2013, the Paris priority date is not the effective date for prior art purposes; the actual U.S. filing date is the effective date. For all patents filed in the United States on or after March 16, 2013, the United States approach is the same as that of the EU: the Paris priority date is the date that the foreign filing becomes a prior art reference. After the effective date of the America Invents Act, the Paris priority date can now be used for both defensive and offensive purposes.

3. NON-OBVIOUSNESS OR INVENTIVE STEP

A second requirement of patent that is closely related to novelty is non-obviousness or inventive step. The term "non-obviousness" is found in U.S. patent law while the term "inventive step" is found in EU law. Footnote 5 of TRIPS makes clear that the two terms are synonymous. Section 103 of the U.S. Patent Code provides that a "patent may not be obtained . . . if the difference between the subject matter sought to be patented and the prior art are such that the subject matter as a whole would have been obvious . . . to a person having ordinary skill in the art." EU Patent Convention Article 56 is similar: "An invention shall be considered as involving an inventive step if, having regard to the state of the art, it is not obvious to a person skilled in the art."

As we have already seen novelty is required because patents are reserved only for those inventions that add to the existing stock of human knowledge. An invention that has never been made before, while novel, may still be ineligible for patent if, based upon prior art, it is obvious. Such an invention does not add to the stock of human knowledge and does not merit a patent.

a. Tests of Non-Obviousness or Inventive Concept

One of the issues with the analysis of non-obviousness or inventive step is the bias of hindsight. The analysis is necessarily retrospective as it asks would the invention have been obvious at some point before it was invented. The problem is that what seems obvious in the present may not have been obvious at the point in time of the invention. History is full of examples of how some crucial event or development that seems obvious in hindsight was missed by everybody at some point in the past. Lower courts have attempted to create tests that will avoid the trap of hindsight. One such test is the "teaching, suggestion, or motivation" (TSM) approach set forth by the Federal Circuit that was discussed and criticized by the Supreme Court in *KSR International v. Teleflex, Inc.*, 550 U.S. 398 (2007).

In *KSR International*, Teleflex sued KSR for infringing a patent claim for combining an electric sensor with a gas pedal of an automobile so that the pedal's position can be controlled by a computer. In its defense, KSR claimed that Teleflex's patent was invalid because it was obvious. To determine obviousness the trial court applied the TSM approach developed by the Federal Circuit, which holds that a patent is obvious only if some teaching, suggestion, or motivation to combine the prior art teachings can be found in the prior art. The Federal Circuit below had applied the TSM test and found Teleflex's patent to be non-obvious. On appeal, the Supreme Court reversed.

The Supreme Court criticized the TSM test as too rigid and narrow. The test requires the patent examiner to scour the prior art to find a TSM and if the examiner, under time pressures to review many applications, does not find a TSM, then the invention is non-obvious. Although the Court criticized the TSM test, the Court did not reject it altogether. In doing so, the Court reaffirmed the principles set forth in *Graham v. John Deere Co. of Kansas City*, 383 U.S. 1 (1966), which set forth an expansive and flexible inquiry that allowed courts to look at secondary considerations, such as commercial success, unsolved needs, and the failure of others.

The *KSR* case established that it is permissible to look beyond the specific problem that the patentee is trying to solve when determining the obviousness of the invention. The issue is not whether the combination was obvious to the inventor but to a person of ordinary skill in the art. The Supreme Court rejected the notion that a person of ordinary skill in the art attempting to solve a problem will look only to those elements of the prior art designed to deal with the specific problem. Many inventors are trying to solve several problems at once and many examine multiple fields of prior art and combine multiple prior art references. Prior art used to solve a different problem might lead to a solution to the problem that the inventor is trying to solve.

The Court further noted that commercial considerations can be relevant in deciding what is obvious. If there is a design need or market pressure to solve a problem and only a few predictable solutions, a person of ordinary skill in the art who pursues those options might successfully solve the problem, but the invention is not an innovation but the obvious use of ordinary skill and common sense. Using this approach, the Court found that the patent claim involved in *KSR* was obvious because a computer-controlled gas pedal had been previously invented. The Teleflex invention to mount a sensor to the pedal was an obvious step to try in response to commercial needs.

As the Supreme Court did not reject the TSM test outright, it is still valid but the Court made clear that it is not the exclusive test. The TSM test is one part of a broad-based approach to determining obviousness.

b. Person of Ordinary Skill in the Art

Another important issue has to do with the perspective that one assumes to evaluate non-obviousness or inventive step. If one assumed the perspective of a ten year old child then nothing will be obvious while if one assumed the perspective of a genius for the ages like Einstein or Newton then all inventions of modern science and technology might be obvious. The standard used in the United States and the EU is a person of ordinary skill in the art (POSA). The POSA is a hypothetical person who is not the inventor. The POSA in patent law stands in a similar position to the reasonable person used for negligence determinations in tort law.

The High Court of Justice of England and Wales offered an interesting and entertaining analysis of the POSA under EU law in *Sandox GMBH v. Roche Diagnostics GMBH*, EWHC 1313 (Ch.), HC–2003–03648 (2004). In that case, Roche Diagnostics had obtained a patent for a combination of two or more of three existing injectable protein formulations. The combination was important because it acted to more effectively preserve the proteins. Claimant Sandoz sought to invalidate Roche's patent on the ground that the combination lacked an inventive step, i.e. that it was obvious to try, and was not qualified for patent.

To be ineligible for patent, combining the existing formulations must have been obvious to a person of ordinary skill in the art. Turning to the issue of what is a POSA, the court referred to the POSA as a "boring nerd." The court noted that while a dictionary definition of a nerd is a person of awkward social skills, the concept in patent law referred to a skilled technician with an unlimited capacity to absorb information but without any imagination or inventive capacity. The POSA can even be a team of boring nerds although the court found it unnecessary to posit such a team in this case. The court found that even if a team is posited the POSA would most likely rely on the opinion of the protein scientist in the group. The court found that the concept of combining the protein formulations was the result of hindsight. Nothing at the time would have made it obvious to a POSA to take single doses of injectable protein to make a combination of preservatives.

Even though the Court engaged in a witty discussion of the POSA as a boring nerd or team of boring nerds, the EU formulation is not very difficult from the U.S. position that the POSA is a "skilled mechanic" that was first set forth in *Hotchkiss v. Greenwood*, 52 U.S. 248 (1851): a hypothetical person who has the ordinary skills in the field and who is technically proficient but not particularly imaginative.

c. Paris Priority Date and Obviousness

Countries generally agree that a Paris priority date cannot be used to evaluate obviousness. This can lead to a court two using two different dates in evaluating a patent: one for novelty and one for non-obviousness.

Illustration 3-23. Maximus company sues Nexus company for patent infringement. Nexus argues

> that the Maximus's patent is invalid for lack of novelty or, in the alternative, for obviousness. Nexus asserts a patent owned by Professor Walters to "knock out" Maximus's patent. Walters's patent was first filed in the UK on February 1, 2024 and then in the United States on February 1, 2025. For the lack of novelty claim, Nexus is able to assert the Paris priority date of February 1, 2024 as the date on which Walters's patent application became a prior art reference. (See the discussion above on offensive uses of Paris priority.) For the obviousness claim, Nexus must assert the February 1, 2025 actual U.S. filing date.

The reason for the difference in treatment may be that in a novelty claim, one single prior art reference must contain all of the elements of the invention while in an obviousness claim several different prior art references can be combined. The more relaxed standard for non-obviousness may have led the courts restrict the use of Paris priority filings.

4. UTILITY OR INDUSTRIAL APPLICATION

A third requirement of patent is utility or industrial application. Footnote 5 of TRIPS states that utility and industrial application are synonymous. The terms "useful" or "utility" are found in U.S. law while the terms "industrial application" are used by the EU.

Although TRIPS refers to the terms as synonymous, they may not be equivalent in practice. Useful may be a broader term than industrial application. The terms "industrial application" connote a public sphere of industry and commerce while the term useful can apply both in a public sphere as well as a purely private and personal sphere. For example, a method of smoking or personal grooming can be useful but is not a method that is capable of industrial application. This disparity could lead to inventions that will obtain a patent in the United States, but not in the EU. No case of this type has arisen but the possible disparity between the two sets of terms has led the World Intellectual Property Organization to draft articles to harmonize them.

5. ENABLEMENT

The three requirements of patent that we have examined so far—novelty, non-obviousness or inventive step, and useful or capable of industrial application—are substantive elements. TRIPS Article 29 adds a fourth requirement that is procedural in nature. Article 29(2) states that "[m]embers shall require that an applicant for a patent shall disclose the invention in a manner sufficiently clear and complete for the invention to be carried out by a person skilled in the art." Section 112(a) of the U.S. Patent Code contains the enablement requirement. Failure to meet the enablement requirement under U.S. law results in an invalid patent. The basic idea behind the enablement requirement is the quid pro quo of patent: in exchange for monopoly rights, the patent owner fully discloses the invention so that it can become part of the public domain once the patent has expired.

A question that may arise is whether a country can impose disclosure requirements for patent applications that go beyond the requirements of Article 29. TRIPS sets forth minimum standards so in theory a country can go beyond the requirements of Article 29. Suppose, however, that a country requires an extreme amount of specificity and detail in its applications. If the additional requirements impose unreasonable burdens on inventors so as to discourage or prevent patent applications, then the requirements are in violation of TRIPS. If such excessive requirements are imposed only on foreign applications, then the requirements will violate the most favored nation principle of TRIPS Article 4. If such requirements are imposed on all applications, then they may violate Article 27(1), which states that "patents shall be available for any inventions." Excessive requirements limit the availability of patents.

G. PATENT RIGHTS

Aside from Paris priority and national treatment, the Paris Convention did not create significant rights for patents. Countries of the Paris Union could not reach agreement on substantive patent rights, leaving patent rights up to each country to decide for itself.

TRIPS breaks new ground by setting forth minimum substantive rights for patents in Article 28.

TRIPS

Article 28
Rights Conferred

1. A patent shall confer on its owner the following exclusive rights:

(a) where the subject matter of a patent is a product, to prevent third parties not having the owner's consent from the acts of: making, using, offering for sale, selling, or importing for these purposes that product;

(b) where the subject matter of a patent is a process, to prevent third parties not having the owner's consent from the act of using the process, and from the acts of: using, offering for sale, selling, or importing for these purposes at least the product obtained directly by that process.

Article 28(1) divides patent rights into two categories: (a) patent rights for products and (b) patent rights for processes. For products, the patent owner has the right to prevent unauthorized third parties from making, using, offering for sale, selling or importing the product. For process patents, the patent owner has the right to prevent the use of the process. If products are made from the use of the process, the owner then also has the right to prevent the use, sale, or importing of the product.

1. PATENTS AND TERRITORIALITY

In the modern world economy, products, production methods, and processes often have a connection with more than one country as manufacture and supply chains have become global in scope. These developments give rise to recurring issues relating to the territorial limits on U.S. patent law. Some of the most common issues are discussed below.

In *Deep South Packing Co., Inc. v. Laitram Corp.*, 406 U.S. 518 (1972), the defendant produced and shipped from the United States all of the component parts of machinery used to de-vein and process shrimp to locations abroad where the parts were assembled into complete machines. The machines were covered by U.S. patents. The Supreme Court held that the defendant's acts in the United States of producing and shipping the component parts abroad did not violate the patents because the patents covered the assembled or finished machines. The assembly of the machines abroad did not violate the patents as this activity occurred outside the United States and the reach of the U.S. patent laws.

The result in *Deep South* led Congress to amend the patent statute to its current version, which reads as follows

35 U.S.C. § 271

* * *

(f) (1) Whoever without authority supplies or causes to be supplied in or from the United States all or a substantial portion of the components of a patented invention, where such components are uncombined in whole or in part, in such manner as to actively induce the combination of such components outside of the

> United States in a manner that would infringe the patent if such combination occurred within the United States, shall be liable as an infringer.

Under the current statute, supplying components from the United States that are later assembled abroad can be a violation if the parts are supplied in a manner to induce the combination abroad.

A more recent case that involved an attempt to expand the scope of § 272(f)(1) is *Pellegrini v. Analog Devices, Inc.*, 375 F.3d 1113 (Fed. Cir. 2004). The plaintiff claimed that the defendant violated its patent for a computer chip under § 272(f)(1) even though the defendant never engaged in any manufacturing or sales of the chips in the United States. The defendant had its chips manufactured and assembled abroad and sold them abroad. Pelligrini, the patent owner, argued that the defendant had its headquarters in the United States, designed its chips in the United States, and provided instructions from the United States for the production and sale abroad of the chips. Pelligrini argued that these actions were acts within the United States that triggered liability under § 272(f)(1). The Federal Circuit rejected this argument and drew a bright line. The court ruled that the components must be physically present in the United States and then shipped abroad where they are assembled and sold.

NTP, Inc. v. Research in Motion, Ltd., 418 F.3d 1282 (Fed. Cir. 2005) involved territorial limitations applied to both a product claim and a process claim under § 271(a), the provision of the U.S. Patent Code that sets forth what constitutes infringement. Section 271(a) provides that an infringement occurs whenever an unauthorized party "makes, uses, offers to sell, or sells any patented invention, within the United States." Plaintiff NTP had a U.S. product patent for a telecommunications system for e-mail and a U.S. process patent for the method used by the system. Defendant Research in Motion (RIM) provided e-mail service for its customers in the United States that used a relay network located in Canada.

The Federal Circuit found that RIM had used NTP's patented telecommunications system in the United States when its U.S. customers received and sent e-mails even though the RIM e-mails used a relay network located in Canada. The court found that because RIM customers manipulated their handheld devices in the United States to send and receive e-mails, the use of the telecommunication system was in the United States.

The Federal Circuit found, however, that RIM had not violated the process claim. Citing precedent, the court emphasized that a process claim is not violated unless each step of the process is utilized. The court further found that for a use to be infringing, each step of the process must occur within the United States. In this case, one step, the interface with the relay network occurred in Canada, outside the reach of U.S. patent law. The court concluded that RIM did not infringe the process claim.

The court also noted that although § 271(a) refers to several acts: makes, uses, offers to sell or sells any patented invention, the only act that directly pertains to a process is "use." The court arrived at this conclusion through an examination of legislative history and emphasized that TRIPS Article 27 only directly prohibits use of process patents.

2. PATENTS AND FOREIGN PROFITS

The U.S. Supreme Court weighed in on the application of § 271 by awarding foreign lost profits to the U.S. patent owner in *WesternGeco LLC v. ION Geophysical Corp.*, 585 U.S. 407 (2018). WesternGeo claimed that ION Geophysical Corp. violated § 271(f)(2) by shipping components of a competing system for surveying the ocean floor to countries abroad for assembly into complete systems indistinguishable from WesternGeo's patented system. Section 271(f)(2) is similar to § 271(f)(1) involved in *Deep South* and *Pellegrini* except Section 271(f)(2) refers to shipment of a specialized component or components abroad instead of a complete set of parts as required by § 271(f)(1). The district court awarded WesternGeo damages of $93.4 million in lost profits due to losing 10 specific survey contracts from companies abroad. The Federal Circuit reversed, holding that that foreign lost profits could not be recovered as that would be an extraterritorial application of § 271(f)(2).

On appeal, the Supreme Court reversed the Federal Circuit, holding that foreign profits are recoverable. The Court found that the focus of the relevant statute, § 271(f)(2), was on domestic conduct, i.e., the act of infringement that occurred in the United States, even though other conduct may have also occurred abroad. The act of infringement was the supplying of the specialized components from the United States with an inducement to assemble them abroad in breach of § 271(f)(2). Section 284, the damages provision in the U.S. Patent Code, provides that the court "shall award the claimant damages adequate to compensate for the infringement." The Court found that the award of lost foreign profits compensates for the infringing conduct that occurred in the United States. Awarding lost foreign profits does not involve an exterritorial application of U.S. patent law. In his dissent, Justice Gorsuch disagreed. He argued that awarding foreign lost profits was an illegitimate extraterritorial application of U.S. patent law.

H. EXCEPTIONS TO PATENT

This section covers exceptions to patent rights under TRIPS. Two articles deal with exceptions to patent, Article 30 and Article 31. Article 30 is a general exceptions provision. Article 31 deals with compulsory licenses.

1. GENERAL EXCEPTIONS

TRIPS

Exceptions to Rights Conferred

Article 30

Members may provide limited exceptions to the exclusive rights conferred by a patent, provided that such exceptions do not unreasonably

> conflict with a normal exploitation of the patent and do not unreasonably prejudice the legitimate interests of the patent owner, taking account of the legitimate interests of third parties.

A WTO panel engaged in an extensive interpretation and analysis of Article 30 in *Canada—Patent Protection of Pharmaceutical Products*, WT/DS114/R (March 7, 2000). The dispute concerned whether two exceptions contained in the Canadian Patent Act that applied to pharmaceuticals from the European Community (EC) were consistent with Article 30. The first exception was the so-called "regulatory review" exception contained in § 55.2(1) of the Act, which permitted unauthorized third parties to "make, construct, use or sell the patented invention solely for . . . the development and submission of information . . . required under any law of Canada . . . that regulates the manufacture, construction, use or sale of any product." The second exception was the "stock-piling exception" set forth in § 55.2(2) of the Act, which permitted the "making or use of the invention during the patent term for the manufacture and storage of articles intended for sale after the date on which the term of the patent expires." The EC challenged these exceptions before a WTO panel.

Canada enacted these exceptions due to the special set of circumstances surrounding the patenting and marketing of pharmaceuticals. Under a first to file system, inventors file for patents as soon as possible to prevent competitors from obtaining the patent first. After the inventor or patent owner obtains the patent, the patent owner must then first obtain regulatory approval from government authorities before the drug can be sold to the public. In the case of Canada, the approval process normally takes 8–12 years. Since the 20-year patent term runs from the date of filing, the approval process will leave only 8–12 years or about 40–60 percent of the patent term left in which the patent owner can commercially exploit the patent. Once the patent has expired, generic drugs will then enter the market usually at much lower prices. Generic pharmaceuticals must also undergo a regulatory approval process. Normally the process for generic drugs takes 3 to 6½ years.

For generic drug makers to obtain regulatory approval, they would have to make copies of the patented drug. If copies are made during the term of the patent, these actions would normally constitute an infringement of the patent. If generic drug makers had to wait until the expiration of the patent to make the drugs and begin the process of obtaining regulatory approval, it would cause a delay of 3 to 6 ½ years after the expiration of the patent before their generic drugs could be sold. The purpose of the regulatory review exception was to allow generic drug makers to make the drugs and obtain regulatory approval of the drug during the term of the patent so that the generic drugs can be sold as soon as the patent expires.

A similar reasoning lies behind the stockpiling exception. To manufacture a commercial supply of generic drugs and to deliver them to pharmacies could take several months. If drug makers had to wait until the patent expired to begin producing commercial quantities, generic drugs might not reach pharmacies and become available to consumers for several months. The stockpiling exception allows generic drug makers to produce a commercial supply starting six months before the expiration of the patent and to keep the supply in storage until the patent expires. This way if the patent expires on a Friday, the generic drugs could be on the shelves of the pharmacies on Monday, if not sooner.

The EC argued that both exceptions violated Article 30 of TRIPS, the general exceptions provision. The panel concluded that the stockpiling exception violated Article 30 but that the regulatory review exception did not.

The panel analyzed TRIPS Article 30 and found that it contained three conditions.

(1) The exception must be "limited;"

(2) The exception must not "unreasonably conflict with a normal exploitation of the patent;" and

(3) The exception "must not unreasonably prejudice the legitimate interests of the patent owner taking account of the legitimate interests of third parties."

The conditions are cumulative; each must be satisfied. Failure to satisfy one condition means that the measure in question fails and there is no need to go on with an analysis of the other conditions.

Turning first to the stockpiling exception, the panel considered that the word "limited" must refer to a small diminution of rights. In this case, the stockpiling exception allowed the generic drug makers to make any quantity of drugs with no limit on volume. In the panel's view, this was not a "limited" exception. As the three conditions are cumulative, the failure to meet the first condition meant that the stockpiling exception was in breach of TRIPS Article 30.

The panel reached a different conclusion on the regulatory review exception. The panel found that the regulatory review exception was "limited" within the meaning of the first condition. Generic drug makers were allowed to make and use the patented invention but only for the purposes of submitting information for review by government approval authorities. The drug makers were not allowed to make drugs for sale or use the drugs for any purpose other than obtaining approval. Also making and using drugs for regulatory review would involve small quantities, certainly not commercial quantities as was involved in the stockpiling exception. The panel found that the limitations on what the generic drugmakers could do in making and using the patented drug qualified the exception as limited.

The panel then turned to the second condition that the exception cannot unreasonably interfere with a normal exploitation of the patent. Most patents have a de facto period of marketing exclusivity after the expiration of the patent. A de facto period of marketing exclusivity occurs because competitors are not allowed to make or use the patent during its term but must wait until the patent expires. At this point, competitors will need a start-up period before they are ready to manufacture a competitive product that copies the now expired patent. In the case of pharmaceutical patents, the de facto period of exclusivity can last up to 6 ½ years as generic drug makers undergo regulatory approval. Canada argued that this de facto period of marketing exclusivity is not a normal exploitation of the patent. If Canada's argument is correct, then Canada's regulatory review exception, which removes the de facto period of post patent exclusivity by allowing regulatory review during the patent term, is not an interference with the normal exploitation of a patent.

The panel found that for many patents a brief period of market exclusivity after the patent expires is not abnormal. In the case of pharmaceutical patents, however, the lengthy period required to obtain marketing approval after the expiration of the patent was not a "normal exploitation" of the patent. The lengthy period of regulatory approval involved is created by the confluence of patent law and food and drug laws requiring government approval of pharmaceuticals before they can enter the market. This is a fortuitous consequence of the intersection of patent law and a regulatory regime that does not exist for patent cases outside of pharmaceuticals. So the delay cannot be viewed as a normal exploitation of the patent to burden a generic drug maker with the full length of the regulatory approval process.

Canada's removing the approval delay through a regulatory review exception does not conflict with the patent owner's normal exploitation of the patent.

The panel then considered the third condition: that the regulatory review exception "must not unreasonably prejudice the legitimate interests of the patent owner taking account of the legitimate interests of third parties." The EC argued that requiring innovator drug makers to obtain the required regulatory approvals during the patent term reduced the effective period of exclusivity to 40–60 percent of the 20-year patent term. The EC argued that patent owners should be able to impose the same type of delay on generic drug makers when they obtain regulatory approval for competing products.

The panel considered this to be a normative claim, i.e. a claim based what norms should be for the activity in question. The issue with the normative claim is that the norms in this area are unclear among nations, which have taken differing approaches on how to compensate the owner of pharmaceutical patents for the reduction in patent term. Some countries have enacted de jure extensions of the patent term, i.e. countries have extended the patent term at the back end to compensate for the reduction in the front end caused by having to seek regulatory approval. This group includes the EC, Switzerland, the United States, Japan, Australia, and Israel. The EC and Switzerland have granted patent extensions while also allowing patent owners to prevent generic drug makers from seeking regulatory approval during the term of the patent. This approach places the patent owner in a better position than they would have just under the patent alone. Other countries have issued patent extensions while also permitting a regulatory review exception, which has the effect of offsetting the negative effects of the regulatory review exception for both patent owners and generic drug makers. The final group of countries, which includes Canada, have adopted a regulatory review exception while not providing patent extensions. This approach places patent owners in a worse position by imposing the costs of the delay of regulatory review on patent owners but not on generic drug makers.

The panel found that the differing positions adopted by countries on how to deal with the delays of regulatory approval meant that there were no universal norms on the subject. Overall, the panel concluded that the claims of the EC patent owners whose effective period of marketing exclusivity was reduced were not so widely recognized as to be a "legitimate interest" within the meaning of the third condition. Since no legitimate interest of the patent owners had been breached, the regulatory review exception was consistent with Article 30.

Subsequently to *Canada—Patent Protection of Pharmaceutical Products,* Canada enacted a patent extension for pharmaceuticals to offset the diminution in patent term caused by the need to obtain regulatory approval. The combination of a regulatory review exception to benefit generic drug makers and a patent extension at the back end to benefit patent owners offsets the negative effects of the lengthy period necessary to obtain regulatory approval for both patent owners and for generic drug makers. Other countries adopting the same approach include the United Sates, Japan, Australia, and Israel. In the United States, the regulatory review exception was enacted by the Hatch-Waxman Act and is contained in 28 U.S.C. § 271(e).

2. TRIPS ARTICLE 31

a. Limits Imposed by Article 31

Article 31 is the provision that authorizes compulsory licenses. Compulsory licenses are used by some governments to redress perceived abuses in the use of patents. We have already encountered compulsory licenses in the discussion of local working requirements. In that context, governments sometimes issue compulsory licenses if a foreign patent owner refuses to use the patent in the country that granted the patent. This section will discuss compulsory licenses in connection with access to medicines.

Compulsory licenses, i.e. a license imposed on the patent owner by governmental authority, are viewed unfavorably by patent owners. When patent owners choose to enter into licenses, they carefully screen their licensees to ensure that the licensee will not abuse the licensing relationship by misusing or stealing the technology. Some license arrangements may also require the licensor to work with the licensee in a continuing relationship. Most licensors do not wish to be forced into a licensing arrangement with a licensee not of their own choosing. Compulsory licenses do not allow licensors to have any choice in the matter.

Reflecting the concerns of licensors, Article 31 authorizes compulsory licenses but within strict limits. Article 31 provides in relevant part:

TRIPS

Article 31
Other Use without Authorization of the Right Holder

Where the law of a Member allows for other use of the subject matter of a patent without the authorization of the right holder, including use by the government or third parties authorized by the government, the following provisions shall be respected:

* * *

(b) such use may only be permitted if, prior to such use, the proposed user has made efforts to obtain authorization from the right holder on reasonable commercial terms and conditions and that such efforts have not been successful within a reasonable period of time. This requirement may be waived by a Member in the case of a national emergency or other circumstances of extreme urgency . . . .

* * *

(f) any such use shall be authorized predominantly for the supply of the domestic market of the Member authorizing such use;

* * *

(h) the right holder shall be paid adequate remuneration in the circumstances of each case, taking into account the economic value of the authorization.

The main restrictions, reproduced above, fall into three categories.

First, the proposed licensee has a duty to first bargain with the licensor for a license based on reasonable commercial grounds. The compulsory license can be issued only if the negotiations are unsuccessful after a reasonable period of time. The duty to bargain can be waived in the case of a "national emergency or other circumstances of extreme urgency." Article 31 does not go on to define these terms or provide any further guidelines. This restriction means that a preemptory issuance of a compulsory license without first bargaining with the licensor is a violation of Article 31 unless it can be justified by a national emergency or a situation of extreme urgency.

Second, the use must be predominantly for the supply of the domestic market. The licensee is not authorized to export the licensed product. The drafters of Article 31 did not want the licensee to enter into the business of the international sale of the drugs. This restriction becomes an issue in the case of pharmaceuticals where the licensee seeks to export quantities to a least developing country without the capacity to produce the pharmaceuticals on its own.

Third, the licensor must be compensated for the license "based on the economic value of the license." This standard indicates that the licensor must be compensated for the market value of the license, i.e. royalties comparable to those that the licensor would receive if it voluntarily chose to license the patent.

b. Access to Medicines Debate

The propriety of the strict limits imposed on compulsory licenses by Article 31 erupted into an international controversy over access to life saving medicines. With the development of drugs treating HIV/AIDS, a debate arose on whether multinational pharmaceutical companies should be allowed to charge monopoly prices enabled by patents for the drugs as many developing countries lacked the resources to meet high prices.

Multinational pharmaceutical companies argued that the prices were justified as a means to recoup the substantive investments in research and development for the drugs. An appropriate financial reward for the drugs would encourage companies to develop new drugs for the future while depriving companies of such profits would discourage innovation. Critics of multinational companies responded by claiming that they put profits ahead of people.

At first the U.S. government supported multinational pharmaceutical companies but two high profile cases led the U.S. government to reverse its position. One case involved Brazil's compulsory licensing scheme, which was credited with reducing the mortality rates among Brazil's approximately 536,000 population infected with HIV/AIDS by about 50 percent. The United States brought a challenge against Brazil's compulsory licensing law in the WTO dispute settlement system arguing that the law was inconsistent with Article 31. The Brazilian law allowed for a compulsory license if the patent holder "exercises his rights derived therefrom in an abusive manner, or by means thereof engages in abuse of economic power." The law contained no requirement of a duty to bargain, use predominantly for the domestic market, or adequate compensation to be paid to the licensor.

The WTO case against Brazil ignited concern among non-governmental organizations and developing countries as the Brazilian compulsory licensing law served as a model for how to obtain access to medicines. Brazil had used the threat of a compulsory license to pressure pharmaceutical companies to lower their prices. As noted earlier, many companies find compulsory licenses to be highly objectionable and would rather lower their prices than be forced to submit to such an arrangement. The WTO case threatened to upend this scheme by invalidating the Brazilian law and undermining Brazil's approach. Objections by non-governmental organizations, developing countries, and other critics led the United States to drop the WTO case against Brazil. A similar case involving South Africa's compulsory licensing scheme also followed the same pattern. At first, the United States supported its companies in challenging the South African compulsory licensing scheme, but then withdrew support after public outcry and backlash. Without U.S. government support, the multinational companies' challenges to these compulsory licensing schemes quickly collapsed.

By the time of the fourth ministerial conference in 2001, developing countries had managed to include the access to medicines issue as one of the main topics for discussion at the conference. The result of these efforts was the Doha Ministerial Declaration on TRIPS and Public Health adopted on November 2, 2001. The relevant provisions of the Declaration are set forth below:

DOHA Ministerial Declaration on the TRIPS Agreement and Public Health

1. We recognize the gravity of the public health problems afflicting many developing and least-developed countries, especially those resulting from HIV/AIDS, tuberculosis, malaria and other epidemics.

* * *

4. We agree that the TRIPS Agreement does not and should not prevent members from taking measures to protect public health. . .

5. Accordingly and in the light of paragraph 4 above, while maintaining our commitments in the TRIPS Agreement, we recognize that these flexibilities include:

* * *

b. Each member has the right to grant compulsory licenses and the freedom to determine the grounds upon which such licenses are granted.

c. Each member has the right to determine what constitutes a national emergency or other circumstances of extreme urgency, it being understood that public health crises, including those relating to HIV/AIDS, tuberculosis, malaria and other epidemics, can represent a national emergency or other circumstances of extreme urgency.

The Doha Declaration significantly alters the interpretation and effect of Article 31. Recall that Article 31 includes a duty to bargain with the patent owner that can be waived only in the case of a "national emergency or other circumstances of extreme urgency." Paragraph 5(c) of the Doha Declaration gives each WTO member the right to determine what constitutes a national emergency or circumstances of extreme urgency. In practice, this right means that any WTO country can waive the duty to bargain.

Paragraph 5(b) gives each member "the right to grant compulsory licenses and the freedom to determine the grounds on which such licenses are granted." This provision allows the country granting the license to determine what compensation, if any, is owed to the licensor. In practice, this means that the duty to provide adequate renumeration to the patent owner no longer exists.

The Doha Declaration recognized that certain countries at a low level of development might not have the technical capabilities to use a compulsory license even if one were granted. The ministers recognized this as a special problem and instructed as follows in the Doha Declaration:

> 6. We recognize that WTO members with insufficient or no manufacturing capacities in the pharmaceutical sector could face difficulties in making effective use of compulsory licensing under the TRIPS Agreement. We instruct the Council for TRIPS to find an expeditious solution to this problem and to report to the General Council before the end of 2002.

This instruction led to a decision of the General Council issued on August 30, 2003 entitled "Implementation of Paragraph 6 of the Doha Declaration on the TRIPS Agreement and Public Health." The Implementation Decision authorized the creation of a system in which a country that had issued a compulsory license could export quantities of drugs to a qualified importing member, a least developed country without the capacity to use a compulsory license. The Implementation Decision was careful to indicate that drugs manufactured under the scheme had to be notified to the WTO, be specially labeled and marked, and could not be diverted to other export markets. The Implementation Decision waived the requirement under Article 31(f) that the use of the compulsory license was primarily for domestic purposes only.

Although the Doha Declaration and Implementation Decision authorized a system of compulsory licenses for pharmaceuticals, few compulsory licenses have ever been actually granted. The real value to countries is a credible threat of issuing a compulsory license, not the actual issuance of the license itself. Faced with a credible threat of a compulsory license, pharmaceutical companies lowered their prices. The special problem identified by ¶ 6 of the Doha Declaration is that least developed countries do not have a credible threat since they do not have the capability of using a compulsory license. The Implementation Decision solved that problem by creating a system that gives them a credible threat. Pharmaceutical companies are faced with the nightmare scenario of a thriving international black market created by drugs exported under a compulsory license that were intended for a least developed country but were diverted to developed country markets. Such a threat gives least developed countries the means to pressure pharmaceutical companies to reduce their prices.

The developments concerning access to medicines indicates that developing countries have been able to effectively assert their concerns in the WTO in certain areas of intellectual property. Article 31 was drafted to protect patent owners and to favor developed countries, such as the United States. The Doha Declaration and the Implementation Decision illustrates the ability of developing countries to use the WTO to nullify the strict constraints of Article 31. This is an indication of the growing influence of developing countries and their ability and skill in the WTO to assert their rights effectively in the area of intellectual property. Overall, developing countries have made great strides in the WTO, but it is not possible to state that developing countries have been able to obtain satisfactory results in every area of intellectual property where they have concerns.

CHAPTER 4

TRADEMARKS AND GEOGRAPHICAL INDICATIONS

A. OVERVIEW

Under U.S. law, a trademark is "any word, name, symbol, or device or any combination thereof" used to distinguish goods from those of others and to indicate the source of the goods. 15 U.S.C. § 1127. A trademark refers to the source of goods, while a service mark refers to the provider of services. Despite this historical distinction, the term "trademark" is now used for both goods and services.

Distinctiveness is the touchstone of trademark, just as originality was the hallmark of copyright and novelty was the criterion of patent. A trademark must be distinctive because its function is to signal to consumers that goods or services are from a single source, i.e. a particular manufacturer or provider. The consumer may not know where the manufacturer is incorporated or where it has its headquarters. That is not relevant. What is important is that consumer identifies the products as being from one single source as opposed to another. If the product is from the same source and the consumer had a good experience with the product in the past the consumer can expect that the experience will also be good in the present. The consumer is saved the costs of a new search or investigation every time a consumer decision must be made. Imagine a weary and hungry traveler who arrives late at night after a long plane ride to a city in a foreign country where she does not know the language or the local customs or tastes. Such a consumer might be greatly relieved to find the familiar trademark of a popular chain restaurant from the United States.

Unlike patents and copyright, trademarks do not create exclusive rights. A patent or copyright owner can bring an infringement action against any unauthorized party who has copied the invention or the work. By contrast, a trademark owner cannot sue for infringement against an unauthorized party that copies and uses the trademark unless the use is likely to cause consumer confusion. In the case of an identical or substantially similar trademark that is used on identical or substantially similar goods (i.e. trademark counterfeiting), consumer confusion is presumed. In other cases, the trademark owner must prove likelihood of confusion in order to establish infringement. This rule is qualified for famous trademarks in the United States that receive special protection as further discussed below.

As this discussion suggests, another difference between trademarks and patents and copyrights is that trademarks must be used in commerce. Many jurisdictions provide that trademarks are subject to cancellation after a period of non-use in trade. The United States takes the position that actual use or intent to use is required to obtain a trademark and actual use is required to maintain it. Along with other common law jurisdictions, the United States takes the position that the first to use has the right to a trademark. Most jurisdictions take the position that the first to file acquires the trademark. We will return to this topic in further detail below on trademark priority disputes in the United States.

As trademarks are used in commerce they can be continuously renewed and can last indefinitely so long as they continue to distinguish the goods and services of the trademark owner. This is another distinction between trademarks on the one hand and copyrights and patents on the other. Copyrights and patents are subject to limited terms of protection while trademarks can endure indefinitely.

At common law, protection for trademarks arose as part of the law of unfair competition that prevented unauthorized parties from "passing off" their inferior goods as those of the trademark owner. Today the state common law or statutory law of unfair competition still protects trademark owners from the offense of "passing off" by unauthorized parties. An additional element of unfair competition law is that third parties should not be able to take a free ride on the goodwill created by the trademark. In this context, goodwill refers to the trust that the trademark has earned from consumers that increases its commercial value. A trademark owner that has invested the time and resources necessary to create a successful brand should not be subjected to others who seek to exploit that goodwill for their own gain.

Trademarks in the United States are not only protected by state law, but also by federal law. Unlike patent and copyright, which are explicitly recognized in the U.S. Constitution, no provision of the

Constitution refers expressly to trademarks. Based on the commerce clause, Congress has enacted the Lanham Act of 1946, 15 U.S.C. §§ 1105–1041. The Lanham Act allows trademark owners to register their trademarks with the United States Patent and Trademark Office. Registration has the effect of establishing constructive notice and use of the trademark from the date of registration effective throughout the United States, establishing priority over any junior users of the mark. Registration allows trademark owners to sue in federal court and, under § 526 of the Tariff Act of 1930, to enlist the aid of U.S. customs authorities in seizing counterfeit and infringing imports. The Lanham Act also recognizes a special category of famous marks that are entitled to additional protection against trademark dilution as further discussed below. As a result of the significant advantages of federal registration, the vast bulk of all commercially valuable trademarks are registered in the United States.

In addition to trademarks, this chapter will also consider geographical indications (GIs), which serve a similar function to trademarks. Article 22 of TRIPS defines GIs as "indications which identify a good as originating in the territory of a Member, or a region or locality in that territory, where a given quality, reputation, or other characteristic of the good is essentially attributable to its geographical origin." GIs are especially important for countries of the EU for foods, such as cheeses and meats, and for wines. Countries in Europe often name a wine or a cheese for the place or region that produces the item. This practice has used for hundreds or thousands of years in Europe. Examples include Champagne and Bordeaux for wines, Romano and Rocquefort for Cheese, and Welsh Lamb and Parma Ham for meats.

Including GIs in TRIPS represented a major victory for the EU, which has long pushed for international recognition of GIs as a distinct field of intellectual property. TRIPS does not require, however, a separate legal regime for GIs. Although the United States is bound by TRIPS to recognize GIs, the United States uses trademark and related laws to protect GIs. The United States is not very enthusiastic about GIs while some EU countries, including France, have been major champions of GIs on the international stage. Such a disagreement may not be all that surprising as most of the world's commercially valuable GIs are in EU countries. Some believe that this divergence might be a new world versus old world split. Countries in the EU have been identifying goods by the name of the place where they are produced for thousands of years, long pre-dating the establishment of the United States.

B. PARIS CONVENTION, TRIPS, AND THE MADRID SYSTEM

The preceding chapter examined the application of the Paris Convention to patents. The Paris Convention also applies to trademarks. The basic structure of the Paris Convention as applied to trademarks is the same as that of patents: Trademarks receive the benefit of Paris priority and national treatment. In the case of trademarks, the period of Paris priority is six months. The drafters of the Paris Convention believed that it takes less time to assess the commercial viability of a trademark in a foreign market.

As in the case of patents, the treatment of trademarks under the Paris Convention is independent of treatment in the country of origin. A Paris Union country cannot refuse to register a trademark because it has not been registered in its country of origin. Paris Conv., Article 6(2). Also as with patents, the Paris Convention is not concerned with how countries treat their own trademarks or trademark owners under domestic law but with how countries treat foreign trademarks and foreign trademark owners—with one notable exception. Under the "telle que" (French for "as is") provision of the Paris Convention, Article 6*quinquies*, once a trademark is registered in its country origin, other Paris Union countries must register the trademark "as is" without questioning the form of the trademark. What precisely constitutes the "form" of the trademark is further discussed below.

National treatment for trademarks prohibits countries from discriminating against foreign trademarks and trademark owners. As in the case of patents, the formalities required for trademark registration prevent the national treatment principle from creating a basket of national rights as was possible in the case of copyrights under the Berne Convention (as discussed in Chapter Two). In the case of trademarks, an applicant must file individual trademark applications in each country in which protection is sought or use the Madrid system for international registrations. The Madrid system is composed of two agreements that Paris Union countries have entered into pursuant to Article 19 of the Paris Convention that allows for special agreements. Paris Union countries also used Article 19 to enter into the Patent Cooperation Treaty.

The Madrid system is composed of the Madrid Agreement Concerning the International Registration of Marks (1891) (the Madrid Agreement) and the Madrid Protocol Relating to the Madrid Agreement Concerning the International Registration of Marks (1989) (the Madrid Protocol). The Madrid system facilitates the acquisition of trademark rights in foreign countries through the use of an international trademark registry administered by the World Intellectual Property Organization in Geneva. The United States is a member of the Madrid Protocol, but not the Madrid Agreement, which may explain why the Madrid Protocol has 115 members representing 130 countries while the Madrid Agreement has only 55 members. The members of the Madrid Protocol represent 80 percent of world trade. We examine the Madrid system in detail below.

Article 2(1) of TRIPS requires WTO members to adhere to Articles 1–12 and Article 19 of the Paris Convention covering trademarks. In addition, TRIPS adds Articles 15–21 for trademarks and 22–24 for geographical indications. Articles 15 and 16 of TRIPS treat service marks as trademarks. Both goods and services are covered by the term "trademark."

1. USE REQUIREMENTS AND REGISTRATION

Countries are divided as to whether trademark rights are acquired based on a registration or a use of the trademark. Civil law countries, such those in the EU, the UK, and China, follow a registration system awarding the trademark to the first person or entity to file for a trademark application that results in a registration without any requirement of a prior use of the trademark in commerce. The registration creates the trademark rights. By contrast, common law countries, such as the United States, Canada, and Australia, award trademarks to the first person to use the trademark in commerce without any requirement of a prior registration. The use in commerce creates the trademark, not the registration. The number of first to file countries outnumber first to use countries, although both approaches have numerous adherents.

Although countries follow two different approaches on how to acquire trademark rights, all countries must have a trademark registration system due to the requirement of TRIPS Article 15. Since all WTO countries now must have registration systems the difference between the two systems can be seen through some simple examples.

> Illustration 4-1. In a first to file system, Roman files for a trademark registration on April 1. Calmus files a registration for the same or a substantially similar trademark on April 20. No inquiry is made as to the use of the trademark. Based on the dates of filing, the registration for the trademark will be issued to Roman and

Calmus will be refused a trademark registration.

Illustration 4-2. In a first to use system, Gisela files for and obtains a trademark registration on February 1. Wilhemina has been using the trademark in commerce for the past three years but never files for a trademark registration. Wilhemina can cancel Gisela's trademark registration.

TRIPS does not take sides between the first to register and the first to use systems. TRIPS Article 15(3) states:

TRIPS

Article 15
Protectable Subject Matter

* * *

3. Members may make registrability depend on use. However, actual use of a trademark shall not be a condition for filing an application for registration. An application shall not be refused solely on the ground that intended use has not taken place before the expiry of a period of three years from the date of application.

Article 15(3) provides that while members can require use for trademark registration, they cannot require actual use in order to apply for registration. The result of this rule is that countries that require use, such as the United States, can only require an intent to use as part of the application for trademark registration. Further, if use is required to maintain a registration, then the registration may be cancelled "only after an uninterrupted period of at least three years of non-use unless valid reasons based on the existence of obstacles to such use are shown by the trademark owner." TRIPS, Article 19(1). In the United States, trademark applications can be filed based upon a statement of an intention to use the trademark. Lanham Act, § 1(b), 15 U.S.C. § 1051(b). The applicant must then file a verified statement that the trademark is actually being used in commerce within a specified time or the application will be rejected. 15 U.S.C. § 1051(d). Non-use of the trademark for a period of three years will be treated as an abandonment of the trademark.

In *Direct Niche, LLC v. Via Varejo S/A*, 898 F.3d 1144 (11th Cir. 2018), the court considered what constitutes use of a trademark in the United States by a foreign corporation. The dispute in this case concerned the use of a domain name casabahia.com. Direct Niche, a company based in Minnesota, purchased the domain name casabahia.com at an online auction. Direct Niche was in the business of registering domain names for resale or for selling advertising that is "parked" on the domain name. Via Varejo, a Brazilian company, owns the multi-billion dollar retail brand Casa Bahia with around 22,000 employees and 750 stores throughout Brazil. Via Varejo filed a complaint against Direct Niche under the Uniform Dispute Resolution Policy, a dispute system created to resolve domain name disputes. The system is administered by the World Intellectual Property Organization in Geneva, which issued a decision ordering Direct Niche to transfer the domain name to Via Varejo. Direct Niche then brought an action in federal district court under the Anti-Cybersquatting Consumer Protection Act for a declaratory judgement that its registration of the domain name was not unlawful. Via Varejo appeared in the federal district court action and claimed that Direct Niche registered the domain name in bad faith with the intention to profit from Via Varejo's common law service mark, Casa Bahia.com. The district court entered a declaratory judgment in favor of Via Varejo.

On appeal, the Eleventh Circuit had to consider whether Via Varejo acquired common law rights in the Casa Bahia trademark in the United States through use. If Via Varejo never had a trademark for Casa Bahai, Direct Niche could not have acted in bad faith. Via Varejo had never registered the trademark with the U.S. patent office so the issue turned on whether Via Varejo acquired trademark rights through use in U.S. commerce. As Via Varejo is a foreign corporation, the issue turned on how a business located abroad can acquire common law use rights in a trademark in the United States.

The court found that Via Varejo maintained a Casa Bahia website accessible in the United States and had used the trademark in U.S. commerce through its (1) preferred product placement program; (2) a banner advertising program; and (3) a marketplace seller program. U.S. companies such as Intel, Microsoft, Hewlett Packard, and Black & Decker purchased preferred product advertising that featured their products more prominently than other items regularly listed for sale. Via Varejo also used its banner advertising program to sell ad space to brokers such as Google, which would then populate the space with third party advertising. Via Varejo's marketplace seller program allowed third party vendors to display their products on the Via Varejo website. The court concluded that Via Varejo established use in U.S. commerce through these programs that sell advertising services to U.S. companies.

The court also rejected Direct Niche's argument that Via Varejo failed to satisfy the test for the exterritorial application of the Lanham Act set forth in *Steele v. Bulova Watch Co., Inc.*, 344 U.S. 280 (1952). The *Bulova* test focused on whether infringing acts that occur in a foreign country have substantial effects in the United States that would justify an exercise of exterritorial jurisdiction. The court rejected Direct Niche's argument because there was no act of infringement that occurred in foreign country. The act of infringement occurred in the United States, i.e. Direct Niche's act of registration. Via Varejo's use of the trademark also occurred in the United States through the sales of advertising for its website.

2. PARIS PRIORITY, TRADEMARKS, AND USE

A trademark application is entitled to assert the Paris priority filing date of a previous foreign trademark application. In the case of trademarks, the applicant has six months to file a second trademark application that can assert the Paris priority date of the prior foreign application. Paris Conv., Article 4(C). As in the case of patents, a trademark filing that is a regular national filing under the domestic law of any Paris Union country gives rise to the right of priority regardless of whether a trademark registration is ultimately issued or not. Paris Conv., Article 4(A)(3).

The D.C. Circuit Court of Appeals applied Paris priority to a trademark dispute involving use requirements in *SCM Corp. v. Langis Foods Ltd.*, 539 F.2d 196 (D.C. Cir. 1976). In that case, the dispute concerned who owned the U.S. trademarks for three brands: Lemon Tree, Apple Tree, and Orange Tree. Both Langis, a Canadian corporation, and SCM Corp., a U.S. company, argued that they owned the U.S. trademarks. SCM's claim for the trademarks was based on its prior use of the trademarks in the United States. Although three trademarks were involved, the D.C. Circuit focused its discussion on the Lemon Tree trademark.

On March 28, 1969, Langis filed trademark applications for Lemon Tree, Apple Tree, and Orange Tree in Canada. On May 15, 1969, Langis began using all three trademarks in Canada.

On September 19, 1969, within the six month period of Paris priority, Langis filed trademark applications for Apple Tree, Orange Tree, and Lemon Tree in the United States and obtained a registration for the Lemon Tree trademark.

On May 15, 1969, after Langis's Canadian filing on March 28, 1969, but before Langis's U.S. filing on

September 19, 1969, SCM Corp. began using the Lemon Tree trademark in the United States. Subsequently on June 18, 1969, SCM filed a trademark application for Lemon Tree with the U.S. patent office.

In June 1970, SCM began using Apple Tree and Orange Tree in the United States. On June 22, 1970, SCM filed applications for those two trademarks with the U.S. patent office.

SCM then brought an action in federal district court to cancel Langis's Lemon Tree trademark and to oppose Langis's applications for the Apple Tree and Orange Tree trademarks. The district court cancelled Langis's Lemon Tree trademark and remanded proceedings concerning Apple Tree and Orange Tree to the U.S. patent office. On appeal, the D.C. Circuit reversed the cancellation of the Lemon Tree trademark.

SCM argued that it was the first to use the Lemon Tree trademark in the United States and had acquired trademark rights through the use. As Langis had never used the Lemon Tree trademark in the United States, SCM argued that Langis's Lemon Tree trademark must be cancelled. SCM's argument was based on § 2(d) of the Lanham Act, which provided in relevant part:

> No trademark . . . shall be refused registration on the principal register on account of its nature unless it consists of or comprises a mark which so resembles . . . a mark or trade name

previously used in the United States by another and not abandoned.

The facts were uncontested that SCM first used Lemon Tree in the United States and did not abandon the trademark, and that Langis had never used the Lemon Tree trademark in the United States.

The D.C. Circuit rejected this argument. The court turned first to an examination of § 44(d) of the Lanham Act, which governs the effect to be given to U.S. trademark applications claiming the Paris priority date of a foreign filing. Section 44(d) provides that a U.S. trademark application filed by a foreign national "shall be accorded the same force and effect as would be accorded to the same application if filed in the United States on the same date on which the application was first filed in [the] foreign country." Interpreting § 44(d), the D.C. Circuit ruled that Langis's use of the Lemon Tree trademark in Canada after its foreign filing date on March 28, 1969 but before its U.S. filing date on September 19, 1969 gave it a *constructive* use date in the United States as of the March 28, 1969 Canadian filing date. Langis then had priority since its constructive use date in the United States of March 28, 1969 is prior to SCM's actual use date of May 15, 1969 so Langis should be awarded the Lemon Tree trademark.

The D.C. Circuit still had to deal with § 2(d) of the Lanham Act that prohibits the registration of a trademark "previously used in the United States by another." The D.C. Circuit reconciled the result in the case with the language of § 2(d) by noting that the word "previously" in § 2(d) should be read to mean "before the filing date in the Convention country." If SCM had used Lemon Tree in the United States before March 28, 1969, Langis's Canadian filing date, then SCM would have been awarded the Lemon Tree trademark in the United States.

In the *SCM* case, Langis used the trademarks in Canada so the D.C. Circuit did not have to deal directly with the issue of what would happen if Langis had never used the trademarks. The D.C. Circuit included a discussion of the possible positions on the use issue in a long and detailed footnote 12 to the opinion. Today, the issue appears to be settled. The *SCM* case was decided before TRIPS, which now states in Article 15(3) that "[m]embers may make registrability depend on use. However, actual use of a trademark shall not be a condition for filing an application for registration." As a result of TRIPS, the United States cannot require actual use in Canada to be a condition of obtaining a U.S. trademark through the use of Paris priority. The current U.S. position is that no use of the trademark in the United States needs to be alleged for § 44 applications filed in the U.S. patent office asserting Paris priority, only the allegation of a bona fide intention to use, which is the same requirement for all U.S. trademark applications. The result of these developments results in the following:

> Illustration 4-3. On February 1, Leonardo files for a trademark application for Peach Tree in Canada. Leonardo has never used the trademark and does not allege use. On April 1,

> Salvatore uses the Peach Tree trademark in the United States and sooner thereafter files an application for the Peach Tree trademark with the U.S. patent office. On July 1, within the period of Paris priority, Leonardo files a trademark application in the United States alleging a bona fide intent to use the trademark in U.S. commerce. Leonardo has a U.S. filing date of February 1 and wins the Peach Tree trademark.

No use, allegation of use, or allegation of intent to use is required for a foreign filing in order for the foreign filing date to serve as the Paris priority date of a U.S. filing in the U.S. patent office. The U.S. filing must allege use or intent to use in the United States, but these use requirements do not apply to the foreign filing.

3. ARTICLE 6*QUINQUIES*, THE TELLE QUELLE PROVISION

Similar to its treatment of patents, the Paris Convention provides for the independent treatment of trademarks, but Article 6*quinquies*, the "telle quelle" or "as is" provision, is an exception to that general rule. Trademark applicants who proceed under the telle quelle provision receive a special benefit. Article 6*quinquies*A(1) provides: "Every trademark duly registered in the country of origin shall be accepted for filing and protected as is in the other countries of the Union, subject to the reservations indicated in this Article."

Under the Paris Convention, a trademark owner has two options in registering its trademark in foreign countries. First, the trademark owner can register the trademark directly in the foreign country without first registering the trademark in the country of origin. If the trademark owner chooses this route then the trademark owner is subject to all of the trademark requirements of the foreign nation. Article 6(1) of the Paris Convention provides that "[t]he conditions for the filing and registration of trademarks shall be determined in each country of the Union by its domestic legislation." Suppose, for example, the domestic law of the country of registration provides that trademarks in a certain stylized script will not be eligible for trademark registration or that numerals cannot be registered as trademarks. If the trademark application uses the contested script or numerals, the trademark owner will be denied trademark registration under Article 6(1).

The second route is to first register the trademark in the country of origin and then file an application in the foreign country. Under this route, the trademark owner is entitled to claim the benefit of the telle quelle (French for "as is") provision of Article 6*quinquies*. Under Article 6*quinquies*, if the trademark owner obtains a trademark in script or in numerals in the country of origin, then the foreign country must accept the trademark telle quelle or as is. Even though the foreign nation's domestic law prohibits the use of the script or numerals, the foreign nation is required by the telle quelle provision of Article 6*quinquies* to recognize the script and numerals and accept it for trademark registration.

In *United States—Section 211 Omnibus Appropriations Act of 1998*, WT/DS176/AB/R (January 2, 2002), the WTO Appellate Body made clear that the telle quelle provision applies only to matters of form and not to other matters, such as ownership. The European Community challenged § 211(a)(1) enacted by Congress to prohibit registration by a Cuban national of a trademark that was confiscated by the Cuban government unless the Cuban national had obtained the express consent of the original owner of the confiscated trademark. The purpose of § 211(a)(1) was to prevent the Cuban government or its entities from registering confiscated Cuban trademarks in the United States.

Pernod Ricard, a French company (as part of a joint venture with a Cuban state trading company that obtained the confiscated trademark from the Cuban government) had registered the trademark for "Havana Club Rum" in the United States in 1976 and renewed it in 1996. In 1998, Congress enacted § 211(a)(1), which would prevent subsequent renewals of the Havana Club Rum trademark unless Pernod Ricard could obtain the express consent of the original trademark owners, an unlikely prospect. Pernod Ricard was able to enlist the aid of the EC in challenging § 211(a)(1) in the WTO.

The EC argued that § 211(a)(1) violated Article 6*quinquies* of the Paris Convention, incorporated into TRIPS by Article 2(1) because § 211(a)(1) did not allow the owner of a trademark registered in another country to register the trademark in the United States "telle quelle" or "as is" but the owner was required to first obtain the consent of the previous owner. The EC argued that the "telle quelle" provision was not limited to matters of form but encompassed all aspects of trademarks. The Appellate Body rejected this argument ruling that Article 6*quinquies* dealt with matters of form only. Matters of form encompass trademarks consisting of numbers, letters, surnames, geographical names, and words in a certain language or script. The Appellate Body found that the telle quelle provision does not encompass matters of ownership of the trademark, the subject of § 211(a)(1).

The Appellate Body reached this conclusion by the following reasoning. If the telle quelle provision encompassed all aspects of trademarks as argued by the EC, then a trademark owner from a country that did not require use can circumvent the use requirements in other countries. The trademark owner could register the trademark in its home country, which did not require use, and then use the telle que provision to register the trademark in a country that did require use. If the telle quelle provision applied to all aspects of trademarks then the country requiring use would have to accept the trademark acquired without use for registration. The Appellate Body reasoned that the drafters of the Paris Convention would not have established a global regime that would allow trademark owners to circumvent and undermine a domestic regime of trademarks based on use.

Although the Appellate Body ruled that § 211(a)(1) did not violate the telle quelle provision of Article 6*quinquies*, the Appellate Body found that § 211(a)(1) violated both the most favored nation and national treatment principles contained in GATT and TRIPS. Under § 211(a)(1), only Cuban nationals were required to obtain permission from the original owner of a confiscated Cuban trademark. Section 211(a)(1) violated the most favored national principle because it subjected Cuban nationals to an additional burden that nationals from other WTO countries did not have to meet, i.e. to obtain permission from the original owner of the trademark. Section 211(a)(1) also violated the national treatment principle because it subjected Cuban nationals to an additional burden that no U.S. national had to bear in order to register a trademark from Cuba.

4. INTERNATIONAL APPLICATIONS UNDER THE MADRID SYSTEM

Under the principles of territoriality and independence of trademarks, trademark owners traditionally had to file a separate application for a trademark registration in every country in which protection was sought. To ameliorate the administrative and financial burdens of multiple filings, the Madrid system was created to facilitate the international registrations of trademarks through the use of a single international trademark registry maintained by the World Intellectual Property Organization in Geneva. An applicant can file an international application resulting in protection in all designated states in one language—

English, French, or Spanish—and pay one set of fees in Swiss francs, which could result in substantial cost savings. The Madrid system consists of the Madrid Agreement formed in 1891 and the Madrid Protocol formed in 1989. In 2022, the Madrid system had a total of about 850,000 active international registrations. In 2022, the Madrid system had over 70,000 international applications and about the same number of international registrations.

To be a participant in the Madrid system, a country must be a member of either treaty or both. In many cases, it will not matter which treaty is used. Filing under either the Madrid Agreement or the Madrid Protocol will result in many cases in the use of the same procedures with the same results. In other cases, some significant differences can result from choosing to use the Madrid Protocol instead of the Madrid Agreement. As every member of the Madrid Agreement is also a member of the Madrid Protocol and as the filing fees are the same, the shortcomings of the Madrid Agreement may not be a problem in practice because the member can simply choose to proceed under the Madrid Protocol. Nevertheless, it is still important to understand that there can be some significant differences between the two treaties. The additional flexibility of the Madrid Protocol is a major reason why the United States is a member of the Madrid Protocol but not the Madrid Agreement.

The basic approach of the Madrid system is to allow a trademark owner to register a trademark on the international registry and to designate each

Madrid state (130 states for the Madrid Protocol and 55 states for the Madrid Agreement) in which an extension of protection is sought. Trademark protection is based upon registration in the WIPO international registry and the designation of selected states; national authorities never issue a domestic trademark registration. Once a country has been designated, the country must grant the same protection to a trademark registered in the WIPO registry as it would grant to a trademark that is registered under the domestic laws of that country.

The Madrid system requires that the international application must be based on either a pre-existing basic trademark application or a pre-existing basic trademark registration. This was not required in the case of international patent applications under the Patent Cooperation Treaty. Under the PCT, it was possible to file an international application as the sole application to begin the PCT process. In the case of the Madrid system, the international application must be based on an existing trademark registration or an existing domestic trademark application.

Under the Madrid Agreement, the international application must be based on a basic trademark registration in the domestic legal system of a Madrid Agreement country. This means that the applicant already has a valid and existing trademark in a domestic legal system and now is seeking to obtain international protection for that trademark. Under the Madrid Protocol, the international application can be based either on a basic registration or on one or more basic applications, that is, an existing trademark application in the domestic legal system that has not yet resulted in a trademark registration. The applicant can file the international application and the basic application at the same time. In the case of a U.S. applicant, the applicant can file a U.S. trademark application and an international application with the U.S. patent office or can file the international application within six months of the filing of the domestic application to claim the Paris priority date of the domestic application. Using the Madrid Agreement does not allow for the applicant to use Paris priority since the international filing is based on a basic registration not a prior filing. The international application must indicate the goods and services for which the trademark will be used and, where possible, the corresponding class according to the classification system established by the Nice Agreement Concerning the International Classification of Goods and Services for the Purposes of the Registration of Marks.

The U.S. patent office will then review the international application and then forward it to WIPO in Geneva. If WIPO receives the international application within two months of the date of the filing of the international application in the U.S. patent office then the filing date in WIPO is the filing date of the international application in the U.S. patent office. If WIPO receives the international application from the U.S. patent office after two months, then the filing date of the international application is the date that it is actually received in WIPO.

Once WIPO receives the international application, WIPO will examine the trademark application to determine whether it meets WIPO filing requirements. Once WIPO determines that all requirements have been met, WIPO will register the trademark in the international registry and publish it in WIPO's Gazette of International Marks. What happens next in the Madrid state depends on whether the state uses an examination system for the registration of trademarks. In states that do not use an examination system, trademarks are automatically registered and the validity of the trademark is determined when and if the trademark is later challenged by a third party. In states following an examination system, the trademark office will first determine whether the application satisfies all of the legal requirements for a valid trademark before registration.

In countries that do not use an examination system for trademarks, once the trademark is registered in the WIPO international registry, the trademark is then automatically entitled to the same trademark protection in the Madrid state as if the trademark had been deposited in the state. While the designated Madrid state does not register the trademark, the state may issue a certificate of extension of protection.

In countries following an examination system, the national trademark authorities will conduct an examination of the trademark and must notify WIPO of a decision not to extend protection within 18 months of the date of the notice of extension of protection sent by WIPO. Failure to notify WIPO within 18 months will result in an automatic extension of protection for the trademark in that country.

An international registration under the Madrid system lasts for a 10-year period subject to indefinite renewals of additional 10-year periods. A renewal of the international registration extends to all designated states. The applicant can also extend protection to additional states either in the renewal procedure or on an independent basis.

All registrations under the Madrid system are subject to a "central attack." If the underlying basic application or basic registration from the home country is rejected or invalidated within the first five years of the date of the international registration then the international registration will be cancelled and any protection in the designated states will also be cancelled. If the basic application or registration does not fail within the first five years then the international registration becomes independent of the home country registration and any failure of the basic application or registration thereafter will have no effect on the international registration.

As the consequences of a central attack can be severe, the Madrid Protocol (but not the Madrid Agreement) contains a mechanism to ameliorate its harsh results. Under the Madrid Protocol, if a basic application or registration fails within the first five years, the applicant can transform the international application into national applications by filing separate national applications in each country designated by the international application. Under this procedure, the national applications will be entitled to the filing date of the now cancelled international application. Converting the international application into national applications must occur within three months of the date on which the international registration was cancelled.

5. PROHIBITION OF SPECIAL REQUIREMENTS THAT UNJUSTIFIABLY ENCUMBER TRADEMARK USE

TRIPS Article 20 provides:

> **TRIPS**
>
> **Article 20**
> **Other Requirements**
>
> The use of a trademark in the course of trade shall not be unjustifiably encumbered by special requirements, such as use with another trademark, use in a special form or use in a manner detrimental to its capability to distinguish the goods or services of one undertaking from those of other undertakings.

Article 20 provides that the use of a trademark "shall not be unjustifiably encumbered by special requirements." The interpretation of this clause of Article 20 was involved in *Australia—Certain Measures Concerning Trademarks, Geographical Indications and Other Plain Packaging Requirements Applicable to Tobacco Products and Packaging*, AB–2018–4, AB–2018–6, Report of the Appellate Body (June 9, 2020). The case involved a lengthy dispute involving Australia's plain packaging requirements for cigarettes that was litigated in the WTO for nearly a decade. In 2011, Australia enacted the Tobacco Plan Packaging Act requiring plain packaging for all tobacco products. By the time the act came into effect, Australia was already phasing out all domestic production of tobacco products. By 2015 all tobacco products were imported into Australia. The 2011 Act was aimed at restricting tobacco imports once all domestic production ceased.

The act standardized the appearance of tobacco products and packaging by banning all brand imagery, bright colors, and promotional texts on the package. All packages had to use a standard plain format, drab brown colors, and other designs prescribed by the legislation. Products can be distinguished by the brand name and product name

printed in a standard sized font near the bottom of the front of the package. Related regulations also required the package to carry graphic health warnings covering 75 percent of the front of the package and 90 percent of the back. Some of the health warnings used gruesome images of the ravages of diseases caused by smoking.

The basic approach of the legislation was to strip the packaging of tobacco products of all of its glamorous images and enticing messages used by the tobacco industry to convince consumers to buy their products, especially teenagers and young people. The express purpose of the legislation was to discourage smoking among the public through the use of extremely blunt and forceful messaging. An example of the required packaging appears above. Note that the name of the cigarette brand in the bottom panel is dwarfed by the message warning about health risks. The purpose of the standard format is to make the packaging as unappealing as possible to consumers.

In 2012, Indonesia, Ukraine, Honduras, the Dominican Republic, and Cuba challenged Australia's legislation, arguing that it violated Article 2.2 of the WTO Technical Barriers to Trade Agreement and Article 20 of TRIPS. The argument based on Article 20 of TRIPS was that the Australian act "unjustifiably encumbered" the use of the trademark by imposing "special requirements," but the TRIPS argument was not the main argument by the complainants. The main argument was that the legislation violated Article 2.2 of the WTO Technical Barriers Agreement, which provides:

> 2.2 Members shall ensure that technical regulations are not prepared, adopted or applied with a view to or with the effect of creating unnecessary obstacles to international trade.

> For this purpose, technical regulations shall not be more trade-restrictive than necessary to fulfil a legitimate objective, taking account of the risks non-fulfilment would create.

The WTO Technical Barriers Agreement applies to goods, not intellectual property, and is a specialized agreement created under the auspices of the General Agreement on Tariffs and Trade (GATT), the basic agreement governing trade in goods. The purpose of the Technical Barriers Agreement is to prevent members from using technical regulations that are overly complex or onerous to create barriers to the free trade in goods. If a technical regulation (defined as one that applies to the characteristics of products) is difficult to understand or sets standards that are difficult to meet, the result will be that the regulations become a trade barrier that will impede the free flow of goods in international trade. Such a trade barrier must be justified as necessary to the WTO. Australia clearly intended the plain packaging requirement to create a trade barrier to imports of cigarettes. The issue was whether the trade barrier could be justified as "necessary" under Article 2.2.

The second sentence of Article 2.2 of the Technical Barriers Agreement requires that any technical regulations must not more trade restrictive than "necessary" to fulfill a legitimate objective. In using the term "necessary," the Technical Barriers Agreement invokes an elaborate and longstanding jurisprudence in the WTO created to interpret the term "necessary" that appears in the Technical Barriers Agreement, the GATT, and other WTO agreements. As part of the well-settled jurisprudence of interpreting the term "necessary," the complainant was required to show that there were no available alternatives that were less trade restrictive and that would achieve the same objective or policy. Only if other alternatives that could achieve the same ends were not available could the measure be deemed "necessary."

In the *Australia Plain Packaging* case, the complainants offered four alternatives that they claimed were less trade restrictive but would achieve the same policy goals: (1) an increase in taxation; (2) an increase in the minimum legal purchasing age; (3) an improvement of anti-smoking social marketing campaigns; and (4) the creation of a pre-vetting mechanism for tobacco packaging. The Appellate Body found that these less restrictive measures would not achieve equivalent policy goals. This finding led the Appellate Body to conclude that the measures were not more trade restrictive than necessary under Article 2.2 of the Technical Barriers Agreement and so did not violate Article 2.2. The Appellate Body then turned to an examination of Article 20 of TRIPS.

The Appellate Body emphasized that the standards under Article 2.2 of the Technical Barriers Agreement and Article 20 of TRIPS were different. Article 2.2 of the Technical Barriers Agreement required the restriction to be "necessary" to achieve a policy goal. Under TRIPS Article 20, the requirement was that the special requirements encumbering the use of a trademark were "justifiable." If the requirements are justifiable then they have not violated Article 20. Justifiable means fair and capable of being reasonably explained. By contrast, unjustifiable is not fair and cannot be reasonably explained.

The concept of justifiability provides a degree of regulatory autonomy to a government that is not available under the concept of necessity contained in Article 2.2 of the Technical Barriers Agreement. The degree of connection between encumbrances imposed on a trademark and the policy objective is lower than in the case of necessity. So long as the encumbrances *contribute* to Australia's goal of reducing smoking, they provided the needed connection. In the case of necessity, the measure must be *indispensable* to the goal of reducing smoking. This standard implies that there are no available alternatives that are less trade restrictive and that can achieve the same goals.

If the trademark encumbrances contribute to the goals in question, then in the analysis of justifiability the complainant has to simply show that reasons support the encumbrances. Members have more flexibility and greater discretion under a standard of justifiability than under a standard of necessity.

Unlike in an analysis of necessity, an analysis of justifiability does not require the consideration of less restrictive alternatives. Nonetheless, as the panel focused on Article 2.2 of the Technical Barriers Agreement, the panel also considered the same four alternatives proposed in the necessity analysis (set forth above) in its analysis of whether the special requirements unjustifiably encumbered the use of the trademark. The Appellate Body found that considering the four alternatives in an analysis of justifiability would be in error if the panel just transplanted the examination of the four alternatives under Article 2.2 of the Technical Barriers Agreement to an analysis under Article 20 of TRIPS. The analysis under Article 2.2 of the Technical Barriers Agreement is whether the alternatives are less trade restrictive; the analysis under Article 20 of TRIPS is whether the alternatives are less trademark encumbering. The Appellate Body noted, however, the panel correctly applied the less trademark encumbering standard to its analysis of the four alternatives under Article 20. There was no error in this part of the panel's analysis.

The Appellate Body found that the panel made an error in its analysis of Article 2.2 of the Technical Barriers Agreement in finding that two of the four less trade restrictive alternatives (increases in tax and the legal age for cigarettes) could not achieve the same result as the plain packaging requirement. In making these erroneous determinations, the panel also made factual findings regarding the design features required by the 2011 Plain Packaging Act. The Appellate Body found that the panel made another error when it relied on these findings regarding design in its analysis of the four alternatives under Article 20 of TRIPS.

The Appellate Body found that the errors in the analysis of Article 20 of TRIPS were essentially harmless error. The panel was not required to consider less restrictive alternatives under Article 20 of TRIPS, but only under Article 2.2 of the Technical Barriers Act. The panel's analysis of the less restrictive alternatives under Article 20 of TRIPS was therefore not necessary to its decision to uphold the plain packaging act so long as the panel found another ground based on Article 20 to uphold the 2011 Plain Packaging Act.

The panel had engaged in a separate analysis finding that the plain packaging requirements contributed to Australia's goal of reducing smoking, the standard used for determining whether the requirements were justifiable. This analysis provided an independent ground for the Appellate Body to uphold the plain packaging requirements.

The *Australia—Plain Packaging* case also established that the special requirements that encumber trademarks do not have to be related directly to trademarks. TRIPS provides that members can consider factors outside of intellectual property in formulating their laws and regulations. Article 7 of TRIPS provides in enforcement matters members can consider factors related to social and economic welfare. Article 8 of TRIPS provides that in formulating their laws and regulations, members can consider including matters pertaining to public health and nutrition. Article 5(a) of the Doha Declaration on the TRIPS Agreement and Public Health (2001) requires a treaty interpreter to take into account the context, object, and purpose of the treaty being interpreted. Although there was a controversy as to whether the Doha Declaration applied outside of the access to medicines debate, the

Appellate Body ruled that regardless of the Doha Declaration's legal status, considering the context, object, and purpose of a treaty is a general principle of treaty interpretation. Under this approach, a WTO member can consider public health and social welfare factors in imposing special requirements on trademarks.

6. EU TRADEMARK

A prominent example of a trademark that has effect across national boundaries is the European Union trademark. The EU trademark is a pan-EU trademark that has a unitary character; it is administered by the European Union Intellectual Property Office located in Alicante, Spain. A single application with the EU Intellectual Property Office can result an EU trademark providing protection across all 27 EU countries. The EU trademark is not a creature of the domestic law of any EU country, but is the result of EU legislation, i.e. the EU Trademark Regulation, 2017/1001 (2017). The EU trademark exists independently of and in parallel with trademarks under the domestic legislation of EU member countries. Many trademark owners have an EU trademark and trademarks in individual EU countries under domestic legislation for the same sign or symbol.

The advantage of the EU trademark lies in its uniformity and pan-European character. The EU trademark creates the same legal rights and obligations in all 27 countries of the EU. There is no need to be aware of differences in domestic trademark legislation. With an EU trademark, it is also possible to obtain pan-European relief such as an injunction prohibiting infringing conduct throughout the EU, if certain requirements are met.

The EU trademark can present some enforcement issues. Rather than establishing specialized courts for enforcing the EU trademark, the EU relies on the designation by each EU country of national courts to serve as courts to enforce the EU trademark. This creates some significant differences among EU nations. For example, the UK has designated its High Court as the single EU trademark court of first instance whereas Germany has more than 20 EU trademark courts. Each national court has its own set of procedural rules with the result that remedies, such as the practice of granting preliminary injunctions, may vary from state to state. Despite these issues, the EU trademark has proven to be extremely popular with 161,232 EU trademarks registrations in 2023.

7. OWNERSHIP AND TRANSFER OF TRADEMARKS

Ownership and transfer of trademarks is complicated by the basic concept of trademark law that trademarks are used in commerce to distinguish the goods and services of one undertaking from another. Historically, countries were divided on whether they would allow the trademark to be transferred without also transferring the business assets associated with the trademark. Under the Paris Convention, the assets associated with the trademark are known as the goodwill of the business. In a later discussion below, we will see that the United States defines goodwill more narrowly than the Paris Convention.

The transfer of the naked trademark is called an assignment in gross. Some countries did not permit assignments of trademarks in gross but required the transfer of the trademark to be accompanied by the transfer of goodwill or the business assets associated with the trademark.

The Paris Convention takes a permissive stance on assignments in gross:

Paris Convention

Article 6*quater*
Marks: Assignment of Marks

(1) When, in accordance with the law of a country of the Union, the assignment of a mark is valid only if it takes place at the same time as the transfer of the business or goodwill to which the mark belongs, it shall suffice for the recognition of such validity that the portion of the business or goodwill located in that country be transferred to the assignee, together with the exclusive right to manufacture in the said country, or to sell therein, the goods bearing the mark assigned.

(2) The foregoing provision does not impose upon the countries of the Union any obligation to regard as valid the assignment of any mark the use of which by the assignee would, in fact,

> be of such a nature as to mislead the public, particularly as regards the origin, nature, or essential qualities, of the goods to which the mark is applied.

Under Article 6*quater*, countries are permitted to allow assignments in gross or to prohibit them. For countries that prohibit assignments in gross, i.e. require that the assignment of the trademark be accompanied by the transfer of goodwill or business assets, the Paris Convention limits the transfer of the goodwill or the business assets to those located in those countries. The Paris Convention also allows its members to disregard any assignment of a trademark that would allow the assignee to mislead the public as regards to the goods to which the mark is applied. As an example of a misleading use under Article 6*quater*(2), consider the following:

> Illustration 4-4. North American Motors assigns its trademark "Summit" used for its luxury line of automobiles to Home Decor, a furniture manufacturer. The Summit trademark is associated by the relevant consuming public with luxury automobiles from North American Motors. The transfer is an assignment in gross, i.e. only the trademark is transferred unaccompanied by any business assets and without any limitations on the type of goods with which the trademark can be used. Home Decor uses the Summit trademark for a new line of high-end furniture. Home Decor has acquired the Summit trademark without the goodwill associated with the trademark. The consuming

public becomes confused by the use of the Summit trademark with furniture. Under Article 6*quater*(2), a Paris Union member can find the assignment of the Summit trademark to be invalid.

Unlike the Paris Convention, TRIPS took the position that all WTO members must allow assignments in gross:

TRIPS

Article 21
Licensing and Assignment

Members may determine conditions on the licensing and assignment of trademarks, it being understood that the compulsory licensing of trademarks shall not be permitted and that the owner of a registered trademark shall have the right to assign the trademark with or without the transfer of the business to which the trademark belongs.

TRIPS Article 21 prohibits the compulsory licensing of trademarks and also requires WTO members to permit assignments in gross, i.e. the transfer of the trademark without the transfer of the business associated with the trademark. Article 21 does not mention "goodwill" and an issue that arises is whether goodwill means something other than the business associated with the trademark.

The meaning of goodwill was discussed in *Vittoria North America LLC v. Euro-Asia Imports, Inc.* 278 F.3d 1076 (10th Cir. 2001). Vittoria North America

LLC, an Oklahoma company, sought to block the importation into the United States of Vittoria branded bicycle racing tires by Euro-Asia Imports, a California importer. Euro-Asia had acquired Vittoria bicycle tires abroad; the tires were intended for sale in a foreign country. Euro-Asia then attempted to import them into the United States without the permission of Vittoria North America, the owner of the U.S. Vittoria trademark. Genuine goods imported into the United States without the permission of the trademark owner are known as gray market goods or parallel imports. Section 526 of the Tariff Act of 1930 allows a trademark owner to block the importation of gray market goods by an importer that did not obtain the trademark owner's permission. The district court enjoined Euro-Asia from importing the tires.

On appeal, Euro-Asia argued that Vittoria North America did not have a valid trademark. Vittoria North America had acquired the Vittoria trademark by assignment from the parent company located in Italy. Euro-Asia argued that the assignment of the trademark was invalid because it did not include the transfer of goodwill as required by U.S. caselaw.

The court of appeals found that goodwill represents consumer trust and expectations associated with the trademark and did not necessarily have to include tangible assets. A trademark owner can transfer goodwill without transferring any business assets. Customers of Vittoria tires expected the trademark to be used for high end bicycle racing tires. Vittoria North America took steps to ensure that the trademark continued to signify high end racing tires by placing advertisements, sponsoring professional athletes, attending trade shows and developing a network of sales representatives. As Vittoria North America was using the assigned trademark for identical goods, consumer expectations were protected. The court of appeals upheld the assignment and the injunction.

Under TRIPS, WTO members must permit assignments in gross, i.e. no business assets need accompany the assignment of the trademark. Under TRIPS, countries, such as the United States, can still require that the assignor of the trademark must also transfer goodwill along with the trademark, which in this context means that the assignee must use the assigned trademark on identical or similar goods. A use of the assigned trademark with identical or similar goods will be consistent with consumer expectations and will avoid consumer confusion. This approach is also consistent with Paris Convention Article 6*quater*(2), which allows countries to prohibit assignments that result in uses that are misleading to consumers. Note that the U.S. definition of goodwill appears narrower than the definition in the Paris Convention that refers to goodwill as business assets associated with the trademark.

The rules we have examined so far relate to assignments of trademarks. An analogous rule exists for the licensing of trademarks. To be valid, a licensing agreement must allow the licensor to maintain quality control over use of the trademark by the licensee. For example, a licensor/franchisor of trademarks for use in a fast food restaurant must maintain quality control over the products and service offered by the franchisee through training programs and inspections. Without quality controls, consumers who depend on the goodwill of the trademarks might get confused and be harmed if the goods or services are different from those of the licensor/franchisor or if the quality of the goods or services fail to meet their expectations. *See Dawn Donut Co. v. Hart's Food Stores, Inc.*, 267 F.2d 358, 367–68 (2d Cir. 1959). A licensing agreement without quality controls is considered to be a "naked licensing" agreement that is not only invalid but also results in the abandonment or loss of the trademark by the owner.

8. SUBJECT MATTER OF TRADEMARKS AND DISTINCTIVENESS

TRIPS Article 15 sets forth the subject matter that must be eligible for trademarks:

TRIPS

Article 15
Protectable Subject Matter

Any sign or any combination of signs capable of distinguishing the good or services of one undertaking from those of other undertakings, shall be eligible for registration as trademarks. Where signs are not inherently capable of distinguishing the relevant goods or services, Members may make registrability depend on distinctiveness acquired through use. Members may require, as a condition of registration, that signs be visually perceptible.

As this language suggests, the subject matter of trademark under TRIPS is broad. "Any sign or combination of signs" can be a trademark. The key element is distinctiveness so that the trademark can serve to indicate to the consuming public that the product or service originates from some particular undertaking.

Distinctiveness in a trademark can be inherent or be acquired through use. Certain trademarks, such as Microsoft and Google, are inherently distinctive due to their fanciful (i.e. made up or coined) and arbitrary nature. Other trademarks are not inherently capable of distinguishing relevant goods or services. An example is the sign "α", the Greek letter for alpha, that was used for wines in the EU, but members can provide that the sign can acquire distinctiveness through use in the perception of the relevant public. *See Office for Harmonization in the International Market v. Borco-Marken-Import Matthiesen GmbH & Co. KG*, [2011] E.T.M.R. 4, C–265/09 (Sept. 9, 2010).

TRIPS Article 15 allows members to require trademarks to be visually perceptible. Such a requirement would preclude smells and sounds from serving as trademarks. The United States does not impose this restriction so sounds and smells can be registered as trademarks with the U.S. patent office.

The Court of Justice for the European Union discussed the EU approach to inherent and acquired distinctiveness in *Louis Vuitton Malletier v. EUIPO*, T–105/19, ECLI:EU:T:2020:258 (June 10, 2020). An applicant challenged the validity of an EU trademark that Louis Vuitton Malletier had obtained for a checkerboard design consisting of alternating dark and light squares with a weft and warp textured pattern for leather goods, including luggage, vanity cases, toiletry bags, and handbags. The EU trademark is a trademark that is effective throughout all of the 27 countries of the EU and co-exists with any trademarks obtained under the domestic law of any EU country. In assessing the inherent distinctiveness of Louis Vuitton's EU trademark, the court noted that inherent distinctiveness is present "when a mark . . . departs significantly from the norm or customs of the sector of the goods and services at issue and thereby fulfills its essential function of indicating origin." *Id.* at ¶ 17.

The court agreed with the board of appeal that the checkboard pattern and the weft and warp pattern applied to the goods at issue was a commonplace and everyday pattern that did not diverge from the norms or customs of the sector concerned. The court then reviewed the board of appeal's decision that the Louis Vuitton trademark had not acquired distinctiveness through use. As Louis Vuitton's trademark was an EU trademark, Louis Vuitton had to demonstrate that the trademark had acquired distinctiveness throughout the entire territory of the EU. The board of appeals, however, chose to focus narrowly on evidence that applied to a group of countries in eastern Europe in which Louis Vuitton did no business and found that the Louis Vuitton trademark had not acquired distinctiveness. The court found fault with this approach and ruled that the board should have carried out a global assessment of all of the evidence. The board should have assessed all of the evidence whether it applied to the EU as a whole or to groups of countries or to the particular group of countries in question. As a whole the evidence might have allowed the board to extrapolate and find that evidence outside of the region in question supported a finding that the trademark had acquired distinctiveness in the group of states that was the focus of the board's inquiry.

a. Non-Traditional Trademarks

The scope of TRIPS Article 15 on the subject matter of trademarks is broad: "*any* sign capable of distinguishing goods and services" is eligible for trademark and, if permitted by domestic legislation, the sign does not have to be visually perceptible. Both the United States and the EU do not require trademarks to be visually perceptible. These broad parameters have given rise to many non-traditional trademarks in the United States and the EU: colors, sounds, and smells. Several cases have considered under what conditions shapes can be trademarked.

i. Shapes

An issue that arose in *Koninklijke Philips Electronics NV v. Remington Consumer Products Ltd.*, [2002] ECR I–5475, Case C–299/99 (June 18, 2002) was whether a shape can qualify as a trademark. Philips Electronics had developed a three headed rotary electric shaver with three circular heads with rotating blades in the shape of an equilateral triangle. In 1985, Philips was able to register the graphical representation of the shaver as a trademark in the UK. Remington, a competitor, began selling a shaver of the same shape in the UK. Philips sued Remington for trademark infringement and Remington counterclaimed for the revocation of Philip's trademark. As issues of EU law were raised, the UK court referred to the case to the European Court of Justice.

Article 2 of the EC Trademark Directive expressly recognized that the shape of goods can qualify as trademarks but subject to certain conditions. The European Court of Justice rejected a suggestion that the shape must contain some capricious addition such as an embellishment that has no functional purpose. The court made it clear that a shape can qualify for trademark protection so long as it has achieved a distinctive character, i.e., a substantial proportion of the relevant class of persons associated the shape with the trader and no other undertaking.

Article 3(1)(e) of the Directive also contained a condition that shape cannot be a trademark if the shape is "necessary to obtain a technical result." The meaning of this clause is that a shape cannot be a trademark if the shape is functional, i.e. the shape is used to obtain a practical result, in this case, a close shave. Article 3(1)(e) is meant to prevent traders from extending the use of a sign that is meant to distinguish goods and services to creating an obstacle that would prevent competitors from freely offering products that also achieve the same technical solution, i.e. a close shave. The court noted that as the shape of the Philips shaver was functional, it could not be protected by trademark and Remington was free to use a shaver with the same shape. The court further held that although other shapes might also give a close shave that possibility does not change the result that the Philips trademark for the shape of the razor is invalid under EC law.

In *Traffix Devices, Inc. v. Marketing Displays, Inc.*, 532 U.S. 23 (2001), the U.S. Supreme Court considered whether it was possible to use trademark law to protect a shape that was protected by a patent that had expired. Marketing Displays had patents on a mechanism built on a dual spring design that displayed road signs and that would stay upright in adverse wind conditions. After the patents expired, a competitor Traffix Devices copied the dual spring design and began selling a product under the name "Windbuster," which was similar to Marketing Display's name for its product, "WindMaster." The district court found that Traffix's name was confusingly similar. On appeal to the Sixth Circuit Court of Appeals, the court upheld the ruling on the name and also held that Traffix infringed Marketing Display's protected trade dress for the shape of the mechanism.

The Supreme Court reversed that part of the lower court ruling related to the shape of the mechanism. Trade dress protects the design or packaging of a product and is treated similarly to trademarks under the Lanham Act. The Court found that trade dress cannot be claimed for shapes that are functional. As Marketing Display had patents for the mechanism the expired patents created a presumption that the shapes were functional and Marketing Display had the heavy burden of rebutting the presumption of functionality. Regarding functionality, the Court reiterated its formula that a product feature is functional and cannot serve as a trademark "if it is essential to the use or purpose of the article or if it affects the cost or quality of the article." 532 U.S. at 24. A functional feature is one that would put competitors at "a significant non-reputation-related disadvantage." *Id.* The Court concluded that Marketing Displays did not and could not overcome the presumption that the shape was functional.

ii. Movements as Trademarks

Not only can shapes quality for trademark but, in theory, a movement can also qualify. A movement and a shape are related in that a movement can take the form of a shape. In *Automobili Lamborghini Hold S.P.A.'s Application*, E.T.M.R. 43, Case R 772/2001–1 (September 23, 2003), the issue concerned whether Lamborghini, a producer of high performance sports cars, could obtain an EC community wide trademark for the movement of its doors. The doors of the Lamborghini car opened by swinging forward and upward around a swiveling axis from a closed position to an open position. The Office of Harmonization denied the application for a trademark for the movement on the ground that the movement is functional under Article 7(e)(ii) of the Community Trademark Regulation. Although the test of functionality under Article 7(e)(ii) had been applied only to shapes in the past, the Office found that movements and shapes were sufficiently similar that if a movement is functional, i.e. the movement opened a car door, the movement was also ineligible for trademark protection.

The Office also found that the movement was not distinctive as required by Article 7(1)(b) because various other manufacturers of high performance sports cars also had doors that opened in a similar movement. The Office found that upward swiveling car doors were perceived by the relevant trade circles as a feature of a certain category of high performance sports cars and not as a feature of a particular manufacturer.

b. Generic Terms

Generic terms do not qualify for trademark protection. Generic terms are those terms by which the goods are designated in the language. The term "apple" is generic when referring to the fruit, the term "chicken" is generic when referring to the bird, and the term "water" is generic when referring to the liquid that forms the oceans, lakes, and rivers. No one can claim a trademark for apple used for the fruit, chicken used for the bird, or water for the liquid because that is the term that is commonly known and used for the product. Anyone can use the term. The rule protects the consuming public in understanding the nature of the goods for sale as well as competitors who are free to use the name of the product by which it is best known to the public. One can argue that a generic term is by is nature non-distinctive and cannot qualify for trademark.

In *Otokoyama Co. Ltd. v. Wine of Japan Import, Inc.*, 175 F.3d 266 (2d Cir. 1999), the court had to consider whether a term that is generic in a foreign language can be registered as a trademark in the United States. Otokoyama Co. had acquired a U.S. trademark for the word "otokoyama," which in Japanese refers to saki, a type of strong rice wine. When the defendant attempted to import rice wine from Japan using the term otokoyama, Otokoyama Co. obtained a preliminary injunction from a federal district court blocking the imports. In issuing the injunction, the district court refused to consider that the term otokoyama might be a generic term in Japan. The court also ignored a ruling of the Japan patent office that refused to issue a trademark for the term because it was generic.

The court of appeals vacated the injunction and remanded the case. The court ruled that under the doctrine of foreign equivalents, foreign language words that are generic are ineligible for trademark protection in the United States. The rule is based on the notion that there are or will be consumers in the United States who speak the foreign language. If otokoyama in Japanese signifies a type of strong rice wine, no single merchant in the United States can be given the exclusive right to use the term for the product by which it is best known to Japanese consumers.

The court of appeals also held that the district erred in refusing to consider the decision of the Japan patent office that declined to issue a trademark for the term because it was generic. The plaintiff had represented to the U.S. patent office that otokoyama was an arbitrary and fanciful term that had no meaning and could not be translated. The decision of the Japan patent office is evidence that the plaintiff was acting in bad faith and was misrepresenting the meaning of the term. The district court should have considered the decision as it was relevant to the issue of bad faith on the part of the plaintiff.

9. EXCLUSIVE RIGHTS

a. Likelihood of Confusion

TRIPS Article 16(1) states:

TRIPS

Article 16
Rights Conferred

(1) The owner of a registered trademark shall have the exclusive right to prevent all third parties not having the owner's consent from using in the course of trade identical or similar signs for goods or services which are identical or similar to those in respect of which the trademark is registered where such use would result in a likelihood of confusion. In case of the use of an identical sign for identical goods or services, a likelihood of confusion shall be presumed.

An unauthorized use constitutes trademark infringement when the use results in "a likelihood of confusion." This standard is found in both U.S. and EU law and required for all WTO members. Actual confusion is not the standard. Proof of actual confusion would require the trademark owner to wait until actual harm was manifested in large enough numbers to support proof by consumer surveys before bringing an action against the infringer. By contrast, the likelihood of confusion standard allows a trademark owner to enjoin a use without wanting for the harm to occur. In cases involving likelihood of confusion courts often find customer surveys to be the most reliable proof of confusion and some courts will consider the absence of survey evidence as proof that confusion cannot be shown. Trademark owners that do not have consumer surveys must make sure that alternative sources of proof are compelling, such as interviews, e-mails, and other communications from consumers.

The last part in the text of Article 16(1) set forth above provides that where identical or similar signs are used on identical or similar goods or services, then likelihood of confusion is presumed. This text refers to what are commonly known as counterfeit goods where the counterfeit product is either completely or substantially indistinguishable from the genuine product. In the case of counterfeits, all the trademark owner needs to show is that the use of the trademark was without authorization.

An EU case also indicates that the likelihood of confusion is not equivalent to a likelihood of association. The EU Trademark Directive provided that "the likelihood of confusion includes the likelihood of association." The European Court of Justice has held that the mere association in the mind of consumers of a junior trademark with a senior trademark is not infringement unless there is also consumer confusion, i.e. consumers believe or are confused about whether the two trademarks refer to the same source of the goods. *See Sabel BV v. Puma AG*, [1997] ECR I–6191, Case C–251/95 (November 11, 1997).

The position by the European Court of Justice in the *Sabel BV* case applies to ordinary trademarks. In the case of famous trademarks, a higher level of protection is available, as further discussed in the next section. For famous trademarks, the mere association of the famous trademark with another trademark, even if there is no likelihood of confusion, can in some circumstances constitute a breach of the rights of the famous trademark.

b. Famous Trademarks

Trademarks that have achieved fame are given special protections under the Paris Convention and TRIPS. Article 6*bis* of the Paris Convention provides:

Paris Convention

Article 6*bis*
Marks: Well-Known Marks

(1) The countries of the Union undertake, ex officio if their legislation so permits, or at the request of an interested party, to refuse or to cancel the registration, and to prohibit the use, of a trademark which constitutes a reproduction,

> an imitation, or a translation, liable to create confusion, of a mark considered by the competent authority of the country of registration or use to be well known in that country as being already the mark of a person entitled to the benefits of this Convention and used for identical or similar goods.

Article 6*bis* has been incorporated into TRIPS by Article 2(1) and is binding on all WTO members. Under this provision, a famous trademark will be protected in a country in which the trademark has not been registered. The prior fame achieved by the trademark will allow the owner of the trademark to block or cancel a registration of an identical or substantially similar junior trademark. Famous trademarks are an exception to the principle of territoriality and are able to overcome the limits of the principle of territoriality.

A good example of the application of the famous marks doctrine is *McDonald's Corp. v. Joburgers Drive-Inn Restaurant (Pty) Ltd.*, 1997 South African Reports 1, Case No. 547/95 (1996). In that case, McDonald's Corp., the American fast food restaurant, registered 52 trademarks in South Africa from 1968 to 1985. Although McDonald's registered its trademarks, McDonald's did no business in South Africa due to prohibitions imposed by U.S. federal laws. U.S. policy prohibited U.S. companies from doing business in South Africa due to its apartheid racial policies. McDonald's registered its trademarks in anticipation of the day when due to changed conditions, it would be free to operate in South Africa.

Joburgers Drive-Inn Restaurant (Pty) Ltd., a South African company, also in the fast food business, began operating a fast food business using the McDonald's trademarks. George Sombonos, an astute and ambitious businessman and the managing director of Joburgers, then applied to register the McDonald's trademarks and at the same time applied to cancel the trademarks previously registered by McDonald's on the ground of non-use. McDonald's opposed Sombonos's trademark applications and his attempt to cancel the existing registrations on the ground that its trademarks were protected by the famous marks doctrine. The trial court rejected McDonald's claims. The trial court ruled that Sombonos could register the McDonald's trademarks and also ordered that the existing McDonald's trademarks be cancelled.

On appeal the appellate court reversed the trial court. South Africa had recently enacted a new Trademarks Act that became effective on May 1, 1995. Under the old Act, in order to assert the famous marks doctrine, the trademark owner had to have a goodwill in South Africa. In this context, goodwill meant having business operations in South Africa. The new Act removed the requirement of having a goodwill in South Africa in order to assert the famous marks doctrine. McDonald's could assert the famous marks doctrine even though it had never done any business in South Africa and had no business assets in South Africa.

The appellate court found evidence of McDonald's worldwide fame established through its 13,993 restaurants spread over 70 countries, its more than $900 million annual advertising and promotion budget, its extensive marketing and promotional campaigns, and its sponsorship of the 1984 Los Angeles and 1992 Barcelona summer Olympics. The appellate court concluded that McDonald's had some of the best known trademarks in the world and that in all probability this fame spilled over into South Africa.

The appellate court also held that interviews of some 202 persons showed that McDonald's had achieved fame in South Africa with the relevant group of consumers, affluent people consisting of white adults who would be both potential customers and potential franchisees. The appellate court concluded that the fame of the McDonald's trademarks precluded Sombonos from registering any of the McDonald's trademarks. The appellate court also reversed the cancellation of the McDonald's trademarks. Cancellation was not necessary as Sombonos could not in any event register the McDonald's trademarks.

McDonald's was able to prevail not because of its trademark registrations in South Africa but because of the fame that its trademarks registered in the United States had achieved in South Africa. The fame of the trademarks, achieved before Sombonos attempted to register his McDonald's trademarks, created a priority right in McDonald's that precluded the registration of the Sombonos applications. The fame of the trademarks allowed McDonald's to overcome the limitations imposed the principle of territoriality. McDonald's trademarks were able to achieve priority rights in South Africa without ever having to rely on the registrations in South Africa.

The *McDonald's* case involved the owner of U.S. trademarks asserting the benefits of the famous marks doctrine in a foreign country. In *Grupo Gigante S.A. De C.V. v. Dallo & Co.*, 391 F.3d 1088 (9th Cir. 2004), the Ninth Circuit set forth a test for determining when a foreign trademark achieves fame in the United States. The dispute concerned the use of the trademark "Gigante" meaning Giant in Spanish for a chain of grocery stores. Beginning in the 1960s, Grupo Gigante S.A. de C.V. operated a large chain of grocery stores in Mexico under the Gigante tradename that was first registered in Mexico in 1963. When Grupo Gigante decided to enter the U.S. market in 1998, it discovered that the Dallos brothers had been operating grocery stores in San Diego using the Gigante tradename. A dispute arose with both parties claiming rights to the Gigante trademark in the southern California area. The district court held for Grupo Gigante but the Ninth Circuit found that the lower court had applied the wrong test for determining the fame of the trademark and vacated and remanded the case.

The Ninth Circuit ruled that in dealing with a foreign trademark seeking the protection of the famous marks doctrine, the first step is to determine whether the Gigante trademark had achieved secondary meaning. Some trademarks are inherently distinctive such as those that are fanciful, arbitrary, or suggestive. Others like Gigante are descriptive and must achieve distinctiveness before trademark protection can be granted. Grupo Gigante would have to show that Gigante had come to signify Grupo Gigante's particular chain of stores to consumers and was not merely descriptive of Grupo Gigante's stores and other large stores.

The court further held that the plaintiff must show that the trademark achieved secondary meaning in the geographical region of the United States where the defendants used the allegedly infringing trademark. The plaintiff must show that a substantial percentage of American consumers in the San Diego market are familiar with the foreign trademark. Factors to be considered are whether the copying by the defendants was intentional and whether American consumers think that they are patronizing the same firm that uses the Gigante trademark in Mexico.

10. EXTERRITORIAL APPLICATION OF THE LANHAM ACT

The *McDonald's* and *Grupo Gigante* cases involved an exception to the territoriality principle for famous trademarks. The United States has developed other exceptions to the principle of territoriality allowing U.S. courts to apply U.S. trademark law to territories outside of the United States.

Trader Joe's Co. v. Hallatt, 835 F.3d 960 (9th Cir. 2016) involved a defendant from Canada who traveled to Trader Joe's stores in Washington state to purchase goods that he later resold in Canada. The defendant Hallatt set up a store in Canada with an exterior sign "Pirate Joe's" using a font similar to that used by Trader Joe's. The store's design also mimicked Trader Joe's south pacific-themed trade dress. Hallatt also operated a website accessible from the United States. He resold the Trader Joe's goods in Canada without maintaining quality controls used by Trader Joe's. When Trader Joe's refused to serve him, he began donning disguises and hiring third parties to buy goods from Trader Joe's. As Hallatt was a Canadian citizen with legal permanent residence status in the United States, he was able to live and work legally in the United States if he wished. In all, Hallatt purchased some $350,000 of goods from Trader Joe's for resale in his store in Canada.

Trader Joe's sued Hallatt in federal district court in Washington state. As the resales of the products occurred in Canada, the court had to decide whether the facts justified the exterritorial application of U.S. trademark law to reach the conduct in Canada. The district court refused to extend the Lanham Act to Canada and dismissed the case.

On appeal the Ninth Circuit reversed the district court and upheld an exterritorial application of the Lanham Act to Hallatt's conduct in Canada. The court of appeals explained that U.S. laws can have exterritorial application if the case satisfies the three-prong test set forth in *Timberland Lumber Co. v. Bank of America National Trust & Savings Association*, 549 F.3d 597 (9th Cir. 1976): There must be (1) an effect on U.S. commerce; (2) the effect creates a cognizable injury under the Lanham Act;

and (3) international comity supports exterritorial jurisdiction.

The Ninth Circuit found that all three elements were satisfied in the case. As to prongs (1) and (2), the court found that the Hallatt's poor quality control practices could lead to consumers becoming ill and news of the illness could travel to the United States. Such news could harm Trader Joe's reputation and cause loss of sales. Hallatt's store also charged inflated prices and had poor customer service. The risk of reputational harm is particularly high in this case because Hallatt had adopted Trade Joe's trade dress for his store leading some consumers to believe it was an authorized Trader Joe's store. The court also found that Hallatt engaged in commercial activity in the United States as he purchased hundreds of thousands of dollars of inventory in the United States to resell in Canada. His activities might have been facilitated by his permanent residence status. The court found these activities to create a nexus to U.S. commerce.

On the third factor of international comity, the court engaged in a multifactor balancing test. Of these factors, the most important were that there was no conflict between the Lanham Act and any Canadian laws; U.S. courts would able to effectively enforce a remedy against Hallatt by an injunction prohibiting him from purchasing goods from Trade Joe's U.S. stores and from engaging in conduct in Canada if that conduct was found to violate the Lanham Act; Hallatt's actions could potentially mislead Canadian consumers who make up a substantial part of Trader Joe's business in its U.S. stores; and Hallatt intended to harm Trader Joe's and to trade on its goodwill. Finally, the court found that Hallatt's activity in the United States was significant, although the conduct most important to causing the harm was in Canada. This last factor weighed against exterritorial application of U.S. law to some extent, but overall these factors supported the exterritorial application of U.S. law.

11. TRIPS EXTENSION OF THE FAMOUS MARKS DOCTRINE

TRIPS Article 16 extends the protection for famous marks set forth in Article 6*bis* of the Paris Convention as follows:

TRIPS

Article 16
Rights Conferred

* * *

2. Article 6*bis* of the Paris Convention (1967) shall apply, *mutatis mutandis*, to services. In determining whether a trademark is well-known, Members shall take account of the knowledge of the trademark in the relevant sector of the public, including knowledge in the Member concerned which has been obtained as a result of the promotion of the trademark.

3. Article 6*bis* of the Paris Convention (1967) shall apply, *mutatis mutandis*, to goods or services which are not similar to those in respect

> of which a trademark is registered, provided that use of that trademark in relation to those goods or services would indicate a connection between those goods or services and the owner of the registered trademark and provided that the interests of the owner of the registered trademark are likely to be damaged by such use.

We have previously examined TRIPS Article 16(1) that prohibited the unauthorized use of a trademark on identical or substantially similar goods that would lead to a likelihood of confusion. TRIPS Article 16(3) provides additional protection for famous marks, including for services, by prohibiting the unauthorized use of the trademark on *dissimilar* goods and services in certain circumstances.

> Illustration 4-5. Premier Sports owns a famous trademark "Premier" for sneakers and other athletic shoes. Gen-Z Electronics uses Premier's trademark on a new line of mobile phones without Premier's authorization. Consumers are not confused into thinking that Premier is the producer of the mobile phones. Instead, many consumers assume that there is an economic relationship between Premier and Gen-Z. The use of its trademark on electronic goods damages the value of Premier's trademark, which is no longer perceived as used exclusively on athletic shoes.

Consumer confusion as to the source of the goods, the touchstone of trademark infringement, is not necessary for the infringement of a famous mark under Article 16(3).

The United States has implemented TRIPS's extended protections for famous marks in the Lanham Act provisions dealing with dilution claims. The main Lanham provisions are set forth as follows:

15 U.S.C. § 1125—False designations of origin, false descriptions, and dilution forbidden

* * *

(c) Dilution by blurring; dilution by tarnishment

(1) Injunctive relief

Subject to the principles of equity, the owner of a famous mark that is distinctive, inherently or through acquired distinctiveness, shall be entitled to an injunction against another person who, at any time after the owner's mark has become famous, commences use of a mark or trade name in commerce that is likely to cause dilution by blurring or dilution by tarnishment of the famous mark, regardless of the presence or absence of actual or likely confusion, of competition, or of actual economic injury.

(2) Definitions

(A) For purposes of paragraph (1), a mark is famous if it is widely recognized by the general consuming public of the United States as a designation of source of the goods or services of the mark's owner. In determining whether a mark possesses the requisite degree of recognition, the court may consider all relevant factors, including the following:

(i) The duration, extent, and geographic reach of advertising and publicity of the mark, whether advertised or publicized by the owner or third parties.

(ii) The amount, volume, and geographic extent of sales of goods or services offered under the mark.

(iii) The extent of actual recognition of the mark.

(iv) Whether the mark was registered under the Act of March 3, 1881, or the Act of February 20, 1905, or on the principal register.

(B) For purposes of paragraph (1), "dilution by blurring" is association arising from the similarity between a mark or trade name and a famous mark that impairs the distinctiveness of the famous mark.

(C) For purposes of paragraph (1), "dilution by tarnishment" is association arising from the similarity between a mark or trade name and a famous mark that harms the reputation of the famous mark.

A cause of action for dilution arises there is a likelihood of dilution, not actual dilution as was the case under the prior version of the statute. The current standard now makes dilution actions consistent with trademark infringement actions where the standard is likelihood of confusion.

The Lanham Act divides dilution claims for famous trademarks into dilution by blurring (§ 1125(c)(2)(B)) and dilution by tarnishment (§ 1125(c)(2)(C)). Blurring is an unauthorized use that weakens or impairs the distinctiveness of the famous trademark. If someone used Google on laundry detergent or McDonald's for a line of sneakers the use would impair the distinctiveness of those famous trademarks that are known for internet software and fast food. Consumers are not likely to believe that Google has branched into the business of making detergent or that McDonald's is making sneakers so there is no danger of consumer confusion as to the source of the goods. Nevertheless, the association of those famous trademarks known for certain products with other types of goods will blur their distinctiveness.

Dilution by tarnishment is when an unauthorized use of a famous trademark is offensive or denigrating. If someone used Tiffany's for a discount store that would harm the famous trademark known for expensive high-end jewelry. Nike used for a brand of cigarettes would harm the shoe company, which is associated with a healthy lifestyle. Victoria's Secret, a famous brand of women's lingerie and clothing, is harmed by Victor's Little Secret used for an adult novelty store. Consumers are not likely to believe that Tiffany's is now selling discount merchandise, that Nike is now selling cigarettes, or that Victoria's Secret has entered the adult novelty business.

Nevertheless, the association of the famous trademarks with unflattering uses will bring them into disrepute.

The current version of § 1125(c) is part of the Trademark Dilution Revision Act of 2006 that replaced the version contained in the Federal Trademark Dilution Act of 1995. Under the previous law, the legal standard for dilution by blurring applied by the courts was that the junior mark must be identical or nearly identical to the senior famous trademark. In *Levi Strauss & Co. v. Abercrombie & Fitch Trading Co.*, 633 F.3d 1158 (2d Cir. 2011), the Second Circuit ruled that this standard did not survive the enactment of the current version of § 1125(c). Nothing in the plain language of the current version of § 1125(c) requires a plaintiff to establish that the junior mark is identical or nearly identical to the senior mark. The current language of § 1125(c)(2)(B) defines blurring as "the association arising from the similarity between a mark and . . . a famous mark that impairs the distinctiveness of the famous mark." The emphasis in the current version is on the *degree* of similarity. Moreover, § 1125(c) makes clear that similarity is only one of several factors that must be considered in a determination of blurring.

Section 1125 (c)(B) provides:

> In determining whether a mark or trade name is likely to cause dilution by blurring, the court may consider all relevant factors, including the following:

(i) The degree of similarity between the mark or trade name and the famous mark.

(ii) The degree of inherent or acquired distinctiveness of the famous mark.

(iii) The extent to which the owner of the famous mark is engaging in substantially exclusive use of the mark.

(iv) The degree of recognition of the famous mark.

(v) Whether the user of the mark or trade name intended to create an association with the famous mark.

(vi) Any actual association between the mark or trade name and the famous mark.

The analysis set forth by § 1125(c)(2)(B) is a balancing test consisting of six factors of which the degree of similarity is only one. Nothing indicates that courts are required to give degree of similarity greater weight than the other factors.

The change in the legal standard under the current version of § 1125(c) is a welcome development because under the prior legal standard, a cause of action based on blurring used the same legal standard—likelihood of confusion—as a cause of action for trademark infringement for non-famous marks. If a junior trademark used on similar goods is identical or nearly identical to a senior trademark then the cause of action lies in trademark infringement and there is no need for a separate cause of action for dilution by blurring. Using the same legal standard only causes confusion between the two causes of action.

12. KEY WORD ADVERTISING ON THE INTERNET AND TRADEMARK RIGHTS

The rise of the internet has given rise to many challenges as trademark law has been forced to adapt to unanticipated new technologies. One area of dispute concerns the use of a keyword referencing service provided by search engines such as Google. The keyword service allows an advertiser to designate a competitor's trademark as a keyword. When viewers search the competitor's trademark the results of the search will include a link to the advertiser's own ad for its products and services.

Illustration 4-6. Premium Leather Accessories, a company that makes luxury handbags, pays Google a fee so that a link to an advertisement for its products appears whenever a viewer searches for Louis Vuitton handbags. Premium reserves certain keywords such as "Louis Vuitton" and "LV." When the viewer enters "Louis Vuitton handbags" into a Google search, the search returns results for Louis Vuitton handbags but also includes a link to an advertisement for Premium that will appear under the heading "sponsored links" on the right-hand side of the webpage. Clicking on the link will bring the viewer to Premium's advertisement. Louis Vuitton claims trademark infringement as its trademarks "Louis Vuitton" and "LV" have been used without its permission.

In the above illustration, liability issues arise concerning two entities: (1) the liability of the user or advertiser (Premium in the illustration above) for using a competitor's trademark as a keyword to create a link to its own advertisement and (2) the liability of the internet service provider (Google in the illustration above) for contributory infringement for providing the search engine that creates a link between the keyword and a link to the user's advertisement. The EU dealt with both issues in the following two cases.

In *Google France SARL v. Louis Vuitton Malletier SA*, [2010] E.T.M.R. 30, C–236/08, C–237/08, C–238–08 (March 23, 2010), the European Court of Justice held that Google did not infringe trademark rights when it allowed parties to use a competitor's trademark as a keyword in a search service.

As a preliminary matter, the court found that an advertiser's purpose in purchasing a keyword identical to a competitor's trademark is to display a link to its advertisement. This constitutes a use of the trademark in commerce by the advertiser. The court further found that a referencing service provider is engaging in commercial activity when it stores trademarks as keywords and displays ads on the basis of the keywords.

Turning to the liability of Google, the court referred to Article 14 of the of the EC Directive on Electronic Commerce, 2000/31/EC (June 8, 2000), which provides a safe harbor from liability for internet service providers that offer services for the processing and storage of data to recipients for renumeration. Article 14 states that the "provider of such a service cannot be held liable unless the service provider, after having become aware . . . of the unlawful nature of those data or of activities of that recipient, fails to act expeditiously to remove or to disable access to those data." To qualify for the safe harbor of Article 14, the service provided must be "of a mere technical, automatic and passive nature," which implies that the service provider "has neither knowledge of nor control over the information that is transmitted or stored."

The court went on to find that Google's keyword referencing service is passive and automatic. The court considered Google's keyword advertising service to be an information storage service that is accessed by keywords in a process that is mechanical. Google cannot be held liable unless Google had knowledge that the advertiser engaged in illegal conduct and failed to expeditiously to cancel the keyword search. The court suggested that Google's participating in the drafting of the commercial message accompanying the advertising link might not be merely passive and indicated that it is up to the national courts to fully assess Google's role in drafting of the message.

In *Interflora Inc. v. Marks & Spencer PLC*, [2012] E.T.M.R. 1, C–323/09 (2011), the European Court of Justice replied to a referral of the case from a national court on issues involving the interpretation of the EU Trademark Directive, 2015/2436 (Dec. 16, 2015). The court did not rule on the merits of the case but issued interpretations that would guide the lower courts in deciding the merits. The court considered the liability of an advertiser who uses a competitor's trademark as a keyword. Interflora Inc., a company incorporated in Michigan, operated a world-wide flower delivery business. Interflora did business in the UK through Interflora British Unit. Interflora is a registered trademark in the UK and is also an EU Trademark. The Interflora trademark has a substantial reputation in the UK and in the EU.

Marks and Spencer (M&S) is a retail company in the UK and is also in the flower delivery business. M&S selected "Interflora" and a few variants such as "Interflora Flowers," "Interflora Delivery," Interflora.com," and "Interflora co UK" as keywords in the Goggle search engine. When viewers entered any of the Interflora keywords into a Google search the results would include a link to an M&S advertisement that appeared under the sponsored links section of the webpage.

Interflora brought a lawsuit against M&S arguing that its use of Interflora's trademarks as keywords violated Article 5(1)(a) of the EU Trademark Directive, which provides that a trademark owner is entitled to prohibit a third party from using without the owner's consent a sign that is identical to the owner's sign on identical or similar goods.

The court found that use by M&S would violate Article 5(1)(a) if the M&S advertisement did not allow reasonably well-informed and observant internet users to discern, or to discern only after great difficulty, whether the goods originated from the owner of the trademark (Interflora) or from an undertaking economically linked to it or from a third party. For example, if M&S's use of the keyword led an internet user to believe that M&S is a subsidiary or affiliate of Interflora and part of its global commercial network of flower delivery services or that M&S is economically linked to Interflora (such as by being a franchisee or licensee) then the use of the trademark is confusing and a violation of Article 5(1)(a). On the other hand, if the user is able to discern that the goods and services do not originate from Interflora, but from M&S, a separate undertaking, then there is no violation of Article 5(1)(a) of the Trademark Directive.

The court also found that the use will interfere with the investment function of a trademark if the use interferes with the owner's efforts to create a trademark capable of attracting consumers and their loyalty. However, no interference exists if the only consequence of the use of the trademark by a third party is that the trademark owner must adjust its efforts to attract consumers and their loyalty.

The court then turned to the issue of whether there was a violation of Article 5(2) of the EU Trademark Directive protecting trademarks with a reputation or famous trademarks. The court found a use takes unfair advantage of the goodwill of a famous trademark if it causes the trademark to lose its distinctiveness by turning it into a generic term. If M&S's use of the word in a referencing service will gradually lead viewers to believe that Interflora is a generic word for any flower delivery service then the use is a dilution of a famous trademark and a violation of Article 5(2). On the other hand, if the use of the trademark as a keyword allowed viewers to determine that the goods originated from a competitor of Interflora, the trademark owner, then there is no dilution and no danger of genericide. Article 5(2) also prohibits free-riding on the goodwill of a famous trademark. The court found that no unfair advantage or free riding on the goodwill of the famous trademark will occur if a viewer can discern from the use of the keyword by M&S that it is offering an alternative to the goods and services of Interflora, the owner of the trademark.

In the United States, courts have held that keyword searches using trademarks constitute a use in commerce of the trademark by both the advertiser and the internet referencing service provider. The critical issue for liability purposes is whether the keyword ad is likely to cause consumer confusion. This is a fact specific inquiry to be made by the trial court. Some courts have found confusion while others have not. *Cf. Rosetta Stone Ltd. v. Google, Inc.*, 730 F. Supp. 2d 531 (E.D. Va. 2010) (no likelihood of confusion found for use of "Rosetta Stone" in keyword search) with *Storus Corp. v. Aroa Marketing, Inc.*, 2008 WL 449835 (N.D. Cal. 2008) (likelihood of confusion found for use of trademark "smart money clip" by competitor for identical goods).

13. TERMINATION OF RIGHTS AND EXCEPTIONS

a. Abandonment

TRIPS Article 19(1) provides: "If use is required to maintain a registration, the registration may be cancelled only after an uninterrupted period of at least three years of non-use, unless valid reasons based on the existence of obstacles to such use are shown by the trademark owner." Valid reasons for non-use include government actions banning the use. For example, if a government prohibits imports of the trademarked goods into a country then the trademark owner has a valid reason for not using the trademark in that country.

In the EU, when a trademark has not been in use for the required period then a third party can bring an action to revoke the trademark in the EU Intellectual Property Office. The burden then shifts to the trademark owner to prove genuine use within the relevant period. That was the posture of the case in *AREs Performance AG v. Ferrari S.p.A*, European Union Intellectual Property Office, Cancellation Division, No. C 30 743 (2018). On November 29, 2008, Ferrari obtained an EU trademark registration for the shape of a Ferrari sports car known as the 250 GTO that was produced from 1962 to 1964. Only 39 units were ever produced, all of which were still in existence at the time of the trademark dispute. Ferrari had obtained registrations for the trademark in various classes: class 12 (vehicles), class 25 (clothing), class 28 (games and playthings), and class 28 (toy vehicles and scale-model vehicles).

Under EU law, a trademark is subject to cancellation if it has not been used for a continuous period of five years. Ferrari was able to show genuine use only for toy and scale-model vehicles for the relevant five year period. Ferrari submitted extracts from websites, catalogues, and five receipts of sales of 56 units for the toy model of the G-250 during the relevant period and of 120 units dated shortly after the end of the relevant period. For clothing, Ferrari was able to show extracts from websites but no evidence of any sales. The EU office found that no genuine use had been shown for clothing.

Ferrai faced a special problem with respect to the GT-250 sports car itself. The sports car was intended to be produced in limited numbers for a very small target group of extremely wealthy persons. (A vintage GT-250 sold for $70 million in 2018.) The car was then expected to become a collectible vintage car that would be constantly maintained and sold and resold at very large sums on the vintage car market. The car was never intended to be mass produced, to result in numerous sales, and then disposed of after a period of use. For this type of specialty car, there would only be a few sales and resales of the car due to its highly selective target audience.

The EU Intellectual Property Office provided guidance on how products of this type could meet the use requirement. Even though the trademark had not been used on a new car since 1962–64, the trademark could be used in connection with after sales service such as the sale of accessories, parts, and the supply of maintenance and repair services. The trademark could be used in connection with services for reconditioning and certifications of used GT-250 cars. However, Ferrari did not use the GT-250 trademark in any of these circumstances but used the umbrella Ferrari brand instead. As for the resales of the cars, the resales occurred through private transactions and cannot be considered to a use of the trademark by Ferrari. With enough planning, Ferrari might have been able to take part in the sales and auctions of used GT-250 cars.

The case indicates that it is possible with sufficient planning to maintain use of a trademark even in the highly specialized market for extremely expensive sports cars. Fulfilling the use requirement for such products, however, requires careful planning and can require more effort than for ordinary consumer goods.

b. Exceptions

TRIPS Article 17 provides that "[m]embers may provide limited exceptions to the rights conferred by a trademark, such as fair use of the descriptive terms, provided that such exceptions take account of the legitimate interests of the owner of the trademark and third parties."

Trademark law has always offered a comparably weaker form of protection than copyrights or patents. Trademark law does not grant exclusive rights but only prevents the unauthorized use of a trademark when it is likely to lead to consumer confusion. As a result, some uses of a trademark will not be considered infringement but as fair use. For example, some trademarks are descriptive, i.e. they describe one aspect of the product, but acquire secondary meaning or distinctiveness in the minds of consumers through use. Some examples of descriptive trademarks are creamy for yoghurt, crispy for French fries, fresh for milk, and crystal clear for distilled water. To the extent that a third party uses the term for a descriptive purpose only and not as a source identifier, the use is descriptive fair use and is not an infringement of the trademark. If a competitor of the "Creamy Yoghurt" brand states that its own yogurt is creamy then the use is descriptive and a fair use. The risk to the trademark owner of choosing a descriptive trademark is that others may be able to use the trademark to describe some quality of their own goods.

A second type of fair use is nominative use of the trademark. Nominative fair use occurs when a third party uses the trademark to refer to the branded product itself because there are no other words that can be reasonably used to do so. If a soft drink company has a television commercial claiming that a blind test of consumers shows that its soft drink tastes better than Coca-Cola, the use of Coca-Cola is nominative fair use. The competitor is using the trademark Coca-Cola not as a source identifier for its own products but to describe Coca-Cola products because those are only words that can describe the product.

The Supreme Court has made clear that in cases of descriptive fair use, the defendant has no obligation to show the lack of consumer confusion and that in some cases of descriptive fair use some confusion must be tolerated. In *KP Permanent Make-Up Inc. v. Lasting impression I, Inc.*, 543 U.S. 111 (2004), Lasting Impression I sued KP Permanent Make-Up Inc. for using the term "micro-color." Both companies sold permanent makeup, which uses an injection of color pigments and liquids under the skin to mask injuries and to hide unwanted natural features. In 1992, Lasting Impression had obtained a registration for "Micro Color" from the U.S. Patent and Trademark Office and in 1999, the registration became incontestable. (Under 15 U.S.C. § 1065, after a period of five years, a trademark becomes incontestable, meaning that various aspects of the trademark cannot be challenged by third parties, such as the validity of the trademark. Incontestability applies only to federally registered trademarks.) Also in 1999, KP produced a 10 page brochure for its products using micro-color in large-stylized letters. When Lasting Impression asked KP to stop using micro-color, KP sought a declaratory judgment that its use of micro-color was descriptive fair use and did not infringe Lasting Impression's rights.

The district court granted KP's request for a declaratory judgment. On appeal, the Ninth Circuit vacated the lower court judgment, holding that no finding of fair use is possible if there is a likelihood of consumer confusion. The court also placed the burden of showing a lack of consumer confusion on KP, the party asserting the fair use defense.

The Supreme Court reversed the Ninth Circuit. The Court found that nothing in the language of the Lanham Act created a burden on the part of the defendant asserting a fair use defense to show lack of consumer confusion. The Court also noted that in trademark litigation, the plaintiff must prove likelihood of confusion as an essential element of its case. Given this burden on the plaintiff, it makes no sense to require the defendant to affirmatively prove lack of consumer confusion. All the defendant needs to show is that the plaintiff has not carried its burden of proof.

As the plaintiff bears the burden of proof to show consumer confusion in descriptive fair use cases, there will be cases where fair use is found although some confusion exists. This can occur when there is confusion that does not arise to the legal standard of likelihood of confusion or where the plaintiff has failed to provide probative evidence, such as a consumer survey, to the court. The Supreme Court noted that some confusion is compatible with fair use. The trademark owner made the choice to use a descriptive term as a trademark but that decision cannot deprive the public from continuing to use the term in a descriptive sense.

14. INTERNET DOMAIN NAMES AND TRADEMARKS

With the rise of the internet in the 1990s, thousands of disputes began to arise concerning the use of internet domain names that copied or used trademarks. Many of these disputes concerned cybersquatting, i.e. the use of a trademark by an unauthorized party as a domain name with the intention to profit off that use. These cases soon flooded the courts and a need arose to create an alternative and stream-lined procedure to handle these disputes. In 1999, the World Intellectual Property Organization recommended that the Internet Corporation for Assigned Names and Numbers (ICANN), the non-profit organization set up in 1998 to oversee the international registry for internet domain names, create a policy and a mechanism to deal with these disputes. The result of these efforts was the Uniform Dispute Resolution Policy established on October 24, 1999.

The Dispute Policy created an arbitration process for the resolution of domain name disputes. Arbitration is an informal dispute resolution process outside of the courts and conducted by private persons. Under the Dispute Policy, arbitration is not an exclusive remedy. Any party can also bring a lawsuit before or after the arbitration process. However, if a party files an arbitration claim under the Dispute Policy, anyone who registered a domain name had to submit to a resolution proceeding before a panel of arbitrators and to abide by its decision. A party that did not wish to abide by the decision must bring a lawsuit in a court.

In any arbitration under the Dispute Policy, the complainant must show three elements:

> (1) the domain name is identical or confusingly similar to the complainant's trademark;
>
> (2) the respondent has no rights or legitimate interests in respect of the domain name; and
>
> (3) the domain name was registered and is being used in bad faith.

Dispute Policy, ¶ 4(a). The last element is critical. The Dispute Policy can decide disputes only when the registration and use of the domain name is in bad faith. To establish a bad faith registration and use under the Dispute Policy, the complainant must show:

> (i) circumstances indicating that you have registered or you have acquired the domain name primarily for the purpose of selling, renting, or otherwise transferring the domain name registration to the complainant who is the owner of the trademark or service mark or to a competitor of that complainant, for valuable consideration in excess of your documented out-of-pocket costs directly related to the domain name; or
>
> (ii) you have registered the domain name in order to prevent the owner of the trademark or service mark from reflecting the mark in a corresponding domain name, provided that you have engaged in a pattern of such conduct; or

> (iii) you have registered the domain name primarily for the purpose of disrupting the business of a competitor; or
>
> (iv) by using the domain name, you have intentionally attempted to attract, for commercial gain, Internet users to your web site or other on-line location, by creating a likelihood of confusion with the complainant's mark as to the source, sponsorship, affiliation, or endorsement of your web site or location or of a product or service on your web site or location.

Dispute Policy, ¶ 4(b).

If the arbitrators find a bad faith registration and use, the arbitrators have the authority to order the cancellation, transfer, or changes in the registration. ICANN will implement the arbitrators' decision after 10 business days unless a party notifies ICANN that it has filed a case in court within the 10-day period. Once notified of the court case, ICANN will not implement the arbitration decision and will take no further action unless it receives notification that the parties have settled the case, the case has been dismissed, or that a court order has been issued that the respondent has no right to use the domain name.

An example of how a complainant was able to prove bad faith and obtain a transfer of the domain name from the respondent is *Madonna Ciccone, P/K/A Madonna v. Dan Parisi and "Madonna.com"*, WIPO Case No. D2000–0847 (October 12, 2000). The complainant was the well-known singer and entertainer Madonna who was the owner of trademark registrations for MADONNA for entertainment and related services. Some of Madonna's work has been controversial and has involved sexually explicit content. Respondent Parisi was in the business of developing websites for profit. On or about May 29, 1998, Parisi purchased the registration for the domain name Madonna.com for $20,000. On June 4, 1998, Parisi registered Madonna as a trademark in Tunisia, a country in north Africa. A few days later, Parisi began operating an adult entertainment website with explicit sexual content under the Madonna.com domain name. The website included a disclaimer that it was not affiliated with or endorsed by Madonna. By March 4, 1999, Parisi removed the sexual content and by May 31, 1999 the website was effectively shut down. On June 9, 1999 through her attorneys, Madonna objected to the respondent's use of the Madonna.com domain name and sought arbitration under the Dispute Policy. As the domain name and the trademark Madonna are identical, the arbitrators' decision focused on whether Parisi had legitimate rights in the domain name and on bad faith registration and use.

The arbitrators found that Parisi could offer no reasonable explanation for his choice of the Madonna domain name for an adult content website. They concluded that the only possible explanation is that he chose the name with an intent to capitalize on the fame of the complainant for commercial gain. The arbitrators rejected Parisi's argument that the registration of the trademark in Tunisia created legitimate trademark rights. Parisi did not reside in Tunisia and did not make any use of the trademark in Tunisia. The registration might in fact be seen as evidence of bad faith. At a minimum, it did not show any legitimate rights in the domain name under the facts of the case.

Parisi also claimed that he made a legitimate non-commercial use of the trademark when he made an offer to transfer the domain name to the Madonna Hospital in Lincoln, Nebraska. The arbitrators also rejected this claim noting that the offer was made after Parisi had been contacted by lawyers for the complainant. The negotiations to transfer the domain name were also inconclusive.

Turning to the issue of bad faith registration, the arbitrators could find no explanation for why Parisi chose the domain name other than for the specific purpose of trading on the fame of the complainant for commercial gain. Parisi could offer no explanation why he paid $20,000 for the domain name or why that name was valuable as an attraction for an adult content website. The disclaimer on the website that it was not affiliated with the complainant was not deemed to effectively negate bad faith. The disclaimer might not be understood by some viewers and the disclaimer would be available only after a viewer had already been attracted to the website. While Parisi did not actually register the domain name but purchased it from a third party, the arbitrators treated the purchase as equivalent to a bad faith registration.

Parisi made an argument that Madonna was being disingenuous in claiming that her reputation could be tarnished by his actions since she had already associated herself with sexually explicit content in her work as an entertainer. The arbitrators pointed out that her reputation can be tarnished if she is associated with sexual content not of her own making and not in accordance with her creative intent and standards of quality. Having found that Parisi had no legitimate rights in the domain name and that he acted in bad faith, the arbitrators ordered the respondent to transfer the domain name to the complainant.

In another case involving a famous singer and similar facts, the arbitrators reached the opposite conclusion and found that the registration of the domain name was not in bad faith. In *Bruce Springsteen v. Jeff Burgar and Bruce Springsteen Fan Club*, Case No. D2000–1332 (January 25, 2001), the respondent Burgar registered the domain name brucespringteen.com through the Bruce Springsteen Fan Club of which Burgar was the administrator. Clicking on the domain name would route the viewer to Burgar's other website "celebrity1000.com." The singer Bruce Springsteen subsequently challenged Burgar's use of the domain under the Dispute Policy.

As the first element of identity or similarity of the domain name and the complainant's name was not at issue, the arbitrators focused on the second and third elements of the complainant's case: whether Burgar had a legitimate interest in the domain name and whether he acted in bad faith.

The arbitrators found that Burgar had a legitimate interest in the domain name. The complainant has the burden of proof of showing that Burgar had no legitimate interest in the domain name. In this case, the arbitrators focused on why it was difficult to find that Burgar's registration was misleading. The arbitrators found that any viewer searching Bruce Springsteen on the internet will get thousands of hits and no viewer would assume that all of the hits are authorized or official sites. The arbitrators concluded that a viewer clicking on the domain name and being diverted to celebrity1000.com would just conclude that the hit was of a non-affiliated site and would not feel misled.

The arbitrators also found no evidence of bad faith. A key element of this finding was that Burgar never attempted to sell the domain name to Springsteen. Burgar also never attempted to block Springsteen from using his name for a domain name. When Burgar registered his domain name, he also could have registered the name using the suffixes .net and .org if he wanted to prevent Springsteen from using his name for a domain name. As an experienced internet user, Burgar was surely aware of these options but he chose not to use them. In fact, Springsteen later registered the domain name "brucespringsteen.net." The arbitrators also found that Burgar never intended to use the domain name for commercial gain. The arbitrators found that it was unlikely that a viewer seeing the domain name "brucespringteen.com" would automatically assume that it was the official site. Anyone clicking on the site would find that it was not official and then just move on with searching.

One significant difference between Burgar and Parisi, the respondent in the *Madonna* case, is that Burgar does not seem to be motivated by financial gain. He seemed to be an odd character who was keenly interested in and possibly obsessed with celebrities. While his eccentricity may make Burgar stand out, eccentricity is not the same as bad faith.

One aspect of the case deserves some further discussion. Early in the decision the arbitrators stated that it was not possible to register Springsteen's name as a trademark and that he could assert common law or state law rights in his name only. It is not entirely clear whether the arbitrators were suggesting that proper names cannot be registered as trademarks under the Lanham Act. To be clear, there is no reason why a proper name cannot be a trademark if it has acquired secondary meaning as an indicator of a source of goods or services. For example, Martha Stewart is a registered trademark for wine and Ralph Lauren is a registered trademark for men's clothing and accessories in the United States.

C. GEOGRAPHICAL INDICATIONS

Geographical indications (GIs) are modern intellectual property rights that recognize rights created by longstanding or, in some cases, ancient production processes related to food and wine associated with particular geographical locations. Long before the first trademark law was passed by the Parliament of England under the reign of King Henry III in 1266, countries in Europe were making products that were identified with particular geographical regions. Prosciutto di Parma or Parma Ham dates back thousands of years with the first recorded reference to a distinctive ham from the town of Parma in Italy traced to 100 B.C. The name Bordeaux has been used continuously to refer to wine from the Bordeaux region of France for nearly 2,000 years since the Romans planted the first vineyards. Champagne can be traced to the Roman vineyards in the Champagne region of France planted in the 5th century B.C., although the modern sparkling version of Champagne was invented by the French monk Dom Perignon in 1688.

TRIPS now requires all WTO members to protect GIs although TRIPS does not require a separate legal regime for GIs. Many countries protect GIs using trademark and related doctrines. The EU has a separate legal regime for GIs, the most complex and sophisticated in the world.

1. GEOGRAPHICAL INDICATIONS AND PROTECTED DESIGNATIONS OF ORIGIN

a. TRIPS Provisions

Under TRIPS Article 22, a GI indicates a good "as originating in the territory of a Member, or a region or locality in that territory, where a given quality, reputation or other characteristic of the good is essentially attributable to its geographical origin."

TRIPS Article 22 provides that GIs are entitled to the following protections:

TRIPS

Article 22
Protection of Geographical Indications

* * *

2. In respect of geographical indications, Members shall provide the legal means for interested parties to prevent:

(a) the use of any means in the designation or presentation of a good that indicates or suggests that the good in question originates in a geographical area other than the true place of origin in a manner which misleads the public as to the geographical origin of the good;

(b) any use which constitutes an act of unfair competition within the meaning of Article 10*bis* of the Paris Convention (1967).

3. A Member shall, *ex officio* if its legislation so permits or at the request of an interested party, refuse or invalidate the registration of a trademark which contains or consists of a geographical indication with respect to goods not originating in the territory indicated, if use of the indication in the trademark for such goods in that Member is of such a nature as to mislead the public as to the true place of origin.

4. The protection under paragraphs 1, 2 and 3 shall be applicable against a geographical indication which, although literally true as to the territory, region or locality in which the

goods originate, falsely represents to the public that the goods originate in another territory.

Under TRIPS Article 22(1), members are to provide the judicial or administrative means to prevent the use of geographical terms that mislead the public about the geographical origins of the good.

Illustration 4-7. A supermarket in Pennsylvania sells a distinctive style of blue cheese with the label "Roquefort Cheese," a geographical indication currently registered and owned by French entities. If the cheese does not actually originate from the Roquefort-sur-Soulzon region of France, the use of the geographical indication "Rocquefort" would violate Article 22(1). The United States must provide the means for the owner of the Rocquefort geographical indication to enjoin or otherwise prevent its use. However, if the label of the product indicated its true geographical origin such as "Roquefort Cheese made in Pennsylvania," there would be no violation because there would be no consumer confusion.

Article 22(2) requires a member to provide the judicial and administrative means to prevent unfair competition as defined in Article 10*bis* of the Paris Convention (unfair competition is discussed in the next chapter). Article 22(3) requires members to invalidate or refuse to register a trademark consisting of a misleading geographical indication. Article 22(4), extends these protections to "a geographical indication which, although literally true as to the territory, region or locality in which the goods originate, falsely represents to the public that the goods originate in another territory." An example of this type of use would be representing that a ham from the town of Parma, Ohio (located outside of Cleveland) is a Parma ham, suggesting that the ham is from the Parma region of Italy.

TRIPS Article 24 contains important exceptions to Article 22. Article 24 provides in relevant part:

TRIPS

Article 24
International Negotiations; Exceptions

* * *

5. Where a trademark has been applied for or registered in good faith, or where rights to a trademark have been acquired through use in good faith either:

(a) before the date of application of these provisions in that Member as defined in Part VI; or

(b) before the geographical indication is protected in its country of origin;

Measures adopted to implement this Section shall not prejudice eligibility for or the validity of the registration of a trademark, or the right to use a trademark, on the basis that such a trademark is identical with, or similar to, a geographical indication.

6. Nothing in this Section shall require a Member to apply its provisions in respect of a

geographical indication of any other Member with respect to goods or services for which the relevant indication is identical with the term customary in common language as the common name for such goods or services in the territory of that Member. . . .

* * *

8. The provisions of this Section shall in no way prejudice the right of any person to use, in the course of trade, that person's name or the name of that person's predecessor in business, except where such name is used in such a manner as to mislead the public.

9. There shall be no obligation under this Agreement to protect geographical indications which are not or cease to be protected in their country of origin, or which have fallen into disuse in that country.

Article 24(5) requires countries to "grandfather" trademarks applied for, registered, or used in good faith before TRIPS became effective or before the GI was protected in its country of origin. Article 24(6) allows a country to deny protection for GIs that have become generic, i.e. the customary term by which the good or service has become known to the public. Article 24(8) provides that GIs cannot prejudice a person's right to use that person's name or the name of a predecessor in business except when to do so would mislead the public. Article 24(9) provides that a country can deny protection to a GI that is no longer protected in its country of origin.

b. GIs in the EU

The EU protects GIs through the use of a registration system that creates the most extensive protections for GIs in the world. Within this system, the EU distinguishes between geographical indications and protected designations of origin (PDOs) that are subject to stricter requirements and receive higher protections.

PDOs describe a foodstuff that has certain qualities and characteristics that are a result of the inherent and natural features of a particular geographical environment. For example, due to natural factors, a certain type of grape can be grown only in one region. In addition, for a PDO, every part of the production, processing, and preparation of the good must take place in the region. For PDOs for wines, all of the grapes must come from the region and all steps of the process of making wine from the grape must also occur in the region. GIs are less restrictive; GIs also indicate that a product's quality is significantly linked to a geographical location but the link for PDOs is stronger and more exclusive. Some of the grapes for a GI for wine and some of the stages of production of the wine can occur outside of the region.

Consorzio Del Prosciutto Di Parma v. ASDA Stores Ltd., [2003] ECR I–5121, Case C–108/01 (May 20, 2003) concerned a dispute about the PDO for Prosciutto di Parma (Parma Ham) registered by the Consorzio di Prosciutto di Parma, an association of producers of Parma ham from the Parma region of Italy. Hygrade Foods, a UK importer, had imported deboned whole hams from a member of the Consorzio. Hygrade then sliced, packaged, and labeled the ham as "Genuine Italian Parma Ham." Asda Stores, a supermarket chain, sold the hams to the public. The Consorzio challenged these practices on the ground that its PDO required the slicing and packaging of the ham to occur in Parma under the supervision of the Consorzio.

In their defense, the UK entities argued that the PDO was invalid. The UK entities claimed that by requiring the slicing and packaging of the ham in Parma in order to be able to use the PDO, the PDO discouraged exports in violation of Article 29 of the EC Treaty that prohibited export restrictions. The PDO led to export restrictions that favored domestic trade over exports in violation of Article 29. The Consorzio countered that under an exception to Article 29 of the EC Treaty, export trade restrictions are justified if they are necessary to protect intellectual property rights. As the case involved an interpretation of EU law, the UK courts referred the case to the European Court of Justice.

The European Court of Justice found that the conditions of slicing and packaging in Parma were justified because they were necessary to protect the PDO and that the PDO justified the export trade restrictions. The conditions of the PDO were necessary to maintain the quality of the product. Only deboned whole hams that satisfied certain conditions as to quality may be sliced. The slicing process involved an additional selection process made during the slicing operations as certain hams that have anomalies such as dots and areas of blankness may be rejected. These anomalies cannot be detected without slicing the ham. At all times during the slicing and packaging, representatives of the Consorzio are present to make special assessments of the quality of the operations and the ham. The court found that fewer guarantees of quality were present if these operations occurred outside of Parma and without the supervision of the Consorzio.

The UK entities argued that the Consorzio allowed its members to export whole hams and as the ham is normally consumed in slices, the Consorzio must have known that slicing operations would occur abroad. The Consorzio exported the ham based on the assumption that all slicing would occur at the retail level. The court distinguished between the type of slicing by Hygrade at the wholesale level and slicing of the whole ham at the retail level by supermarkets and restauranteurs outside the Parma region. Retail slicing operations normally occur in front of the consumer (or at least for those that demand it). Consumers can witness the slicing by the supermarket behind the counter or by the restaurant chefs at the front of the table. If the slicing by these business operators led to an inferior final product, the consumer would attribute its inferior quality to the UK business operator and would not blame the Consorzio. The reputation of its PDO would remain intact.

The problem was with slicing operations upstream in the chain of commerce by a wholesale distributor such as Hygrade. These operations occurred at a point in commerce not visible to the consumer and where the quality controls of the Consorzio were lacking. If the consumer receives an inferior final product due to upstreaming slicing the consumer might assume that all hams from Parma are of poor quality, harming the PDO's reputation. (On a technical issue, the PDO did not bind Hygrade or Asda because the Consorzio failed to give them proper notice as required by the EC Regulation.)

The issue of whether a PDO has lost protection due to becoming a generic term was involved in *The Federal Republic of Germany and The Kingdom of Denmark v. Commission of the European Communities*, [2005] ECR-I, C–465/02, C–466/02 (October 25, 2002). Germany and Denmark argued that "feta" had become a generic term for a certain type of goat cheese and that the PDO for feta obtained by Greece was invalid.

The European Court of Justice first noted that the term "feta" in Greek can be traced to an Italian word "fetta" meaning slice that entered the Greek language in the seventeenth century. The EC regulation in effect at the time of the case provided that certain non-geographical names can be PDOs if they met the conditions of PDOs set forth in other parts of the regulation. That is, similar to trademarks, a non-geographical name can become a PDO if it fulfills the conditions of PDOs and also if it acquires a secondary meaning in the minds of consumers as referring to a region. (The current regulation effective as of May 13, 2024 takes a similar position.) The court found that the PDO for feta met these conditions.

The court then turned to the issue of whether the geographical area defined for the production of feta meets the requirements of Article 2(2)(a) for PDOs that "the quality or characteristics" of an agricultural foodstuff "are essentially or exclusively due to a particular geographical environment with its inherent natural and human factors." The court found that the PDO for feta covered a geographical area for mainland Greece and Lesbos, an island, that is mountainous or semi-mountainous, that had mild winters, hot summers and a great deal of sunshine, and that had typical vegetation of the Balkan medium mountain range. These features distinguished it from the adjoining areas. The distinctive natural features of the geographical area gave the feta cheese made from ewes and goats milk from this area distinctive organoleptic qualities and characteristics.

As to whether "feta" had become a generic term, the court looked at several factors. Greece produced 115,000 tons of feta annually while Denmark produced 27,640 tons in 1988. Germany's production varied from between 19,757 and 39,201 from since 1985, and France's production varied from between 7,960 to 19,964 tons from 1988–1998. While Greece's production of feta according to some accounts dates back some 8,000 years, production in Germany (1972), France (1931), and Denmark (1930s) is recent. In addition, some 85 percent of all feta consumption occurs in Greece. The court also noted that feta cheese sold in the EU is commonly adorned with labels referring to Greek cultural traditions and heritage.

The court noted that data indicated that the majority of Greek consumers considered feta to carry a geographical indication while a majority of consumers in Denmark believed that it did not. However, Danish legislation does not refer to "feta" but to "Danish feta" a designation that suggests that the term feta used alone indicated a Greek origin. Based upon all of these facts, the court concluded that feta had not become a generic term and did not lose its status as a PDO.

Several of the factors cited by the court, such as the production and consumption figures, indicate the economic importance of feta to Greece but they are not directly related to the issue of whether feta has become a generic term. Although the economic and cultural significance of the product are not explicitly stated as factors in the case, these factors seemed to have some bearing on the court's final decision that feta is not a generic term. If the court had found feta to be generic such a finding could have caused significant economic and cultural harm to Greece. The potential harm to Greece of an adverse ruling may have played a role in the court's decision.

2. TRIPS PROVISIONS FOR WINES AND SPIRITS

a. Heightened Protection

TRIPS provides for an increased level of protection for wines and spirits beyond what is required by Article 22, which applies to all goods.

Article 23 provides:

TRIPS

Article 23
Additional Protections for Geographical Indications for Wines and Spirits

1. Each Member shall provide the legal means for interested parties to prevent use of a geographical indication identifying wines for wines not originating in the place indicated by the geographical indication in question or identifying spirits for spirits not originating in the place indicated by the geographical indication in question, even where the true origin of the goods is indicated or the geographical indication is used in translation or accompanied by expressions such as "kind", "type", "style", "imitation" or the like.

Article 22 prohibits the use of geographical indications that are misleading. Article 23 prohibits the use of a geographical indication for wines and spirits even when it is not misleading.

Illustration 4-8. A supermarket sells a wine with the following label: "Bordeau-Style Red Wine made from grapes grown in Hudson Valley, New York." Bordeaux is a PDO (since 1973). The use of the PDO is prohibited under TRIPS even though the label indicates that the wine is from New York so there is no consumer confusion about the origin of the wine. The use of the expression "style" does not cure the violation.

Article 23 is subject to the general exceptions contained in Article 24 discussed previously. In addition, Article 24 contains two exceptions that apply in particular to wines and spirits. Article 24(4) grandfathers the use of GIs for wines if used in a continuous manner for at least 10 years before April 15, 1994 or in good faith preceding that date. Article 24(6) allows countries to continue uses of geographical indications using grape varieties that have become generic terms as of the date of entry of the WTO (January 1, 1995).

The United States divides wines into three categories: "generic, semi-generic, and non-generic designations of geographic significance." 24 CFR § 4.24. Only those wines that are non-generic are entitled to the full protection of Article 23 of TRIPS, i.e. they cannot be used unless the wine originates from the region even if the true origins of the wine are disclosed and there can be no consumer confusion. The United States has also invented a new category called "semi-generic" that is not found anywhere in TRIPS. Into this category fall wines that are protected by PDOs in their country of origin but can be used in the United States if the true origin of the wine is disclosed. Such current PDOs as

Champagne, Burgundy, and Chablis fall into the semi-generic category as set forth in 24 CFR § 4.24(b)(2). All of these PDOs are owned by French entities. Under the U.S. semi-generic classification, "California Champagne" is a permitted use. Under TRIPS, "California champagne" is a violation of Article 23. Champagne can be used only for wines from the Champagne region of France even if the true origins (California) are disclosed.

As the semi-generic category appears to be a violation of TRIPS, the question may arise as to why France has not challenged the "semi-generic" category in the WTO. Although there may be a number of reasons, one practical reason may be that France considers the current situation with the United States to be satisfactory even if less than ideal. The United States is one of the world's most important markets for French wines and many French wines are included in the non-generic category entitled to full Article 23 protection. France may realize that if it challenges the semi-generic classification, nothing prevents the United States from reclassifying champagne, burgundy, and chablis as generic terms free for anyone to use under any conditions. France may have accepted the status quo based on a realization that any provocations of the United States might result in a worsening of the situation. In 2006 France and the United States reached an agreement that semi-generic wines would be limited to the 16 wines then listed in 24 CFR § 4.24 and that no new names would be added to the list. This agreement appears to have resolved the issue for now.

An example of the extensive protections enjoyed by PDOs for wines under EU law is exemplified by *Les Grand Chais de France SAS v. Consorzio Di Tutela Della Denominazione Di Origine Controllata Prosecco*, [2020] England and Wales High Court 1633 (Chancery Division) (June 24, 2020). Les Grand Chais de France, a French company, filed for a trademark registration in England for its mark "Nosecco" for non-alcoholic sparkling wines. The Consorzio Di Tutela Della Denominazione Di Origine Controllata Prosecco opposed the registration. The Consorzio was formed to protected "Prosecco," a PDO registered under EU law for a type of sparkling wine. Prosecco was first produced in Prosecco, Trieste Italy in 1382 and was registered as a PDO under EU legislation on August 1, 2009. The Consorzio argued that "Nosecco" violated Article 103(2)(b) of an EC regulation that protects PDOs against "any misuse, imitation or evocation." The UK was required to apply EU law under the relevant provisions of its trademark law. A hearing in the UK was held at which the hearing officer upheld the Consorzio's opposition to the trademark registration for Nosecco. The case was then appealed to the England and Wales High Court.

The court's decision focused on the element of "evocation" prohibited by the EC regulation. Evocation occurs when a term used to designate a product incorporates part of a PDO and the use of the term evokes the PDO in the mind of the consumer. No consumer confusion is necessary for evocation. All that is required is that the contested term calls the PDO to mind.

The court affirmed the hearing officer's order, finding that evocation was present. In discussing the evidence, the court pointed to numerous posts written by consumers on Instagram, Twitter and Facebook linking Nosecco to Prosecco, including numerous posts referring to Nosecco as "non-alcoholic Prosecco." These posts from the public seemed to be particularly persuasive to the court as representing the genuine and unprompted perception of ordinary consumers. The court noted that these posts were not prepared for litigation and so had distinct advantages over evidence specifically prepared for litigation. The link between Nosecco and Prosecco seem to be an instant reaction of the public. There were also articles in the press and social media making the same connection. The court concluded that the evidence supported the hearing officer's conclusion that Nosecco evoked the PDO.

In its defense Les Grand Chais argued that "Nosecco" was a coined novel name to highlight the non-alcoholic nature of its beverage. The term "secco" means "dry" in Italian so "Nosecco" means not dry or sweet. Les Grand Chais argued that it never borrowed any part of the PDO Prosecco for its trademark Nosecco and never tried to take advantage of Prosecco's goodwill. Les Grand Chais claimed that the origins of the Nosecco trademark were entirely innocent and any similarities between the two names was coincidental. Whether or not this dubious claim is true, the result is still the same. Under EU law, it does not matter that a third party does not intend to evoke a PDO or that the evocation is innocent, coincidental, or fortuitous. No matter what the cause, if there is evocation the use violates EU law.

Protection against evocation prohibits a third party trading on the goodwill of the PDO. There is no need to show consumer confusion. The mere association with the PDO in the mind of the consumer is an unlawful trading on the PDO's goodwill. The association does not have to be offensive or denigrating.

Comparing evocation with U.S. law illustrates some important contrasts. In the United States, federal law protects famous trademarks from blurring or tarnishment, which also does not require consumer confusion but evocation seems to go beyond both doctrines. There was no tarnishment involved in the *Prosecco* case because associating Nosecco with Prosecco will not bring disrepute to the latter. Nonsecco is a non-alcoholic wine that appears to be quite popular and fashionable among young people and health conscious persons. There was also no blurring, which occurs when a mark that is similar or identical to a famous mark is used on a different product. Nosecco and Prosecco are not similar marks as no one would believe that they are the same. The importance of the name Nosecco for Les Grand Chais is that the name immediately evokes a comparison with Prosecco in a clever and witty way, but that evocation is not permitted because it trades on the goodwill of Prosecco. Evocation is a type of protection that goes beyond what is offered under U.S. trademark law.

b. TRIPS Negotiations and the Future of Protection for Wines and Spirits

TRIPS Article 23(4) provides that WTO members should enter into negotiations for an international system of notification and registration of GIs for wines. Article 24(1) provides that members will also engage in negotiations for increasing protections for wines. Negotiations under these TRIPS articles were commenced in the WTO but no agreements could be reached before the negotiations ceased altogether in 2011. No new negotiations have been implemented in the WTO since 2011 so these negotiations seem to have permanently stalled.

As multilateral efforts seem to have failed, the EU has pursued a path of increasing protections for wines outside of the WTO. The EU has entered into numerous bilateral and regional free trade agreements with its trading partners. In its free trade agreements, the EU requires its trading partners to commit to "TRIPS plus" standards, i.e. higher levels of protections for wines than that available under TRIPS. This can be an effective strategy as the EU has many dozens of agreements with trading partners all over the world. By contrast, the United States has never been enthusiastic about GIs and has entered into free trade agreements that contain minimalist protections for wines through certification and collective trademarks. The conflicting approaches of the EU and the United States to the protection for wines and spirits will now likely continue to be played out in the bilateral and plurilateral level for the foreseeable future.

The EU also helped to create and is a proponent of the Geneva Act of the Lisbon Agreement on Appellations of Origin, which came into effect on February 26, 2020. The Geneva Act modernizes the Lisbon Act of 1958 and creates an international registry for GIs that is administered by the World Intellectual Property Organization in Geneva. Once an appellation of origin (similar to a designation of origin explained above in the discussion of GIs in the EU) or geographical indication is registered, it is entitled to protection in all of the member states of the Geneva Act. As of this writing, the Geneva Act has 21 contracting parties and covers up to 57 countries. So far the Geneva Act has not attracted major wine consuming states outside of the EU. Aside from the EU, the other signatories include smaller states such as Albania, Bosnia and Herzegovina, Burkina Faso, Cambodia, Congo, Gabon, Hungary, Mali, Nicaragua, Peru, Romania, and Togo. Many countries that are major markets for French and European wines did not join the Geneva Act including the United States, China, and Japan.

The Geneva Act creates the international system of notification and registration contemplated in TRIPS Article 23, but this was done outside the auspices of the WTO when it became clear that WTO members were unable to agree on creating the registration system. The United States vehemently opposed the Geneva Act and expressed "grave concerns" about the process that led to its adoption. The U.S. antipathy towards the Geneva Act maybe one reason why it has not attracted more adherents.

3. THE RELATIONSHIP BETWEEN TRADEMARKS AND GEOGRAPHICAL INDICATIONS

Article 24(5) of TRIPS contemplates the co-existence of GIs and trademarks by grandfathering in trademarks registered before the effective date of TRIPS in that country or before the GI is protected in its country of origin. In that case, Article 24(5) provides that TRIPS provisions dealing with GIs "shall not prejudice eligibility for or the validity of the registration of a trademark, or the right to use a trademark, on the basis that such a trademark is identical with, or similar to, a geographical indication." Article 24 provides that a trademark will be able to co-exist with a subsequently registered GI for the same sign, but it does not deal with the issue of conflicts between trademarks and GIs that can arise if the two are identical. For example, suppose that a subsequently registered GI causes consumer confusion. What, if any, rights can the trademark owner assert against the GI?

TRIPS is silent on this issue but the EU dealt with the issue of conflicts in the EU Regulation Governing GIs, No. 2081/92 (July 14, 1992). Article 14(2) of the EU regulation provides that trademarks and GIs can co-exist if the trademark is registered either before the GI is protected in its country of origin or before the date an application for protection as a GI or protected designation of origin is submitted to the EU competent authority. Under the EU regulation, in the case of co-existing trademarks and GIs, the trademark owner has the right to enforce trademarks rights against anyone except for the GI owner even when the use of the GI may lead to a likelihood of confusion.

The curtailment by the EU regulation of the rights of the trademark owner against GI owners is in conflict with Article 16.1 of TRIPS, which provides that

TRIPS

Article 16
Rights Conferred

> 1. [T]he owner of a registered trademark shall have the exclusive right to prevent all third parties not having the owner's consent from using in the course of trade identical or similar signs for goods or services which are identical or similar to those in respect of which the trademark is registered where such use would result in a likelihood of confusion.

The right of the trademark owner set forth in Article 16.1 applies to *all* third parties. There is no exception for GI owners.

The United States and Australia challenged the EU regulation before a WTO panel as a violation of TRIPS Article 16.1 in *European Communities—Protection of Trademarks and Geographical Indications for Agricultural Products and Foodstuffs*, WT/DS174/R (March 15, 2005). The panel agreed that the EU regulation was in conflict with TRIPS Article 16.1. The panel also decided that TRIPS Article 24(5) was not applicable to the dispute.

Article 24(5) permits the co-existence of trademarks and GIs in a WTO member when the trademark is "grandfathered" as discussed at the beginning of this section. Article 24(5) applies only to a small group of trademarks and does not answer the question of whether a grandfathered trademark can enforce its rights against a GI for the same sign.

The panel found that the more relevant provision was TRIPS Article 17, which recognizes exceptions to trademark rights. The EU regulation would be lawful if it met all of the requirements of TRIPS Article 17, which provides that "[m]embers may provide limited exceptions to the rights conferred by a trademark, such as fair use of descriptive terms, provided that such exceptions take account of the legitimate interests of the owner of the trademark and of third parties." The focus of the panel's report was whether the EU regulation met the requirements of Article 17 as a "limited exception" and whether it takes into account the "legitimate interest of the owner of the trademark and third parties."

The panel found that a limited exception refers to a narrow or small diminution of rights. The EU regulation only limits the right of the trademark owner to prevent uses of GIs on foodstuffs that are likely to cause confusion. The rights of the trademark owner against all other goods are not curtailed. The panel found that this curtailment was a "limited exception" for the purposes of Article 17.

The panel then turned to a consideration of the legitimate interest of the trademark owner and third parties. Their interest is in preserving the distinctiveness of the trademark. Various provisions of the EU regulation required a refusal to register a GI if the registration would jeopardize the existence of a trademark. The EU regulation also required refusal in light of a trademark's reputation, renown, and length of time it has been used. The panel concluded that these provisions of the EU regulation took into account the legitimate interests of the trademark owner and third parties. The panel concluded that the EU regulation was lawful as it was justified by TRIPS Article 17.

The result of the panel's decision is that in the EU, GIs can still be acquired for a sign even after a trademark for the same sign has been registered. Once the GI is registered, the trademark owner cannot enforce its rights against the GI. In the EU, the inverse is also possible but more difficult. EU law makes it difficult, although still possible under certain conditions, to obtain a trademark for a sign that is part of a GI. One could conclude from these positions that the EU elevates GIs above trademarks in areas where they overlap.

The most famous and longstanding trademark and GI battle involves Anheuser-Busch InBev, a U.S. company, and Budweiser Budvar, a company from the Czech Republic, for the right to use the name "Budweiser" as a trademark and a GI for beer. The dispute has been ongoing since 1907 and has resulted in over 100 legal cases fought around the world with victories and defeats for both parties. As of 2025, Budweiser Budvar has the right to use Budweiser in most of Europe through its protected designation of origin and Anheuser-Bush InBev has the right to use Budweiser in North America through its trademarks. Unless the parties reach a universal settlement of their rights, their battle will continue to rage on.

CHAPTER 5

UNFAIR COMPETITION AND TRADE SECRETS

A. UNFAIR COMPETITION

In common law countries such as the United States and the United Kingdom, the law of unfair competition originally arose to deal with trademark infringement or when a party was "passing off" its trademark as that of another. Passing off involved confusing or deceiving a consumer into believing that the trademarked product was actually a different and usually more commercially valuable trademarked product. Preventing consumer confusion was the principal concern in the development of the law of unfair competition in the United States and UK. Protection of the consumer remains the central focus of the law of unfair competition, which has developed to encompass other areas outside of trademarks such as false or deceptive advertising. The law of unfair competition in the United States is a mix of common law and statutory law, both federal and state.

In the European Union, unfair competition is statutory law. A major source is the EU Directive on Unfair Commercial Practices, 2005/29/EC (May 11, 2005), which provides in relevant part:

EU Directive on Unfair Commercial Practices

Article 5: Prohibition of unfair commercial practices

1. Unfair commercial practices shall be prohibited.

2. A commercial practice shall be unfair if:

(a) it is contrary to the requirements of professional diligence, and

(b) it materially distorts or is likely to materially distort the economic behavior with regard to the product of the average consumer whom it reaches or to whom it is addressed, or of the average member of the group when a commercial practice is directed to a particular group of consumers.

Article 5 refers to a vague and ill-defined concept of unfair commercial practices that are contrary to the requirements of "professional diligence." The unfair practice distorts the economic behavior of consumers or consumer groups. The EU directive does not mention deception or consumer confusion, which is not a required element in the EU. The overall approach of the EU is to promote an ambiguous standard of honest and ethical conduct in commercial practices.

Article 5(3) singles out certain consumers for special protection:

> 3. Commercial practices which are likely to materially distort the economic behavior only of a clearly identifiable group of consumers who are particularly vulnerable to the practice or the underlying product because of their mental or physical infirmity, age or credulity in a way which the trader could reasonably be expected to foresee, shall be assessed from the perspective of the average member of that group. This is without prejudice to the common and legitimate advertising practice of making exaggerated statements or statements which are not meant to be taken literally.

The statute identifies vulnerable persons, including the young and the old, who might be more susceptible to unfair practices. In this respect, the EU statute adopts a paternal and moralistic tone that also differs from the U.S. approach, which focuses on protecting fair economic competition in a market economy.

In the EU, unfair competition has become a catch-all term for a number of practices that violate notions of fair and honest behavior, including bait and switch selling tactics, cold calling consumers, using a loss leader (i.e. charging a low price to attract consumers), commercial bribery, and some forms of comparative advertising. In France and Germany, imitations of products are actionable even if the product is not protected by intellectual property and there is no consumer confusion. The protection of fashion designs from otherwise lawful imitations through the law of unfair competition is based on the concept that the imitator is improperly appropriating another's creative efforts. Although there has been some convergence of the two approaches in recent years, the divide between the U.S. and the EU approaches can still be understood as marked by the requirement of consumer confusion or deception under the U.S. approach and the absence of these elements from some of the unfair practices of the EU.

1. COMPARATIVE ADVERTISING

An understanding of the differences in approaches to unfair competition in the EU and the United States can be gleaned from a study of comparative advertising. In the United States, comparative advertising has become a staple of the advertising industry and has become an important part of commercial speech. So long as it is truthful, comparative advertising is permitted. An advertisement indicating that in a blind taste test, most consumers prefer Pepsi to Coke is lawful if the results are supported by facts. Many other advertisements using variations of this side by side comparison of competing products have aired. Other types of comparative advertising deal with imitations of well-known brands. For example, many store brands will have labels comparing the store brand to a more well-known brand. A store brand might have a label stating that it has the same ingredients as a well-known brand of medication. A store brand or discount brand of perfume might have a label stating that it smells just like Chanel No. 5. All of these types of comparative advertising are common and lawful in the United States so long as they are supported by the facts.

U.S. comparative advertisements often ridicule or disparage competitors; this practice is permitted so long as there are no factual misrepresentations. A 1984 Wendy's television commercial featured the 81-year old actress Clara Peller who, after being served with a giant hamburger, lifted the huge bun to reveal a comically tiny hamburger patty, and exclaimed, "Where's the beef?" The narrator's voice stated that there was more beef on the Wendy's burger than on "the Whopper" or the "Big Mac," trademarks of competitors Burger King and McDonald's. The advertisement was a smash hit, increased Wendy's sales dramatically, and became a cultural phenomenon.

In the EU, comparative advertising is subject to many restrictions. The Wendy's "where's the beef" advertisement would not be permitted under Article 4(d) of the EU Misleading Comparative Advertising Directive, 2006/114/EC (December 12, 2006), which prohibits ads that "discredit or denigrate the trademarks, trade names, other distinguishing marks, good, services, activities or circumstances of a competitor." Another important restriction is contained in Article 4(f) providing that an advertisement cannot "take unfair advantage of the reputation of a trademark, trade name or other distinguishing marks of a competitor." Article 4(f) would also be an obstacle for the Wendy's ad as it explicitly invokes trademarks owned by its competitors.

Article 4(f) of the EU comparative advertising directive was the key provision involved in *L'Oréal SA v. Bellure NV*, [2010] RPC 23, ETMR 47, a decision by the England and Wales Court of Appeal. This is an important decision indicating the limits of comparative advertising in the EU. L'Oréal SA and other plaintiffs brought an action in a UK court against Bellure and other defendants for using comparative advertisements claiming that the defendants' cheap perfumes smelled just like the expensive luxury perfumes of the plaintiffs. For example, defendants' advertisement stated that "Stitch No. 7 smells like Trésor," a brand owned by L'Oréal. The plaintiffs did not claim that the defendants were misleading consumers or that the defendants' claims were false. The plaintiffs also did not claim that their products would be tarnished by the advertisement. The plaintiffs' arguments were based on the EU directive on comparative advertising.

In a previous litigation, the case was referred to the European Court of Justice on various trademark law issues. The ECJ found that the defendants' use of the plaintiffs' trademarks was not purely descriptive but was for comparative advertising purposes. This use violates the EU trademark directive unless it is protected by the EU directive on comparative advertising. The ECJ returned the case to the English court to decide the comparative advertising issue based on the ECJ's interpretative guidance on the EU directive on comparative advertising.

The English court found itself bound to declare the advertisement to be in violation of the EU comparative advertising directive. The English court found that under existing interpretations, the use by the defendants of the trademarks of one of the plaintiffs in the advertisement "Stitch No. 7 smells like Trésor" was free riding or taking advantage of the trademark of the plaintiff in violation of Article 4(f) of the EU directive. In this context, free riding refers to exploiting the goodwill attached to a highly desirable and valuable brand like Trésor to draw attention to the defendants' own product.

The English court was quite troubled by this result but the court felt compelled to reach it as a matter of precedent. The imitation or replica by the defendants was not a counterfeit but a lawful imitation. The statement that defendants' perfume smelled like plaintiff L'Oréal's perfume was truthful. Nonetheless, the statement is not permitted under EU law.

One has to question whether any comparative advertisement can be permitted in the EU given the broad interpretation of Article 4(g) of the EU directive that an advertisement cannot "take unfair advantage of the reputation of a trademark, trade name or other distinguishing marks of a competitor." If the mere mention of the trademark or tradename of a competitor, even if entirely truthful, can constitute free riding then it appears difficult to imagine any comparative advertisement that can survive the test set forth by the European Court of Justice.

In the United States, many imitation perfumes are available for sale with labels that compare the imitation to the luxury brand name perfume. No one seriously believes that the luxury brand is harmed by these imitations as the consumer groups for the two products are not the same. Luxury brands do not lose sales to any appreciable extent to imitation perfumes because the persons who purchase the luxury brands do not purchase the cheap imitations. A consumer who is willing to purchase a bottle of Chanel No. 5 for $500 is not likely to forgo the purchase and buy an imitation claiming that it is "inspired by Chanel No. 5" for $17.99 at the local drugstore. The image or reputation of the luxury brand is not harmed by imitations and in a way may even be enhanced by imitations that are indications of the appeal of the luxury brand. Consumers know the difference between the imitation and the genuine product.

Most consumers also would not be bothered by the point made by Lord Justice Jacob in the *L'Oréal* case that a cheap imitation that smells the same as a luxury brand might reveal that "the price of the real thing may be excessive and that the luxury image may be a bit of a delusion." One can argue that the luxury image is not a delusion at all but the result of an investment of many millions or hundreds of millions of dollars spent on advertising and promotion. Many consumers value the brand's prestige and are generally not concerned about its manufacturing costs. While the luxury brand is not harmed by an imitation, the benefit to society is that the imitation allows more products to be created and a group of consumers who would otherwise not have access to the luxury brand to enjoy some benefits associated with the brand.

2. THE PARIS CONVENTION AND UNFAIR COMPETITION

The Paris Convention deals with unfair competition as follows:

Paris Convention

Article 10*bis*
Unfair Competition

(1) The countries of the Union are bound to assure to nationals of such countries effective protection against unfair competition.

(2) Any act of competition contrary to honest practices in industrial or commercial matters constitutes an act of unfair competition.

(3) The following in particular shall be prohibited:

(i) all acts of such a nature as to create confusion by any means whatever with the establishment, the goods, or the industrial or commercial activities, of a competitor;

(ii) false allegations in the course of trade of such a nature as to discredit the establishment, the goods, or the industrial or commercial activities, of a competitor;

(iii) indications or allegations the use of which in the course of trade is liable to mislead the public as to the nature, the

> manufacturing process, the characteristics, the suitability for their purpose, or the quantity, of the goods.

Article 10*bis*(1) of the Paris Convention provides that members must ensure "effective protection against unfair competition." Article 10*bis*(3) contains a non-exclusive list of examples of unfair competition, each of which involves deception, consumer confusion, or use of false allegations. Article 10*bis*(2) prohibits acts contrary to "honest practices in industrial or commercial matters." This language refers to the EU's liberal construction of unfair competition, which refers to a broad panoply of dishonest commercial practices that do not involve consumer confusion or deception. An issue that has arisen is whether the U.S. Lanham Act incorporates the language of Article 10*bis*(2) so that plaintiffs can assert the EU's broad version of unfair competition in litigation in the United States.

The incorporation issue was involved in *General Motors Corp. v. Lopez De Arriortua*, 948 F. Supp. 684 (E.D. Mich. 1996). Plaintiffs General Motors and Opel AG, a European subsidiary of General Motors, brought a lawsuit in federal district court in Michigan against defendants Volkswagen, a German corporation, its wholly owned American subsidiary, and former employees of General Motor's European affiliates and of Opel. The plaintiffs claimed that Lopez, a high-level executive at General Motors' subsidiary in Spain, agreed with Volkswagen to secretly collect confidential information from General Motors. Lopez then led an exodus of several employees from General Motors' European subsidiaries taking a large number of files containing confidential information. Lopez and his group were given jobs at Volkswagen in Germany at substantially higher salaries. Volkswagen obtained the confidential files.

The plaintiffs sued in federal district court under the Lanham Act and the Copyright Act. The defendants moved to the dismiss the complaint, which was denied by the court. The Lanham Act claims based on unfair competition referred to trademark infringement and false designation of origin or passing off. The narrow claims would not entitle plaintiffs to sue for the conspiracy to steal confidential information. To assert that claim, the plaintiffs argued that § 44(b), § 44(h), and § 44(i) of the Lanham Act incorporated Article 10*bis* of the Paris Convention.

Article 44(b) of the Lanham Act provides that

> Any person whose country of origin is a party to any convention or treaty relating to trademarks [or] unfair competition, to which the United States is also a party . . . shall be entitled to the benefits of this section ... to the extent necessary to give effect to any provision of such convention . . . in addition to the rights to which any owner of a mark is otherwise entitled by this chapter.

One of the plaintiffs, Opel, is a German corporation, and Germany is a party to the Paris Convention. Plaintiffs argued that § 44(b) incorporates Article

10*bis*(2) of the Paris Convention that "[a]ny act of competition contrary to honest practices in industrial or commercial matters constitutes an act of unfair competition." Section 44(h) provides that foreign citizens are entitled to protection against unfair competition and § 44(i) provides that U.S. citizens, which includes General Motors, have the same benefits as those granted to foreign citizens.

The plaintiffs argued that the combined effects of §§ 44(b), 44(h) and 44(i) are that General Motors and Opel can assert the broad European version of unfair competition in their lawsuit against the defendants. Such a broad view of unfair competition would allow General Motors to claim that a conspiracy by Volkswagen and the individual defendants to steal confidential information in exchange for higher paying jobs is a dishonest act and an act of unfair competition. The defendants disagreed with this approach, arguing that the Lanham Act does not incorporate any substantive rights but only requires that Paris Union countries provide national treatment to foreign nationals and foreign trademarks.

The district court agreed with the plaintiffs, relying on several cases that the Lanham Act incorporates the substantive provisions of the Paris Convention, including Article 10*bis* and denied the motion to dismiss. The position of the court in *General Motors* is a minority position in the United States. Most federal courts hold that the Lanham Act does not incorporate any substantive rights under the Paris Convention apart from those independently recognized by the Lanham Act and that the broad European approach to unfair competition does not apply in the United States. If the *Lopez* case arose today, the plaintiffs would not need to rely on the Paris Convention. The plaintiffs could assert subsequently enacted federal laws against the theft of trade secrets, the Economic Espionage Act (1996) and the Defend Trade Secrets Act (2016), both discussed in the following sections below.

B. TRADE SECRETS

1. TRIPS AND TRADE SECRETS

TRIPS broke new ground in going beyond the Paris Convention by including a provision that expressly protects trade secrets. No previous international treaty had ever recognized rights in trade secrets.

TRIPS Article 39 provides in relevant part:

TRIPS

Section 7: protection of undisclosed information

Article 39

1. In the course of ensuring effective protection against unfair competition as provided in Article 10*bis* of the Paris Convention (1967), Members shall protect undisclosed information in accordance with paragraph 2 and data submitted to governments or governmental agencies in accordance with paragraph 3.

2. Natural and legal persons shall have the possibility of preventing information lawfully within their control from being disclosed to, acquired by, or used by others without their consent in a manner contrary to honest commercial practices so long as such information:

(a) is secret in the sense that it is not, as a body or in the precise configuration and assembly of its components, generally known among or readily accessible to persons within the circles that normally deal with the kind of information in question;

(b) has commercial value because it is secret; and

(c) has been subject to reasonable steps under the circumstances, by the person lawfully in control of the information, to keep it secret.

To constitute a protectable trade secret, the information (1) must not be generally known or accessible to persons that normally deal with that information; (2) must have commercial value because it is secret; and (3) is subject to reasonable steps to keep the information secret. These three elements are similar to the elements provided by trade secret law in the United States. The obligation to use reasonable steps to keep information secret imposes an active duty to maintain secrecy. The owner of a trade secret who carelessly fails to maintain secrecy measures could lose rights to the trade secret.

One of the basic decisions that many owners of commercially valuable know how must make is whether to seek a patent or to protect the information as a trade secret. The trade-off is that a patent provides much stronger protection but it has a term of 20 years after which the information enters the public domain. For example, a drug that is protected by a patent cannot be independently discovered by a third party or reversed engineered by a third party. Those protections are not available under trade secret law. On the other hand, while a patent expires after 20 years, know how that is protected by a trade secret can be protected indefinitely. One of the most famous examples of a decision to protect know how by trade secret law is Coca-Cola's formula for its Coca-Cola soft drink. The formula was first invented in 1886 and would have entered the public domain long ago if Coca-Cola had obtained a patent. Instead, the formula has been protected as a trade secret since 1886. The formula is kept locked in a massive 10-foot vault at the Coca-Cola museum in Atlanta, Georgia, which has become an attraction for fans of Coca-Cola and the curious. No doubt the extreme measures that Coca-Cola has boasted about using over the years to maintain the secrecy of its formula has added to its mystique.

The growing importance of the commercial value of know how and the interest of foreign governments in obtaining such know how led the U.S. Congress to pass the Economic Espionage Act of 1996, which criminalizes certain acts of theft of trade secrets. The Act applies not only to acts by foreign governments but also to individuals who steal trade secrets from

U.S. businesses. Under the Act, the defendants in the *General Motors* case discussed in the preceding section might have been liable for criminal prosecution in addition to civil penalties.

2. UNDISCLOSED DATA AND MARKETING APPROVALS

TRIPS Article 39(3) is a provision designed to specifically deal with information and data that must be submitted for regulatory approval of the marketing of pharmaceuticals and agricultural chemical products:

TRIPS

Article 39

* * *

3. Members, when requiring, as a condition of approving the marketing of pharmaceutical or of agricultural chemical products which utilize new chemical entities, the submission of undisclosed test or other data, the origination of which involves a considerable effort, shall protect such data against unfair commercial use. In addition, Members shall protect such data against disclosure, except where necessary to protect the public, or unless steps are taken to ensure that the data are protected against unfair commercial use.

The concern addressed by Article 39(3) relates to the requirement of many countries that pharmaceutical companies submit data and information and obtain approval by government authorities before their drugs can be sold to the public. Pharmaceutical companies are concerned about the confidentiality of the information that they submit. Companies will obtain a patent for their new drugs but the patent will not protect the information and data that they must submit for marketing approval. This information normally consists of the results of clinical trials of the drugs showing that the drugs are effective and safe for human consumption. Pharmaceutical companies claim that obtaining this data involves tests on animals and clinical trials with people that takes years and costs hundreds of millions of dollars.

Pharmaceutical companies are concerned that the submitted information will be disclosed to third parties and competitors and become the subject of unfair commercial use. For example, suppose that a pharmaceutical's patent term has expired. Generic drug makers can now manufacture the drug but they must still obtain government approval before marketing the drugs to the public. If generic drug makers were able to use the original clinical data submitted to obtain marketing approval for the original drug then the generic drug makers could take a free ride on the substantial investments of the innovator pharmaceutical company.

The argument against prohibiting the use of the data is that to force generic drug makers to reproduce the data is not only wasteful but unethical. Recreating the data will require additional tests that harm and kill many animals and additional clinical trials on people that could cause unwanted health problems and side-effects. *See* Aaron Fellmeth, *Secrecy, Monopoly, and Access to Pharmaceuticals in International Trade Law: Protection of Marking Approval Data under the TRIPS Agreement*, 46 Harv. Int'l L. J. 443, 473–74 (2004).

In the end, the United States and other countries protected the clinical data by implementing a period of data exclusivity. In the United States, the period is generally five years. Generic drug companies must generally wait five years before they can use the data of the innovator pharmaceutical company to obtain marketing approval. Other countries, such as China, have a general six year period of exclusivity. The period of data exclusivity has been contentious in the past with the United States seeking longer periods than its trading partners. The other issue that has been debated is that TRIPS Article 39(3) provides that only data for products "containing new chemical entities" must be protected. The meaning of these terms has also been the subject of disagreements. Currently, the United States negotiates for periods of data exclusivity as part of its free trade agreements with its trading partners.

3. PROTECTING TRADE SECRETS INTERNATIONALLY

a. Transnational Litigation

U.S. owners of intellectual property rights often face problems of infringement that occur overseas. Many U.S. companies do not relish the prospect of suing in foreign jurisdictions due to differences in legal systems and problems with enforcement. The topic of suing in the United States for infringing conduct that occurred abroad by a foreign defendant is a complex one that is studied in depth in courses on international dispute resolution. Fortunately, in the area of intellectual property, the United States has created a mechanism that allows U.S. owners of intellectual property to bring lawsuits under some circumstances in the United States for infringing conduct abroad.

In *Tianrui Group Company Ltd. v. International Trade Commission*, 661 F.3d 1322 (Fed. Cir. 2011), the Federal Circuit Court of Appeals reviewed an exclusionary order issued by the International Trade Commission barring the importation of goods manufactured by Tianrui Group, a company in China, into the United States. After Tianrui was unable to license proprietary know how from Amsted Industries, a U.S. company, Tianrui hired nine employees from Amsted's licensee in China who allegedly brought proprietary know how with them in violation of various confidentiality obligations in their employment contracts. The trade secrets concerned a process for manufacturing cast steel railway wheels that had been developed by Amsted. The commission found that acts committed by Tianrui occurring in China constituted a method of unfair competition that led to the theft of trade secrets. Under § 337 of the Tariff Act of 1930, 19 U.S.C. § 1337, the commission has the authority to issue an order blocking the importation of goods that violate intellectual property rights.

On appeal, Tianrui argued that the acts by the commission in applying U.S. law to conduct in China was an unlawful exterritorial application of U.S. law. Tianrui argued that this exterritorial application would interfere with the application of Chinese law and would intrude upon China's sovereignty.

The court of appeals rejected these arguments. While there is a presumption against exterritorial application of U.S. law, this presumption can be overcome by evidence of legislative intent. Congress clearly intended for the commission to look to conduct abroad as a basis for issuing an exclusionary order barring the importation of articles violating U.S. intellectual property rights. Moreover, § 337 does not sanction purely exterritorial conduct; it sanctions the importation of those articles into the United States so § 337 has a domestic component and is not purely aimed at foreign conduct. Section 337 applies only to conduct that affects imports into the United States and not conduct generally in China. Section 337 also does not directly affect any foreign persons, only the goods that are intended for import into the United States. Section 337 does not hinder Tianrui's ability to sell the products in China or to any other countries. Finally, the court of appeals found that as China is a member of the WTO, China also has an obligation to obey Article 39 of TRIPS covering trade secrets and unfair competition.

Section 1337 was intended to subject foreign conduct to the reach of U.S. law protecting intellectual property rights. In addition to providing protection against acts of unfair competition, including the theft of trade secrets, § 1337 allows a petitioner to seek an exclusionary order from the commission banning imports that violate U.S. patent, copyright, trademark, mask work, or design law. As the exclusionary order blocks the importation of goods violating intellectual property rights from entering into the United States, the infringing conduct must have occurred overseas and outside of the territory of the United States. The purpose of § 1337 is to apply U.S. intellectual property law to such foreign conduct. The justification for the exterritorial application of U.S. law is that the conduct leads to infringing imports targeted at the United States. In this respect, § 1337 is consistent with the effects principle of exterritorial jurisdiction. Under the effects principle, in any case that conduct occurring outside the United States has substantial effects in the United States, the United States is justified in exercising exterritorial jurisdiction over the foreign conduct.

b. New Developments in Trade Secret Law in the United States and the EU

The increasing importance of know how, i.e. commercially valuable knowledge, in the conduct of business in both the national and international arenas has given rise to a need for new protections for know how in the form of trade secret law. The Economic Espionage Act, enacted in 1996, has already been discussed. The Economic Espionage Act is primarily a criminal statute. An amendment to the Economic Espionage Act, the Defend Trade Secrets Act came into effect on May 11, 2016. The Defend

Trade Secrets Act created a federal civil law regime for trade secrets, which had been primarily governed by state law with the exception of the Economic Espionage Act. The Defend Trade Secrets Act creates a private civil cause of action in federal district court for the violation of trade secrets. The act confers federal jurisdiction in federal district court over trademark cases so the plaintiff will not need to rely on diversity jurisdiction or general federal question jurisdiction. The act contains a very broad definition of trade secret:

The Defend Trade Secrets Act of 2016

* * *

(3) A trade secret includes all forms and types of financial, business, scientific, technical, economic, or engineering information, including patterns, plans, compilations, program devices, formulas, designs, prototypes, methods, techniques, processes, procedures, programs, or codes, whether tangible or intangible, and whether or how stored, compiled, or memorialized physically, electronically, graphically, photographically, or in writing if

(A) the owner thereof has taken reasonable measures to keep such information secret; and

(B) the information derives independent economic value, actual or potential, from not being generally known to, and not being readily ascertainable through proper means by, another person who can obtain economic value from the disclosure or use of the information.

Although many states have adopted the Uniform Trade Secret Act, states still have variations in their trade secret laws, creating a lack of uniformity that hampers enforcement. In addition to creating a uniform legal regime, the Defend Trade Secrets Act empowers the federal district court to order the ex parte seizure of property and to issue an injunction to prevent the theft of a trade secret. An ex parte seizure order is one that can be obtained by the plaintiff without prior notice to the defendant. The lack of prior notice preserves the element of surprise as the defendant will first receive notice of the seizure order only at the moment that the goods are being seized. An ex parte order is critical to prevent the destruction or disappearance of evidence in trade secret cases. By providing federal remedies and a uniform federal law, the Defend Trade Secrets Act is a significant improvement over the existing state law regimes.

In the EU, a similar movement towards harmonization is taking place. The EU implemented a new EU Trade Secrets Directive, 2016/943 (June 8, 2016), for the purpose of harmonizing trade secret law throughout the EU. Prior to the directive, trade secret law had been governed by the national laws of each EU country. National laws created barriers to enforcement as trade secret cases often had connections to more than one EU nation, creating complex problems of choice of law and conflicting jurisdiction among national courts. Harmonization in the EU should also facilitate the enforcement of trade secrets.

4. DESIGN PROTECTION

a. The U.S. Approach

Under U.S. law, a design patent protects the appearance of industrial products. A chair, lamp, or shoe may have a visual appearance, such as its shape, configuration, or surface ornamentation, that has commercial value and that the manufacturer wants to protect. To qualify for a U.S. design patent, the design must be new, original, and ornamental. 35 U.S.C. § 171. The design must also be non-functional. Examples of design patents include the curvy Coca-Cola bottle, the Addidas shoe, and a sports bottle in the shape of a dumb-bell weight.

The same industrial design might also be eligible for copyright and trademark protection under U.S. law, but a design patent provides more extensive protections. A copyright for works of applied art does not provide for protection against independent creation while a design patent under U.S. law does provide such protection. Trademark protects against unauthorized use only if there is a likelihood of consumer confusion. An unauthorized use violates a design patent regardless of consumer confusion.

While design protection in the United States has traditionally lagged the other areas of intellectual property rights covered in this book, increased interest in industrial designs has led to a sharp rise in recent years in the number of U.S. patent design applications. This trend could reflect an awareness that the appearance of industrial products has important and increasing commercial value as a marketing tool.

b. TRIPS and Design Protection

TRIPS requires its members to provide protection for designs:

> **TRIPS**
>
> **Section 4: industrial designs**
>
> **Article 25**
> **Requirements for Protection**
>
> 1. Members shall provide for the protection of independently created industrial designs that are new or original. Members may provide that designs are not new or original if they do not significantly differ from known designs or combinations of known design features. Members may provide that such protection shall not extend to designs dictated essentially by technical or functional considerations.

Article 25(1) provides that members must protect designs that are new or original. Members may exclude from protection "designs dictated essentially by functional considerations." The concern is that functional inventions are protected by utility patents and that design patents should not become a backdoor to obtaining protection for inventions that do not meet the more rigorous requirements of utility patents. For this reason, design law typically excludes designs that are functional. However, TRIPS opens the door to protection for designs that are at least somewhat functional by its high standard that "protection shall not extend to designs *dictated by* essentially technical or functional considerations." This standard suggests that some functionality is permitted. Ultimately, it is up to each nation to interpret the terms "dictated by" as narrowly or as expansively as they wish in accordance with their domestic policies.

TRIPS Article 25(2) specifies the required protections for textile designs:

> 2. Each Member shall ensure that requirements for securing protection for textile designs, in particular in regard to any cost, examination or publication, do not unreasonably impair the opportunity to seek and obtain such protection. Members shall be free to meet this obligation through industrial design law or through copyright law.

Article 25(2) is written to deal specifically with textiles or clothing. The concern is that fashions in clothing are seasonal and ephemeral so if obtaining design protection for fashions is too costly, burdensome, or time consuming such protection will be of little value.

While TRIPS requires protection for industrial designs, TRIPS does not require any specific legal regime. The United States uses a design patent while the EU uses a *sui generis* right called a Community registered design. In both legal regimes, the applicant for design protection is required to submit a graphic depiction of the design in the form of drawings, a photographic reproduction of the design, or a computer assisted design. In the EU, the graphic depiction cannot be accompanied by any explanatory text. The United States allows accompanying text but treats the drawings as more important as they define the scope of the design patent's protection.

TRIPS Article 26 provides:

TRIPS

Article 26
Protection

> 1. The owner of a protected industrial design shall have the right to prevent third parties not having the owner's consent from making, selling or importing articles bearing or embodying a design which is a copy, or substantially a copy, of the protected design, when such acts are undertaken for commercial purposes.

TRIPS requires that owners of protected designs have three basic rights: to prevent unauthorized parties from "making, selling, or importing articles" bearing a copy of a protected design when used for commercial purposes. The use of the word "copy" suggests that independent creation does not violate the design protection. However, as TRIPS sets forth minimum standards a country could provide that independent creation does violate a protected design. This is the position of the United States: independent creation is no defense to a claim of infringement of a U.S. design patent.

c. Infringement of a Protected Design

To find an infringement under U.S. design patent law, the court must make a comparison between the protected design and the accused design to determine if they have the same general appearance so that the ordinary observer will be deceived into confusing the accused design with the protected design. Under this standard the identity of the "ordinary observer" is critical to the infringement determination.

In *Arminak and Associates, Inc. v. Saint-Gobain Calmar, Inc.*, 501 F.3d 1314 (Fed. Cir. 2007), overruled on other grounds, *Egyptian Goddess, Inc. v. Swisa, Inc.*, 543 F.3d 665 (Fed. Cir. 2008) (en banc), the Federal Circuit Court of Appeals had to determine the identity of the ordinary observer in a dispute over a design for a shroud used in a trigger sprayer bottle. A trigger sprayer is a common device attached to a bottle with a tube that extends downward into the bottle. The tube draws the liquid in the bottle that is discharged as a spray by the trigger mechanism. The outside top cover behind the nozzle and behind the trigger is called the shroud as it hides the tube that extends downward into the liquid. The shroud is typically made of molded plastic. Saint-Gobain Calmar had design patents for its shroud. Fearing that Calmar might sue for breach of its design patents, Arminak peremptorily filed a lawsuit for a declaratory judgment that its trigger shrouds did not infringe Calmar's design patents. The district court held for Arminak, finding no infringement. Calmar then appealed the ruling to the Federal Circuit.

One of the grounds of Calmar's appeal was that the district court erred in its determining who was the ordinary observer. The district court found that the ordinary observer was the manufacturer of trigger sprayers that purchased parts, including the shroud, that are then assembled into a trigger sprayer bottle containing liquids that is sold to retail consumers. Calmar argued that the ordinary observer should be the retail consumer.

The identity of the ordinary observer was critical in this case. At the trial, there was ample evidence that the manufacturers of trigger sprayers would be able to easily discern the difference between the two shrouds and would not be confused. By contrast, retail customers have far less experience or technical expertise than the manufacturers and might be less able to discern the difference between the two products and more likely to confuse them.

The Federal Circuit held that the district court was correct to find that ordinary observer was the manufacturer of the trigger sprayers. The decisive factor related to the point of sale. Neither Arminak nor Calmar ever sold the shroud to retail consumers. They always sold the shroud to manufacturers. The court of appeals determined that at the point of sale, the ordinary observer was the manufacturer of the trigger sprayer bottle and that the manufacturer would not confuse the two designs. The court upheld the district court's declaratory judgment in favor of Arminak.

The issue of how to make the comparison between the protected design and the accused design was discussed by the UK Supreme Court in *Magmatic Ltd v. PMS International Group PCL* [2016] UKSC 12, [2016] R.P.C. 11. The design at issue concerned a ride-on suitcase for children. Magmatic Ltd., a UK company, had acquired Community registered designs by submitting monochrome and color computer assisted designs for a ride-on suitcase in the form of an animal with horns, four wheels, and a handle. PMS International Group began importing into and selling in the UK a ride-on suitcase that also looked like an animal. Magmatic sued PMS seeking damages and an injunction.

The trial court found that it must make a comparison of the "overall impression" created by the Community registered design and the accused design. In making the comparison, the trial court focused on the monochrome design that had shades of gray, some black, and no surface ornamentation and concluded that Magmatic's registered design was for the shape of the suitcase only. A comparison of the shapes of Magmatic's design and the ride-on suitcases of PMS created an overall impression that they shared the same appearance. The judge accordingly issued Magmatic's requested injunctive relief.

The trial court was reversed on appeal and the reversal was then appealed to the UK Supreme Court. The court found that the first step was to characterize the overall impression of Magmatic's registered design, which the court found to be that of a horned animal. The court then disagreed with the trial judge that Magamatic's design was for a shape only. The UK Supreme Court focused on the monochrome computer assisted design images that showed different shades of gray and black wheels. The court concluded that the design was not only for the shape but also surface colors and ornamentation. Once surface colors and ornamentation became relevant the court then pointed out that the PMS suitcases were bright colored and had surface ornamentation showing that one resembled a ladybug and the other a tiger. The court then compared the overall appearance of the Magmatic suitcase as that of a horned animal with the PMS suitcases as those of a ladybug and a tiger. The court concluded that the Magmatic and PMS designs were not similar and upheld the reversal of the trial court.

The approach of the EU and the United States share the common element that the test for infringement is a comparison of the overall visual appearance of the two designs, but important differences remain. The U.S. approach allows the application for a design patent to include explanatory text that can be used to clarify the exact scope of protection. The EU approach is to completely exclude explanatory text (other than allowing the indication "top" to be displayed). The absence of explanatory text could result in cases like *Magmatic Ltd.* where there is disagreement over the scope of protection based on the design image alone. Of course, TRIPS allows each member to create its own system for design protection as well as to set forth the requirements for design applications.

d. International Protection Under the Hague Agreement

The Hague Agreement Concerning International Registrations of Industrial Designs, first concluded in 1925, offers a simple mechanism for acquiring protection for industrial designs in all 80 members (that cover 97 countries) of the agreement. The Hague agreement is similar to the Madrid system for trademarks and the Patent Cooperation Treaty for patents. An applicant can file a single international application in a single language (English, French, or Spanish) that can result in protection for up to 100 designs in 97 different countries, including the EU. The administering body of the Hague agreement is the World Intellectual Property Organization in Geneva, which also administers the Madrid system for the international registration for trademarks and the Patent Cooperation Treaty.

Once the international application under the Hague agreement is submitted, WIPO will review the application to determine whether it complies with formalities. If all formalities have been met, WIPO will publish the application. At that point each nation designated for an extension of protection in the application will conduct its own novelty review of the design. Each designated nation has six months to decide whether to grant the extension of protection and, in some cases, 12 months by sending a notification to WIPO. Failure of national offices to respond within the prescribed time period will result in an automatic extension of protection in that country.

Like patent and trademark applications, applications for design protection are also entitled to Paris priority. In the case of design protection applications, the period of priority is six months. Paris Conv., Article 4(C)(1). An international application is also entitled to the benefits of Paris priority and can assert the Paris priority date of an earlier national filing as the filing date in the Hague agreement system.

CHAPTER 6

TRANSNATIONAL ENFORCEMENT OF INTELLECTUAL PROPERTY RIGHTS

A. INTRODUCTION

This chapter deals with private enforcement of intellectual property rights in a transnational context. Private enforcement refers to the use by U.S. and other business entities of court-based civil litigation and administrative action by government agencies. Private enforcement also refers to pursuing criminal sanctions imposed by police and prosecutorial authorities. This type of enforcement also includes the use of private detective and investigation companies, marketing companies, and lawyers. The enforcement actions examined in this chapter are transnational in character, i.e. the enforcement action and the intellectual property rights involved will have connections with more than one nation. This chapter will not focus on purely domestic enforcement in the United States.

Enforcement of intellectual property rights requires study as a topic of its own apart from the previous chapters that focused on substantive rights and obligations. Of course, substantive laws are important but such laws are of little value if they are not enforced. In the area of international intellectual property, effective enforcement has been a longstanding problem, but it has been exacerbated significantly in recent decades by the rise of trademark counterfeiting and copyright piracy on an unprecedented scale around the world. In recognition of the importance of enforcement, TRIPS devotes the entirety of Part III to enforcement obligations, the first time in history that any intellectual property treaty has directly dealt with enforcement. We will examine TRIPS enforcement obligations that WTO members are required to implement in their domestic legal systems in detail in this chapter.

The focus in this chapter is on private enforcement not governmental enforcement at the level of the World Trade Organization. Many of the cases discussed in this book are the result of litigation at the WTO. The parties to WTO disputes are governments and the disputes usually concerned whether WTO members are fulfilling their obligations required by TRIPS and other WTO agreements. A WTO panel or Appellate Body will issue an opinion after the dispute is resolved. Of course, businesses are interested in WTO litigation and governments often represent business interests in WTO litigation. These types of disputes are important at the macro level as they will impact national and international regulation of intellectual property, but on a daily basis, most owners of intellectual property are more concerned with the micro level of on the ground enforcement of their rights against particular violations and violators. In this chapter, our focus is on the many complex and difficult decisions that an owner of intellectual property faces in enforcement on the ground level.

In the next sections we take a closer look at trademark counterfeiting and copyright piracy, the most serious problem facing many multinational companies in the area of intellectual property. The rise of the internet and sales of counterfeit and pirated goods through electronic commerce adds a new and daunting challenge for intellectual property owners. The chapter then turns to an examination of TRIPS enforcement obligations, many of which were designed to combat counterfeiting and piracy. This chapter will then examine private enforcement through court-based litigation and, finally, enforcement against gray market goods or parallel imports.

B. COUNTERFEITING AND PIRACY

1. OVERVIEW

The International Chamber of Commerce, based in Paris, France, claims on its website that the economic and social costs from counterfeiting and piracy were about USD $2.8 trillion in 2022. These losses include the international trade in counterfeit and pirated goods ($991 billion), domestically produced counterfeit and pirated goods ($524–$959 billion), digital piracy in movies, music, and software ($384 to $856 billion) and net job losses (4.2 to 5.4 million jobs). Other costs for which economic figures are not available include displacement of legitimate economic activity, loss of sales tax revenue, damage to the formal economy, and financial revenues for criminal networks. Although already unprecedented in size and scope, counterfeiting and piracy continue to grow and costs continue to mount.

While the terms counterfeiting and piracy are often used loosely to refer to all types of intellectual property law infringements, it is necessary to distinguish between the various rights involved to obtain a clearer picture of the problem. In fact, there are usually three types of problems involved that are very different in scope, magnitude, and legal consequences.

a. Copyright Piracy

When the term "piracy" is used in this book, the term refers to copyright piracy or the unauthorized copying of works of authorship such as books, movies, music, and business and entertainment software. In copyright piracy, there is usually no attempt to hide that the copy is unauthorized as the purchaser or recipient of the pirated work is seeking the content of the work. Copyright piracy has been facilitated by modern technology. In many cases, pirated works are exact or high-quality copies of the original work. Modern technology makes it easier to produce exact digital copies of works through compact disks and electronic digital files.

The latest available data from the software and entertainment industries show that the most serious losses from copyright piracy occur in the area of business software ($46.3 billion in 2017) and entertainment software ($2.65 billion in 2007). Next are losses from music ($14.9 billion in 2009) and movies ($1.97 billion in 2005) and then books ($531 billion in 2005). Unfortunately, more recent figures are not available as business organizations have stopped providing them. A separate study (see above) by the International Chamber of Commerce claims losses from pirated movies, music, and software to be as high as $856 billion per year.

b. Trademark Counterfeiting

Counterfeiting refers to the unauthorized use of an identical or substantially similar trademark on identical or substantially similar goods. In the case of counterfeiting, the knock-off impersonates the genuine product and some consumers will mistakenly purchase the counterfeit instead of the genuine article. Only some consumers are confused, however, as many consumers actively seek out counterfeits for certain types of products such as designer handbags, luxury watches, and luxury clothing brands.

The vast bulk of the losses in the billions or trillions of dollars (see the figures above) from counterfeiting and piracy can be attributed to trademark counterfeiting. Copyright piracy is limited a few categories of products (movies, music, and software) and most losses are concentrated in the area of computer software. In the case of counterfeiting, the types of products that can be counterfeited are almost limitless, constrained only by whether the counterfeiter believes that it can make a profit. Counterfeit auto parts, computers, phones, chemical fertilizer, baby formula, laser printer cartridges, and even entire cars are all available for purchase.

In China, studies indicate that 15–20 percent of all goods available for purchase are counterfeits. The involvement of organized crime in counterfeiting (further discussed below) and the vast profits to be made have caused some experts to label counterfeiting as the crime of the twenty first century.

c. Patent Infringements

Patent infringements refer to the unauthorized copying of a patent. Some loosely use the term "counterfeit patents," but counterfeits are technically limited to trademarks. Although fake pharmaceuticals are widespread and have been the most serious problem in the area of patent infringements, these unauthorized copies of drugs have always been treated differently by policy makers. For many years before the WTO and TRIPS, some countries, such as Thailand and India, did not extend patent protection to pharmaceuticals for public policy reasons as drugs can be lifesaving. Thriving generic drug industries developed in Thailand and India as a result. Some viewed the unauthorized copying of pharmaceutical patents as justified by policies in favor of protecting public health.

The drafters of TRIPS were reluctant to treated unauthorized copying of patents in the same fashion as trademark counterfeiting and copyright piracy, which have no arguable justification. For this reason,

Article 61 of TRIPS requires criminal penalties for copyright piracy and trademark counterfeiting on a commercial scale but not for unauthorizing copying of patents.

d. Methods Used for Determining Scope and Losses

As multinational companies and business groups claim that the size and scope of counterfeiting and piracy are unprecedented and that annual losses are in the trillions of dollars, the question arises as to the methods by which these figures are calculated. All studies use a variation of the following methods.

In calculating the scope of counterfeiting or piracy loses for a location, such as a city or region, multinational companies will first conduct a market survey of all products of a certain brand found in the market. For example, a survey concludes that there are 10,000 items of a certain trademarked product for sale in a city. The company or brand owner then determines how many genuine products were shipped to the location. Let us assume that the brand owner's records indicate that 8,000 genuine items were shipped to that particular location. The company will conclude that 2,000 items are counterfeit and that the rate of counterfeiting is 20 percent.

To calculate the losses caused by counterfeiting, the company will now assume that the presence of 2,000 counterfeit items on the market will displace 2,000 sales of the genuine products at the retail price. Let us assume that the genuine product sells for

$100. The company will claim that its losses due to counterfeiting and piracy are lost sales of 2,000 items of the genuine products at $100 per item for a total loss of $20,000. These methods will be repeated on a wider scale to reach numbers for a particular country or region of the world.

These methods use several questionable assumptions. Relating to size and scope, the method does not account for horizontal movement of genuine products from one market to another. For example, even though a company may have supplied only 8,000 units of the genuine products to a city, a local distributor from another location might sell genuine products to the retailers in question. In a country like China, there are many middle-men distributors who can move products without the knowledge of the manufacturer. Retailers with more than one store may also shift products between stores. In many busy and high-volume locations such horizontal movements are common.

Regarding losses, the assumption that each counterfeit product on the market represents a loss of a sale of a genuine product at the retail price is highly dubious. A consumer who purchases a counterfeit Louis Vuitton handbag for $150 is not likely to purchase a genuine item for $3,000 but for the availability of the counterfeit. A purchaser of pirated business or entertainment software for $50 is not likely to purchase genuine software for $750 but for the availability of the pirated copy.

The doubtful assumptions and crude methods used by multinational companies lead many observers to conclude that the size and scope and the losses from counterfeiting and piracy are greatly exaggerated. Many critics claim that industry groups have an incentive to portray themselves as victims and to make the problem appear as large as possible to justify the higher prices that these companies claim they must charge to compensate for their losses.

In their defense, industry groups claim that much of this criticism is unfair. The companies argue that they are using the only methods that are available because no scientific study is possible. Counterfeiters and pirates operate clandestinely and hide in an opaque underworld. Counterfeiters are either petty criminals or are affiliated with criminal organizations and most are never caught. There is no data available on their profits and sales. The industry groups argue that they are doing their best within the constraints of the lack of information and transparency of an illegal, underground activity.

2. PROBLEMS FACED BY A HYPOTHETICAL MULTINATIONAL COMPANY IN CHINA

As many multinational companies are confronted with problems of counterfeiting and piracy, this section presents an overview of the organizational responses and challenges that they face in China, the world's epicenter of counterfeiting and piracy. Dealing with counterfeiters in China present some special challenges and frustrations.

Multinational companies that are accustomed to dealing with legitimate business disputes over intellectual property rights face a different challenge altogether in dealing with pirates and counterfeiters. A multinational company may have a legitimate legal dispute with another multinational company or a local business over trademark, copyright, patent, or trade secret issues. The parties are law abiding entities that disagree in good faith over the rights involved. The parties hire law firms and litigate their disputes in court. The parties obey the rules of litigation and procedure and interact with each other directly during the litigation. Multinational companies are accustomed to these types of disputes and they follow a predictable pattern. In problems of counterfeiting and piracy, however, there is a legitimate business, a multinational or domestic company, on one side and an illegal, clandestine, and criminal counterfeiter or pirate on the other side. These types of infringers do not hire lawyers and do not appear in court. They do not respect or follow any laws or regulations. To the contrary, as their liability is clear, their response to any legal action is to disappear at the first sign of trouble. Many multinational companies are not accustomed to dealing with this type of adversary.

Let's us now follow a hypothetical multinational company in its struggles in China. For the multinational company, the first step in any enforcement action against pirates and counterfeiters is to identify and locate the culprits. Counterfeiters and pirates fear detection and capture and so use many means to operate clandestinely and to hide their identities. In China, most multinational companies find it necessary to hire private investigation companies to find the counterfeiters.

Not only do private investigators have experience in tracking down these perpetrators but the work can also be dangerous so most multinational companies would rather outsource this work than subject their own employees to these risks. The investigative work of private investigators can take weeks or months, and usually involves the use of one or more investigators using false identities to gain the confidence of the counterfeiters in order to penetrate into their network. This work can be expensive, costing the multinational company tens of thousands of dollars or more for any single product. Some multinational companies conduct multiple investigations at once.

Once the investigators believe they have located the counterfeiter's manufacturing operations, usually the next step is to conduct a raid and seizure. The benefits of such a procedure are that it occurs expeditiously and time is always of the essence in tracking down counterfeiters. The multinational company and its investigators will appear at the offices of an administrative enforcement entity, usually the local branch of the Administration of Market Regulation. The investigators will often be able to convince the authorities to initiate an enforcement action expeditiously, usually within the hour. Waiting until the next day is usually too late because the counterfeiter will receive tip offs and will have disappeared. The representatives of the multinational company and its private investigators will accompany enforcement officials in cars and vans heading to the location. The investigators will reveal the exact location only when the vehicles are en route to avoid tip offs.

The goal of the raid is to surprise and capture the counterfeiter and to seize all contraband, cash, and equipment found on the premises. If caught, the counterfeiter is usually questioned by the authorities on site and then released. Administrative authorities have no police powers and are unable to arrest or detain suspects in custody. The authorities do have the power to auction off the equipment and the contraband after eradicating the counterfeit trademark.

While the raid itself can be dramatic and exciting, multinational companies complain that the results are frustrating and disappointing due to the lack of deterrence. The administrative authorities will usually impose a fine on the counterfeiter of about $2,000 or less with no further consequences. Many counterfeiters are able to return to operations, sometimes with a vengeance, within several weeks. Some brand owners even claim that associates of the counterfeiter buy the seized equipment at the public auctions. One brand owner claimed that enforcement actions are like scratching an itch that makes the condition worse: the more enforcement actions the company brings, the more counterfeiting that occurs.

In cases involving contraband that crosses the threshold for criminal liability, many brand owners seek to pursue criminal prosecution. To do so, the administrative authorities must transfer the case to the police, known in China as the Public Security Bureau. However, the brand owner may find that administrative authorities are not cooperative. Administrative authorities and the police compete for prestige, power, and resources. If the administrative authorities transfer all of the goods, cash, and equipment seized to the Public Security Bureau, the administrative authorities will have less to report to their superiors and will also lose whatever proceeds they can realize in an auction. In addition, the primary responsibility of the Public Security Bureau is the suppression of violent crime and threats against the state. Suppression of counterfeiting is a low priority so the Public Security Bureau might not be willing to pursue a criminal prosecution without receiving a bribe.

Such bribes are known to be made without the direct knowledge of the brand owner. In some cases, private investigation companies will make a payment and call it a "miscellaneous expense" in its bill to the brand owner. Many brand owners may not even be aware that the private investigation industry is an unregulated industry that exists in a gray zone in China. The industry is technically illegal because private investigators engage in police work, which is the sole responsibility of the government. However, China tolerates the industry because PRC government authorities lack the resources and motivation to engage in time consuming investigations of counterfeiters. The industry falls into a gray area with companies that have business licenses for marketing and research serving as private investigators. As the industry is not regulated, it attracts persons of nefarious backgrounds willing to ignore legal rules. A private investigation firm that pays a bribe to the police, other law enforcement entities, other government bureaucrats, or a judge may achieve results not otherwise attainable. The private investigation company successfully resolves the case and the brand owner never finds out about the illegal payments. Some brand owners also tell their investigators that they do not want to know all the details of enforcement.

The long term risks of pay offs is the further corruption of certain segments of China's law enforcement system, such as the Public Security Bureau. The short term risk is that the brand owner may be subject to criminal and civil liability under laws pertaining to corruption. China has laws against official and commercial corruption and the United States (and other countries) also have laws against companies involved in foreign government corruption. In the United States, the U.S. Justice Department aggressively enforces the Foreign Corrupt Practices Act, 15 U.S.C. §§ 78dd–1 et seq. that covers bribes given by companies to foreign government officials to obtain or retain business. Some recent cases cover bribes given by U.S. companies in China, although to date no case has been brought for payments given in enforcement actions against counterfeiters and pirates.

Some companies bemoan what they perceive as the double losses they suffer with counterfeiting and in dealing with an intractable enemy. The company suffers losses of sales of the genuine product to counterfeits and knock-offs and the company suffers another loss in the expenditure of significant funds in pursuing counterfeiters. Companies claim that they must follow legal rules in a battle against an adversary that freely ignores them. Some multinational companies have multi-million dollar budgets spent just on enforcement actions with additional amounts for legal services and lobbying.

Another frustrating problem for brand owners is that in some cases counterfeits with authentic looking packaging appear on the market within a few days or a week of the launch of the genuine product. Such a rapid response of counterfeiters is not possible without the cooperation of persons working for the brand owner and the cooperation of third party manufacturers of the packaging. The brand owner is then faced with the problem of internal corporate security, of rooting out perfidious employees who are actively themselves engaging in counterfeiting, and the involvement of dishonest third party manufacturers hired by the company.

The reaction to the many complex and daunting problems surrounding the battle against counterfeiting and piracy has led some companies to form their own internal brand protection groups. These groups consist of representatives from the legal, government affairs, marketing, and sales departments. Some groups have formed relationships with local law enforcement officials who have created special programs giving the company priority in enforcement against the company's brands. Anecdotal evidence indicates that local law enforcement entities receive computers, phones, and other gifts from some brand protection groups as part of the special program. These programs raise issues of legality under PRC and U.S. anti-corruption laws as already discussed above. Despite these issues, some companies continue to maintain brand protection groups that use extremely aggressive tactics.

3. COUNTERFEITING IN CHINA

a. Origins of Counterfeiting

The origins of counterfeiting in China can be traced back to the first opening of its economy to foreign investment and trade in the 1980s. For 30 years after the founding of the People's Republic of China in 1949, China closed itself off from the rest of the world in order to focus on the internal goals of self-purification and self-introspection in pursue of revolutionary ideals. China maintained ties only with the Soviet Union but after Mao Zedong felt slighted by Stalin, he cut off relations with the Soviet Union and China became a hermit country. Isolationism left China's economy without the benefits of international trade and it stagnated. From the 1960s until Mao's death in 1976, China was convulsed by political terror campaigns instigated by Mao to destroy his enemies. Unrelenting political turbulence for more than a decade contributed to the decline of China's economy and the nation became mired in poverty and backwardness.

After Mao's death, China's paramount leader Deng Xiaopeng signaled a new national focus on economic development when he opened China's borders in 1979 that invited an unprecedented influx of foreign investment and capital from the world's largest multinational companies. Enticed by the prospect of China's huge market, one of the first multinational companies to invest in China was Procter & Gamble, the consumer products company. In the 1980's, Procter & Gamble opened its first factories in the southern port town of Guangzhou in southeast China in a special economic zone set up with incentives to attract foreign investment.

b. Manufacture of Counterfeit Goods

Soon after Procter & Gamble began its manufacturing operations of shampoos, laundry detergent and other daily use products, counterfeits appeared on the market. Some counterfeits were crude knock-offs that could fool no one but some were high quality, using some of the same formulas found in Procter & Gamble's shampoos and nearly identical packaging. Soon this became a pattern: in areas where foreign companies set up legitimate manufacturing operations, counterfeiting soon appeared nearby. It became clear that in some cases employees within the company with access to formulas and marketing plans were working with counterfeiters. Third party manufacturers that produced plastic containers, bottles, and packaging were known to engage in nights shifts to produce additional packaging for counterfeiters.

When companies with valuable brands like Procter & Gamble rushed to enter China in the 1980s, China had only recently emerged from the chaos of Mao's Cultural Revolution that ended with his death. The legal system had been destroyed by zealots during the Cultural Revolution. Existing intellectual property laws were crude by international standards and enforcement was weak. In the 1980s, China was not a member of any major international intellectual property treaties such as the Berne and Paris Conventions. China did not become a member of the WTO and subject to TRIPS requirements until 2001. The combination of a rapid inflow of advanced technology in China provided by multinational companies in the form of trademarks, patents, copyrights, and trade secrets and a weak legal regime created a legal environment where counterfeiting and piracy could flourish. By the end of the last millennium, in the span of just a couple of decades, China emerged as the world's largest producer of counterfeit goods.

Criminal organizations in China began to migrate to counterfeiting due to the high profits involved and the low penalties. These organizations are known to be involved the counterfeiting of cigarettes that are then smuggled into the United States and other countries. Counterfeit cigarettes have a high profit margin rivaling that of illegal narcotics, but with penalties that are far less severe by comparison to drug trafficking laws. The costs of the trade in counterfeit cigarettes are also lower since the contraband can be moved during daylight hours using ordinary trucks and stored in ordinary warehouses, none of which is possible with illegal narcotics. Only a large criminal organization has the resources to grow or procure the tobacco in China, package and brand the cigarettes, load them in shipping containers with false documentation, and distribute them in the United States. Industry studies indicate that China produces up to 400 billion counterfeit cigarettes to meet international demand.

Counterfeit cigarettes from China are continuously smuggled into the United States in shipping containers using false documentation. It is very difficult to interdict counterfeits at the border at U.S. ports of entry. U.S. customs authorities will not inspect a container unless the brand owner has specific intelligence that a particular container has contraband. Overall U.S. customs authorities inspect only about five percent of all containers or else international trade with the United States will grid to a halt. Everyday shipping containers containing smuggled cigarettes with a street value in the millions of dollars clear the port of Los Angeles.

c. Distribution of Counterfeit Goods

In a country the vast size of China, the manufacturing of counterfeits must operate in conjunction with a distribution system so that the goods can reach retail outlets and ultimately end-use consumers. Without a nationwide distribution system, counterfeits cannot reach consumers and will become not be a serious threat to genuine products. Counterfeits cannot use the legitimate distribution channels that large companies like Procter & Gamble have established for its products. Counterfeits are never found in large retail stores in China such as

Walmart, Carrefour, Costco, and many state-owned department stores. These stores obtain their supply of products from legitimate and qualified distribution channels that cannot be penetrated by counterfeits. Instead, counterfeiters had to develop an alternative and parallel distribution system that would cater to counterfeits, copyright pirated goods, smuggled goods, and inferior quality products.

Distribution systems for counterfeits depend on large wholesale markets established in large cities or in towns with easy access to multiple highways and transport routes. A wholesale market can be a large open air market or a large fully enclosed space on the lower floor in a commercial building. A wholesale market can be populated by thousands of wholesale distributors. The Tianyi wholesale market in Beijing offers 60,000 small products and is in a densely populated area within easy reach of thousands of retail outlets. Many of the products are counterfeits. Retailers with bicycles, small trucks, and vans travel to Tianyi and then back to retail locations to sell the counterfeits to consumers. There are similar sizeable wholesale markets in large cities throughout China that serve as distribution centers for counterfeit and other illegal goods.

d. Yiwu City, Privatization, and the China Small Commodities Group

A sense of the size and scope of some of these wholesale market can be gleaned from an examination of the China Small Commodities Wholesale Market in Yiwu City, Zhejiang Province, a city on the eastern coast of China near Shanghai. Yiwu presents an important study because it shows how counterfeiting has been integrated into nearly every facet of the economy of the city. It is no exaggeration to say that the entire city is built on the edifice of counterfeit and infringing goods. *See* Daniel C.K. Chow, *Organized Crime, Local Protectionism, and the Trade in Counterfeit Goods in China*, 14 China Econ. Rev. 473 (2003).

In the 1980s, the Yiwu City Administration of Industry and Commerce (AIC) established the China Small Commodities Market, a wholesale market selling small commodities and products, many of which later turned out to be counterfeit goods. The State Administration of Industry and Commerce (now renamed the State Administration of Market Regulation) and their local counterparts are charged with regulating commercial activity. The Yiwu AIC invested about USD $10 million in setting up the wholesale market and would also collect fees from vendors for licenses and use of the space. These fees could amount to hundreds of thousands of dollars. As part of its duties, the Yiwu AIC was also charged with enforcement of trademarks against counterfeiting. As the Yiwu AIC was both the investor and the regulator/enforcer, there arose a conflict of interest, although no one in Yiwu ever seemed to see the conflict as problematic.

Yiwu is an almost ideal location for a huge wholesale distribution market. Accessible highways allow travel by truck to reach the three most populous cities in China. Yiwu is a short drive to

Shanghai, China's largest city by population, and is about equidistant from Beijing to the north, the second most populous city, and Guangzhou to the south and east, the third largest city. The highways to Yiwu are clogged with trucks 24 hours a day with incoming trucks delivering counterfeit goods manufactured by factories in southern China and outgoing trucks delivering counterfeits purchased by buyers at the wholesale market to ship to their ultimate destinations for retail sale to consumers.

The rapid growth of the China Small Commodities Market led the Yiwu government in 1993 to privatize the management and operation of the wholesale market by incorporating the Small Commodities Market as a limited liability stock company owned by private investors and state-owned entities. Privatization accomplished several important goals. So long as the Yiwu government operated the Small Commodities Market, all revenues earned had to be transferred to the central government in Beijing with some portion of the funds being rebated to the local government as its share of national revenues. Once the Small Commodities Market became a private entity then all revenues were owned by the limited liability company and could be distributed to its investors. Privatization had the benefit of allowing the private investors to gain access to the substantial wealth generated by the wholesale market.

Privatization also had the benefit of allowing the Small Commodities Market to branch out into other businesses as subsidiaries and affiliates could be formed as part of a corporate group under the umbrella of the China Small Commodities Market management company. New subsidiaries and affiliates were established for internet and information services, property management, real estate, highway construction, finance, credit, trade, and hotels. After privatization, the revenues of the China Small Commodities Market soared through the decade of the 1990s when it abruptly stopped disclosing any additional financial information on its operations.

e. Local Protectionism

Although the Yiwu City Administration of Industry and Commerce privatized the China Small Commodities Market, the entity continued to have the cloak of government authority. Many former and some current government officials served on the boards of the China Small Commodities Market and its subsidiaries. Some business cards had the name of the privatized entity along with the name of a Yiwu government entity. The comingling of government authority with the private company created the impression that the China Small Commodities Market corporate group was an extension of the city government. This connection indicated to outside observers that any attempt to suppress counterfeiting by brand owners would be strongly defended at local levels.

The ability of the China Small Commodities corporate group to branch out into other businesses further integrated counterfeiting into the local economy. The Small Commodities Market's trade in counterfeit and infringing goods was supported by local restaurants and hotels used by the same 200,000 buyers who traveled daily to Yiwu. Warehousing and storage facilities, transportation companies, and real estate development were all supported by the trade in counterfeit goods. The China Small Commodities Market was also the largest taxpayer in the city, accounting for about 25 percent of all tax revenues for the city in the late 1990s.

The integration of counterfeiting into all facets of the local economy meant that the total suppression of counterfeiting would in effect shut down the local economy. Faced with the importance of counterfeiting to the entire local economy and the cloak of government authority enjoyed by the China Small Commodities Market, brand owners found that enforcement against counterfeiting in Yiwu was a largely futile task. While it was possible to obtain enforcement actions, such actions had only a superficial effect and no long term deterrence was possible given the economic and political conditions of the city.

The issues of local protectionism and government corruption, while appearing in an extremely powerful form in Yiwu, can be found throughout many local cities and towns in China. Such problems are generally not found in large cities like Beijing, which are subject to strict oversight by central level authorities. In areas outside large cities, however, local protectionism and government corruption remain the most serious and stubborn problem for brand owners seeking to enforce their intellectual property rights in China.

f. New Challenges

The rise and dominance of the internet and electronic commerce in the new millennium have created daunting new challenges for brand owners. *See* Daniel C.K. Chow, *Alibaba, Amazon, and Counterfeiting in the Age of the Internet*, 40 Northwestern J. Int'l L. & Bus. 157 (2020). In China, Alibaba operates the world's largest e-commerce market with over 1.3 billion active consumers, with about one billion active consumers in China and over 300 million outside of China. Brand owners have accused Alibaba of knowingly selling counterfeits on its various e-market sites. In the United States, brand owners have asserted the same allegations against Amazon and other internet platforms.

The use of the internet to sell counterfeit and infringing goods has created unanticipated new problems for brand owners. In the past, consumers in China had to travel to undesirable locations on side streets or to unsanitary wholesale markets to purchase counterfeits. Now any consumer can purchase goods on the internet from the safety and comfort of home or office. Counterfeiters who sold their wares in brick and mortar establishments were exposed to detection and capture. The internet provides the protections of anonymity and the ability to disappear into the vastness of cyberspace at the first sign of trouble. Counterfeiters now have what they have always wanted: a legitimate distribution channel using e-commerce sites to reach potential consumers anywhere in the world.

Brand owners who complain about counterfeits to operators of e-commerce platforms such as Alibaba and Amazon claim that they do not find a sympathetic forum. Brand owners claim that they face a cold, vast, and faceless bureaucracy. Most e-commerce platforms have notice and take down procedures that require a three strikes policy, i.e. the brand owner must demonstrate at least three instances of illegal activity by a web merchant before a website must be taken down permanently. Brand owners claim that these procedures are labyrinthine, burdensome, and frustrating. One small technical mistake can unravel months of work and force the brand owner to restart the process. Brand owners bemoan that the oppressive experience of dealing with unsympathetic internet platforms only compounds their misery.

Most brand owners have focused their attention on working with e-commerce platforms to simplify notice and takedown procedures. While these efforts are ongoing, the use of the internet to sell counterfeit goods is a continuing problem for which there does not appear to be an effective solution at present.

C. TRIPS ENFORCEMENT OBLIGATIONS

TRIPS broke new ground by including provisions in Part III of TRIPS, Articles 41–61 on enforcement of intellectual property rights. No international treaty on intellectual property had ever previously created enforcement obligations. TRIPS Part III was a long overdue recognition of enforcement as a separate field of its own right, especially in light of the growing problem of counterfeiting and piracy. As will be further explained in the discussion that follows, many of the enforcement provisions in TRIPS are modeled after procedures available under U.S. law.

Part III of TRIPS consists of five sections: (1) general obligations, (2) civil procedures and remedies, (3) provisional measures, (4) border measures, and (5) criminal liability and penalties. Several of these sections were aimed specifically at counterfeiting and commercial piracy.

General enforcement obligations are set forth in Article 41, which provides in relevant part:

TRIPS

Part III: Enforcement of Intellectual Property Rights

Section 1: General Obligations

Article 41

1. Members shall ensure that enforcement procedures as specified in this Part are available under their law so as to permit effective action against any act of infringement of intellectual property rights covered by this Agreement, including expeditious remedies to prevent infringements and remedies which constitute a deterrent to further infringements. These procedures shall be applied in such a manner as to avoid the creation of barriers to legitimate

> trade and to provide for safeguards against their abuse.
>
> 2. Procedures concerning the enforcement of intellectual property rights shall be fair and equitable. They shall not be unnecessarily complicated or costly, or entail unreasonable time-limits or unwarranted delays.
>
> 3. Decisions on the merits of a case shall preferably be in writing and reasoned. They shall be made available at least to the parties to the proceeding without undue delay. Decisions on the merits of a case shall be based only on evidence in respect of which parties were offered the opportunity to be heard.
>
> 4. Parties to a proceeding shall have an opportunity for review by a judicial authority of final administrative decisions and, subject to jurisdictional provisions in a Member's law concerning the importance of a case, of at least the legal aspects of initial judicial decisions on the merits of a case. However, there shall be no obligation to provide an opportunity for review of acquittals in criminal cases.

The approach of TRIPS is to require members to have certain administrative and judicial procedures in place and available to owners of intellectual property. TRIPS does not specify that any member must achieve a certain level of results from the uses of the procedures. The drafters of TRIPS believed that mandating results would have been overreaching and unrealistic.

1. CIVIL AND PROVISIONAL REMEDIES (TRIPS ARTICLES 42–50)

Sections 2 and 3 of Part III of TRIPS, Articles 42–50, require members to provide the legals tool for private civil enforcement of intellectual property rights through court-based litigation or through administrative means. To support civil enforcement, TRIPS requires members to create evidentiary presumptions against parties that destroy evidence (Article 43), to make available injunctions to prevent the entry of counterfeit and pirated goods into commerce (Article 44), to provide compensatory damages for intellectual property infringements (Article 45), and to create a means to dispose of counterfeit and pirated goods outside the channels of commerce (Article 46).

One of the most important provisions contained in TRIPS requires that members make available provisional measures, i.e. remedies that are temporary and that can be obtained before the conclusion of the legal proceeding. Article 50 provides:

TRIPS

Article 50

1. The judicial authorities shall have the authority to order prompt and effective provisional measures:

(a) to prevent an infringement of any intellectual property right from occurring, and in particular to prevent the entry into the channels of commerce in their jurisdiction of goods, including imported goods immediately after customs clearance;

(b) to preserve relevant evidence in regard to the alleged infringement.

2. The judicial authorities shall have the authority to adopt provisional measures *inaudita altera parte* where appropriate, in particular where any delay is likely to cause irreparable harm to the right holder, or where there is a demonstrable risk of evidence being destroyed.

3. The judicial authorities shall have the authority to require the applicant to provide any reasonably available evidence in order to satisfy themselves with a sufficient degree of certainty that the applicant is the right holder and that the applicant's right is being infringed or that such infringement is imminent, and to order the applicant to provide a security or equivalent assurance sufficient to protect the defendant and to prevent abuse.

4. Where provisional measures have been adopted *inaudita altera parte*, the parties affected shall be given notice, without delay after the execution of the measures at the latest. A review, including a right to be heard, shall take place upon request of the defendant with a view to deciding, within a reasonable period after the notification of the measures, whether

> these measures shall be modified, revoked or confirmed.
>
> * * *
>
> 6. Without prejudice to paragraph 4, provisional measures taken on the basis of paragraphs 1 and 2 shall, upon request by the defendant, be revoked or otherwise cease to have effect, if proceedings leading to a decision on the merits of the case are not initiated within a reasonable period . . . , not to exceed 20 working days or 31 calendar days, whichever is the longer.
>
> 7. Where the provisional measures are revoked or where they lapse due to any act or omission by the applicant, or where it is subsequently found that there has been no infringement or threat of infringement of an intellectual property right, the judicial authorities shall have the authority to order the applicant, upon request of the defendant, to provide the defendant appropriate compensation for any injury caused by these measures.
>
> 8. To the extent that any provisional measure can be ordered as a result of administrative procedures, such procedures shall conform to principles equivalent in substance to those set forth in this Section.

Article 50 of TRIPS is based on procedures set forth in Rule 65 of the Federal Rules of Civil Procedure. TRIPS Article 50(2) requires members to permit a party to obtain the equivalent of an ex parte temporary restraining order (TRO) under federal civil practice in the United States. Under Federal Rule of Civil Procedure 65(b)(1), a party is able to appear ex parte, i.e. without the presence of the other side, and obtain a seizure order or an injunction from a court. The opposing party is given no prior notice of the TRO and receives notice only when the TRO is being served on the party. The ex parte nature of this procedure is essential to preserve the element of surprise. In dealing with counterfeiters, surprise is a necessity. Prior notice to a counterfeiter of a judicial proceeding will usually result in the immediate flight of the counterfeiter and the disappearance or destruction of the goods.

TRIPS Article 50(3) requires that the applicant for a TRO post security to compensate the defendant in the event that the TRO is later shown to be without basis. Article 50(4) requires that once a TRO has been issued a hearing must be held within a reasonable period. Article 50(6) requires the TRO to be dissolved if a hearing on the merits of the case is not initiated within 20 working days. These provisions parallel those in Rule 65 of the Federal Rules of Civil Procedure. Rule 65(b)(2) allows a plaintiff to apply for a TRO that will suspend any illegal activity and that will be in effect for 14 days. Rule 65(b)(3) then requires a notice of a hearing at which both parties will appear and at which the plaintiff can apply for a preliminary injunction that will take effect as soon as the TRO expires. The preliminary injunction will be in place for the duration of the trial at the end of which the court can issue a permanent injunction that will replace the preliminary injunction. These procedures under Rule 65 of the Federal Rules of

Civil Procedure are designed to allow a plaintiff to immediately suspend illegal counterfeiting activity by a defendant at the start of a lawsuit and to continue the suspension until the conclusion of the lawsuit when a final judgment or permanent injuction is entered.

As a practical matter, most legal actions against counterfeiters in the United States end with a successfully executed TRO. The liability of the counterfeiter is usually never in doubt. Either the counterfeiter does not appear in court for the hearing on the preliminary injunction and a default judgment is entered or a settlement is reached. These procedures have proven effective against counterfeiters in the United States. TRIPS Article 50 now requires that similar procedures must be made available by each WTO member. The importance of the element of surprise is so critical that the United States will challenge the laws of countries that provide for injunctive relief but not ex parte injunctive relief. *See Notification of Mutually Agreement Solution (June 1, 2001) of Denmark—Measures Affecting the Enforcement of Intellectual Property Rights*, WT/DS83/1 (May 14, 1997) (Denmark agreed to make ex parte injunctive relief available in intellectual property enforcement actions).

2. CRIMINAL LIABILITY AND PENALTIES

TRIPS was the first international treaty to require criminal liability and penalties for trademark counterfeiting and copyright piracy:

TRIPS

Section 5: criminal procedures

Article 61

> Members shall provide for criminal procedures and penalties to be applied at least in cases of willful trademark counterfeiting or copyright piracy on a commercial scale. Remedies available shall include imprisonment and/or monetary fines sufficient to provide a deterrent . . . . In appropriate cases, remedies available shall also include the seizure, forfeiture and destruction of the infringing goods and of any materials and implements the predominant use of which has been in the commission of the offence.

Article 61 mandates criminal penalties for willful trademark counterfeiting and copyright piracy on a commercial scale. TRIPS does not require criminal liability for violations of other intellectual property rights. In particular, TRIPS does not mandate criminal liability for patent infringements. An earlier discussion noted that unauthorized copying of patents for pharmaceuticals are controversial as some countries believe that such copying is justified for public health reasons. This debate over drug patents meant that the drafters of TRIPS could not agree on criminal liability for patent infringements. As TRIPS sets minimum standards, nothing prevents a member from imposing criminal liability for patent infringements or violations of other intellectual property rights. The United States has implemented federal criminal liability for theft of trade secrets.

TRIPS Article 61 requires criminal liability for counterfeiting and piracy "*on a commercial scale.*" The meaning of these terms was at issue in *China—Measures Affecting the Protection and Enforcement of Intellectual Property Rights*, WT/DS362/R, Report of the Panel (January 26, 2009). China's criminal laws used monetary thresholds for imposing criminal liability. For example, Article 213(1) of the PRC Criminal Law imposed criminal liability for trademark counterfeiting for sales of 50,000 yuan (about USD $7,000) or above and profits of 30,000 yuan (about USD $4,200) or above. Article 5 of Judicial Interpretation No. 19 (2004) interpreted Article 217 of the PRC Criminal Law to impose criminal liability for copyright piracy where the profits were 30,000 yuan or above and sales were 50,000 yuan or above. The reproduction of computer software and other works of 1,000 copies or more also triggered criminal liability.

The United States argued that amounts slightly below these thresholds should also be considered to be "on a commercial scale" and that China's laws were therefore in violation of TRIPS Article 61. The United States also argued that counterfeiting that involved any commercial activity must be criminalized under Article 61. The panel rejected this argument. The panel noted that the terms used were "commercial scale" not just "commercial" as was proposed by the United States in the negotiation of TRIPS. The panel found that the term "scale" indicates a certain size. The panel further found that "commercial scale" is the magnitude or extent typical of commercial activity. The panel concluded that counterfeiting on a commercial scale indicates counterfeiting of a product on a scale typical of the sales of a genuine product.

As the United States argued that China failed to impose criminal sanctions on counterfeiting on a commercial scale in violation of TRIPS Article 61, the United States had the burden proving commercial scale. On the issue of counterfeiting on a commercial scale, the United States failed to provide sufficient evidence. The United States produced scattered statistics and newspaper articles on the size and scope of counterfeiting in China. The panel found that this evidence lacked probative value and concluded that the United States failed to establish that China's use of criminal thresholds was inconsistent with TRIPS Article 61.

The evidentiary problems for the United States can be traced to the reluctance of multinational companies to provide detailed information about the counterfeiting of their products in China. Only the multinational companies had information about the scale of the counterfeiting of their products. Although multinational companies urged the United States to bring the WTO case, they were reluctant to provide detailed information on the extent of the counterfeiting of their products for fear that this would create negative publicity for their products. This conduct appears to be a pattern among multinational companies. They issue general complaints about counterfeiting but do not provide detailed accounts involving their products. Either the companies fear that providing such information would harm the reputation of their products or the companies do not have reliable information.

3. BORDER CONTROL MEASURES (TRIPS ARTICLES 51–60)

TRIPS continued to break new ground by requiring border enforcement measures for the protection of intellectual property rights.

> **TRIPS**
>
> **Section 4: special requirements related to border measures**
>
> **Article 51**
> **Suspension of Release by Customs Authorities**
>
> Members shall, in conformity with the provisions set out below, adopt procedures to enable a right holder, who has valid grounds for suspecting that the importation of counterfeit trademark or pirated copyright goods may take place, to lodge an application in writing with competent authorities, administrative or judicial, for the suspension by the customs authorities of the release into free circulation of such goods. * * *

Article 51 requires members to allow a right holder to file an application with customs authorities or other authorities to prevent the importation of trademark counterfeit and copyright pirated goods. As in the case of criminal penalties, only these two types of illegal goods must be interdicted although members can choose also to prevent other types of goods infringing intellectual property rights from passing through customs. The United States also allows for the prohibition of imports that infringe patents or trade secrets. 19 U.S.C. § 1337. The key is to prevent the illegal goods from clearing customs and entering the internal market. Once contraband enters a nation's internal market, the task of interdicting the illegal goods becomes nearly impossible.

Note that there are two "choke" points in the international trade in counterfeit and pirated goods. One is at the point of exportation and the other is at the point of importation. TRIPS only requires border measures at the point of importation. The negotiators of TRIPS could not agree on imposing restrictions at the point of exportation. Many nations favor and encourage exports as they lead to a favorable trade balance and can also earn hard currency. Nations are wary of imposing procedures that could restrict exports and that might negatively affect their economic interests. Unfortunately, for political and economic reasons, nations could not agree to impose export restrictions. This oversight means that only one choke point is constrained by TRIPS while some nations can freely export counterfeits. One has to ponder how effective import restrictions that are not accompanied by export restrictions can be to stem the trade in counterfeit goods.

TRIPS Article 53 requires the right holder to post security and to compensate for an injury caused by wrongful detention of the goods by customs authorities. A detention of the goods cannot exceed 10 days unless a proceeding on the merits has been initiated (Article 55). Under Article 59, government entities must have the authority to order the destruction or disposal of the goods outside the channels of commerce as specified in Article 46. Article 59 also provides that in the case of counterfeit goods, the authorities "shall not allow for their re-exportation in an unaltered state or subject them to a different customs procedure, other than in exceptional circumstances." The concern of multinational companies that is captured in both Articles 46 and 59 is that disposal procedures should not permit counterfeit goods that are not destroyed to be reused in a way that will harm the right holder. One particularly worrisome possibility is that the counterfeiter or another counterfeiter can acquire or reacquire the goods and reaffix a counterfeit trademark before selling the goods.

The interpretation of Article 59 was the main issue in *China—Measures Affecting the Protection and Enforcement of Intellectual Property Rights*, WT/DS362/R, Report of the Panel (January 26, 2009). (A different part of this opinion has already been examined in connection with the discussion of counterfeiting "on a commercial scale" above.) The United States claimed that several of China's customs regulations violated TRIPS provisions dealing with disposal of counterfeit goods. China's customs regulations provided for several methods of disposal of counterfeits: (1) donation to a social welfare organization, (2) sale to the right holder, (3) auction of the goods after eradicating infringing features, and (4) destruction of the goods when eradicating infringing features is not possible.

The United States argued that these regulations created a mandated sequential ordering of disposal methods and that (4) destruction cannot occur unless the first three methods were unavailable. The United States claimed that this required sequential ordering violated Article 59, which provides that authorities must be able to order the destruction of the goods. The panel rejected this argument. The panel did not find that the PRC regulations required a sequential ordering of methods and accepted China's contention that customs authorities had discretion and inherent authority to order the destruction of counterfeit goods at any time.

While the United States lost on this issue, the panel did agree with the United States that the regulation's method of auctioning off the goods after removal of infringing features violated TRIPS Article 46 (incorporated by Article 59). Article 46 states that "[i]n regard to counterfeit trademark goods the simple removal of the trademark unlawfully affixed shall not be sufficient, other than in exceptional cases, to permit release of the goods in the channels of commerce." China's regulations violated Articles 46 and 59 because the regulations did not require any exceptional circumstances for the sale of the goods after the simple removal of the counterfeit trademark. China's regulations allowed goods to be sold in all cases as soon as the counterfeit trademark was erased.

a. U.S. Border Controls

The United States has implemented TRIPS border requirements through various provisions contained in the U.S. Code and in the Code of Federal Regulations. These provisions permit U.S. right holders to prevent the importation of trademark counterfeit and copyright pirated goods in accordance with the requirements of TRIPS Article 51.

Under 19 CFR § 133, the owner of a trademark registered with the U.S. Patent and Trademark Office can record the trademark with U.S. customs authorities. Once the trademark is recorded, customs authorities must seize and forfeit all goods that are counterfeits of the recorded trademark. In this context, a counterfeit involves an unauthorized use of the recorded trademark on an identical or substantially similar product with identical or substantially similar packaging to that of genuine product. Sometimes this type of product is referred to as a "dead counterfeit." The seized goods are then destroyed unless the trademark owner consents to a different form of disposal. 19 U.S.C. § 1526(e). Even though a trademark is not recorded, customs authorities are empowered to seize and destroy counterfeit goods under a different statutory provision, 15 U.S.C. § 1595a(c) (dealing with seizure of goods violating a variety of federal statutes).

If the suspect goods are not counterfeits but are trademark infringing goods then U.S. customs authorities will seize and forfeit the goods only if the trademark is recorded. In this context, a good that infringes a trademark in one that uses a confusingly similar (but not identical) trademark on goods that may also use confusingly similar packaging. Trademark infringing goods that are seized are subject to forfeiture, but the importer can seek to enter the goods by removing the trademark. Depending on the circumstances of the case, customs authorities have been known to permit goods with eradicated trademarks to enter against the protests of the right holder. Goods that infringe a trademark that has not been recorded are not detained but are permitted to enter the United States. The right holder has the option to bring a civil action in court against the importer.

U.S. customs authorities use a similar procedure for copyrighted works. If the right holder registers the copyright with the U.S. copyright office and then records the copyright with customs authorities, U.S. customs will then seize and forfeit any copyright pirated goods (identical copies) or copyright infringing goods (similar copies). As in the case of trademarks, customs authorities also have authority to seize copyright pirated goods (identical copies) even when the copyright has not been recorded. However, customs authorities will not seize copyright infringing goods (similar copies) unless the copyright is registered and recorded.

The simple recording procedure with customs authorities for trademarks and copyrights is not available for patents and trade secrets. A right holder seeking to prevent the importation of goods violating patents and trade secrets must file an action with the International Trade Commission under 19 U.S.C. § 1337 for a hearing and an exclusion order.

U.S. customs authorities provide a procedure that importers can use to obtain an advance ruling on whether imports will violate the rights of recorded trademarks or copyrights. In *Ross Cosmetics Distribution Centers Inc. v. United States*, 18 C.I.T. 979 (Ct. Int'l Trade 1994), the plaintiff Ross Cosmetics sought an opinion from customs authorities on whether products that it sought to import violated trademark rights. Ross's bath oils and fragrances were imitations of the luxury trademarked products "Giorgio," "Youth Dew," and "L'Air Du Temps." Ross's products referred to the trademarked products by name on the packaging of its imitation products and urged the consumer to compare Ross's products with "Giorgio," "Youth Dew," and "L'Air Du Temps." Customs authorities found that the use of these trademarks without authorization on Ross's own products was a counterfeit use and that Ross's counterfeit products, if imported, would be subject to seizure and forfeiture.

The Court of International Trade reviewed the ruling and disagreed that Ross's product "Gorgeous" was a counterfeit of "Giorgio." Counterfeits use the same trademark and packaging and are exact duplicates of the genuine product. Gorgeous was not an exact duplicate of Giorgio and while Gorgeous used the Giorgio trademark on its packaging, the use was to urge the consumer to compare Gorgeous with Giorgio and not for the purposes of passing the Gorgeous product off as a Giorgio product.

Although Gorgeous was not a counterfeit of Giorgio, the court found that Gorgeous infringed the Giorgio trademark because consumers would likely confuse Gorgeous and Giorgio products. Gorgeous used a background design, a crest, and a name that was similar in appearance to Giorgio. All three of these elements (background design, crest, and name) were registered Giorgio trademarks. The similar appearance of Gorgeous products was intentional and was likely to confuse consumers. The court found that a disclaimer that was on the Gorgeous product package that it was not associated with Giorgio was ineffective. The disclaimer was in smaller type at the bottom of the front panel and could be easily overlooked by consumers. As Giorgio was a recorded trademark, Gorgeous products would be subject to seizure and forfeiture by customs authorities.

The court used a similar analysis for the registered trademark "L'Air Du Temps." The court found that Ross's product "Love Birds" was not a counterfeit but was a confusingly similar use and a trademark infringement. L'Air Du Temps was not a recorded trademark, however, so customs authorities will not seize and forfeit Love Birds products. Ross's Love Birds products could enter the United States but the owner of the L'Air Du Temps trademark had the option of bringing a civil action for trademark infringement.

b. EU Border Controls

The EU has implemented border controls in compliance with TRIPS Article 51 in EU Regulation, No. 608/2013 (July 22, 2003). The EU Regulation allows right holders to file an application with customs authorities to seize and forfeit or destroy goods suspected of violating intellectual property rights, including trademarks, copyrights, patents, and geographical indications. The EU does not have its own customs authorities but relies on the customs authorities of each member nation.

The issue of border measures in the EU is complicated by one of the fundamental principles of the EU, the freedom of transit for goods between member states set forth in Article 28 of the Treaty on the Functioning of the European Union. The EU creates a single internal market consisting of its 27 member states. To maintain the single market it is essential that all internal borders be eliminated and that barriers to the movement of goods between member states be removed. Seizing goods in transit conflicts with these basic policies.

The conflict between freedom of transit and border measures was involved in *Administration Des Douanes et Droits Indirects v. Rioglass SA, Transremar SL*, [2003] European Court of Justice, Case C–115/02 (October 23, 2003). Two Spanish companies were involved in the shipment of auto parts from Spain to Poland. The auto parts included windows and screens intended for use on Peugeot, Citroen, and Renault cars. The manufacturer of the auto parts included its own trademark and the trademarks of these cars on the auto parts in order to indicate the cars that could be fitted with the parts. The French trademark owners enlisted the aid French customs in seizing and detaining the parts based on a claim of trademark infringement. The trial court upheld the seizure order but was reversed by the appeals court. The case then went before the Cour de cassation, France's highest court, which referred the case to the European Court of Justice as it involved the freedom of transit within the EU.

The European Court of Justice refused to uphold the seizure order. Article 28, freedom of transit, is subject to exceptions if necessary to protect intellectual property rights. The court found that trademarks have a marketing function, allowing the right holder to place the goods on the market for the first time so as to protect the right holder from competitors taking advantage of the trademark by selling goods with similar trademarks. As the goods in this case were in transit and not being placed on the market, the marketing of the goods was not involved and so no trademark rights were infringed. The seizure order was an unjustified interference with the freedom of transit and so was illegal.

It is worth noting that the freedom of transit within the internal market is viewed as sacrosanct in the EU and that a different result may occur under similar circumstances in the United States. For example, if a party challenged the seizure of goods with unauthorized trademarks in interstate commerce in federal court, the court could to a different conclusion and uphold the seizure.

D. PRIVATE ENFORCEMENT BY RIGHT HOLDERS IN COURTS

1. CHOICE OF FORUM, JURISDICTION ISSUES, AND CHOICE OF LAW

Multinational companies and right holders sometimes have the option of filing a lawsuit against defendants in federal or state courts in the United States. For the reasons discussed in the last section, lawsuits are not a viable option against counterfeiters and pirates who do not appear in court but take flight instead. Lawsuits can be an option against a defendant that is a legitimate business entity when a transnational business dispute arises between the parties.

If a U.S. plaintiff sues a foreign defendant in a U.S. court, the plaintiff will need to establish that the court has personal jurisdiction over the defendant. The test for personal jurisdiction over a foreign defendant is the same standard as that used for U.S. defendants: the defendant must satisfy the minimum contacts test for personal jurisdiction first established by *International Shoe Co. v. State of Washington*, 326 U.S. 310 (1945) and applied to foreign defendants in *Asahi Metal Industry Co., Ltd v. Superior Court*, 480 U.S. 102 (1987). A foreign defendant that has offices or operations in the United States or that does business in the United States will likely satisfy the tests for personal jurisdiction.

The U.S. court will also need to have subject matter jurisdiction over the case. In federal district court, a U.S. plaintiff suing a foreign defendant can establish subject matter jurisdiction based upon diversity of citizenship. 28 U.S.C. § 1332(a)(2). Federal district courts have subject matter jurisdiction for trademark infringement cases under the Lanham Act, 15 U.S.C. § 1121. In cases involving a U.S. patent, federal district courts have exclusive subject matter jurisdiction under 28 U.S.C. § 1338. These are some specific examples, but in all cases in federal district court, the plaintiff must plead and establish the subject matter jurisdiction of the court.

If the court has both personal and subject matter jurisdiction and the lawsuit can proceed, the court will likely next encounter choice of law issues. A transnational intellectual property litigation in the United States involving a foreign defendant will usually involve the laws of the United States as well as the laws of a foreign nation. The U.S. court will need to engage in a choice of law analysis to determine whether the intellectual property laws of the United States apply to the dispute, whether the laws of the nation of the foreign defendant apply, or whether both apply to different aspects of the case. A U.S. federal district court exercising diversity jurisdiction will make this determination using the choice of law rules of the state in which the court sits under the rule established by *Klaxon v. Stentor*, 313 U.S. 487 (1941).

These types of preliminary issues will be involved in any transnational litigation in U.S. courts and similar issues will be involved if the litigation occurs in a foreign court involving a U.S. defendant. This has been a brief overview of these issues, which are examined in greater detail in courses on transnational litigation or international business transactions.

2. U.S. COURTS ADJUDICATING INTELLECTUAL PROPERTY CLAIMS INVOLVING FOREIGN CONDUCT

If a right holder decides to file a lawsuit against a defendant that involves transnational elements in a U.S. court, the court may be confronted with the adjudication of intellectual property claims for conduct that occurs abroad. In two cases with similar facts, involving this issue, and the courts reached opposite results.

In *London Film Productions Limited v. Intercontinental Communications, Inc.*, 580 F. Supp. 47 (S.D.N.Y. 1984), the plaintiff, London Films Production Limited was a UK company that produced motion pictures in the UK for distribution around the world. The defendant was Intercontinental Communications, Inc., a New York corporation, which allegedly licensed the rights to show London Films's movies in Chile, Venezuela, Peru, Ecuador, Costa Rica, and Panama. The court held that under the Berne Convention, when London Films acquired a UK copyright for its films, it also acquired copyrights under the Berne Convention in all of the South American countries where its films were being distributed. London Films sued Intercontinental for breach of its copyrights in the South American countries. The court decided to exercise jurisdiction over the copyright claims in the foreign countries.

In *Voda v. Cordis Corp.*, 476 F.3d 887 (Fed. Cir. 2007), the plaintiff Voda was an Oklahoma resident. The defendant Cordis Corporation was a U.S. corporation incorporated in Florida. Cordis and the foreign affiliated Cordis entities were all part of the group of companies owned by Johnson & Johnson, the pharmaceutical company. All of the Cordis entities were separate legal entities and none of the foreign Cordis entities was named as a defendant in the lawsuit. Voda had three U.S. patents for the use of catheters in heart surgery. Voda also had a European patent (a basket of national patents of all EU countries), as well as British, Canadian, French, and German patents. Voda sued Cordis in federal district in Oklahoma for the violation of his U.S. patents and added claims for breach of his patents in the European countries.

The district court had subject matter jurisdiction over Voda's U.S. patent claims pursuant to 28 U.S.C. § 1338 (exclusive federal jurisdiction over U.S. patent law) but did not have subject matter jurisdiction over the foreign patent claims. The district court decided to exercise supplemental jurisdiction over the foreign patent claims pursuant to 28 U.S.C. § 1367. A federal district court can exercise supplemental jurisdiction over claims over which it does not have original federal jurisdiction when the supplemental claims arise out of the same transaction so that the supplemental claims and the U.S. patent claims form one case or controversy for the purposes of Article III of the Constitution.

On appeal, the Federal Circuit Court of Appeals found that the district court had abused its discretion by assuming jurisdiction over the foreign patent claims. Under § 1367(c) even when the court has supplemental jurisdiction, the court should decline to exercise jurisdiction when there are other compelling factors against such exercise. These factors include comity, judicial economy, convenience, and fairness. The court of appeals found that the Paris Convention provided for the independence of each country's patent system from others and that TRIPS Part III required members to provide for effective enforcement procedures for intellectual property rights, including patents, in their domestic legal systems. The court of appeals concluded that nothing in international treaties indicated that one jurisdiction should adjudicate the patents of another. The district court's exercise of exterritorial jurisdiction would harm international comity.

One way of explaining the different results reached in the two cases is that *London Films* represents a line of cases holding that copyright infringement is a transitory cause of action. In this context, a transitory cause of action is one that can be brought in any court that has personal jurisdiction over the defendant regardless of where the defendant's conduct occurred. Traditional examples of transitory actions are breach of contract and tort cases. So long as a court has personal jurisdiction over the defendant, the defendant can be sued for a breach of contract or for a tort that occurred in a different state or jurisdiction. Some commentators, such as Nimmer, and some courts, such as the court in *London Films*, believe that copyright infringement also belongs in the category of transitory actions but this is not a view that is held by all courts. In the case of patents, the traditional rules of jurisdiction as exemplified by *Voda v. Cordis* will apply: the claim must be adjudicated in the legal system where the conduct occurred or under the laws of the legal system that granted the patent.

In the case of trademarks, some courts will exercise exterritorial jurisdiction over foreign conduct involving a U.S. trademark if the foreign conduct has substantial effects within the United States. *Steele v. Bulova Watch Co., Inc.*, 344 U.S. 280 (1952). A modern application of the effects doctrine justifying the exterritorial application of the Lanham Act to conduct in Canada was involved in *Trader Joe's Co. v. Hallatt*, 835 F.3d 960 (9th Cir. 2016) discussed in an earlier chapter of this book on trademarks.

3. ENFORCEMENT OF FOREIGN COURT JUDGMENTS

In transnational litigation, a party that has obtained a judgment in one nation may need to enforce the judgment in another nation. This need arises when a defendant does not have any assets in the nation that rendered the judgment. Suppose, for example, that a U.S. plaintiff sues a Chinese company in the United States. While the Chinese defendant does business in the United States and is subject to personal jurisdiction, the company may have only a small office and no other assets in the United States. If the U.S. plaintiff receives a judgment from a U.S. court and seeks to collect on the judgment, the plaintiff will need to enforce the judgment in China where the defendant has assets. The U.S. plaintiff will need to appear in a Chinese court and ask the Chinese court to recognize the U.S. court judgment. Once the Chinese court issues an order recognizing the U.S. court judgment, it becomes enforceable in China.

Whether or not a court will recognize a foreign court judgment depends upon a number of factors. If the two nations involved are signatories to a treaty calling for mutual recognition of judgments, recognition will proceed in accordance with the treaty. China and some other countries will apply a reciprocity test, i.e. Chinese courts will recognize a foreign court judgment only if the foreign nation will recognize Chinese court judgments. Aside from these situations, the general approach for recognizing foreign court judgments followed by most nations, including the United States, will focus on (1) whether the foreign court has jurisdiction; (2) whether the foreign case satisfied due process concerns such as proper notice to the defendant and did not involve any fraud or misconduct in the case; and (3) whether the foreign judgment is inconsistent with an important public policy of the forum.

In analyzing the last factor, consistency with U.S. public policy, U.S. courts have cautioned that the analysis cannot be a fuzzy general policy analysis but must be specific and tailored to the particular cause of action involved in the foreign court. In *Sarl Louis Feraud International v. Viewfinder, Inc.*, 489 F.3d 474 (2d Cir. 2007), the federal district court refused to recognize a French court judgment against the defendant Viewfinder, Inc., a Delaware corporation, on the ground that the judgment was inconsistent with the policies underlying the First Amendment. Viewfinder had posted photographs of plaintiffs' new seasonal fashions on a website. The plaintiffs, fashion houses in France, claimed that Viewfinder's unauthorized posting of photographs of plaintiffs' fashions breached their copyrights, which, under French law extends to seasonal clothing fashions (U.S. copyright law does not protect fashions). When Viewfinder failed to appear in French court, the court entered a default judgment. The French plaintiffs then sought recognition of the French court judgment in the federal district court for the Southern District of New York in order to enforce it against Viewfinder.

The district court applied New York law and refused to recognize the French court judgment on the ground that Viewfinder is a news magazine reporting on a public event and that its conduct in posting the photographs is protected by the First Amendment. To enforce the French court judgment would be repugnant to U.S. public policy so the district court refused recognition.

The Court of Appeals for the Second Circuit found fault with the general approach used by the district court and required a more refined analysis. The court of appeals found that New York law required the district court to analyze the cause of action on which the foreign court judgment was based. The court of appeals found that the district court should have analyzed whether the intellectual property law regime upon which the French judgment was based impinged upon the First Amendment. To make this determination, the district court should have analyzed the level of First Amendment protection required by U.S. public policy and then determined whether the French intellectual property legal regime provided comparable protections.

Under U.S. law, First Amendment considerations under copyright law are entirely encompassed by the fair use doctrine. The court of appeals held that the district court should have analyzed whether Viewfinder's activities constituted fair use under U.S. law. If the publication of the photographs would not be fair use under U.S. law then the French court judgments would not be repugnant to U.S. public policy. By contrast, if the posting was fair use then the French court judgments would be inconsistent with U.S. public policy and should not be recognized. The court of appeals remanded the case to the district court for further proceedings.

E. ENFORCEMENT AGAINST GRAY MARKET GOODS

1. GRAY MARKET GOODS AND PARALLEL IMPORTS

This section now turns to an examination of enforcement by right holders against gray market goods or parallel imports. Enforcement in the context of gray market goods usually refers to efforts by right holders to block the importation of the goods into the United States. Let us first begin with a basic question: what is a gray market good?

Illustration 6-1. Lois goes to an electronics store to buy a mobile phone. She finds Lotus, a well-known U.S. brand, at a substantial discount but sees that the packaging of the phone has English language labels pasted over the text in French. Later, she discovers that Lotus had first sold the phones to a distributor in Canada and that the distributor imported the phones into the United States. She uses the phone and is annoyed when some features of the phone are different from Lotus phones used by her friends. When a problem arises, she contacts Lotus but finds out that the phone is not covered by Lotus's warranty, only by the store warranty. Lois submits a consumer complaint to Lotus and tells her friends that she should have bought an Apple phone instead. Lotus now attempts to block the importation of the phones by the electronics store.

In the illustration, Lois has bought a gray market good. The product is a genuine product, not a counterfeit. Lotus has manufactured the phones in the United States and has exported them to a country abroad. A distributor has purchased the phones outside of the United States and has imported them into the United States without authorization from the manufacturer for sale at a discount store. Gray market goods are also sometimes called parallel imports. Assume that Lotus has its phones manufactured abroad for importation into the United States. When there are unauthorized imports, i.e. gray market goods, the imports are called parallel imports because they are a second unauthorized channel of imports parallel to the first authorized channel. In this chapter, the terms gray market goods and parallel imports are synonymous.

2. BLOCKING THE IMPORTATION OF GRAY MARKET GOODS

A U.S. company that exports some of its products to be sold in a foreign market does not wish to have those goods re-imported into the United States at discount prices and enter into intra-band competition with sales of its goods intended for the U.S. market. Aside from the unwanted price competition, there is also the issue of consumer confusion and dissatisfaction (see Illustration 6-1 above). U.S. right holders often attempt to block the importation of gray market goods. The right holder will assert that part of its intellectual property rights in the product is the right of importation, which allows the right holder to ban imports of the product without its authorization.

Whether a right holder can ban imports of gray market goods depends on whether the intellectual property right involved in the particular item, i.e. trademark, copyright, or patent, has been exhausted under the first sale doctrine. If the right involved is subject to a rule of international exhaustion, then the first sale of the product anywhere in the world exhausts the right in that particular product and it can be imported without the permission of the right holder. If the right involved is subject to a rule of national exhaustion, only first sales in the nation of origin of the product will exhaust the right. Under a rule of national exhaustion if the first sale occurs abroad, the right has not been exhausted and the right holder can block the importation of the product. Finally, under a principle of regional exhaustion followed by the EU, a first sale anywhere in the EU exhausts the right and the product can be imported into any country in the EU.

Illustration 6-2. Returning to the facts of problem 6-1 above. Lotus attempts to block the importation of the Lotus phones by the electronics store. The United States follows a principle of national exhaustion for trademarks (but subject to many exceptions). The first sale of the Lotus phones occurred abroad so the Lotus trademarks have not been exhausted. Lotus can record its registered trademark with customs authorities and block the importation of the gray market goods. If Lotus first sold the goods to a distributor in the United States who then sold them to a second distributor abroad, the trademarks rights would have exhausted by the first sale in the United States and Lotus would be unable to block the imports.

3. APPROACH IN THE UNITED STATES AND THE EU

The United States follows a principle of national exhaustion for trademarks, although the principle is subject to so many exceptions that it operates almost as a principle of international exhaustion. Recent cases now establish that the United States follows a principle of international exhaustion for copyrights and patents.

The EU follows a principle of regional exhaustion for trademarks, copyrights, and patents. Although the rules can be easily summarized, exhaustion for each category of intellectual property rights is subject to many complexities as explained in the following discussion.

4. EXHAUSTION OF TRADEMARKS

Exhaustion of trademark rights is the most complex of the intellectual property rights. This results from the practice by many multinational companies of having the same trademark used on products manufactured by different corporate affiliates, such as a parent and a subsidiary, within a single corporate group. This practice gives rise to situations where one affiliated corporate entity may try to block imports of the trademarked good produced abroad by another corporate affiliate. These complexities are examined in both the EU and the United States below.

a. EU approach

In *IHT Internationale Heiztechnik GMBH v. Ideal Standard GMBH*, [1994] ECJ I–2789, Case C–9/93 (June 22, 1994), the French subsidiary of American Standard, a U.S. company, sold the French trademark "Ideal Standard" to an unaffiliated French company Société Générale de Fonderie, which then assigned the trademark to another unaffiliated French company named CICh.

American Standard also had a German subsidiary, Ideal Standard GmbH, which used the German trademark "Ideal Standard" in Germany. IHT, a German subsidiary of CICh, began importing heating equipment manufactured in France and sold under the French trademark "Ideal Standard" into Germany. Ideal Standard GmbH opposed the importation and sought an import ban. Article 30 of the EC Treaty prohibits obstacles to the movement of goods between member states. An import ban would on its face violate Article 30. However, Article 36 of the EC Treaty permits exceptions to Article 30 for the purpose of protecting intellectual property rights. The issue was whether the import ban was justified to protect Ideal Standard GmbH's German trademark. As the issued involved one of EU law, the German courts referred the case to the European Court of Justice.

The European Court of Justice found that the import ban was justified. The critical element for the court was that the American Standard French subsidiary sold the trademark to an unaffiliated third party. So long as the Ideal Standard trademark was owned by the French subsidiary of American Standard, the German subsidiary of American Standard would be unable to block the imports. As all of the entities were economically linked and formed part of a single corporate group, the placing of goods on the market by one subsidiary would not cause consumer confusion. When the American Standard French subsidiary sold the French trademark to an unaffiliated third party, the sale severed the economic link between the new owner of the French trademark with the German subsidiary and with American Standard, the U.S. parent company. Importation of the French Ideal Standard products are now from a different source and could cause consumer confusion in Germany.

The approach of the EU is to allow gray market imports when the party seeking to block the imports and the manufacturer of the imports abroad are economically linked. This linkage exists when the entities are corporate affiliates such as subsidiaries of the same parent. The EU also considers a licensing agreement to create an economic link. Suppose that the licensor located in one EU country and the licensee located in another EU country are unaffiliated corporate entities. The licensor cannot exclude imports from the licensee because the two entities are economically linked by the licensing agreement. The EU approach to licenses differs from the U.S. approach. In the United States, a licensor can block imports from a licensee. This is further explained below.

One other aspect of this case deserves discussion. Most U.S. multinational companies would not allow their foreign subsidiaries to be the registered trademark holder of a global trademark. Instead, the normal practice is for the multinational parent company to register the trademark in the foreign country and to license the trademark to each of its foreign subsidiaries. If the U.S. parent registered the Ideal Standard trademark in France and licensed the trademark then the French subsidiary would not be able to sell the French trademark to a third party. The sale by the French subsidiary created serious headaches for the U.S. parent and the German subsidiary as one of American Standard's global trademarks, Ideal Standard, is now owned by an unaffiliated third party. If the U.S. parent company registers all global trademarks around the world and then licenses them, there is never an issue of who owns and controls the company's intellectual property assets.

b. U.S. Approach

The origins of the U.S. approach to gray market trademarked goods can be traced to *A. Bourjois & Co. v. Katzel*, 275 F. 539 (2d Cir. 1921), rev'd, 260 U.S. 689 (1923). A U.S. company purchased the business, goodwill, and U.S. trademark for a face powder from a French company at a premium. Afterwards, the defendant began to import products from the French company using the same trademark and similar packaging and sold them in the United States. The Second Circuit declined to enjoin the importation of the French face powder but was reversed by the

Supreme Court. In response to the Second Circuit decision, Congress enacted § 526 of the Tariff Act, 15 U.S.C. § 1526, which provides in relevant part:

> [I]t shall be unlawful to import into the United States any merchandise of foreign manufacture if such merchandise ... bears a trademark owned by a citizen of, or by a corporation or association created or organized within, the United States, and registered in the Patent and Trademark Office by a person domiciled in the United States ... unless written consent of the owner of such trademark is produced at the time of making entry.

In *K Mart Corp. v. Cartier, Inc.*, 486 U.S. 281 (1988), the Supreme Court considered the validity of 19 C.F.R. § 133.21(c), an administrative interpretation by U.S. customs authorities of § 526 of the Tariff Act of 1930. Section 133.21(c) provides three exceptions to the rule in § 526 blocking imports of gray market goods:

> (c) *Restrictions not applicable.* The restrictions [of § 526] do not apply to imported articles when:
>
> (1) Both the foreign and the U.S. trademark or trade name are owned by the same person or business entity; [or]
>
> (2) The foreign and domestic trademark or trade name owners are parent and subsidiary companies or are otherwise subject to common ownership or control. . . .[or]

> (3) the articles of foreign manufacture bear a recorded trademark or trade name applied under authorization of the U.S. owner. . . .

19 CFR § 133.21(c) (1987). The Supreme Court upheld §§ 133.21(c)(1) and 133.21(c)(2) but rejected § 133.21(c)(3).

The Supreme Court found that § 133.21(c)(1) set forth above is a valid administrative interpretation of § 526 due to the ambiguity in its text providing for the exclusion of a gray market good that "bears a trademark *owned by a citizen of, or by a corporation or association created or organized within, the United States.*" The ambiguity is that when a U.S. subsidiary that registered the trademark is owned by a foreign parent, it is unclear whether the U.S. subsidiary owns the trademark or the foreign parent owns the trademark because the foreign parent owns the U.S. subsidiary. Section 133.21(c)(1) has resolved this ambiguity by finding that the foreign parent owns the trademark so therefore the U.S. subsidiary cannot prohibit the imports of the gray market goods as it is not the owner of the trademark and cannot invoke § 526.

The Supreme Court found a similar ambiguity in the language of § 526 referring to "*any merchandise of foreign manufacture.*" This language could mean goods manufactured in a foreign country, goods manufactured by a foreign company, or goods manufactured in a foreign country by a foreign company. Section 133.21(c)(2) interprets this ambiguity to mean that goods manufactured in a foreign country by a foreign subsidiary of a U.S.

company are not "merchandise of foreign manufacture" and therefore cannot be excluded under § 526.

The Supreme Court found, however, that there was no statutory ambiguity in § 526 that would allow it to uphold § 133.21(c)(3), the "authorized use" exception. As a result, the Supreme Court found that exception to be invalid. A U.S. trademark owner can exclude imports of the trademarked product manufactured abroad by a licensee. Note that the EU applies a different rule to authorizes uses. The *Ideal Standard* case discussed above indicates that a licensing agreement creates an economic link between the licensor and the licensee. The economic link prevents the licensor from blocking the imports from the licensee.

Having examined the reasoning of the Court, we can now review the three hypothetical cases (with three subparts) posited by the Supreme Court at the beginning of the *K-Mart* decision:

(1) A domestic firm purchases a U.S. trademark owned by foreign firm. The foreign firm then begins to import goods using the trademark into the United States or a foreign distributor buys the trademarked goods produced by the foreign firm and imports them into the United States.

(2) A domestic firm registers a U.S. trademark for goods that are manufactured abroad by an affiliated manufacturer. Based on

this basic fact pattern, there are three variations:

(2)(a) The domestic firm is a subsidiary of a foreign firm that wants to control distribution of its goods in the United States. To achieve this goal, the domestic firm registers a U.S. trademark that is identical to the foreign trademark owned by the foreign parent. A third party buys the trademarked goods broad and imports them into the United States.

(2)(b) A U.S. parent establishes a subsidiary abroad to manufacture the goods and imports them for domestic distribution but the subsidiary also sells the goods abroad. A third party buys the goods and imports them into the United States.

(2)(c) The U.S. company establishes a branch office abroad to manufacture the goods for domestic distribution but the branch also sells them abroad. A third party buys the goods and imports them into the United States.

(3) A domestic holder of a U.S. trademark authorizes an unaffiliated party abroad to manufacture the goods. A third party buys the goods abroad and imports them into the United States.

The Supreme Court concludes that the U.S. trademark owner can block gray market imports in case (1). This is the fact pattern from *A. Bourjois &*

Co. v. Katzel. Section 526 was enacted to block imports in just this situation. The right holder cannot block imports in cases (2)(a), 2(b), and 2(c). These are all encompassed by the common ownership and control exception set forth § 133.21(c)(2) and upheld by the Supreme Court in *K Mart*. The right holder can block imports in case (3). Customs wanted to let these goods in under the authorized use exception but the Supreme Court ruled that this exception was invalid.

Section 133.21(c)(2), the exception upheld by the Supreme Court, is known as the common ownership or control exception and is also referred to as the affiliate exception. If the U.S. company that is the holder of the registered trademark and the foreign company manufacturing the goods are under a common ownership or control, the U.S. company cannot block the importation of the gray market goods. As multinational companies have many corporate affiliates today, this exception is in practice very broad and could result in many cases where gray market imports cannot be banned.

The D.C. Circuit imposed some limitations on the common ownership or control exception in *Lever Brothers Co. v. United States*, 981 F.2d 1330 (D.C. Cir. 1993). In that case, Lever Brothers Company, a U.S. company, and its British affiliate Lever Brothers Limited, both manufactured soap and detergent under the "Shield" Trademark. The soap and detergent from the UK had different physical characteristics, such as smells, and different packaging. The British version produced less suds and was designed for "hard" water (i.e., water with minerals) whereas the American version produced more suds and was designed for soft water. The packaging was also different as different fonts and decorative patterns were used.

The unauthorized influx of the British Shield products in the United States caused consumer confusion, leading to U.S. Lever Brothers receiving numerous complaints from American consumers. U.S. Lever Brothers sought to ban the importation of the British Shield products but U.S. customs authorities refused the request based on the affiliate exception (i.e., the common ownership or control exception). U.S. Lever Brothers challenged the customs ruling and won in the district court. U.S. customs authorities appealed to the D.C. Circuit Court of Appeals.

U.S. Lever Brothers's argument for blocking the imports was based on § 42 of the Lanham Act, 15 U.S.C. § 1124, which provides:

> [N]o article of imported merchandise which shall copy or simulate the name of any domestic manufacture, or manufacturer . . . or which shall copy or simulate a trademark registered in accordance with the provisions of this chapter . . . shall be admitted to entry at any customhouse of the United States.

Customs argued that § 42 did not apply to this case because it refers to merchandise "which shall copy or simulate a trademark" and in this case the trademark on the British Shield products was genuine. The court of appeals disagreed finding that trademarks applied to physically different products are not genuine from the point of view of the consumer. The court also noted that nothing in the legislative history of § 42 discussed an exception for materially different goods when the trademarks were owned by affiliated companies. The D.C. Circuit affirmed the district court's ruling in favor U.S. Lever Brothers and blocked the imports.

Following *Lever Brothers,* U.S. customs authorities amended the pertinent regulations to include the "Lever Rule." The current version, 19 C.F.R. § 133.23, provides for the denial of entry of goods by "a party subject to common ownership or control that the Customs Service has determined to be physically and materially different from the articles authorized by the U.S. trademark owner for importation or sale in the U.S." 19 C.F.R. § 133.23(a)(3). However, such goods covered by the "Lever Rule" shall not be detained

> where the merchandise or its packaging bears a conspicuous and legible label designed to remain on the product until the first point of sale to a retail consumer in the United States stating that: "This product is not a product authorized by the United States trademark owner for importation and is physically and materially different from the authorized product."

19 C.F.R. § 133.23(b). U.S. customs authorities will permit the importation of a physically and materially different gray market good produced abroad by a

corporate affiliate of the U.S. trademark holder if the product contains a clear disclaimer.

5. COPYRIGHT EXHAUSTION

a. EU Approach

Consistent with its approach to trademarks and patents, the EU applies a rule of regional exhaustion to copyrights. Article 4(2) of the Information Society Directive, EC Directive 2001/29/EC (May 22, 2001), provides in relevant part:

> **EC Information Society Directive**
>
> **Article 4**
> **Distribution right**
>
> * * *
>
> 2. The distribution right shall not be exhausted within the Community in respect of the original or copies of the work, except where the first sale or other transfer of ownership in the Community of that object is made by the right holder or with his consent.

A sale of a book or a compact disk containing music or movies anywhere in the EU exhausts the copyright in that particular item. The item can be resold (i.e. distributed) anywhere in the EU or in the world without the permission of the copyright holder.

b. U.S. Approach

A recent Supreme Court decision makes clear that the United States applies a rule of international exhaustion to copyrights. Until this case, further discussed below, U.S. courts grappled for years with finding the proper approach to copyright exhaustion.

In *Kirtsaeng v. John Wiley & Sons, Inc.*, 568 U.S. 519 (2013), the plaintiff, Kirtsaeng, a citizen of Thailand and a student at Cornell, asked his relatives to purchase copies of English language textbooks in Thailand and mail them to him in the United States. Kirtsaeng then sold the books at a profit. One of the publishers of the books sold in Thailand, John Wiley & Sons, Inc., sued Kirtsaeng in federal district court for copyright infringement. In his defense, Kirtsaeng argued that the books were acquired after a first sale in Thailand. The first sale exhausted the copyright in the books so Kirtsaeng was free to import the books into the United States and to sell them in the United States. The district court rejected this argument and the Second Circuit Court of Appeals affirmed. Kirtsaeng appealed the case to the U.S. Supreme Court, which reversed.

Section 106 of the Copyright Act grants the right holder certain exclusive rights, including the "right to distribute copies" to the public. Section 106 is subject to the first sale doctrine set forth in § 109, which states that the "owner of a particular copy . . . *lawfully made under this title* . . . is entitled, without the authority of the copyright owner, to sell . . . that copy." Section 602(a)(1), dealing with importation, considers the right of importation as part of the right of distribution. Section 602(a)(1), 17 U.S.C. § 602(a)(1), provides that "[i]mportation into the United States of copies . . . of a work that have been acquired outside of the United States is an infringement of the exclusive right to distribute . . . *under section **106**.*"

If the first sale of the copy in Thailand exhausted the copyright in the copy under § 109 then the right to distribute under § 106 has also been exhausted and no longer exists. The exhaustion of the right of distribution also exhausts the right of importation under § 602(a)(1). According to this line of reasoning, Kirtsaeng would be free to import the books and sell them in the United States.

The debate in the Supreme Court concerned the meaning of the terms "lawfully made under this title" in § 109. The U.S. government argued that this term imposed a geographical limitation requiring the copies to be made in the United States. The government interpreted "made under this title" to mean "in conformance with the Copyright Act where it is applicable," i.e. in the United States. An earlier case *Quality King Distributors, Inc. v. L'anza Research International, Inc.*, 523 U.S. 135 (1998) held that the first sale abroad exhausted the copyright but Quality King involved copies manufactured in the United States. The books in involved in *Kirtsaeng* were manufactured abroad. The Supreme Court had to decide whether the approach set forth in *Quality King* also applied to copies that were manufactured abroad.

The Supreme Court accepted Kirtsaeng's non-geographical reading of the clause "lawfully made under this title." Section 109 says nothing about geography. The non-geographical reading was simple and made sense. The geographical limitation argument seemed strained. Accordingly, Kirtsaeng's purchase of the books in Thailand completely exhausted Wiley's copyright and Kirtsaeng was free to import the copies into the United States and to sell them.

6. PATENT EXHAUSTION

Consistent with its approach to trademarks and copyrights, the EU also applies a rule of regional exhaustion to patents. Complications can arise when the decision of the patent holder to market a product in the EU is not voluntary.

In the United States, *Impression Products, Inc. v. Lexmark International, Inc.*, 581 U.S. 360 (2017) makes clear that the United States follows a rule of international exhaustion for patents, consistent with the approach for copyright set forth by *Kirtsaeng* discussed above. The Supreme Court indicated that some of the policy reasons in *Kirtsaeng* also supported the same approach for patents. The Supreme Court has brought much needed clarity on exhaustion of copyrights and patents, ending many years of uncertainty.

a. EU Approach

In *Merck & Co. v. Primecrown Ltd.*, [1996] ECR I–6285, Case C–267/95 (December 5, 1996), Merck accused Primecrown of violating Merck's UK patents when Primecrown imported several Merck drugs that were first sold in Spain and Portugal. Beecham made similar claims against Europharm that imported Beecham drugs. Spain and Portugal had acceded to the EU but did not yet provide patent protection for pharmaceuticals when Merck and Beecham first sold their drugs in those two countries. Merck and Beecham argued that their UK patents should allow them to oppose parallel imports from a countries where the drugs can be marketed but not patented.

As the case involved an issue of EU law, the case was referred to the European Court of Justice. A ban on parallel imports is on its face a breach of Article 30 of the EC Treaty prohibiting quantitative restrictions at the border unless the restriction is justified as protection for intellectual property rights under Article 36.

The ECJ rejected the arguments by Merck and Beecham. The patent holders voluntarily put their products on the market in the EU, i.e. Spain and Portugal, knowing that their relevant laws did not provide for patent protection for their pharmaceuticals. Merck and Beecham must accept the consequences of their decisions and the free movement of goods that follows from putting their goods on the market in the EU. The ECJ noted that if they were compelled to put their goods on the market as by a compulsory license then their patent rights would not be exhausted and they could oppose importation of the parallel imports.

b. U.S. Approach

In *Impression Products, Inc. v. Lexmark International, Inc.*, 581 U.S. 360 (2017), Lexmark

International, Inc. sought to enforce its patent rights to its products after first sales in the United States and abroad. Lexmark manufactured toner cartridges for use in laser printers in the United States and around the world. After the Lexmark toner cartridges ran out of toner or ink, remanufacturers acquired the empty cartridges refilled them with toner and sold them at lower prices than the new ones that Lexmark sold. To combat this practice, Lexmark sold some lower priced cartridges that the consumer contracted to return only to Lexmark. These cartridges had microchips that prevented reuse once the toner ran out.

The remanufacturers soon devised ways to disable the microchips and then acquired the lower priced cartridges in both the United States and abroad, refilled them, and sold them at a lower price. Lexmark brought a lawsuit against the remanufacturers for patent infringement. All of the remanufacturers eventually dropped out of the lawsuit leaving only one defendant, Impression Products, which asserted that the first sale of the cartridges in the United States and abroad exhausted Lexmark's patent rights in the cartridges. Impression moved to dismiss both claims. The lower courts dismissed Lexmark's claim on the domestic sales but denied the motion on the cartridges sold abroad. A prior case, *Jazz Photo Corp. v. International Trade Commission*, 264 F.3d 1094 (Fed. Cir. 2001) held that a sale abroad did not exhaust patent rights.

On appeal, the Supreme Court held that both the domestic sales and the sales abroad exhausted the patents under the first sale doctrine. When Lexmark sold the cartridges in the United States, the sale terminated Lexmark's patents. Lexmark may have a contract claim against the customers who resold the cartridges but no patent rights.

The Supreme Court also found that the first sale abroad exhausted Lexmark's patent rights. The Court referred to its decision in *Kirtsaeng v. John Wiley & Sons, Inc.*, which held that the first sale of a copy abroad exhausted the copyright in that copy. The Court cited the common law rule against restraints on alienation, which invalidates efforts to prevent the transfer of real or chattel property. The common law rule has no geographical limits. The Court cited the rule as a policy supporting the result in *Kirtsaeng* and ruled that the same policy supported exhaustion by a first sale abroad for patents.

The Supreme Court rejected an argument made by Lexmark that as its products were not protected by U.S. patent law abroad, the sale could not occur at the same monopoly price that Lexmark could charge in the United States. Lexmark argued that the inability to charge a high price abroad meant that Lexmark had not received the reward guaranteed by U.S. patent law. The Court found that patent rights do not guarantee some unspecified premium for the right holder. The patent gives the patent holder the right to receive one reward for the sale at whatever amount the patent holder deems satisfactory.

INDEX

References are to Pages